MY YEARS WITH AYN RAND

MY YEARS WITH AYN RAND

Nathaniel Branden

o

Jossey-Bass Publishers
San Francisco

Jossey-Bass books and products are available through most bookstores. To contact Jossey-Bass directly, call (888) 378-2537, fax to (800) 605-2665, or visit our website at www.josseybass.com.

Substantial discounts on bulk quantities of Jossey-Bass books are available to corporations, professional associations, and other organizations. For details and discount information, contact the special sales department at Jossey-Bass.

TCF Manufactured in the United States of America on Lyons Falls Turin Book. This paper is acid-free and 100 percent totally chlorine-free.

Library of Congress Cataloging-in-Publication Data

Branden, Nathaniel.
  My years with Ayn Rand / Nathaniel Branden. —
1st ed.
    p. cm.
    Includes index.
    ISBN 0-7879-4513-7 (acid-free and chlorine-free)
    1. Rand, Ayn—Friends and associates. 2. Branden, Nathaniel—
Friends and associates. 3. Women novelists, American—20th
century—Biography. 4. Women philosophers—United States—
Biography. 5. Psychologists—United States—Biography.
6. Objectivism (Philosophy) I. Rand, Ayn. II. Title.
    PS3535.A547 Z564 1999
    813'.52—ddc21   98-25440
    [B]

FIRST EDITION

PB Printing   10 9 8 7 6 5 4 3 2 1

AUTHOR'S NOTE

A MEMOIR IS THE RE-CREATION of certain events in one's life as seen through the lens of memory. In re-creating the events described here, I have had the help not only of a keenly vivid memory—made stronger by my having recounted the incidents many times—but also by a variety of materials, such as letters, diaries (Patrecia Branden's), tape recordings of Ayn Rand as she talked about her life, such publications as *The Objectivist Newsletter* and *The Objectivist* (which reported many of Ms. Rand's and my public activities), and Barbara Branden's biography, *The Passion of Ayn Rand.*

When I reproduce conversations that took place many years ago, I am not suggesting that all the words have been reported verbatim, but I am confident they are faithful to the essence of what was said and to the spirit and mood of the occasion. This conviction has been reinforced by those, acknowledged below, who knew one or more of the people about whom I write and who affirm that my characterizations match their own memories of the individual's attitudes, beliefs, behavior, and spoken style. I am especially gratified by the response of people who knew her and who praised the accuracy with which I captured Ayn Rand's "voice."

Prior to our break, Ms. Rand said publicly and on more than one occasion that I knew her thoughts more profoundly and specifically than any other human being and that I was qualified to speak for her on virtually any aspect of her ideas or convictions. Only the internal logic of my narrative can assure the reader that I am reliable in reporting on the more intimate aspects of our story.

Certain individuals read all or portions of this manuscript prior to its original publication, shared recollections with me, checked my memory, or offered editorial or other suggestions. Those people include Joseph Barber, Roger Callahan, Reva Fox, Florence and Hans Hirschfeld, Jonathan Hirschfeld, Leonard Hirschfeld, John Hospers, Elayne and Harry Kalberman, Ralph Roseman, Lawrence Scott, and Lee and Joyce Shulman. I thank them all. Thanks also to many former students who helped me recreate details about the atmosphere of the Nathaniel Branden Institute.

Obviously, there are events I write about that no one else is in a position to affirm or disaffirm. In any event, I alone am responsible for any errors that may have escaped notice.

Originally published in 1989 under the title *Judgment Day*, the present volume represents a newly edited and significantly revised edition. This new publication has offered me the opportunity, on the one hand, to eliminate some unnecessary material that impeded the flow of the action and, on the other, to include new material that adds, I believe, to the story's richness. Furthermore, revising this book has offered me the opportunity to correct a number of minor factual errors, to modify or eliminate passages that contained unintended and misleading implications, and, I hope, to present a more balanced portrait of certain people with whom my relationships were at times adversarial.

With regard to correcting factual errors and eliminating some unintended and misleading implications, I especially want to thank Barbara Branden for her input. She invested considerable time and energy in this effort, and it is much appreciated. This acknowledgment, however, carries no implication that she would agree with all the viewpoints expressed in this book; she would not.

The concept and approach of this memoir are difficult to convey. They are unconventional in a number of ways, and I shall always be grateful to Marc Jaffe of Houghton Mifflin, editor of the original edition, for the speed with which he grasped my basic intention and for his sensitivity and insightfulness in helping me to fulfill it.

I am equally appreciative of the book's new editor, Alan Rinzler, of Jossey-Bass Publishers, whose suggestions have been enormously valuable and often inspiring and whose enthusiasm for the project has done much to make the process of revision a joy for me.

Finally, my greatest debt is to my wife, Devers, whose contribution to this book—both editorial and psychological—is immeasurable. She provided inspired input from the first page to the last. Not only did she encourage me to write freely and openly about my intimate relationships with three other women but she lovingly and mercilessly challenged me to keep going deeper into self-disclosure. This book is dedicated to her in love and gratitude.

MY YEARS WITH AYN RAND

To Devers Branden

INTRODUCTION

I MET HER a month before I turned twenty. She was forty-five. I was study-ing psychology at UCLA. She was already famous as the author of *The Fountainhead* and was now engaged in writing a new novel, *Atlas Shrugged,* which would make her still more famous—and more controversial—not only as a novelist but also as a philosopher. Our relationship lasted eigh-teen years, coming to an explosive parting of the ways in the summer of 1968. During the course of those eighteen years, the relationship went through many transformations; we went from student and mentor to friends to colleagues and partners to lovers—and, ultimately, to adversaries.

At the time of the break, neither she nor I (for different reasons) chose to disclose to the world its actual cause. In her case, she chose to with-hold the truth even from her closest friends. But everywhere I went I was assailed with questions: "What really happened between you and Ayn Rand? What could possibly have broken you two apart? How could two people who were so close find themselves in irreconcilable conflict?" I had been the foremost exponent of her philosophy. She had described me as its most consistent embodiment. What could have happened? The ques-tions never stopped.

Because I thought the facts were of some importance as a matter of intellectual history, I decided that I would eventually write a book about our relationship. The problem was, the project did not overly excite me. My world was the present and the future, not the past. And then, one day, in a single shift of perspective, my attitude changed. I suddenly saw that our story had all the elements of a well-constructed novel. It had a range of characters whose lives, choices, and actions were all integrated in a cen-tral story line, events that propelled the "plot" forward to the logical explosion of its climax, and a resolution that satisfied all the requirements of high drama. Seeing the story through the eyes of a dramatist ignited my enthusiasm to write it.

Although I would not begin to work on it until some years later, I first announced my intention to write the book in a lecture I gave in 1982 at the University of San Diego. Called "The Benefits and Hazards of the Philosophy of Ayn Rand," the talk was published in 1994 in the *Journal of Humanistic Psychology* (it is also available on my Web site: www.nathanielbranden.net). Many people conveyed that they found the talk helpful and even liberating, which gave me further encouragement to write this book.

I conceived the project as a memoir in the form of a novel in the form of a memoir. If you wish to understand the literary method of the book, that is the key.

There are many reasons one might choose to write a memoir, and one does not necessarily know all of them consciously. But this much I do know. I wanted to write as accurate a portrait of my relationship with Ayn Rand as I could, as a matter of historical record. I wanted to capture the essence of a brilliant, innovative thinker and artist, an exalted and tortured woman, neither allowing the positives to obscure the negatives nor the negatives to undercut the positives. I wanted to write about the dynamics of intellectual movements and about why and how even the best of movements can bring out the worst in people as well as the noblest. I wanted to examine anew the choices I made and the actions I took during those years; some of those decisions were disastrous. I wanted to take a fresh look at old wounds and perhaps heal old traumas. I wanted to explore the process of my own individuation—more specifically, my development through my relationships with three women, of which the relationship with Ayn Rand is the dramatic centerpiece that integrates all the events of the story. I wanted to write about the experience of being in love—with individuals, with ideas, and with causes. I wanted to celebrate the woman and the love that, in the end, precipitated the break from a life that had become destructive of my growth and well-being.

I offer very little psychological analysis in this book. That is intentional. I wanted to relate the facts as accurately as I could—to let the story speak for itself—and let the reader draw his or her own conclusions.

Ayn named her philosophy Objectivism. I was the person chiefly responsible for launching Objectivism as a philosophical movement. How that happened and what it led to are part of this narrative.

Among establishment intellectuals, there has always been ferocious resistance to acknowledging Ayn's achievements or the importance of what she spoke to in people. In 1991, however, the *New York Times* reported that the Library of Congress in cooperation with the Book-of-the-Month Club did a national survey to learn which books had had the biggest impact on readers—which books changed people's lives. Number 1 on the list was the Bible; number 2 was *Atlas Shrugged*. Did anyone conduct a study aimed at understanding the nature of or reasons for *Atlas*'s impact? Not that I know of. But I believe this memoir will shed light on the question.

I hope this memoir will deepen the reader's understanding not only of Ayn Rand's work but also of Ayn Rand as a person. Ideally, it will help the reader get past the misconceptions circulated by both her blind worshipers and her blind detractors. I also hope that the reader will find value in one man's willingness to write rather intimately about the experience of being in love—with three very different kinds of women in three very different kinds of ways—because although this book is a work of intellectual history, it is also a love story.

PART ONE

1

"'I WANT TO SLEEP with you. Now, tonight, and at any time you may care to call me. I want your naked body, your skin, your mouth, your hands. I want you—like this—not hysterical with desire—but coldly and consciously—without dignity and without regrets—I want you—I have no self-respect to bargain with and divide me—I want you—I want you like an animal, or a cat on a fence, or a whore.'"

The girl who was reading these words aloud to her friends was trying, it seemed to me, to contain and deny her excitement. I was puzzled by her unconvincing attempt, just as I was puzzled by the slightly nervous laughter of the other two girls. The book to which they were reacting was clearly an object of their intense fascination.

One of the girls was my oldest sister, Florence, age twenty-one, seven years older than I.

That summer afternoon in 1944, far from Toronto, Canada, where we lived, wars were being fought; human beings were killing and dying. In Paris, German troops were surrendering to French and American forces. In the Pacific, General MacArthur was unleashing devastating bomb attacks against Japanese shipping. To me, it was all rather remote.

That afternoon, the radio and newspaper reports did not capture my interest. Nothing seemed able to capture it.

I sat in a large armchair in our living room, my legs stretched over the side. As usual, I was gazing off into space. I did not expect my sister Florence or her two friends to pay any attention to me, and they didn't. I had wandered into the room a few minutes before, in response to the mysteriously hushed and excited sounds of their voices. With nowhere to go and nothing to do, I listened, thinking that there was something silly about such behavior from twenty-one-year-olds. At fourteen, I felt detached and faintly superior.

A few minutes later, without saying a word to me, they walked out of the room.

They had left the book behind on a coffee table.

I walked over a little disdainfully, picked it up, and glanced at the title. *The Fountainhead,* a novel by Ayn Rand. I read the dust jacket and gathered that the book's central idea was that the ego, meaning the independent mind, "is the fountainhead of all human progress." I was intrigued. I studied the author's photograph on the back of the jacket. Nothing about the face reminded me of anyone I had ever seen. Perhaps it was the dark, perceptive, intense eyes, conscious in some heightened way, that imparted a glamorous, even exotic cast to the face.

I vaguely recalled the boy up the street mentioning the book to me months earlier. I tried to recall what he had said—something about an architect with a very unusual philosophy of life. I turned to the first page.

"Howard Roark laughed." That was how it began.

There are extraordinary experiences in life that remain permanently engraved in memory. Experiences that represent turning points. Moments, hours, or days after which nothing is ever the same again. Reading this book was such an experience.

The writing had the most marvelous purposefulness and clarity. I had the sense that every word was chosen with excruciating care; the book seemed absolutely devoid of the accidental. This was stylization of a kind I had never seen before, and it was maintained down to the smallest detail. The author's ability to provide an experience of visual reality was instantly evident, and it was visual reality of the highest level of luminosity and precision.

The author's constructions, images, and rhythms all took hold of me in some profound way. The style reflected a manner of interpreting experience, a way of being conscious, that I had never encountered and yet seemed intimately familiar.

Six years later, at one of my early meetings with Ayn, I told her, "My excitement wasn't just at the stylization of the writing—your particular way of seeing and recreating reality, which runs through everything—it was like being in a *stylized universe.*" She clapped her hands in appreciation of this image and later referred to it many times.

The first chapter of the novel establishes the basic character and context of Howard Roark. A young man passionately committed to becoming an architect, he has just been expelled from school for designing buildings that represent a total break with tradition. Unmoved by the expulsion, he knows he will not be stopped. His direction comes not from the opinions or values of others but from his own inner vision and convictions.

The novel covers nearly two decades in Howard Roark's life. The plot-theme of *The Fountainhead* is the battle of a great innovator, an architect of genius, against a society geared toward and committed to tradition and mediocrity. In terms of its abstract theme, the novel is a dramatization of the morality of individualism.

Every work of art is an act of psychological self-disclosure. An artist declares to the world, "This is what I think is important—important for me to project and for others to perceive." By the same token, an intense response to a work of art is also psychological self-disclosure. More often than not, the roots of our responses lie deep in our subconscious, but our values, philosophy, and sense of life are necessarily engaged when we encounter a work of art and fall in love.

As I read *The Fountainhead,* I was aware that Ayn Rand had reached me in some unique way and that in the cardinal values of the novel—independence, integrity, love of one's work, and a sacred sense of mission about one's life—I had found a world more interesting, more energizing, more challenging, and in a way more real than the world around me.

I was what psychologists call an "alienated adolescent." Certainly, I felt radically different from everyone I knew, to the point of sometimes feeling that I had almost nothing in common with anyone. At times I felt almost unbearably lonely. However, the concept of alienation is somewhat troublesome. To some extent, any thinking person experiences alienation as a by-product of independence, although I do not believe that independence was the only reason for my alienation.

By my teenage years, my sense of distance from other people had grown stronger. My recollection of those years is not so much that I was unhappy as that I was questioning, searching. What I wanted, without the words to name it, was a world that would somehow match what I had felt as a child running down the street. I longed for a place of laughter and challenge and high-energy excitement. I wanted to find heroes. What I saw instead was a world in which life was perceived not as an adventure but as a burden and in which growing up was equated with giving up.

My feelings of progressive isolation and estrangement provided the psychological backdrop for the events that were to follow—even events twenty or more years in the future.

Living in the predominantly Anglo-Saxon city of Toronto, my parents were Russian Jewish immigrants who had never really assimilated into Canadian culture. A sense of rootlessness and disorientation was present in our home from the beginning. I had no sense of belonging, in Toronto or anywhere else, and I was not even aware of what a sense of belonging would mean. To me, the void seemed normal.

I was aware that neither of my parents felt effective in practical matters. My mother was by far the more this-worldly of the two. An action-oriented woman with no outlets for her energy, she had a sense that life is to be "taken," but she had no sense of how to seize it, and she felt enraged at my father because he did not know either. My father, more passive, was a dreamer. His favorite recreation and escape from my mother was his garden, where he loved to work, especially when my mother was yelling that he come and deal with some matter of family business.

My mother's greatest preoccupation was, "What will people think?" Reality for her was only what others believed it to be. In retrospect, I can see that she existed in a condition of chronic anxiety.

However, she provided the minimal grounding that existed in our home. Father's contribution, apart from supporting us, was of a different order; he brought music and literature into our lives—the voice of Caruso and the plays of Shakespeare, for instance.

My father owned a men's clothing store in a blue-collar suburb of Toronto. I was obliged to work there most Saturdays, which I disliked, wanting more free time for myself. He evidently believed that leisure time, music and literature aside, was only for small children and perhaps for girls; a man *worked*.

I can remember times when he attempted to be physically affectionate with my mother; I cannot remember a single occasion on which he was not rebuffed. They fought a good deal, chiefly over my father's tendency to disappear mentally, to start talking about birds or flowers, when Mother wanted to discuss some matter of money or family.

If Mother suffered from an anxiety disorder, then Father was passive-aggressive. I did not feel close to either of them, although at times I felt sorry for what I perceived to be the joylessness of their lives.

Once, when I was sixteen years old and had failed to do a chore, my father, frustrated and angry to the point of fury, struck me with his open hand. We stood looking at each other. He appeared bitterly forlorn; he could not control his family, he could not win respect from his wife or children, and he could not even get his son to perform a simple task satisfactorily. I felt neither pain nor anger. For him to resort to a physical blow seemed like a confession of impotence, and in that moment I felt older than my father. It was not a happy feeling.

As the only son, I received many messages to the effect that all important family expectations centered on me; I was the one who was supposed to achieve something noteworthy in life. On the other hand, I also received messages to the effect that I might be a failure, because I did not

Author at the age of four, 1934

seem interested in money, business, or most things that the "world" regarded as important.

One of my earliest impressions of grown-ups in general was that they did not say what they thought or felt but rather whatever they believed would serve some particular purpose. When I was young, this sometimes distressed me. As I grew older, I tried to understand it, believing that understanding is protection, that understanding is power. Often, it seemed to me, they themselves did not know what they thought or felt and just made up explanations as they went along. I felt starved for the rational and the straightforward. I grew up being slow to trust.

I loved physical activity—bicycling, tree climbing, archery—but it was almost always as solitary as my reading. I rarely admitted to myself how much I longed for human companionship. I wanted to like and admire people, but I was indifferent to my contemporaries' values and concerns: winning love from Mother or Father, being popular, or cloning oneself in the image of whatever was currently fashionable. Others my age probably thought my indifference was an affectation.

I knew no one to whom I could talk about what most mattered to me, no one who felt as strongly about the importance of ideas or the great questions of life. With the exception of two or three girls to whom I felt attracted for a while, there was no one my own age who seriously interested me.

Occasionally, I would meet someone with whom I might have several exciting conversations. I would think I had found a friend, but at some point either I would decide that this person was not really "serious" or the person would drift away, evidently losing interest in our high-intensity discussions.

Also—and this puzzled and troubled me—the people who did seem serious were typically depressed. I was the only person I knew whose interest in ideas felt joyful. Apart from differences in our outlook, it was my happiness far more than my suffering that estranged me from other people.

From time to time, I would have interesting conversations with my cousin Allan Blumenthal. Allan was an A student, a model son, the essence of decorum in just about every conceivable respect. The irony was that although my mother wished I were more like Allan, his mother wished Allan were more like me, because of my aggressiveness; he and I would joke about that. Two years older than I, Allan would sometimes drop pompous rebukes to the effect that I should be more family oriented and "more conventional," meaning more compliant. But he was intelligent, and we could talk about such subjects as why people believed in

God and whether there were grounds for free will. Allan introduced me to a novel by Romain Rolland, *Jean-Christophe,* which deals with the life and struggles of a musician of genius. It reinforced a conviction already forming in me, especially after I read *The Fountainhead,* that a hero is one who perseveres. *Jean-Christophe* was very meaningful to Allan because he dreamed of becoming a concert pianist. His parents intended for him to become a physician, and a physician is what he eventually became, and after that, a psychiatrist.

During those years I lived in a void, but, without having lived any other way, I did not always recognize it. So it was easy, at times, to be oblivious to signs of both hostility and friendship. My protection was my exuberant conviction that it was great to be alive and my hope that someday in the future I would find my kind of people.

Between the ages of fourteen and eighteen, I read and reread *The Fountainhead* almost continuously with the dedication and passion of a student of the Talmud. *The Fountainhead* was the most important companion of my adolescence. When I opened its pages, I was transported into a world where the issues I cared about really *mattered.*

There were particular scenes I returned to again and again, like favorite pieces of music. One such scene occurs at the conclusion of Part One. At a time when he is struggling and destitute, Roark receives an enormously important commission, one that could make his career. But there is one condition—that he modify the unconventional design of his building. Roark explains why it is as important for a building as for a man to have integrity, why a building cannot borrow pieces of its soul. They concede that he may be right, but in practical life one can't always be so consistent. They give him an ultimatum: "Yes or no, Mr. Roark?" After a long, agonizing moment, Roark says, "No." Appalled, one member of the board of directors cries, "You need the commission. Do you have to be so fanatical and selfless about it?" Pressing his architectural drawing to his body, Roark answers, "That was the most selfish thing you've ever seen a man do."

In first reading this, I knew immediately what Roark meant. Placing the integrity of his own convictions, values, and commitments above fame, worldly success, or money was not an act of self-sacrifice but a supreme expression of selfishness in the noblest possible meaning of that word. If he had perceived his action as self-sacrificial, it would have lost all moral stature.

Everything I had ever heard about the virtue of self-sacrifice and selflessness became preposterous and irrelevant. It missed the point of what life—and greatness—demanded. Not to sacrifice the self but to remain true to it at all costs—that was the heroic vision *The Fountainhead* offered.

Another scene of great personal meaning to me was the "boy on the bicycle scene" at the beginning of Part Four. A young man, newly graduated from college, is wheeling his bicycle through a forest, thinking about his future. He wants to love and admire others, but he is happiest when he is alone. This saddens him, because he longs for the experience of human joy and achievement as fuel and inspiration. He comes to a clearing and stands overlooking a valley; he sees a series of breathtaking structures, a magnificent symphony in stone. Lost in contemplation of this answer to his longing, he finally notices a man sitting alone on a rock and looking at the same sight. "Who built this?" the boy wants to know. "I did," the man says." "What's your name?" the boy asks, and the man answers, "Howard Roark." The boy thanks Roark and walks away. "Roark looked after him. He had never seen that boy before and he would never see him again. He did not know that he had given someone the courage to face a lifetime."

There was one scene in *The Fountainhead* that I reread a hundred times. For one sentence only, this one scene was more important to me than any other in the book. Peter Keating, a parasitic yet successful fellow architect, asks Roark to design the government housing project Cortlandt Homes and to let Keating take the credit. Years earlier, Keating graduated from architectural school with honors on the day Roark was expelled. Later, when they were both in practice—Roark struggling desperately, Keating rising to the top of his profession—Keating went to Roark again and again for help with his work. Keating is the "second-hander," the man without independent values or judgment, the man who lives through and by others. Roark, the innovator, the egoist, the man who lives for his own sake and by his own mind, has fought an eighteen-year battle against the society around him. Now his architectural ideas are beginning to win; clients are coming to him in increasing numbers. Keating, having ridden for years on a prestige he did not earn, is now slipping. Roark, inspired by the challenge of Cortlandt Homes, agrees to design the project for Keating on one condition—that it be built exactly as Roark designs it. In a rare, pathetic groping for honesty, Keating struggles to understand Roark's motive. "Everybody would say you're a fool. . . . Everybody would say I'm getting everything. . . ." Roark answers, "You'll get everything society can give a man. You'll keep all the money. You'll take any fame or honor anyone might want to grant. You'll accept such gratitude as the tenants might feel. And I— I'll take what nobody can give a man, except himself. I will have built Cortlandt."

To me, age fourteen, fifteen, sixteen, seventeen, and eighteen, those words, "I will have built Cortlandt," were like a hymn or a battle cry, celebrating my almost reverential feeling for the activity of creative work and the self-sufficiency of the creative process. This feeling has never changed in me.

In an introduction to the twenty-fifth anniversary edition of *The Fountainhead,* Ayn said that her novel is a confirmation of the spirit of youth. My own experience of reading it quite supports this assessment. It confirms the spirit of youth—and the conviction that joy is possible for human beings, that doom and defeat are not our inevitable fate.

I cannot discuss the impact of *The Fountainhead* on me without discussing its much-debated climax, Roark's blowing up of Cortlandt Homes. How many discussions—how many arguments!—among how many readers that event must have inspired! On my first reading of the novel, and at each rereading through my teenage years, I was inspired by the integration of the various characters and their conflicts at the climax and by the story's resolution.

Ellsworth Toohey, the architectural critic who secures the Cortlandt Homes commission for Peter Keating, is Ayn Rand's first major literary portrait of evil. Toohey is a socialist who preaches self-surrender, self-sacrifice, and collectivism as a means to gain power over other human beings. Now, after years of plotting and scheming, his goal is to control the Wynand newspaper chain for which he works as a columnist. His boss, and the target of his manipulations, is Gail Wynand.

Gail Wynand is projected as the great tragic figure of *The Fountainhead.* Having succumbed in his youth to the belief that virtue and integrity have no chance in human society, he concludes that one's only choice is to rule or be ruled—and he chooses to rule. He pours his energy and genius into creating a vast newspaper syndicate that does not express his own values or convictions but panders to the lowest values and tastes of the mob. With the exception of the *Banner,* his New York paper, Wynand finds only two passions in life: Dominique Francon, whom he marries, and Howard Roark, whom he first attempts to corrupt and later virtually worships. Roark is the embodiment of the impossible—a man of integrity. But Wynand begins to realize that if Roark can be practical *and* successful on his own moral terms, then there is no justification for Wynand's life.

Wynand does not know that Dominique and Roark are in love. Dominique left Roark years earlier, before she met Wynand, because she could not bear to witness the destruction to which she felt certain he was doomed. Like Wynand, she believes that the good has no chance in human society, but she does not seek anything from a world she despises. She marries Wynand, whom she views as the embodiment of evil, in a deliberate act of self-destruction as she seeks to kill her own ecstatic sense of life. Then she witnesses Keating's disintegration, sees Roark winning his battle, observes Wynand's helplessness before him, and begins to grasp the impotence of evil.

The book dramatized for me, and no doubt for many young people seeking a rational view of life, that the moral and the practical are not in conflict, provided one knows what is, in fact, moral. This was hardly what I was hearing from my peers and elders.

When the first Cortlandt Homes building is completed, Roark discovers that it has been totally disfigured. The government officials have used Roark's structural and engineering plans, without which the project would have been impossible, but they have drastically altered the design for petty and personal reasons. No legal recourse is available to Keating or Roark; the government bureau cannot be sued or forced to honor its contract.

Roark dynamites Cortlandt and waits at the scene of the explosion to be arrested. The storm of public indignation against him, led by Ellsworth Toohey, emphasizes Cortlandt's status as a housing project for the poor. Roark's motive is of no concern.

Peter Keating (who has made a final, desperate effort to save his career through another act of parasitism) is publicly disgraced and fully realizes his own emptiness and mediocrity. From my teenage perspective, Keating's characterization illuminated the conventional mentality I found so inimical—all those forever preoccupied with "What will people think?"

Gail Wynand attempts to use the *Banner,* for the first time in his life, to support a cause in which he believes—his defense of Roark. His readers desert him, and Wynand learns that it is not he who has directed public opinion but public opinion that has controlled and directed him. To save his newspaper, he finally joins the voices denouncing Roark. Recognizing, however, the futility of his career and recognizing that his pursuit of power has enslaved him, he finally closes the *Banner.* He sees that a man cannot sacrifice his values all his life and expect to escape the consequences.

In my later teenage years, I would have many arguments with people who accused Ayn Rand of being a Nietzschean. By the time I knew who Nietzsche was, it seemed obvious that the character of Gail Wynand was intended to be an indictment of Nietzsche—a conviction that Ayn would subsequently confirm. "A true and consistent egoist," she would say in conversation, "would never seek power over other human beings. He would be too independent for that. And power seeking always means dependency." To me, from reading her book, this could not have been clearer.

The dynamiting of Cortlandt puts Dominique to the severest test possible; the thing she values most, Roark, is in far worse danger than he has ever faced before. But she is not afraid for him. She knows that he is right, that he has won, no matter what happens. She makes peace with her love for him and joins him.

I found the character of Dominique the most troublesome in the book; I could not really make sense of her psychology. She must be read very abstractly, very symbolically. Once, Ayn rather bluntly acknowledged, "If you take Dominique literally, she's quite stupid. You have to see her more as the projection of a certain attitude taken to an extreme—an idealist paralyzed by disgust." But what nonetheless attracted me was Dominique's passion and her spirituality. She was a priestess run amok and was certainly more interesting than the "normal" girls I met in Toronto.

Dominique's love for Roark raised another issue that influenced me profoundly—the supreme importance of admiration in romantic love, as contrasted with the mixture of affection and contempt that seemed to pass for love with so many people. This total dedication, I thought, is what I want to feel for a woman one day and what I want her to feel for me.

At his trial, Roark's statement to the jury is a summation of the novel's philosophy: that all progress and achievement come from the independent mind; that altruism, the doctrine that self-surrender in service to others is the highest ideal, is a device for controlling and ultimately enslaving productive men and women; that a human being is not a sacrificial animal but has a right to exist for his or her own sake; and that society depends on the work of creators and has a right to that work only on the creator's terms. Roark is acquitted.

I listened to the boys on the block talk about girls and popular songs and baseball. I sat in class while teachers talked about geography and social studies. I listened at family dinners as my parents argued with each other or lectured my sisters or me. But what I was seeing and hearing were the events and characters of *The Fountainhead,* the ecstatic laughter underlying the book's sense of life.

This, of course, is precisely the inspirational power of romantic art. Contrary to the claims of naturalism, a young person does not require descriptions of the people next door but an escape from them to a wider view of life's possibilities.

The Fountainhead was for me an invaluable aid to psychological survival. Not many novels have that power.

Although my three sisters liked and admired the book, each in her own way, Florence and Elayne sometimes teased me about it. Florence, who was a socialist for a while, was intrigued by the book but insisted that it was intended to provide an ethical justification for capitalism. I, who did not really know what capitalism was, told her she was crazy. Although she was not correct literally, her observation disclosed a perceptiveness for which, years later, Ayn complimented her.

My youngest sister, Reva, four years older than I, seemed most touched by the book emotionally, and occasionally we would try to talk about it. We were both a little shy and inhibited about sharing our intimate feelings, even though at that time I was closer to Reva than to anyone in our family.

All four of us seemed to inhabit private worlds and were all preoccupied with different goals and concerns. In the summer of 1944 when I first discovered Ayn Rand, Florence was employed in an office, Elayne was preparing to study nursing at the University of Buffalo, Reva was about to enter the University of Toronto, and I was approaching my second year of high school, impatient to know my future.

That fall, my mother noted my obsession with *The Fountainhead*. Although she had not read it (unlike the rest of the family, she did not read books), she became slightly alarmed. She wanted an outside opinion and invited Selena Herman, a teacher of Hebrew studies and an "intellectual," for dinner and a discussion of *The Fountainhead*. The evening was to have extraordinary consequences for my future.

I welcomed the opportunity to discuss the book with someone who might be genuinely interested. As Selena had not read the novel, I proceeded to synopsize the story. Then I handed her the novel and waited silently while she read Roark's courtroom speech.

"Well, there's nothing new in this. This is a well-known philosophy. It is called anarchism."

The next day I skipped school, later forging a note from my mother saying I had been sick. I went down to the Bloor Street branch of the Toronto Public Library and discovered Bertrand Russell's *Proposed Roads to Freedom*, an examination of socialism, anarchism, and syndicalism. I read the book in its entirety that day and confirmed my judgment that Selena had been wrong. Ayn Rand's message in *The Fountainhead* was a completely different one; it was primarily ethical and psychological. But I did become interested in anarchism and in philosophy. I began reading other books by Russell, then by other philosophers.

As for politics and economics, I never did discover capitalism (during those years) or the Founding Fathers' concept of government as the protector of inalienable rights or the idea of a free-market economy. I decided that if coercive power over other human beings is evil, anarchism is the only defensible political philosophy. I wondered if Ayn Rand would agree with me.

I kept skipping school, forging excuses from my mother, and spending my days at the library. It was as if I had been set loose in a candy store.

Eventually, a book on psychology fell into my hands. I recall looking through it, slowly grasping the kinds of issues and questions that psychology addressed. What causes our emotions? Are any of our choices truly free? What are the origins of genius? It was the beginning of a life-long passion.

That year, at the age of fourteen, I made two decisions: I wanted to be a psychologist, and I wanted to be a writer: a psychologist because of the things I wished to understand, a writer because of my desire to give objective form to the things I felt, believed, understood, and envisioned.

That same year, I failed to get passing grades in high school. I had skipped too many classes and spent too much time reading books absolutely unrelated to my curriculum.

I did not feel the slightest bit guilty about how I had chosen to spend my time, but the idea of failing in school nonetheless rankled. I convinced my mother to let me enroll in a special school that offered four years of high school in one year. At this school, there were no sports, there were no social activities, and many of the students were adults. Everyone was treated with the respect due a grown-up. We were there for one purpose only, which everyone understood—to learn. It was the most satisfying school year I had ever known, and I graduated with the highest marks of my life.

My extracurricular studies did not stop; they were merely confined to evenings and weekends.

In *The Fountainhead*, there was a reference to a playwright whom Ayn Rand obviously admired—Henrik Ibsen. So I went to the library and discovered drama. I would borrow my sisters' library cards so I could take ten or twelve books of plays home at one time. Between the ages of fifteen and seventeen, I easily read two thousand plays. I wrote several plays of my own. It was as if drama had disclosed itself to me as a separate category of existence more stimulating than any other.

I had been an atheist since the age of twelve. One day that year, walking down my street, I looked up at the sky and had an electrifying experience. I had a sudden sense of the universe as a totality, and I thought, If God is needed to explain the existence of the universe, then what explains the existence of God? If God does exist, he's at least as marvelous and impressive as the universe—and no less in need of an explanation. But then who created whatever created God? Isn't it more reasonable to accept the existence of the universe as the starting point of everything? Whatever stages of development it may go through, whatever its forms at different points in time, in an ultimate sense the universe *is*. We begin there. I felt a great rush of exhilaration and as I looked at the blue sky overhead, at the green of the trees on our block, at people and cars and at children playing, I felt a love of a kind I had never consciously experienced before—a love for being. A love for existence itself. I felt a great sense of serenity.

"The smartest men believe in God!" my mother yelled at me that night at dinner. "*Einstein* believes in God! How can you not believe in God?"

I countered, "But *why* do people believe?"

"They're brilliant men. They must know."

I had heard the same kind of argument at school: "Do you think you're the only one who knows what's true—and everyone else is wrong?" I began to think that most people believed in God only because others did, rather than because of any perception, knowledge, or experience of their own. I wondered if this might not be the grounds for most of their beliefs.

I decided that nothing was more important than to protect the sovereignty of my own mind—against family, teachers, and anyone who might try to get me to see the world their way rather than the way it appeared to my own eyes. "That's why *The Fountainhead* meant so much to you," Ayn later said to me. "You were already on the track of its basic premise."

The way I applied the idea of independence was not positive, however. In encounters with other people, I screened out too much. I prevented myself from learning things from my teachers that could have been helpful to me. In later years, I often struggled to reinvent the wheel.

And there was another way in which I misconstrued the idea of independence. After reading *The Fountainhead,* I began to reproach myself for my loneliness. I told myself that it was a weakness. I imagined that an ideally evolved man could enjoy people without suffering over the absence of satisfying relationships. I struggled to repress my desire for human companionship. Interestingly enough, it was Ayn who helped me to understand the nature of my error. "I can see how you could have gotten that idea from *The Fountainhead,*"she would say to me. "But it's a mistake." It was a mistake, I learned later, that a great many people had made after reading *The Fountainhead.*

One consequence of my repression was that I sometimes failed to see that girls I liked returned my feelings. Signs of interest or warmth could pass right over my head. Once, in my twenties, I remarked to Ayn, "As a teenager, I was not a great success with the opposite sex. Perhaps I was too serious. Anyway, I don't think girls liked me." She stunned me by the insightfulness of her response: "Would you have known if they did?"

The kind of woman I admired was not like Dominique but like Kira, the heroine of Ayn's first novel, *We the Living,* which I discovered when I was sixteen. Kira struck me as far more rational, far more psychologically healthy—a young woman of "purposefulness, contempt for the inconsequential, and furious innocence." She is committed to work, love, and personal freedom, and she is completely unconfused about these issues. That, I understood.

We the Living is about the struggle of three young and talented people to live and achieve happiness in Soviet Russia and the manner in which the system destroys all three of them, not in spite of but because of their virtues. When I first read the book, I did not know that Ayn Rand had emigrated to the United States from Soviet Russia.

"Can you imagine what it was like to read your novel," I said to Ayn some years later, "while hearing people talk about Soviet Russia as a 'noble experiment'?" Ayn answered, "Can you imagine what it was like to *write* it, having *come* from that hell, and hear Americans talk about Russia that way—with absolutely no understanding of, or appreciation for, their own country?"

At the same time that I found *We the Living,* I discovered another early work of hers. *Anthem* was a novella written a few years prior to *The Fountainhead.* In *Anthem*'s world of the future, the word *I* has disappeared from language and the concept of ego has vanished. An individual refers to himself or herself as "we" and to another individual as "they." The hero's struggle to identify and name himself is developed with such tension that when, after pages of "we," I saw the opening line of the climactic chapter, my emotional experience was one of unsurpassable violence and power: "I am. I think. I will."

I related this struggle to my own, viewing both struggles not in political terms but in psychological ones. The struggle, so acute in adolescence, was to carve out a sense of identity and a view of life unsurrendered to the opinions and values of others. To me, Ayn Rand was the ultimate champion of autonomy and was therefore a shield against the world to protect the process of my own growth.

No one can understand the appeal of Ayn Rand to youth—or to readers of any age—who does not understand how profoundly she speaks, on many different levels, to the quest for individuation, autonomy, and self-actualization.

One of the most meaningful memories of my adolescent years concerns a conversation I had with my sister Florence one evening when we talked about what we wanted from life. This was a rare occasion. Ordinarily, we did not have much contact and would have said we shared few common interests.

"What I would like to find, someday," I said, "is a great issue, a battle, a crusade. . . . Something really worth fighting for. . . . Something that would require and demand everything I am and everything I've got to give. . . . Something *important*. Something that would really be challenging."

Florence, who could be very protective of me, observed thoughtfully, "In battles, people sometimes get hurt."

A battle worth fighting—that was precisely what I was destined to find in the world of Ayn Rand. I struggled to express the fulfillment of that very longing to Florence. But real battles, I would discover, are very different from the battles of our dreams.

In 1948, at the age of eighteen, I knew *The Fountainhead* so thoroughly that if someone read me any sentence in the book, I could recite the gist of the sentence immediately preceding and following. This had one practical consequence, which would assume so much importance later; I had become intimately familiar with the workings of Ayn Rand's consciousness. It was as if there were a direct line from her psyche to mine. I was two years away from our first meeting.

After high school, I spent twelve months in Winnipeg, Manitoba, working in the jewelry store owned by my uncle, David M. Copp. While my father had maintained his usual detachment, my mother had begged me to forget about psychology and accept the opportunity her younger brother offered me to join him in business. Uncle Dave had become wealthy in his jewelry business and in real estate. He had no children of his own and was prepared to offer me a virtually guaranteed future if I would live and work with him in Winnipeg.

"You do have brains," Uncle Dave said. "And you have a good gift of gab." I think he also enjoyed my energy and assertiveness. When I thanked him for his generosity and explained that I had other ambitions, he was kind and gracious. He did not push, in spite of his obvious disappointment. He told me that if I wanted to go to college, to become a psychologist or anything else, and if my parents found the expense difficult, he would take care of it. My mother implored me to work in Uncle Dave's store for a year before making a decision. I agreed, knowing that at the end of a year I would proceed precisely as I had planned.

In the fall of 1948, when I was just settling into Winnipeg, I met Earl Hyman, a passionate reader whose father had a splendid library. I enjoyed visiting their home, where we all talked about books. One day Earl said

Author at the age of eighteen, 1948

to me, "I've been thinking. There's an old friend of mine you've got to meet. She's nineteen years old and she's in college. She wants to be a writer, and she talks about *The Fountainhead* the way you do. Her name is Barbara Weidman."

Initially, he had difficulty setting up the meeting. Barbara was rather elusive. Later she would tell me, "He talked so much about how brilliant you were that I pictured you as maybe five foot two with thick glasses and very, very sensitive—you know, an 'intellectual.' I really wasn't curious."

Earl prevailed. We drove to Barbara's home, which was on one of the "best" streets in Winnipeg. We were greeted at the door by a slender girl with blond hair, green eyes that flashed intelligence, a warm and somewhat shy smile, and an innocent vulnerability that I found appealing.

"Nathan," said our friend, "I want you to meet Barbara Weidman. Barbara—Nathan Blumenthal."

2

BARBARA AND I sat in her den, mutually assessing each other, mutually intrigued. I felt more adult and male than I had ever felt in my life. I spoke about my reasons for being in Winnipeg. She spoke about her studies in college and her desire to be a writer. She mentioned her love for Thomas Wolfe, whom I had not read; I liked the quiet enthusiasm with which she spoke of him. I looked at the books on the shelves and was pleased to learn that most of them were hers. I told her I thought she would enjoy *Jean-Christophe*. She asked me if I liked Oscar Wilde.

I had absolutely no idea that my life was about to change in an irrevocable way. At most I might have guessed that I was on the verge of an interesting romance. Barbara was a year older than I was, and I found that appealing.

I liked her voice. Warm and musical, it promised a depth of feeling she might not yet know how to express. I liked the slenderness of her body and the fluidity of her movements; they, too, hinted at passion underneath her somewhat shy and formal manner.

When she talked about books or ideas, she did so as if they mattered with a childlike earnestness incongruously combined with an obvious effort to look and sound sophisticated. I was impressed when she told me that she intended to major in philosophy.

The three of us drove off to an afternoon gathering, the nature of which I do not remember. Barbara and I were acutely aware of each other. I thought I sensed some muted, distant sadness within her, which in no way impeded the excitement rising within me. I felt exhilarated, challenged in a way I had not experienced before.

Later, when I asked her about *The Fountainhead,* she remarked simply that she liked it very much. Our conversation on this subject was rather restrained; our enthusiasm showed chiefly in the exaggerated casualness of our discussion. Perhaps we were testing each other.

The next time we met for a date, however, our reticence began to melt. "What do you think of Dominique?" "How do you interpret her?" "Isn't Steven Mallory a terrific character?" "What do you say when people want to argue about Roark blowing up Cortlandt Homes?" "I wonder what Ayn Rand is like as a person."

Throughout December, we saw each other frequently, and our encounters became more and more intimate. We were clearly going to have an affair. It would be my first.

Since my own mother and father were rarely in my thoughts, I was rather surprised that Barbara spoke so frequently about her parents. They struck me as very decent people. They always treated me graciously and kindly. Unfortunately, Barbara's father had little or no grasp of her dreams and ambitions and didn't know how to defend her when she clashed with her mother. Her beautiful, glamorous mother seemed to have little time for her and clearly preferred Barbara's older brother, who was handsome and far more socially adept. I wondered why a nineteen-year-old girl would still have so much energy invested in her mother's and father's approval—an insensitivity that no doubt reflected my alienation from my own family.

She spoke about her previous relationships with boys and about her desire for someone who would not try to change her. I could not see why someone would want to change her, I said. She spoke of having had one sexual relationship in her life, which had ended a few months ago; she suggested that the young man had been too conventional for her, and she expressed some pain over the intensity of her past feelings for him.

Our actual affair began on an evening in January when Barbara appeared at my apartment on a subzero night, bringing with her a beautiful smile and the scent of perfume.

When a man makes love to a woman for the first time in his life, he feels aligned with the forces of the universe in a new way and aligned with the internal energies of his own maleness. The connection feels cosmic. I felt a deepening sense of internal integration and power. Sensuality and spirituality fused in an experience of shattering force. When the first experience of sex is a happy one, as mine was, it is an experience of waking up, of being enlightened, of giving birth to a new self. Through the act of sex I discovered my own body, as if it had only now come into full existence.

The intensity of my feelings—for Barbara, for sexual intercourse, for the exquisite miracle of a woman's body—were almost overwhelming— irresistible and yet disorienting. I was flung out of my isolation—and out of control. A few days after our first sexual encounter, driving through streets piled high with snow, I announced to Barbara in a matter-of-fact voice, "I want you to know that I am not in love with you."

When we mentioned this incident to Ayn a few years later, she shook her head and grunted, "Emotional repression." Barbara laughed and said, "That was when I knew he was in love with me."

I rarely went to sleep without telephoning Barbara to say good night. Sometimes I would call her in high excitement to read her some poem I had found and liked. We met frequently for lunch, and when I saw her walking toward me through the snow, smiling, carrying her textbooks, bundled in boots and fur coat. I laughed in unbearable happiness. I did not think about our future. The present was a magnificent gift, an end in itself, and it seemed to me that of all of nature's blessings, the phenomenon of woman was the greatest.

If we sometimes had small clashes or disagreements, they were resolved swiftly, gracefully, and effortlessly—or else dismissed as unimportant. "What do couples fight about?" I once asked Barbara wonderingly, adding, "You're so easy to get along with." And she would ask, "Don't you ever have moods? Aren't you ever grouchy or on edge?" I would answer, "No, I'm happy."

A few times, some small piece of her behavior would confuse and trouble me. She might avoid eye contact while telling me something important, for instance. She might respond with unexpected sharpness when I questioned some action of hers, or fall into puzzling fits of sadness, or reminisce with strange dreaminess about some former boyfriend, or look at me as if she expected to be reproached when no such thought was in my mind. When I saw this apprehension in her glance, I told myself that she had been hurt and needed time to learn to trust me. A moment, an hour, or a day later, she would be so warm, loving, and joyful that I almost believed none of it had happened. "God, life is wonderful," we would say, melting into each other's arms.

Barbara claimed passion as her highest value. She would say that one of the things she most appreciated about me was how intensely I felt about things, about life, about myself, about her. She was very moved by *Tristan and Isolde*. "I *know* it's tragic, but who cares? They *felt* things." I could not articulate my reasons, but I did not quite share her perspective.

Whatever our differences, we agreed on the most important thing—there was nothing in the universe that compared to *The Fountainhead*. Like the skyscrapers it celebrated, it rose above everything.

I brought her my copies of *We the Living* and *Anthem,* which she devoured with great enthusiasm. The hero of *We the Living* is called Leo. When Barbara said to me, "Leo is not an Ayn Rand name. I can't explain how I know that, but I know it," I agreed with her. Then she went on, "I'll bet that Leo is the name of some man Ayn Rand actually knew and probably cared for, perhaps was in love with." Later, when we met Ayn, she told us that Barbara had been right and expressed astonishment at such perceptiveness.

At the age of eighteen, I continued to feel like it was a miracle that I was having such discussions with a girl in an erotic context. Watching her as she spoke, her eyes alive with an intensity that was almost enraptured, her gestures delicate yet firm and decisive, I thought her feminine, sexual, intellectual. At such times, my faint doubts and misgivings seemed unreal. I was in love.

One evening, we met two male friends of hers in a restaurant. One of them, Wilfred Schwartz, who was several years older than I, was a former boyfriend of Barbara's. He was also an admirer of *The Fountainhead*. Sitting with them in the restaurant, I remembered Barbara's recounting of their stormy relationship. She said she had broken it off "because I was always made to feel guilty." It was obvious that whatever they had once meant to each other had not died. Most of Wilfred's comments to her had a sarcastic undertone. Barbara remained warm and friendly, but I sensed an underlying hurt and helplessness.

Wilfred and his friend were curious about the new man in Barbara's life. One moment they were polite to me in a guarded sort of way. The next moment one of them would say something outrageous. I laughed with them and remained cordial.

When we were alone again, I asked her, "Are you really such a heartbreaker?" She answered sadly, "In this case, perhaps I was. He really cared about me." A little while later she made a remark that I thought extraordinarily revealing. She wondered aloud how Wilfred would explain her and my relationship, since this time she was with someone he would have to respect. Evidently he did not respect her other boyfriends.

I slipped once, badly. We were out somewhere, and she pointed out a former boyfriend. I prided myself on seeing a lot when I looked at a person. I didn't like anything about what this old boyfriend projected and foolishly told her so. I was not without jealousy; I could not bear the idea of anyone else touching her. But I lacked the wisdom—or the courage—to say so in plain language. Subsequently, she told me that she had been deeply hurt by my remarks.

I had it in me to be insensitive and critical at times without knowing it. Although I no longer remember my words, I am sure I said some things to Barbara that were unkind and inappropriately judgmental, reflecting my own fears about the instability of our relationship.

One night, lying in my arms, she suddenly whispered, "Don't judge me. Just love me." My whole system went on alert; at the same time, I felt myself pulling away emotionally and reproached myself for it. Had she been hurt that badly by her mother's rejection and by Wilfred's continuing disapproval? Holding her tightly, I felt alone, helpless, and miserably confused.

But when we made love, all of these concerns vanished. My hunger for union after so many years of isolation could sweep everything else out of my consciousness. Through the act of sex I shattered the walls of an invisible prison. I became connected not only to this human being who had become so precious to me but also to nature, to the world. These were not the words in my mind but the feelings in my body. I was not yet able to express myself through work, but when I was with Barbara, my love, my excitement, my sense of power, my life force, had an outlet. I was eighteen years old, and in the egocentricity of my joy, it did not occur to me to wonder what the act of sex meant to Barbara.

I felt only that she was desperately important to me—and that, for reasons I did not understand, we were in danger.

Wilfred and I remained curious about each other and met a couple of times on our own. He seemed more intelligent and serious than at our first meeting, and I liked him more. Also, I could not help but be touched by his pain over Barbara. Whatever their story was, he had loved her, and that gave us a kind of bond.

One day, he invited me to join him and a friend for lunch. They were already seated and stopped talking when I arrived. After a half hour of casual conversation, undoubtedly prompted by demons of his own, Wilfred suddenly asked me, "Has Barbara ever told you about her great love affair with —?" He named the young man Barbara had pointed out to me, the one about whom I had made some negative comments. She had told me they had never slept together. Now, Wilfred was saying—what was Wilfred saying? I struggled to follow his somewhat oblique and rambling discourse. This, I gathered, was the man to whom Wilfred felt he had lost her—the first of several, he stressed. But Barbara had told me that she'd only had one lover. If Wilfred was telling the truth, why hadn't she told me about it?

Her response was devastating. "I knew Wilfred would try to turn you against me," she said sadly, looking at me with wounded eyes. Whether I recognized it or not, she chided me, I was puritanical. Before she could safely talk about her past experiences, I needed to know her better. Later, I realized Wilfred had given me an exaggerated idea of what her experiences had been. Wilfred, for one, had never actually been her lover.

Spring was coming, and Barbara and I continued to take walks and drives and make love and talk about books and life and the future. We made plans to go to Los Angeles in September—to UCLA. She would study philosophy; I would study psychology. But something had changed between us, and we both knew it. The ease and serenity of our beginning had vanished.

Fairly early in our relationship, she began to drop remarks to the effect that at times she felt something was wrong with her, that her mind and body were split. At first I did not take her seriously, or I imagined that in my presence problems would magically dissolve. But part of Barbara projected that she was a "bad girl." Further, she conveyed that she expected disapproval. Often I felt the need to reassure her, but if I tried to question her, wanting to understand, she would become gently defensive or soulfully tragic or so confused and forlorn that my heart would melt and I would feel self-reproachful or retreat in frustrated silence. What is apparent to me today is that attitudes such as hers do eventually turn into self-fulfilling prophecies. When we expect others to disapprove of us, we often behave in ways to bring this about.

In my bewilderment and impatience, I at times reinforced her worst fears. Two confused children struggling in the dark.

By late April, Barbara was finding reasons to see less of me. She swung between intense demonstrativeness and mystifying withdrawal. Hurt and bewildered, I responded by pursuing her more vigorously. The frequency of our quarrels escalated—about dates, about sex, about her friends. In some way I could not define, I felt as if her allegiance was switching to something unnamed but utterly alien to me. Our times together left me in despair. I felt myself being pulled back into the loneliness I thought I had escaped.

Then, in the midst of our struggles, I contracted a form of pneumonia and was advised to take a month off from work, to go home to Toronto and convalesce. I spent most of May in Toronto, lying around the house or in the backyard under a blanket when it was warm enough, consuming endless quantities of my mother's chicken soup, reading books, day-dreaming about the future, talking to Barbara on the telephone and writing her letters, trying to determine whether the tone of her voice or of her letters signaled any shift in her feelings, never being certain, and missing her to the point of physical pain.

In June, I returned to Winnipeg. I knew almost immediately that we were at the end. We lasted through the month, with the abyss between us growing wider each day. A sense of doom permeated our every meeting.

One night, near the end of June, sitting in a parked car a few feet off the highway, we agreed that it was over. Barbara initiated the breakup. I did not argue with her; I knew it was useless.

"I would give anything to know *why*," I said. "If only I could understand *why*."

Barbara was not interested in questions of this kind, not at the moment, and perhaps she was right. In any event, if she had grievances against me, she did not tell me what they were. "I will always love you in my own way," she said solemnly. At some level, I believed her.

During July and August, my last two months in Winnipeg, I dreaded weekends. Monday through Friday, I had the distraction of work. In the evenings, I could force myself to go to bed early. But the weekends were especially difficult—hours stretching before me in which there was no escape from my thoughts and feelings. My loneliness for Barbara was agonizing.

One powerful symbol of a rational universe remained—Ayn Rand. On an impulse, motivated perhaps by a desire to give my life some other focus, I decided to write her a letter, care of her publisher, inquiring about her political convictions. What did she believe in? "Certainly not capitalism," I wrote her confidently. I received no answer to my letter.

Finally, in early September, my stay in Winnipeg came to an end, a little more than two months after the breakup with Barbara. I was eager to fly to California to begin my studies at UCLA.

Uncle Dave drove me to the airport, wished me luck, and said goodbye. Approaching the boarding area, I saw Barbara, who was departing for Los Angeles on the same flight as we had previously arranged. We smiled at each other, with unexpected affection. In that moment, without any discussion, we became "friends."

Shortly after arriving in Los Angeles, we enrolled at UCLA. It was impossible not to feel excited at the start of this new life. The brilliant sunlight on the UCLA campus seemed to symbolize unlimited possibilities. I was in the United States. I was beginning college. I felt more like an adult than I ever had. Who knew what might happen now? Whom might I meet? And what might yet happen with Barbara?

Although we saw each other frequently at school, talked on the telephone, and sometimes went to a movie or for a drive together, we did not date and were not physically intimate. At times I missed her badly.

The problem, and it was a serious one, was that I continued to feel that I was moving on a planet of strangers whose language I did not speak and that Barbara was the only one who spoke English. True, she did not speak it all the time—she kept mixing it with that other tongue—but there was nonetheless some sense of kinship, a bond I was reluctant to relinquish fully. To a much lesser extent, she seemed to feel that, too. Sometimes I thought she resented me for the bond she felt.

During the preceding months in Winnipeg, we had evidently forged a connection that was now showing unexpected strength. We were no longer lovers, and we could not really be friends, yet we could not let go of each other. To me, Barbara represented a battle I could not accept having lost. Furthermore, there was no one in my new environment with whom I felt I could share my inner world, although there were people I liked.

To Barbara, my esteem mattered greatly, just as hers mattered to me. If I began to drift away, she would reach out to bring me back, evoking that sense of our special intimacy and even hinting at the presence of unspoken sexual feelings. Some part of me was waiting. I could not decide if she still had some form of love that neither of us understood. I waited. And I hoped.

On arriving in Los Angeles, I had renewed contact with my sister Elayne, who was working as an operating room nurse at Cedars of Lebanon Hospital; she was now twenty-four. We decided to share an apartment in order to have a larger place than either of us could afford alone.

As we approached the end of 1949, I thought of writing Ayn Rand another letter. Perhaps my previous one had not reached her. I wrote asking if she had any works in print other than *We the Living, Anthem,* and *The Fountainhead* that I might have missed.

A couple of months later, I received a brief note from her saying that those were the only books she had published. She added that she could not say when she would complete her next novel. Then she asked me if I were the gentleman who had written her from Canada, asking about her political convictions. If I were, she hoped I had learned that she believed in laissez-faire capitalism.

This response inspired me to write a longer letter, asking her a number of questions about *We the Living*, the nature of free will, and capitalism. As she later told me, although the letter impressed her, she was deeply engrossed in writing *Atlas Shrugged* and had no time for inessential correspondence. Plus, her "fans" had disappointed her too many times. It was her husband, Frank, who felt there was something special about the letter writer and urged her to respond. When her letter arrived—several pages long, single-spaced—I was delirious with excitement. The letter was cool in tone and intellectual in content but direct and personal, concluding with an invitation to further correspondence and even suggesting the possibility of a meeting.

I shot over to Barbara's to show her the letter. Suddenly there were no conflicts between us, no abyss separating us, nothing else that mattered but the bond we shared in what Ayn Rand meant to us.

I fired off a lengthy answer, included my telephone number, and waited. On an evening toward the end of February 1950, I was tired and had gone to bed early. The phone rang a few minutes before nine o'clock, waking me up.

"Mr. Nathan Blumenthal?" said a woman's voice with a thick Russian accent. I could not imagine who this was.

"Yes."

"How do you do. This is Ayn Rand speaking."

3

ON THE EVENING of March 2, 1950, I drove my old La Salle down Mulholland Drive and into the San Fernando Valley, heading toward Chatsworth and an address that had been the target of my thoughts for a week—10,000 Tampa Avenue. There were no freeways or supermarkets in that area then, just a few scattered structures in a small, sleepy California village. I had the sense of being in a country environment far removed from Los Angeles, which was an hour's drive away.

For the past week, I had shifted between two perspectives. On the one hand, this meeting felt like the impossible, like a miracle or a dream. On the other hand, and this response was stronger, the meeting felt natural, normal, and logical, as if life for once was as it ought to be and as if almost everything else up to this night had been unreal.

I found my way to a dirt road lined with trees and stopped when I saw the modern glass-and-aluminum-covered steel house. It looked incongruous in this rustic setting yet absolutely appropriate for its owner; it was somehow an elegant statement of self-assertion, so that at second glance it seemed to transform the setting into a perfect background.

The house was set back about two hundred feet from the road, and I followed the straight driveway down to the entrance. I saw a small moat curving around the front of the house, with flowers floating in the water. The property was actually a modest-sized ranch, but the land beyond the house faded into the evening mist. The beams of my headlights disappeared into shadows.

I felt as if ordinary reality had been left somewhere behind and I was entering the dimension of my most passionate longing. I knew that the abnormal calm of my body meant an excitement so enormous that stillness was its only possible expression. I got out of the car but did not immediately ring the doorbell, because I wanted to freeze this moment in my memory forever

"Would eight o'clock be convenient?" she had asked me in that phone call a week ago, and I had willed my voice to relax when I answered, "That would be fine."

I reached for the doorbell, knowing without words and with absolute certainty that nothing was ever going to be the same again.

Within a moment the door swung open, and a tall, slender man in his early fifties stood facing me. I thought, He looks like the kind of man she writes about. Gray-blue eyes set wide apart, high cheekbones, hair the color of dark sand swept straight back, long legs, and a simplicity of manner that somehow combined friendliness and detachment. He wore slacks and an open-collared shirt. I liked him immediately.

"Mr. Blumenthal?" he said, holding out his hand. "Frank O'Connor. Come in." I walked ahead of him into the living room. "Ayn will be down in a minute."

A single large painting hung in the room—a magnificent portrait of Frank O'Connor set against a jungle background. It endowed him with a subtle power that he himself did not project; his gentle assurance did not match the portrait's larger-than-life certainty. I wondered if the artist had revealed an aspect of Ayn Rand's husband that was not readily visible. "This is marvelous," I said to him. I heard a note of relaxed authority in my voice, the ease in pronouncing a value judgment, and I felt how simple everything was, how free of doubts, hesitancies, or complications in the universe I had now entered.

The dominant colors of the living room were green, turquoise, and peacock blue. The room held a few pieces of oversized furniture that looked custom-designed and large plants that threw dramatic shadows against the walls. Frank stood watching me study the room, his smile good-natured, as if he somehow knew what all this meant to me. I smiled back at him, willing to be transparent.

Then I heard the sound of steps coming down the stairs, and I turned. She was walking toward me, wearing a simple straight skirt and blouse. She had a helmet of dark brown hair, bobbed in the style of the twenties, and the most penetrating eyes I had ever seen, large, dark, and luminous. She was not as slender as she looked in the jacket photograph of *The Fountainhead*, nor as elegant—she was a little stocky and rather more "Russian" than I had imagined—but the intensity was there, and so was the consciousness that was like a searchlight.

I felt myself standing in the path of that light. I liked the experience, and I knew she knew I liked it. There are timeless moments, suspended

between seconds, in which it is possible to know these things. That was
the first connection between us, the first link. Later she told me, "That
first night, you were not afraid of whatever I might see. I knew that immediately. You were not afraid."

"How do you do, Mr. Blumenthal," Ayn Rand said a bit formally but
not without warmth. As we shook hands, I felt more comfortable than I
had ever felt with another human being. I saw myself as having walked
into the world of *The Fountainhead*.

Frank stretched out on a chair, instantly relaxing, while Ayn sat on the
enormous sofa, leaning forward intently, and I sat facing them, completing the triangle, my glance shifting back and forth to absorb them both.

For the next several hours, she and I talked while Frank listened attentively but more or less silently; he disappeared once and returned a few
minutes later carrying a tray with coffee and cookies. "Food for the body
as well as the mind," he said, smiling.

She began by wanting to know how I discovered *The Fountainhead*,
and when I told her the story of Florence and her girlfriends reading from
the scene when Dominique first speaks of her desire for Roark, she chuckled with amusement. I began to talk about what *The Fountainhead* meant
to me and about my favorite scenes and my reactions to the various characters. I knew I was under careful scrutiny from both Ayn and Frank, and
I enjoyed that very much. It was as if their combined glances were challenging me to take a false step, but I knew that was not possible, not this
night.

I felt simultaneously the exhilaration of operating at a very high level
of consciousness and the dreaminess of a somnambulist. Much like an
athlete who has been training for years for one event, I knew that this was
the event and that there was no longer anything to hesitate about or to
doubt.

Ayn's accent was strong, which I found disorienting at first; it did not
seem to go with the author of so streamlined, so American a novel as *The
Fountainhead*. At some point, she mentioned that she was forty-five years
old and had come to the United States when she was twenty-one. "I turned
twenty-one on the way over here, while passing through Berlin," she remarked. I wondered if one of the consequences of her extraordinary independence was a failure to absorb the sounds of American pronunciation.

Ayn asked a few questions about my background: my childhood, my
parents, and my interests as a boy growing up in Toronto. We talked a little about *Jean-Christophe* and Romain Rolland, whom she disliked as
both a literary figure and a thinker. She disapproved of his kind of literary "realism" and of his sympathy for socialism.

I was somewhat surprised by her interest in my adolescent years. "Were there no adults you admired when you were growing up?" she inquired at one point.

Wanting to communicate the support I had found in books, I said, "Perhaps this will strike you as weak, but the characters of Howard Roark and Jean-Christophe helped me. They gave me strength and inspiration, and I have to say I needed that."

I was astonished by the protectiveness I heard in her response. "You foolish child! Of course that's not weak! We all need that fuel. That's what art is for."

To be spoken to so compassionately, to be given such understanding, and then to hear the intimately personal tied to the philosophical was to feel nurtured and cared for in a uniquely satisfying way. In one breath, Ayn had addressed multiple levels of need.

She went on to talk about Aristotle's view that literature is of greater philosophical importance than history. Whereas historical accounts report things as they are, literature presents things as they might be and ought to be. This was the principle of her writing, she explained, the projection of man as he might be and ought to be. "Might be" implies realism, she explained, as contrasted with mere fantasy; "ought to be" implies ethical judgment, a moral vision.

"I call this approach to fiction writing 'romantic realism,'" she said. "*Romantic*, taken by itself, can mean values divorced from reality. You know, just a sea of emotion, or gushy sentimentalism. And *realism* taken by itself can mean naturalism, just the description of things as they are, the folks next door, which doesn't interest me in the slightest. If the folks next door bore me in real life, why would I wish to write about them? But the unusual, the exceptional, the strong, the heroic, that which shows man at his best, at his highest possibility, does interest me, and that's what I choose to write about." She chuckled and added, "And that's why you're here—because that's what interests you."

I listened, intoxicated.

She said that if our relationship were to develop successfully, we would need time to establish "a common vocabulary" so as to allow each of us to learn how the other used words; otherwise, needless misunderstandings would occur. This statement stunned and thrilled me, because I had not permitted myself to assume that I would have more than this one meeting.

Love affairs can begin in many different ways. Ayn's and mine began with discussions of epistemology, metaphysics, and ethics. The initial steps of our courtship dance were formal, cerebral, philosophical. While another kind of drama was playing at the edges of our awareness, with two souls shocked by mutual recognition, the testing and probing continued.

Ayn said that there were three questions she wanted to ask me, questions that touched on the essentials of how one saw human existence: What did I think of reason? What did I think of man? What did I think of life?

Ayn Rand was interested in what I thought about reason, man, and life.

From that point on, I could not stop talking. I assumed she wanted to know my stand on reason versus revelation, so I spoke at length about respect for evidence, facts, logic, and proof and about my disbelief in any form of faith or supernatural claim to knowledge. In my enthusiasm, I jumped up, I paced, I gestured—I came close (as she told me later, laughing) to lecturing her.

She wanted to know what I thought about "the mind versus the heart," thinking versus feeling, and did I agree that feelings by themselves were not a reliable guide to action? Of course I agreed. I thought of Barbara, whose life seemed so largely ruled by feelings she could not account for, and an idea and a hope began to germinate in my mind; I suddenly wished Barbara were in the room to share this experience with me.

Most of Ayn's and my conversation that first evening was abstract and fairly impersonal. Intellectual discussion, after all, is what I had come for. And to Ayn the most important thing about a person was his ideas. Yet we were intimate that evening in a subtle and indirect way. Everything had a subtext; a separate, silent dialogue ran counterpoint to whatever we discussed explicitly. We were falling in love—not romantically, but intellectually.

Ayn was saying, "Because of *The Fountainhead*, people think that the most important issue in my philosophy is individualism versus collectivism, or egoism versus altruism, but these are derivatives, not the starting point. The most important issue, the most fundamental, is reason versus mysticism—the premise that knowledge is based on logic and the evidence of the senses versus claims to some sort of nonsensory, nonrational knowledge."

I said that I had always taken reason so much for granted, as an unquestioned principle, that it never occurred to me think of it as in any way controversial. I had not really grasped the philosophical significance of the issue yet. Of mysticism I actually knew nothing. To me, the basic issue had always been independence or autonomy versus conformity—that is, seeing the world through your own eyes versus uncritically accepting others' beliefs. What was wrong with people, it seemed to me, was that they didn't think for themselves.

"That's true enough," she said, "but it doesn't go deep enough. Psychologically, that idea is important, but philosophically, it isn't where you begin."

"When you ask me what I think of man," I said, proceeding to her second question, "I'm not sure I know what you mean." She explained that she meant, Did I think man was evil by nature or good? I found the question odd; I did not believe either. I thought that we were born with a potential for evil or for greatness. I did not believe in original sin, and I did not believe in original virtue. Frank broke his silence to laugh at this. She said she agreed with me, but this was not what she was asking. Did the concept of human being or man evoke a positive response in me or a negative one? "Put that way, I would say a positive one," I responded. Did I see man as depraved by nature? Of course I didn't. Did I see him as heroic, at least potentially? "Oh, yes." This satisfied her.

As to what I thought of life, this meant, Did I see life as malevolent or benevolent? Again, I thought the question strange, explaining that I thought of life as neutral and as containing both malevolent and benevolent possibilities. But, Ayn asked, I did not think of existence as intrinsically evil? "Of course not." I did not think that the universe was such that man was doomed to defeat and tragedy? "No." Did I think that life was such that success and happiness were in principle possible for man, if man acted rationally and realistically? "Of course." This is what she meant, she explained, by the concept of a benevolent universe. "The benevolent universe premise," she called it.

"I hate the idea," she said in her thick accent, "that the essence of life is frustration, futility, and tragedy. It's very Russian, you know. That's one of the reasons I love America. In the American sense of life, happiness is normal. With all its flaws and contradictions, this is a pro-life culture. In spite of the guff about religion, I believe it's also pro-reason and pro-man, in its deepest 'instincts.'"

Then she added, leaning forward with smiling assurance, "With you it's not 'instinct.' You're pro-reason, pro-man, and pro-life, consciously."

I felt as if I had been knighted. I felt appreciated, recognized, seen to a degree that I never had before in my life. No person my own age could have given me what Ayn was giving me. Later I would understand that one of Ayn's special talents was the ability to evoke such feelings of unique visibility. Watching her mesmerizing impact in personal encounters over the years, I had many opportunities to see this skill in action.

When she asked me about the kind of writing I wanted to do, I answered, "Novels. Perhaps plays. Books on psychology certainly, as my knowledge develops. I'm not certain how to do it all, but these are the things I think about."

"Don't imagine that you have to confine yourself to one kind of writing," she said eagerly. "Don't think you have to be as single-tracked as my heroes. I myself struggle between fiction and philosophy, each of which is really a career in itself. Perhaps you'll learn to integrate fiction and psychology, to combine both. Why not?"

I was struck with the matter-of-factness with which she discussed my ambitions; there was not the slightest suggestion that they might merely be passing dreams. What she projected was the sense of unlimited possibilities, conveyed in the way she said, "Why not?"

We had been talking for several hours and were approaching midnight before I raised the subject of capitalism. This, "officially," had been one of the chief reasons for our meeting—for me to learn about capitalism and its relation to her individualist philosophy. I told her how impressed I was by the books she had recommended and how much I was beginning to understand.

"It was a revelation," I said. "I truly had no idea what capitalism is— and neither does anybody else I know. I would love to see Henry Hazlitt's *Economics in One Lesson* made required reading in the schools." I spoke with enthusiasm about what I had learned from reading Isabel Paterson's *The God of the Machine,* and we agreed that, notwithstanding Paterson's unconvincing attempt to tie capitalism to Christianity, the book was a masterpiece of political economic thinking. I gathered that the two women had been personal friends once and were now estranged, which in no way diminished Ayn's appreciation of the book.

Most people, she explained, think capitalism is the system we have in America today, but what we have today is a mixed economy, part free, part controlled. *Nominal* private ownership with a good deal of regulation by the government. A kind of fascism, in effect.

"If you care to do the research," Ayn said, "and I can give you an excellent reading list, you will discover that virtually every evil ascribed to laissez-faire capitalism is in fact the result not of laissez-faire but of government intervention, government controls, the betrayal of laissez-faire. For example, capitalism is blamed for scarcities that are created by government price controls. Or the government, not the market, establishes monopolies that forbid competitors to enter a particular field, and when high prices result, again capitalism is blamed. What capitalism? Most people are shocked when I tell them this; they think it can't be true. But let them check the facts for themselves—in non-Marxist textbooks and histories. Remember, capitalism means laissez-faire. Not government controls in favor of business but rather no government controls. Hands off. A totally free market."

She went on to say that pure laissez-faire of the kind she advocated has never existed but that the United States in the nineteenth century came closer to it than any other time or place in history, with spectacular results. American capitalism transformed the world.

Rather sheepishly, I mentioned my interest in anarchism, and she said to me, "You thought anarchism was the right system, because you understood the evil of ruling men through physical force, and you thought that was intrinsic to all government. Where were you going to learn that a system existed, at least in principle, that had solved this problem? At college? Most of your professors are leftists. From the conservatives? You'll discover they don't know that much about capitalism, either. They merely favor different controls than the liberals, and when you hear them prattle about God and tradition, you'll be tempted to run to the Marxist camp, if only because it's more intellectual. In my philosophy, the government's only proper job is to protect individual rights against violence by force or fraud, to provide courts for the protection of property and the peaceful settling of contractual disputes, and to provide a military for protection against foreign invaders. The greatness of the Founding Fathers was how well they understood this issue and how close some of them came to understanding it perfectly."

As she talked, she waved her cigarette holder in the air to punctuate what she was saying. Her hand movements struck me as feminine and graceful, in contrast to the masculine sternness with which she sometimes spoke. She smoked throughout most of the evening, but even when she was not smoking, she kept the holder in her hand like a conductor's baton.

"In any event," she was saying, "what really interests me is the job of providing a moral or ethical foundation for capitalism, which we've never had and badly need. That's one of my goals in the novel I'm writing now. But the essence is already in *The Fountainhead*. Let me show you how."

I noticed that although she was functioning in the role of teacher, there was no hint of condescension or disrespect in her manner. She spoke from the premise of absolute equality, the equality of two minds in search of the truth.

She asked, as if preparing to present a syllogism, "Do you believe that man has the right to exist?"

"Yes. Yes, of course."

"Do you understand that means he has the right to exist for himself?"

"Sure. If he has a right to exist only if he serves others or does whatever others want, that isn't a right."

"You understand that already? Good. You're fast. What my philosophy teaches is that a human being is an end in himself, not a means to the ends of others. This means he has a right to exist for his own sake, neither sacrificing himself to others nor others to himself."

I did not yet have the historical context necessary to appreciate how radical this idea was, although at some level I knew it. At the same time, I thought that this idea surely was self-evident to any reasonable person. "I agree completely," I said.

"You would have to, if you understand *The Fountainhead*."

I was enjoying the obvious fact that she liked the way I talked to her. There was a spontaneity and freedom from the beginning. I was enormously impressed by her and yet absolutely happy about being myself.

She said, "If you understand that a man's life is his own, that he's not a sacrificial animal, nor the property of the collective, that he has rights that are not to be sacrificed, then you understand that no person, no group, no government has the right to force him to act against his own judgment."

And then I saw clearly the relationship between the theme of *The Fountainhead* and the advocacy of a free market. I experienced a great rush of excitement, as if a new continent had been disclosed to me. At the edge of my consciousness, I saw her noting and approving of my excitement, which she would interpret to mean that I was a person who took ideas seriously.

"Capitalism is the only *moral* system," she was saying, "because capitalism, in its pure, consistent form, is the only system based on the inviolability of individual rights."

I knew I would need time to digest everything she was saying, to reflect on it and assess it, but there was a clarity and internal consistency to her ideas that were instantly appealing. What I had always wanted was an older person I could respect and from whom I could learn. More important to me by far than the content of what I was learning was the experience of learning itself, of listening to a rational voice speaking in intelligible language about issues that mattered.

When I became aware that it was approaching two o'clock in the morning and that Frank was beginning to drift in and out of sleep in his chair, I stood up apologetically. "I'm sorry for keeping you both up so late. I'd better be going."

"Not if you don't want to," Ayn said brightly. "But perhaps you're tired."

I laughed incredulously. "Right now, I don't know what being tired means."

Ayn spread her hands in a broad, expansive gesture. "Then sit down, Mr. Blumenthal. Or may I call you Nathan?"

"Of course."

"You may call me Ayn if you wish."

We went on talking, about her books, about my experiences at UCLA, about my enthusiasm for Ibsen's plays, until I finally asked her the question that interested me most: "Can you tell me what your new novel is about?"

Her dark eyes flashed with excitement. I could see that this was the most important subject in the world to her, and that her desire to talk about it, tightly controlled at the moment, was fully as powerful as my desire to listen. Looking to Frank for permission, she asked him with unexpected girlishness, "May I tell him a little?" Frank grinned and nodded.

"The novel is called *The Strike,*" she began slowly, "although I'll probably change the title. . . . The background is the world of business, heavy industry, specifically railroads and steel."

I felt the smallest stab of disappointment. "Will the novel be philosophical? Can you make businessmen romantic and interesting?" I asked.

My question seemed to delight her. "Wait and see."

"Come on." I grinned pleadingly. "Tell me something more."

"It's a mystery novel. Not a detective story, of course, but there's a mystery."

"A mystery about what?"

"About what's happening to the world."

There was an air of suppressed excitement about her that was delightful and intriguing; she was like a child with a marvelous secret she was bursting to tell. Again she turned to Frank: "Don't let me say too much." Her deference struck me as strange; I couldn't imagine anyone stopping Ayn Rand. "Would you like to know the hero's name?" she asked provocatively.

I nodded eagerly, gesturing for her to speak.

"John Galt. You don't meet him till the last third of the book. Oh—I shouldn't have told you that!"

"Why not?"

"That's part of the mystery."

"What's his occupation?"

"He's an inventor."

I did not know what was proper or improper to ask, but I could not contain myself. "Can you tell me what the climax of the book is?"

"A scene in which the hero is being tortured by the villains."

I took a moment to consider this, then asked, "Do they want to force him to reveal the secret of some invention of his?" Even as I asked, this did not sound right, not original enough. Not for the author of *The Fountainhead*.

"No," she said, deliberately poker-faced; I could feel, rather than see, the humor in her glance. "They want to force him to become dictator of the country."

I burst out laughing. "Oh, god," I said happily.

Whatever I had wanted out of life I was experiencing at this moment.

Ayn's and Frank's faces were glowing as they looked at me, as if they knew what I felt and were feeling it, too. Beneath everything we were discussing, like background music to the entire evening, I felt the presence of that exhilarating connection among all three of us. I kept thinking, I'm home, I'm home, I'm home.

I had arrived at eight o'clock and left at five thirty in the morning. "You'll come back," Ayn said as we stood up. "But if there are philosophical issues you would like to discuss in the meantime, you can phone me."

"I can?"

"Certainly."

"When?"

"Whenever you like."

I was not shy. There were times when I had been shy with young girls, but there was not one moment when I was shy with Ayn Rand. "Do you mean tomorrow?"

"Tomorrow by all means," she said.

When I turned to Frank, he took my hand in both of his and held it for a long moment with a friendliness and affection that touched me deeply.

The roads returning to Los Angeles were thick with fog as I made my way around twisting curves at fifteen miles an hour. All the while, I felt that I was flying weightlessly through unobstructed space.

I imagined reciting the events of the evening in detail to Barbara, going over and over the lines of dialogue in my mind, never wanting to relinquish them, wanting to hold onto them for the rest of my life.

The next day, when Barbara asked me what Ayn Rand was like, I hesitated for an instant, then answered, "Mrs. Logic." Then I went on to recreate for her, as fully as possible, this incredible night and to describe my vision of this extraordinary personality. "She's more than anything I could have imagined."

In the years that followed, Ayn and I reminisced over that first night many times, quoting each other's lines, delighting in the speed and depth of the connection that formed between us.

"Walking into the living room," she would tell me, "seeing you for the first time, I thought, He's got my kind of face. And then I told myself,

Don't start that again, meaning, Don't start hoping. I'd met too many alleged admirers who seemed intelligent and serious in their values and who turned out to be phonies. But, you see, this time it didn't end in disappointment. This time I was right."

When I returned a week later, I brought Barbara with me.

I had spoken to Ayn on the telephone several times that week and on one occasion had said to her, "May I bring someone? I have a close friend who feels about your work as I do." "By all means, bring him along," Ayn had said. I had answered, "It's not a 'him.'" She had laughed. "Fine. Bring her along."

Driving to the ranch, Barbara was more nervous than I had ever seen her. Feeling very much the hero of the occasion, I urged her to relax, and she looked at me as if I were mad to suggest that anyone could be relaxed under the circumstances.

During the evening, she was visibly enthralled but relatively silent. She listened avidly but seldom spoke except in answer to Ayn's questions. But when she did express herself, it was with precision and clarity; she knew what it meant to talk philosophically. "How does one determine what one can legitimately call an axiom?" she wanted to know. Later she remarked to Ayn, "How I wish my professors could explain issues the way you do."

When Ayn began discussing the idea that all emotions are the product of a person's conscious or subconscious premises and that emotions reflect conscious or subconscious value judgments, I saw that this was a principle of enormous importance to her. It was tied in her mind to the supreme importance of reason in human life.

"Emotions are not tools of cognition," she said. She would say this often, always with great intensity. I deliberately drew her out on this subject, even though what she was saying was clear to me. My hope was that she might accomplish what I could not—a reorientation of Barbara's psychology with regard to thinking and feeling. I imagined that I might be the beneficiary of such a reorientation.

I watched Barbara's face as Ayn spoke, taking pleasure in the eager attentiveness of her expression, feeling as if every value I cared about was sitting in this room.

"When you abandon reason as your standard," Ayn said at another point in the evening, "there's no peaceful way for people to settle their differences, and you open the door to every kind of evil, every kind of atrocity. Look at Hitler, with his hatred of 'bourgeois reason' and 'bourgeois science,' or the communists with their claim to a special 'proletarian logic' that justifies every sort of contradiction and irrationality, that justifies lies, torture, and murder. In both cases, reason is seen as the enemy."

This was a new idea to me, and I thought it of the highest importance. I recognized the same awareness in Barbara. When we glanced at each other, we smiled in the intimacy of shared excitement.

Waving her cigarette holder, Ayn went on. "And, of course, this issue applies in more personal situations, as well. . . . I remember once being at a party and talking to a man who was praising me for *The Fountainhead*. He said, 'On your tombstone it should read, "Ayn Rand, Individualist."' And I said, 'No. It should read, "Ayn Rand, Rationalist."' And he answered, 'Oh, I was afraid of that.' When I asked him why, he answered, 'Because if I go to the doctor and he tells me I have cancer, if I go by reason, I have to take him seriously. I have to believe it. But if I'm not bound by reason, I can deny it. I can go on my way as if it isn't true.' I despise that man's mentality. In my philosophy, nothing is more important than respect for reality."

Seeing the glow of eagerness in Barbara's eyes as Ayn spoke, I felt as if Barbara and I had no conflicts. Wasn't it obvious that this was the world in which we both belonged and that whatever had gone wrong before was only a senseless mistake? How could anything or anyone compete with what we were now experiencing? What I did not allow myself to think consciously was, How could anything or anyone compete with me, the engineer of this event?

Ayn and I jumped from one subject to another, eager to explore everything at once. We were rather more interested in philosophy, psychology, and literature than in political economy, and we talked about the latter as something to be clarified and gotten out of the way so that we could discuss more enjoyable subjects. And yet, learning to understand the nature and workings of a market economy was intensely stimulating. Barbara and I would later agree that the experience was grounding; it connected us to the world.

I brought up the subject of military conscription, certain that Ayn would share my opposition to it; she did. "The draft is a good example of our mixed political system, and of what's wrong with it," she stated. "Military conscription contradicts the basic principle of a free society— a man's right to his own life. It's sickening how many conservatives favor the draft while pretending to be champions of freedom. The bastards."

We went on to talk about Freud. Ayn had never read his work and knew it only from secondhand reports but detested it nonetheless. "Freud sees emotions, for all practical purposes, as primaries, as givens, rather than as proceeding from premises."

We talked about logical positivism, which seemed to be the dominant influence in the UCLA philosophy department. Ayn gave us intellectual ammunition against this idea: "Let me show you some of the contradictions in that so-called scientific philosophy. It's complete nonsense, you know, but vicious nonsense."

We talked about Ayn and Frank's house, which, Ayn told us, had been designed by the renowned modernist architect Richard Neutra. It had belonged to Josef von Sternberg, who lived there with Marlene Dietrich. "Do you want a tour?" she asked.

We were led, first, to the modest office in which Ayn worked. It overlooked a garden. There we were introduced to Oscar and Oswald, two stuffed lion cubs that had been among Frank's first gifts to Ayn many years ago. Evidently important members of the family, they were brought out with their red-and-green hats on all festive occasions. "Oscar and Oswald are our symbols of the benevolent universe," Ayn remarked wryly. Then we walked to the long, narrow kitchen, which inspired Ayn to make a brief monologue on her hatred of cooking; for her, cooking evidently required a form of concentration that she found particularly onerous. Finally, we were led to their bedroom on the upper level, which was made intimate and erotic, as I recall, by great quantities of mirror and glass and by a bidet set down not in the bathroom but in the bedroom. "I believe that was Dietrich's contribution," Ayn joked. "It was not in Neutra's original design."

Downstairs again, we somehow fell into a discussion of our religious background. Ayn mentioned that she was Jewish by birth and that Frank was Catholic, although they were both atheists and felt no tie to religion of any kind. "What matters," Ayn remarked, "is what you accept by choice, not what you are connected with through the accident of your ancestry."

Then she proceeded to tell us with obvious pride how Frank had been taken to church as a young boy, had heard the priest expound on the doctrine that all human beings are born in sin, had thought this idea preposterous, and had rejected Catholicism then and there. Frank listened silently.

"I became an atheist at thirteen for two reasons," she said. "First, because there were no rational grounds for believing in God. Second, and terribly important to me, because God was held to be the greatest entity in the universe. That made man inferior, and I resented the idea that man was inferior to anything." She paused thoughtfully for a moment and then added, "If you were to put a title over everything I have written, or ever will write, it would be, *To the Glory of Man.*"

I loved seeing Barbara in the living room of this house, sitting with Ayn and Frank. I felt that she, too, had at last come home, that whatever she had hoped to find when she was a young girl growing up in Winnipeg was now here before her. I did not mind her relative quietness that first night. Let her take it all in, I thought. Let her discover that everything we talked about in our happiest times together is possible. I felt proud that I could lay all this before her.

Had her passion and enthusiasm for Ayn's world been less than it was—had I not believed that this was the world she wanted—I would have let her go. I would have released her internally. It would not have been without pain, but I would have done it, accepting that I had failed to understand our differences. If we did not share a love for Ayn Rand, I would not have imagined that Barbara and I were actual or potential soul mates. I did not recognize how much more than a mutual passion of that kind was needed to make two people right for each other. I had, to put it gently, a highly simplified view of sexual psychology—and of love.

When Ayn learned that Barbara and I had met because of *The Fountainhead,* she was delighted. "Good fiction," she called it, meaning that this connection among the three of us was the kind of event one might put in a novel.

As we drove home from that first meeting, Barbara was radiant. Now that we were alone, words poured out of her. She felt as if here at last she was going to find the answers to all her questions. "You can ask her anything," Barbara exclaimed. She was overwhelmed by Ayn's sensitivity, clarity, dazzling intellect, and benevolence. "Is it really possible?" she asked. "Is this really happening?" And she struck my arm with excitement. "Are we really here?" she wondered, as we drove through the night, with dawn only a couple of hours away. And I answered, "We're here."

Years later, reflecting on their first meeting, Ayn said that Barbara's combination of fragility and strength made her think of Dominique. "You were very quiet, and so your personality did not come immediately into focus, but it was obvious that you were highly intelligent."

The comparison to Dominique had occurred to me long before Ayn mentioned it. Wasn't Dominique a heroine in spite of her conflicts? I saw a justification of my fight for Barbara and in my hope for a happy outcome. I clung to the dream of a victory that would eventually occur by dint of my brains, character, and perseverance and by what I imagined to be the natural logic of things. I did not yet know that there are victories more terrible than defeat.

4

I DID NOT RECOGNIZE it immediately, but the four of us were on our way to becoming a family. For me, it felt like the first family I had ever had—my first sense of roots. Not that I perceived Ayn and Frank as mother and father figures; that was far from the case. Rather, it was family in the sense of intellectual clan. As part of this experience, my bond with Barbara deepened.

I would visit Ayn and Frank every Saturday night and talk with Ayn almost every evening on the telephone. Sometimes we spoke for several hours, chiefly about philosophy but also about my earlier years. Chatsworth was a toll call away, and I remember my sister Elayne's concern in light of my rather limited budget. I did not care; there was nothing of comparable importance for me to spend money on. When she thought of it, Ayn would suggest that I hang up and let her call me back.

Although Barbara did not initiate phone calls to Ayn, she usually would join me on the Saturday night visits and often on other visits as well. I encouraged Barbara to contact Ayn on her own, rather than route the entire relationship through me, but she never did so; she said she was too shy.

"I don't want you to think of Barbara as my appendage," I once said to Ayn. She answered kindly, "But realistically, for the time being, how else can I think of her? I don't really know her as I know you." Her interest sparked when Barbara mentioned that she wanted to become a novelist.

Once Ayn and I were talking about our childhood heroes and ideals and the role they played in our development, and I told her, "When I was six or seven, my hero was the Lone Ranger. Then, at about eight or nine, it was Superman. When I was twelve, I discovered the novels of Baroness Orczy, and my ideal became the Scarlet Pimpernel." As an aside I remarked, "Interesting, isn't it, that all three were in a sense invisible? Their true identities were not known to people." I went on, "So how do I translate what I admire in these figures into the terms of twentieth-century reality? I had no interest in rescuing French aristocrats from the guillotine, but there was something in those adventure stories that I was in love with and didn't want to let go of. I wondered how I could apply it to my life in the modern world. Then at fourteen I read *The Fountainhead*—and discovered the answer. The adventure of creative work. Individualism as a moral battle."

Ayn became enthusiastic. "Don't you see?" she exclaimed. "You kept the same values—daring, audacity, independence—but you kept adjusting the form of their expression to your growth and developing knowledge. You stayed integrated. A more conventional man would have left it all as a daydream that had nothing to do with his adult life. And observe that you weren't literal-minded; you didn't decide to become an architect like Roark. You responded to the abstraction—passion for one's work— and translated that into terms relevant to your own goals." She added, "Of course, you're right; it is significant that all three childhood heroes were masked or disguised—invisible men. That would strike a chord in your own feelings of isolation."

Gratefully and cheerfully, I answered, "I'm not feeling invisible now."

In my first year at UCLA, I was restless in class a good deal of the time. No professor ever conveyed as Ayn did that the ideas being discussed were matters of life-and-death importance.

One of our most memorable visits during this period was an evening when Barbara brought along *The Rise of Scientific Philosophy*, a textbook from one of the classes we were taking together. The course was taught by the author, Hans Reichenbach, a famous exponent of logical positivism. This philosophy held that the laws of logic are ultimately arbitrary, that the senses are unreliable as sources of information about the world, that nothing can be known for certain, and that any statement made about the nature of reality is meaningless. We enjoyed him as a teacher because of his humor and liveliness but disagreed with almost everything he said. The conversation that ensued that evening was extraordinary.

Ayn had never heard of Reichenbach. She picked up his book and read the first two or three pages, then forecast what Reichenbach's position would be on any number of issues. Then she waited for our confirmation that she was right. Next, she began to teach us how she had done what she had done and, more generally, how to read far-reaching implications into the simplest choice of words. We were astonished by what she was able to know about him, based on what seemed to us to be almost no evidence at all.

"When you speak, when you write, when you read, watch the implications," she said. "Pay attention to the implications of your own statements—and the statements of other people." That was one of the first philosophical lessons she drummed into us.

Never was our energy and enthusiasm greater than that of this woman who was twenty-five years our senior. Sometimes when we arrived at the ranch she would be visibly exhausted from a difficult day's writing, but once the discussion began to flow and her mind became engaged, it was as if she had tapped into some universal energy source. The lines of tiredness vanished, and her face took on the brightness of the dawn. She conveyed an inspiring and electrifying passion for ideas. The best of our professors seemed drained and worn-out by comparison. She was the apotheosis of the philosophically dedicated mind. In future years, we would hear her having discussions with any number of professors who came to visit us, and I cannot recall one who did not comment on this trait of hers, this burning commitment to the importance of ideas.

One of her ideas that particularly impressed me was her identification of free will with the choice to think or not to think—to seek awareness or to avoid it.

She gave inexhaustibly of her time and energy to Barbara and me. I was puzzled by her generosity. "Surely," I said to her, "you must have contemporaries who share your intellectual interests." She replied, "Friends, or more often acquaintances, who share my interest in politics. Conservatives, mainly. Not philosophical thinkers." I remained puzzled. "But Barbara and I haven't accomplished anything in life yet." She chuckled. "You will. Are you concerned about receiving something you don't deserve?" I hadn't quite thought of it that way, but answered, "Well, I suppose so." She said, "Don't be. You and Barbara know how to think. No one had to teach you that. One day you'll understand how important that is—and how unimportant differences of age are by comparison." Ayn and I had various versions of this conversation several times. As we came to know each other better, her perspective seemed more and more natural to me.

At UCLA, I tried to engage some of my professors in the kind of issues I talked about with Ayn. When I tried to persuade a psychology professor that the doctrine of psychological determinism contained insuperable contradictions, he replied, "Don't get philosophical on me." When, in a logic class, I tried to argue that reality was knowable to the human mind, I was told, "No enlightened person believes he can know anything." When, in an obligatory course on government, I challenged a professor who spoke glowingly of Soviet Russia, he informed me, "You're just prejudiced against dictatorships."

Rand's portrait, autographed to Nathaniel,
1951, one year after they met

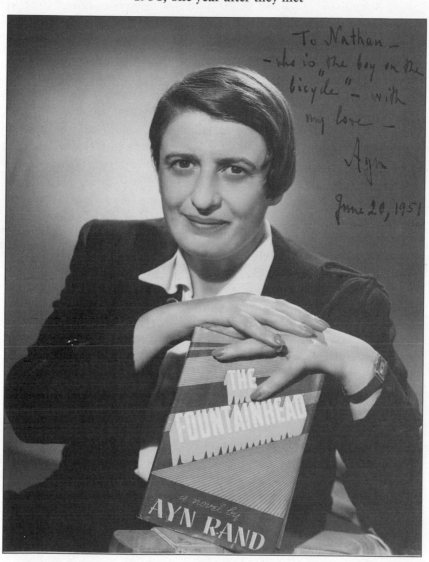

With Ayn I shared my feelings of boredom and impatience with other people. She smiled a little sadly, but she nodded in understanding.

In later years there were many discussions of feelings Ayn did or did not recognize that first year. She would say, "I don't think I would have permitted myself to know, at first. The situation was impossible. Being that unaware of my feelings is out of character for me, isn't it? I was not evading—I would not evade knowingly—but I suppose it was a kind of suppression, or repression, or something. I knew you had my kind of face and that you were my kind of person and had the best mind of anyone I'd met, but I never allowed myself to think further than that. But if I were to read it in a novel, I would certainly have suspected. The dramatist in me would have been on the alert."

She admitted to great caution in approaching our relationship. Her inscriptions in my copies of *Anthem, We the Living,* and *The Fountainhead* were perhaps unusually reserved, for example. Ayn said of these early inscriptions, "I was so cautious in the beginning. So concerned about what was appropriate to say on paper. And yet, wasn't I already feeling . . . almost everything?"

Not long after we met Ayn and Frank, Barbara said to me, "I wonder what their social life is like." I replied, "It's hard to imagine them in ordinary social settings, isn't it? I mean, you know, with ordinary people." Over time, we met a number of their friends.

One of these friends was a young screenwriter, Albert Mannheimer, who was working on the screen adaptation of Garson Kanin's *Born Yesterday.* Ayn had converted him from Marxism. She had been amused by the fact that he had proposed to convert her. She appreciated his intelligence and his seeming enthusiasm for ideas. Under her influence, he became an enthusiastic advocate of laissez-faire.

We learned that Albert was struggling with painful personal problems, involving a good deal of anxiety and depression, and Ayn was attempting to help him, chiefly through philosophical discussions. She seemed fond of him. One of his conflicts was the pull between the values represented by Ayn and those associated with Hollywood. Partly by way of explaining her "tolerance" for his problems, Ayn mentioned that years earlier when she and Frank had been financially desperate, Albert had sent her a check for five hundred dollars, which had been of enormous help to them. She spoke of her gratitude: "I can't forget his help to us when our situation was so bad." I was surprised because I had heard her declare in front of a number of people that no one had ever helped her during her years of financial struggle. Years later, she would repeat this claim to the whole world on the About the Author page of *Atlas Shrugged*. But I did not question her about this evident contradiction.

None of us appreciated that what Albert needed was not an abstract discussion of his "premises" but competent psychotherapy. Among other things, he needed the freedom to explore the roots of his feelings and to say anything that came into his mind without fear of censure, which would hardly have been possible with anyone as given to moralizing as Ayn. Of course, I did not call it "moralizing" then; I called it "moral passion." In any event, Ayn was unable to help him.

One day, she announced that she had become disenchanted with him. Lying on her sofa in miserable depression, Albert had uttered something to the effect that he did not care about ideas, that philosophy did not matter to him. To Ayn, this was anathema. In light of the convictions she thought they shared, she found Albert's utterance incomprehensible. Telling us about it, she projected an almost childlike quality of having been betrayed. She appeared both hurt and angry, and their relationship deteriorated from that point.

Ayn had specific expectations of those she regarded as friends—the closer the friendship, the higher the expectations—and if those expectations were not met, her response could be ruthless. When Albert did not pull out of his depression, when he permitted his "psychology" to get the better of his "philosophy," he lost Ayn's friendship. She did not break with him explicitly, but he lost all stature in her eyes. I fluctuated between feeling sorry for Albert while thinking Ayn had been too severe and feeling unconcerned about Albert and sorry for Ayn.

The collapse of their friendship struck me as rather sad, because her other relationships seemed cordial enough but clearly less intimate. There was Burroughs (Buzzy) Hill, a cancer researcher at UCLA, and his wife, Ruth Beebe Hill, who would later become well known as the author of *Hanta Yo*. There was the economist Henry Hazlitt and his wife, Frances; Ayn had worked with Frances while employed as a reader for Paramount Pictures more than a decade earlier. The Hazlitts lived in New York, and when they visited Los Angeles, Ayn and Frank gave a party for them, where I had an opportunity to tell Henry how much I admired *Economics in One Lesson*. There was Leonard Read, whose small firm was responsible for the first American publication of Ayn's novel *Anthem* and who founded and guided the Foundation for Economic Education, an organization dedicated to the ideals of individualism and political freedom. There was William Mullendore, president of Consolidated Edison of California; he was an older businessman of great integrity who lectured throughout the country on the merits of a free market and for whom Ayn had exceptionally high esteem. Other friends included the actress Janet Gaynor and her designer husband, Adrian, whose rather theatrical clothes Ayn loved and wore on all dressy occasions; and Morrie Ryskind, who wrote *Of Thee I Sing*.

It was exciting to meet people in Ayn's home and to feel that we were almost being shown off, not as Ayn's children (there was nothing maternal in Ayn's manner) but as products of her philosophy. "Certainly not," she snapped when someone asked if she felt like our mother. Then she added, "They're not my children—they're the children of *The Fountainhead*." She felt a need to stress the intellectuality of our relationship.

It was exciting to see Ayn moving among her guests with great charm, warmth, and even humor; to see Frank sitting in a corner with someone, talking with surprising animation, perhaps about his activities on the ranch; and to know that, after all the guests had left, Barbara and I would remain for the postmortem on the evening, which could go on for another six hours.

"They all seem nice, intelligent," I remarked to Ayn, "and they all seem to admire you. But . . ." I felt hesitant and was not certain how to express myself. "Do they actually share your deepest interests and values?" Ayn shrugged. "That's a good question. To answer literally, possibly yes in one or two respects and definitely no in a good many others."

Had I asked that question from some impulse of inappropriate possessiveness? When I conveyed my concern, Ayn laughed. "If you did," she said, "I approve. It's what I would have done in your place. That's what I call the 'Dominique premise'—not wanting to share your values with anyone. As a young girl, I hated it when someone said he liked the same books or music as I did. I wanted my values to be my private possession. In effect, I felt that no one else was good enough to share them. If that's how you feel about me, darling, I'll take it as a compliment."

I was amused by her use of "darling," which I noticed she said frequently—to me, to Frank, to Barbara. It was her one touch of Hollywood. In that moment, I heard only her cheerfulness and warmth. I was oblivious to other implications in what she was conveying—the subtle encouragement of estrangement from the world.

Barbara and I gathered that many brilliant and celebrated people visited Ayn and Frank's home. Yet I agreed with Barbara when she observed, "Have you noticed that they are not really close to anyone? There's always a distance." I agreed rather proudly because I felt no such distance between Ayn and Frank and us.

Ayn made it clear that she preferred the informality of just the four of us sitting around and talking. "I'm not really good at gracious living," Ayn said many times. By "gracious living," she meant anything above the most basic amenities. We noticed that she looked most comfortable with her hair barely combed, snags in her stockings, a casual blouse and skirt, and hastily applied lipstick. It was as if material reality, like cooking, was a boring distraction from writing and having intellectual discussions.

Notwithstanding the passion she conveyed for the physical world in her writing, there was a good deal of the ascetic about her. Her appreciation of physical reality seemed abstract, as when she contemplated the beauty of a distant horizon. As a writer, she was masterful at recreating sensory reality—sight and sound and motion—and many of her descriptions of nature are almost reverential in their lyricism. Moreover, most of her heroes and heroines skillfully manage the physical world. But she herself lived almost entirely in a world of ideas.

Locks that jammed, toasters that malfunctioned, blouses with missing buttons, dresses with falling hems—all seemed to be malevolent adversaries whose sole intention was to frustrate and thwart her. I was sometimes astonished at the intensity of her exasperation over such trivia.

An example of Ayn's estrangement from physical reality was that she never learned to drive an automobile. She was entirely dependent on Frank for transportation, a dependence she professed to hate. He was not a good driver, and Barbara and I witnessed more than one exchange of harsh words when Ayn became agitated and impatient with him. In view of Ayn's independence and her admiration for technology, I couldn't understand how she would not learn to drive. When I told her so, she said, "Oh, Frank tried to teach me, but it didn't go well, and Frank is afraid I'll be thinking about writing and not have my mind on the road, and he's probably right." I had the sense that she was trying to romanticize the situation, and I dropped the subject, mystified. I felt that her self-concept did not include being able to drive a car; that simply did not fit with her relationship to the material world.

There may have been another reason that she did not drive. She was so much more powerful than Frank in virtually all other respects that she may have elected, consciously or otherwise, to remain dependent on him in this one area, whatever the inconvenience. Perhaps that was her way of protecting their relationship.

Although we rarely discussed it, Barbara and I found Ayn and Frank's relationship puzzling. We wondered what they had in common. He never participated actively in our discussions, did not read books, was clearly not an intellectual, and did not have her energy or passion. They had met when he was a struggling actor. Now Frank was operating their thirteen-acre ranch, which he had reconditioned and landscaped, growing flowers and citrus trees as a commercial enterprise. He was most alive and talkative when discussing his ranch activities.

"I never miss acting, never think about it," he told me cheerfully. "I love the ranch."

"Frank believed in me. He saw who I was and what I would become when no one else did, when we were both young and struggling and had nothing," Ayn told us. "We have the same sense of life. But Frank is too disgusted with people to share what he is with the world."

Frank would listen silently to such statements, almost as still as the painting on the wall. If he was not "disgusted" with Ayn, Barbara, or me, I found myself wondering why he was so silent during our meetings. He had great natural dignity and considerable charm and always projected enormous benevolence, and I felt much affection for him. Yet I found his lack of ambition incomprehensible, given that he was Ayn Rand's husband. For another man, operating the ranch would have been a perfectly legitimate occupation. But when Ayn spoke of work and career, she spoke of changing the world, of having an impact on history. "I could never love anyone who was not a hero," she said. Literally, a *hero* meant someone with moral virtue high above the average, but in the contexts in which she used the term, it also usually connoted someone with a range of vision and ambition far beyond anything Frank suggested. I recognized that there was something between them I did not understand.

Yet I made no particular effort to know Frank, which I now badly regret. I would ask an occasional question about his ranch activities or admire the beautiful peacocks he raised or observe that he looked a little tired. But within moments, my attention swung back to Ayn. She was a great light that illuminated anyone in her purview and that left the rest of the world in shadows. She and Frank both seemed to regard this state of affairs as natural. Most people I saw at the ranch treated Frank as I did. He was the man who wasn't quite there.

At this time, I had absolutely no intimation of trouble between Ayn and Frank. Much later, Ayn told me that those years on the ranch had been bad for them. They were quarreling a great deal. She was bothered by his passivity and lack of intellectuality. Then she confided that in the entire history of their relationship, he had never once initiated sex; it was always she who began it. After that, she said, everything went fine; he was involved and uninhibited. But it was not difficult to imagine how that would leave her feeling. Then, there was the plain fact of their enormous intellectual differences—not merely the issue of intelligence but also differences in how their minds worked. She understood only pure, linear, sequential reasoning; he was almost totally intuitive. Although he could appreciate her cognitive style, she was never really comfortable with his. She said that she had been thinking of divorce but wanted to wait until the novel was finished, because she dreaded the interruption of her work. Work came above everything. And yet, years later, she told me that she could not live without him. He was, in his own sad way, her rock.

Ayn loved to talk about the beginning of their relationship. When they met for the first time, they were both in their twenties. Having arrived in America only a few months earlier, she had come to Hollywood. She had hoped to write scripts for silent films while she mastered the English she would need for her future novels. By an extraordinary stroke of good fortune, she fell into a conversation with Cecil B. DeMille, who saw her staring at him near the gate of his studio. "Why are you looking at me?" DeMille had asked, and she had answered in a daze of excitement that she had just come from Russia and was happy to see him. She greatly admired his films, she told him, and wanted to write for the movies. Charmed and intrigued, he invited her to watch the daily shooting so she could learn how films were made, and he gave her a job working as an extra in his current production, *The King of Kings*. Frank had a bit part in the film.

She had seen Frank earlier that day on a streetcar headed for the DeMille studio in Culver City. "I took one look at him," Ayn told us, "and, you know, Frank is the physical type of all my heroes. I instantly fell in love." On the streetcar, she had been terrified that he would get off and that she would never see him again. On the set, determined to attract his attention, she tripped him, which led them to talk for a while and exchange names. "I couldn't think of any other way to make contact," she said, smiling.

Frank did not mention to her that this was his last day on the set. When shooting was finished, he simply vanished. He had found her interesting, it seemed, but he had not been aggressive about it. He had planned to wait for her, but someone offered him a lift and he took it. I thought there was a faint hint of resentment when she mentioned this. "Why couldn't you have waited for me that first day?" she asked Frank in mock reproachfulness. For nine months, she dreamed—and despaired—of finding him again. "You can't imagine how miserable I was," she remarked.

During those nine months, Frank was her obsession. This fascinated me, in view of how little she knew about him. From the perspective of today, I would say that Frank's appearance and manner obviously spoke to a private, inner vision, a male archetype existing within her psyche. When this happens, when we meet someone who seems to embody the traits of our opposite gender archetype, we can be flung instantly into the experience of romantic love. If our perception of the other is realistic, if more detailed knowledge supports our initial impression, love can flourish. If on the other hand, we are merely projecting our own needs and longings, we step into a dream—or a nightmare—from which we may not ever choose to awaken.

One day, while working for DeMille as a junior screenwriter, she wandered into a public library and saw Frank. He looked up and recognized her, and they went out to walk and talk. They spoke about writing and acting and life, and both were hit by an instant sense of profound affinity. It did not take long for them to decide—or for Ayn to decide—that they were "soul mates."

Ayn said, "When Frank began to talk about movies, I could see how much alike we were in our values. He hated the conventional. He loved the daring and the heroic."

"One of the most striking things about her," Frank reminisced, "was the absence of any trace of deviousness. The total honesty. If she liked something, she liked it violently. If she didn't like something, she would communicate that violently, too. She never wondered if she was going to succeed. The only question was how long it would take."

"Frank seemed completely unaffected by other people," she said. "It was as if he existed alone in the world. Like Roark."

Listening to her tell the story of their beginning, I enjoyed her openness; she spoke like a young girl, and I thought that was how a woman should speak about the man she loves. The women in her novels conveyed the same hero worship. It did not matter that I could not fully understand Ayn's worship of Frank. What mattered to me was her capacity to experience love that way.

What Frank conveyed was affection and admiration rather than passion. I took this to be a matter of form rather than content, assuming that at the core their feelings for each other must be of the same magnitude. There was so much I did not grasp.

I gathered that she saw in her kind of hero worship the essential meaning of femininity. One day, I asked her, "Don't men worship women? I mean, the women they love?"

"Oh, I suppose so, but that's not how I would think of it. By 'worship,' I mean our highest capacity for admiration, reverence, looking up. I see man as superior to woman, and . . ."

"Oh, Ayn," I protested. "You don't. You're joking!"

"I am not joking," she answered seriously.

"Superior in what? Intelligence? Creativity? Moral worth?"

"No, of course not. In spiritual or intellectual matters, the sexes are equal. But man is bigger, stronger, faster—better able to cope with nature."

"You mean, at a purely physical level?"

"The physical is not unimportant."

I would return to this issue many times over the years. I did not feel fully comfortable with her point of view. Yet I would discover that many of the most independent, strong-minded women I met shared it.

Ayn would smile good-naturedly at my evident bafflement. Once she said to me, as if to make the matter clear once and for all, "Don't you understand that a truly strong woman wants to see a man as stronger? Certainly her man." When I asked why, she answered, "For the pleasure of surrendering."

I persisted. "So in a way the issue is sexual?"

She laughed. "Of course." Then she added, "And beyond that, the pleasure of being helpless at times, of laying down the burden of strength. In a way, that is also sexual. A woman can't do this with a man she doesn't look up to. Nathan, be honest. You understand me perfectly. That feeling of surrender—that is exactly how you expect a woman to feel about you."

"Maybe so," I conceded reluctantly, "but I wouldn't try to defend my position philosophically."

"I would," she said brightly.

On one visit, I acquainted Ayn with the nature of Barbara's and my situation—the difference in the strength of our feelings for each other. I said that whereas my feelings for Barbara were romantic and sexual, hers for me were not. "What kind of men does Barbara like?" Ayn wanted to know. I muttered something about Barbara's being confused and in transition.

While conveying respectful sympathy toward Barbara, Ayn made it clear that she found Barbara's psychology difficult to understand. In Ayn's view, our sexual desires are the product of our deepest values, and if Barbara's values were the ones she professed and seemed to hold, how could she not be in love with me? I felt acutely uncomfortable listening to this, yet I could not deny that I felt much as Ayn did. Subsequently, she privately conveyed her perspective to Barbara, who later reported it to me a little sadly. I was torn between embarrassment, gratitude to Ayn, pity for Barbara, and misery.

One day, I visited Barbara in her apartment. She'd had some kind of quarrel with her current boyfriend and looked confused and unhappy. She flung her arms around me, pressed her face against mine, and whispered, "Don't give up on me." She had such a look of innocence, vulnerability, and childlike goodness that I felt a rush of tenderness; I also felt uncertainty. Was this merely a mood, or was she genuinely trying to tell me something? The next time I saw her, she was cheerful again, and it was as if the moment had never happened.

During those first months, I looked for opportunities to draw Ayn out on the subjects of love and sex, hoping to gain insights that might illuminate my relationship with Barbara. Ayn told us that she was developing her theory of sexual attraction in her novel and that, in fact, it was important to the plot. The theory is dramatized through the character of Hank Rearden, primarily through his conscious philosophical convictions. This was the level at which Ayn tended to think, and it imposed a severe limitation on the theory. Her view of sex, as I grasped only years later, was badly oversimplified. And yet her core idea is one that many psychologists today recognize as valid—that our deepest vision of ourselves, as well as our most intimately personal values and our underlying sense of life, will inevitably be manifest in our sexual-romantic responses—above all, in the people with whom we fall in love.

In the spring and summer of 1950, the chief result of Ayn's theory of sex (which of course I shared by then) was to increase Barbara's guilt about not being in love with me. I do not think this was Ayn's intention, and she was doubtless unaware of her impact. In her own way, she was laying a foundation for Barbara's and my eventual reconciliation by treating as more and more self-evident the idea that I was, in some sense, a hero. I could not have conceived that a day would come when Ayn's theory of sex would be used not against Barbara but against me.

That summer, Barbara's cousin Leonard Peikoff came to visit us in California. He was seventeen years old.

Leonard struck me as high-strung; he was chronically anxious. He was eager to meet the author of *The Fountainhead,* and we had promised to take him to see her. One evening, we drove together to the ranch. Within a few minutes of arriving, he plunged into the philosophical questions he had come prepared to raise, which we all found delightful.

One question was especially important to him: "Is Howard Roark idealistic or practical?"

In a conversation that lasted over an hour, Ayn ended by saying, "If your ideals are rational, if your moral principles are based on reality, there's no conflict. The moral is the practical. Roark is totally practical— and totally consistent in the principles he lives by. That's why he succeeds.

Whenever you think you have a conflict between the idealistic and the realistic, check your premises about what you've accepted as 'idealistic.'"

This idea, for Leonard, was not merely important but totally revolutionary. It went against just about everything he had ever heard. He was euphoric.

Some months later, he wrote that he had decided against a career in medicine, in defiance of his family's expectations, and that he was going to major in philosophy.

As the months passed and as our friendship with Ayn and Frank deepened, we learned more details of their past—where they had been born, what their relationship with their families was like, and a little about how they had struggled in earlier days.

Ayn was born on February 2, 1905, in the city of Saint Petersburg (subsequently known as Petrograd and then Leningrad before once again becoming Saint Petersburg), which is the setting of *We the Living*. "Ayn Rand was not my original name," she told us. "My first name was Alice. I adopted the name Ayn from a Finnish writer, and I adopted the name Rand soon after coming to America—from my Remington-Rand typewriter! I never tell anyone my original family name, because if I still have relatives living in Russia, they'd be endangered." Many years would pass before I would learn (from Barbara) that her original name had been Alice Rosenbaum.

Discussing her first novel, she said, "*We the Living* is not autobiographical, except in the intellectual sense, but it does give you a good picture of Saint Petersburg—Petrograd—in the years following the revolution. Kira's mother is somewhat patterned after my mother, and Kira's Uncle Vasili after my father. He was a strong, silent, retiring man, but he was intensely anticommunist, unable to adapt, a self-made man now in an impossible situation. Self-made men were unusual at that time in Russia, and my father had been proud of having his own business; he was a pharmacist. Many occupations were closed to Jews, of course, so he chose to become a chemist. The character of Leo was inspired by a man I was in love with. Nothing ever happened between us, just a few dates, certainly not an affair, and when he stopped calling me, I suffered horribly. In some ways, that was the most painful experience of my life. Much later, I heard that he ended up in a conventional marriage. What I saw in him, what he meant to me, is what I gave to the character of Leo in the novel."

In response to a question about her mother, she remarked, "My mother and I didn't get along. She was always encouraging me to do physical exercise, which I hated. 'Make motions, Alice,' she would say. 'Make motions!' And she was very social, very people oriented, which I also disliked. She was totally not my kind of person."

I could not help but notice the detachment with which she discussed her parents, even her father, of whom she was to grow fonder during her adolescent years. But her distance seemed entirely normal to me—I related it to my feelings about my own parents.

On another occasion, Ayn told us, "I would say my childhood was happy, although I really was not close to anyone. I always received enormous recognition for my intelligence, not just from my parents and relatives but also from my teachers. I was always first in the class. I was special—unusual—and everyone seemed to know it. So that kind of recognition, I got. I was always asking questions. I drove adults crazy. I always wanted to know 'why' about whatever anyone said."

If any adult had ever cuddled her or told her she was pretty or treated her in any real sense as a little girl, she did not mention it, and somehow I felt certain that no one ever had. Or perhaps it was simply that she remembered only the kind of nurturing that paid tribute to her intelligence This perspective did not strike me as unnatural, either. Hadn't I also wondered on many occasions why people insisted on taking their childhoods so seriously?

On yet another evening, she spoke of the pleasure she took in family summer vacations, usually in the Crimea, and of her excited discovery one summer of what she called "tiddlywink" music. By this she meant music that was bright, aggressively cheerful, and defiantly nontragic. This included certain marches, songs like "It's a Long Way to Tipperary" (one of my father's favorites, which I often heard him sing), several German and American popular tunes, and, as she grew older, some selections from operettas by Lehár, Kalman, Millocker, Offenbach, and the like. She loved Rachmaninoff, Chopin, and a few other classical composers (or a few of their compositions), but not as she loved her tiddlywink music.

Sometimes, when Barbara and I arrived in the evening, we found Ayn listening to this tiddlywink music, dancing around the room and waving a bamboo stick. It was as if she wanted to laugh at all the suffering she had ever endured, to proclaim that these joyful sounds were the actual essence of life.

In contrast to such moments, on one of our visits she talked about the civil war's horrors, the communist takeover, and her reactions to communist ideology. I recall the implacable severity of her voice as she told us, "I was twelve years old when I heard the slogan that man must live for the state—and I thought right then that this idea was evil and the root of all the other evils we were seeing around us. I was already an individualist. And, you know, hearing what the communists were saying, it wasn't just the idea of sacrifice, which would have been evil enough, but the sacrifice of the highest to the lowest, the intelligent to the mediocre, the exceptional to the substandard, which is the ideal they were really preaching. . . . And for years, up to the present day, all the torture and all the slaughter and all the blood haven't stopped people from calling it a 'noble ideal.' . . . And I saw what it really was when I was twelve."

Then, with that particular brightness she exhibited whenever she could link the personal to the intellectual, she said, "When I saw that my father felt as I did, and he saw my interest in political issues, that was the beginning of a kind of bond between us."

She was convinced, no doubt rightly, that if she could not escape, she would be killed. Adjustment to the Soviet system was out of the question for her. In 1926, when travel restrictions were temporarily loosened, she obtained permission to leave the Soviet Union for a visit to the United States.

"I have to give my mother credit," she said almost reluctantly, "for saving my life. Father was apprehensive about my fate abroad, but Mother knew I had to get out. Mother was the one who got things done. She contacted relatives in Chicago, and they invited me for a visit." Her family understood that her "visit" would be permanent.

For a few months, she lived with her Chicago relatives, about whom she had almost nothing to say except that they were kind to her. Later, in Barbara's biography of Ayn, *The Passion of Ayn Rand,* they were quoted as saying that they were fond of her and admired her but found her self-absorption more than a little dismaying. She typed on the kitchen table noisily, late into the night, oblivious to the ruinous effects on her relatives' sleep. She did not appear interested in anything about their lives. "They were nice," she once told Barbara and me. "Very kind. But we had little in common; they were not really my kind of people." One did not sense that she felt grateful to them.

Ayn moved to Hollywood, where she met and subsequently married Frank, which allowed her to become an American citizen. "That was why I married her," Frank joked. Between difficult periods of unemployment, she worked as a movie extra, waitress, newspaper subscription salesgirl, and studio wardrobe clerk. She wrote short stories, movie outlines, and film scripts, none of which were remotely about the folks next door or in the spirit or style of the times and none of which seemed to arouse anyone's interest sufficiently to allow her career to begin properly.

When she felt ready, she began working on her first novel, which dealt with the subject of man against the state and whose central characters were young people, "because I knew I could not yet handle the kind of

Ayn Rand with husband Frank O'Connor, 1951

fully mature adults I wrote about in *The Fountainhead.*" She added that she wanted to get Soviet Russia out of her system; when *We the Living* was completed, she felt she had achieved that.

After a number of publishers rejected it, *We the Living* was published in 1936. It was attacked for its unsympathetic portrayal of Russia. This was the "Red decade" in America, when sympathy toward Soviet Russia and communism was at its height, especially among intellectuals, the literati, and show business personalities. The book did not sell well. By the time word of mouth had caught on and sales began to climb, the publisher had destroyed the plates, and the novel went out of print. She told us these facts in a dry, uninflected voice; there was no hint of self-pity.

During the same year, a play Ayn had written, *Penthouse Legend,* enjoyed a moderately successful Broadway run under the title *Night of*

January 16th. This helped financially for a while, but she knew that the real mountain she had to climb—attaining success as a novelist—still lay ahead. Her ambition was to make enough money to be able to write full-time without having to support herself through other kinds of work. She described her experience in the theater as "ghastly," chiefly because of endless fights with a producer who was trying to change her material.

When she wrote her novelette *Anthem,* she was unable to find a publisher in this country; the book was published in Great Britain. Nearly ten years went by before *Anthem* was published in the United States, when Leonard Read discovered and published it in 1946.

"To understand how I felt," Ayn remarked, "you have to know what kind of pro-communist books were being published in the thirties and hailed as serious literature."

She spoke of the continuing financial difficulties and intellectual isolation through the years of writing *The Fountainhead.* After being rejected by twelve publishers as "noncommercial" and "too intellectual," *The Fountainhead* was published in 1943 when Ayn was thirty-eight years old. The novel achieved spectacular success and brought her worldwide fame. More than half a century after its original publication, it continues to sell over one hundred thousand copies a year.

Ayn often declared that it was Frank who sustained her through her struggle. "No matter how desperate I was feeling, he would smile and say, 'Nothing that a little writing won't cure.' There was one night when I really wanted to give up. I felt nothing for the world but paralyzing loathing. And it was Frank who pulled me through. I had never seen the point of dedicating a book to a particular person; I always felt that books were dedicated, in effect, to whatever readers were worthy of them. But that night I decided that *The Fountainhead* would be dedicated to Frank."

Frank (Charles Francis) O'Connor was born eight years before Ayn on September 22, 1897, in Lorain, a small Ohio steel town. His father was a steelworker, a passive, unambitious, warm, gentle, and kind man, according to Frank, for whom Frank conveyed quietly restrained love. It was obvious that his mother had been the central power in their family, and what Frank expressed, when Ayn prompted him to talk to us about his childhood, was adoration. We gathered that his mother had been aristocratic in appearance and bearing, ambitious for her sons, strict in their upbringing, and determined that they be "gentlemen."

When his mother died, Ayn informed us, Frank was devastated; he was fifteen years old at the time. "I think the subject is still painful to him," she stated. Frank did not contradict her.

Frank was drawn to motion pictures ever since the first two-reelers came to Lorain. With his older brother, Nick, who would later become a newspaper reporter, Frank organized theatrical productions in the basement of their home. Every aspect of theater interested him: acting, directing, writing, set design. As he grew older, he gravitated specifically toward acting. I say "gravitated" because, listening to him talk about his early years, I never heard that sense of single-tracked purpose that was so evident in Ayn. Unlike her, Frank never saw himself as a person with a destiny. The telling of his life lacked force. And in the living of his life, I could not help but wonder if the man also lacked force.

As he grew older, he held many odd jobs on the way to New York City, where he hoped to find work as an actor. He obtained work from time to time as an extra and did several bit parts. Eventually, he found his way to the D. W. Griffith Studio and got a job as an extra on *Orphans of the Storm*. He admired Griffith and hoped for more roles with him, but they failed to materialize. In 1925, when Frank was twenty-eight years old and still struggling on the fringes of a career, Griffith moved his studio to Hollywood, just as the other movie studios were doing. Frank followed. Not long after, he got a bit part in DeMille's *King of Kings* and met Ayn. In the years that followed, Frank landed a few larger parts but never broke through.

He showed no anger or bitterness in speaking of this; it was as if it had all happened in another lifetime. He had put thoughts of acting behind him. I caught myself thinking that it was success that he would have found astonishing, not defeat.

"Frank is not meant to deal with people," I thought. "He's meant to deal with physical nature, with his peacocks, his flowers, his cypress trees—that's why he's at peace now. And his helplessness with people is part of why Ayn loves him."

"Let me be the one the world batters," I had heard her say. I remember also thinking that, as if by some tacit understanding, they had agreed that she would be the man and he the woman. She was the ambitious, aggressive one, out to conquer the world, and he was the loyal companion, the emotional support system, far more passive in the world.

Ayn spoke of their hardships only rarely and rather reluctantly. It was as if she did not want to grant importance to suffering. Barbara and I wished she had told us more. To us, her struggle was inspiring. What we were given in those first months was only the roughest of sketches. Much more was still waiting to be disclosed.

On September 22, 1950, Frank turned fifty-three, and Barbara and I were invited to a candlelit dinner at the ranch to celebrate—roughly seven months since our first visit there. In honor of the occasion, Ayn did the cooking herself, making what was to become one of my favorite dishes— beef stroganoff. My absolute favorite was chicken Kiev, also introduced to me by Ayn. "You've given me a new appreciation of Russian culture," I told her. Looking from face to face, from the table to the flickering candles to the luminous intensity of Ayn's eyes, I felt drunk with joy.

"The thing I want you to understand," Ayn was saying, "is that no matter how hard the battle, it can be won. You can break through. As long as a society is semifree, you have a chance. Maybe, when your turn comes, it won't be as hard for you. And if I can make it any easier, I would like that."

At moments such as this, my feeling of family was at its strongest. I thought, Here is my home. Here is my space. Here are my roots. I was conscious of longing for roots, and I welcomed what I had found.

Swept by gratitude, I said, "We're so fortunate to have you at the very beginning. You do make everything easier. Whatever happens later, we will have no right to complain about difficulties, because you've paved the way." I felt as if I had broken free of gravity, as if I dwelled in an unobstructed universe where anything was possible. It seemed as if all obstacles could be overcome, all problems could be solved, and no pain needed to be taken too seriously.

A month earlier, Barbara and I had begun reading the manuscript of Ayn's new novel. This was the background to everything I was now experiencing.

I had entered the world of *Atlas Shrugged*.

5

FOLLOWING THE PUBLICATION of *The Fountainhead*, Ayn briefly considered writing a nonfiction treatise on the morality of individualism but quickly found she had no enthusiasm for the project. Isabel Paterson, author of *The God of the Machine* and a close friend at that time, made the mistake of trying to argue Ayn into writing the book on the grounds of her duty to humankind. "Your message is so important for people," she said. If readers didn't find enlightenment in *The Fountainhead*, Ayn responded, if they did not understand its message, why should she wish to help them further? Because people need it, Paterson insisted. To which Ayn replied, "Oh, they do? What if I went on strike? What if all the creative minds of the world went on strike?" She added, as an afterthought, "That would make a good novel." When she hung up the telephone, Frank said, "It *would* make a good novel," and they stayed up all night discussing how the idea might be developed.

By morning, she had decided to make "the mind on strike" her next project. It would be "an action story, a stunt novel, no new ideas beyond what I had presented in *The Fountainhead*, just a dramatization of the importance of freedom to the creative mind." She did not yet grasp the enormousness of the assignment awaiting her. But her casual, throwaway remark to Isabel Paterson became the catalyst for the vision of John Galt, an inventor-philosopher who, in rebellion against the growing statism and collectivism of American society and its underlying morality of self-sacrifice, leads a strike of "the men of the mind."

While she researched this project, she was working six months of the year as a screenwriter for Hal Wallis Productions. She had come back to Hollywood to write the film script of *The Fountainhead*, but the project was delayed because of the war. She wrote two highly successful adaptations—*Love Letters* and *You Came Along*—but as she became more deeply immersed in the new novel, she found this division of her time increasingly intolerable and persuaded Wallis to release her from her contract. For many years to come, far longer than she had imagined, her life would belong entirely to the book that she would regard as the fulfillment of her life's purpose.

Atlas Shrugged is a philosophical novel, expressing all the author's key ideas in dramatic form. As Ayn herself said at one point, it has all the elements of a mystery, which keeps building as the story progresses. Initially, we are presented with a series of events that appear inexplicable. We see these events chiefly through the eyes of the heroine, Dagny Taggart, vice president in charge of operation of Taggart Transcontinental, the nation's largest and most powerful railroad.

The world seems to be moving toward destruction in a manner that neither Dagny nor anyone else can understand. A brilliant industrialist, Francisco d'Anconia, who is the first man Dagny ever loved, appears to abandon all purpose, as well as every character trait that Dagny admired in him; he becomes a worthless playboy. A great composer, Richard Halley, renounces his career, after years of struggle, on the night of his triumph. Businessmen who have been single-tracked in their devotion to their work—Midas Mulligan, Ellis Wyatt, and Ken Danagger—retire without explanation and disappear. A pirate, Ragnar Danneskjold, once a brilliant student of physics and philosophy, is loose on the high seas, attacking and robbing government relief ships. The world's most distinguished philosopher, Hugh Akston, who was once Francisco's and Ragnar's teacher, leaves his university position to work as a cook in a diner. The remnant of a new type of motor that could have revolutionized the economy is abandoned on a scrap heap in the ruins of a factory. And in the growing darkness of a crumbling civilization, in moments of hopelessness, bewilderment, and despair, people are crying, "Who is John Galt?" without knowing what the question means or where it came from.

Ayn had told me the first night we met that John Galt, the inventor of the motor and the man who sets all these events in motion, would not appear until the last third of the book. Yet his presence is felt from the beginning, so that ultimately he dominates the entire book. The question "Who is John Galt?"—asked by a nameless bum—opens the novel. We quickly grasp the emotional meaning of this slang expression—it is a cry of despair and a plea for help. It reflects the ominousness that permeates the atmosphere, the sense of impending doom.

At first, Ayn said she would allow us to see only Chapter One, "just to give you a sense of the novel." Then, because our excitement and enthusiasm were so high, she agreed to show us Chapter Two the following week. Then, the week after that, she showed us Chapter Three. Then all pretense was dropped, and we read all that she had written thus far, which was a little more than half the book.

No one had seen any of it, she told us, except Frank and Archie Ogden, her editor of *The Fountainhead* at Bobbs-Merrill, who had read some of the book during a visit from New York. "How can I resist two readers who react as you do?" Ayn asked happily. She remarked that after working on the book for five years, essentially in isolation, she enjoyed being able to expand the world of her writing to include the two of us. I felt privileged, honored, ecstatic.

Although I admired the literary style of *The Fountainhead*, I gathered within a few pages of the new novel that Ayn was now writing at a much higher level of mastery and control. Thus, for example, we are introduced in the first chapter to a New York City that is strangely unlike the New York City of the present, and the mood must prepare us for what is happening to the world:

> The clouds and the shafts of skyscrapers against them were turning brown, like an old painting in oil, the color of a fading masterpiece. Long streaks of grime ran from under the pinnacles down the slender, soot-eaten walls. High on the side of a tower there was a crack in the shape of a motionless lightning, the length of ten stories. A jagged object cut the sky above the roofs; it was half a spire, still holding the glow of the sunset; the gold leaf had long since peeled off the other half. The glow was red and still, like the reflection of a fire: not an active fire, but a dying one which it is too late to stop.

I lifted my head and looked at Ayn, feeling as if I literally had been hit by these words— "like an old painting in oil, the color of a fading masterpiece" and "not an active fire, but a dying one which it is too late to stop"—feeling myself quietly, irresistibly carried into the atmosphere of a collapsing civilization that precedes the birth of a new one. I wanted the expression on my face to disclose to Ayn the nature of her effect on me. I knew that she saw it, that she understood.

Dagny Taggart, an engineer-industrialist, is the first fully realized portrait of Ayn's concept of the ideal woman. Dominique clearly was not; she was torn by paralyzing inner conflicts. Kira dies at the end of *We the Living* before she achieves full adulthood. Dagny, "the woman who runs a railroad," is passionate, creative, a hero worshiper of exactingly high standards—Ayn's personal ideal. Dagny, Ayn once said, is Kira if she had grown up in America: self-confident, independent, ambitious, action oriented, highly intelligent and energetic, and totally feminine, totally at peace with herself as a woman.

Here is Ayn's description of Dagny, on the day Hank Rearden falls in love with her:

> He saw a girl standing on top of a pile of machinery on a flatcar. She was looking off at the ravine, her head lifted, strands of disordered hair stirring in the wind. Her plain gray suit was like a thin coating of metal over a slender body against the spread of sun-flooded space and sky. Her posture had the lightness and unself-conscious precision of an arrogantly pure self-confidence. She was watching the work, her glance intent and purposeful, the glance of competence enjoying its own function. She looked as if this were her place, her moment and her world, she looked as if enjoyment were her natural state, her face was the living form of an active, living intelligence, a young girl's face with a woman's mouth, she seemed unaware of her body except as of a taut instrument ready to serve her purpose in any manner she wished.

This was one of my favorite scenes in the novel, one that spoke to me at the most intimate level. It addressed my deepest longings.

"Dagny is a man worshiper," Ayn remarked, "as any heroine of mine would have to be. For Dagny, Dominique, and Kira, man is the ultimate, just as he is for me—and I don't have to tell you how important my work is to me or how important Dagny's work is to her." On another occasion, Ayn stated, "Dagny is myself, with any possible flaws eliminated. She is myself without my tiredness, without my chronic, slightly antimaterial feeling, without what I consider the ivory tower element in me, or the theoretician versus the man of action." I thought it typical that she did not say woman of action. I also thought it typical that she spoke of tiredness as a flaw. "Dagny is myself without a moment of exhaustion."

Ayn would make statements of this kind quite often, and I was always surprised; as a total human being, she seemed to be Dagny's superior. Dagny was beautiful; Ayn was not. But Ayn was a genius, a cosmic force so powerful that thoughts of physical beauty rarely entered my mind in regard to her. The only exception were those infrequent moments when I thought how Russian-Jewish she looked. She could have been a family relative, a cousin, say, of my parents, but this was a thought I quickly dismissed, because it did not fit my vision of her. No, she did not have Dagny's appearance nor Dagny's ease with the material world nor Dagny's tireless energy, although I never thought of Ayn's energy as less than awesome. But she was Dagny's creator. She was the source from which Dagny and Francisco and Rearden and all the characters flowed. And in my eyes, that placed her above them all.

When I attempted to convey this perspective to her, she became strangely modest, almost humble, as if she did not want to think herself superior to her own characters; as long as she could look up to them, she felt relief from her aloneness. She said, "A man, conceivably, could adjust to the knowledge that he was at a higher level than those around him, although no rational man could possibly enjoy that perspective. But to a woman it would be unbearable."

Ayn did have two striking physical attributes: dark, enormous eyes, alive with consciousness and passion, and beautiful legs, in scale with her height, which was about five two or three. She was proud of both these features, but apart from that she did not like her appearance. Dagny was the incarnation of Ayn's physical ideal and frustrated yearnings. Dagny was tall and slender with long legs and a sculptured face. "I see Dagny more or less as Katharine Hepburn looked in her thirties," Ayn told me.

To see a woman in heroic terms seemed natural to me. I had never been impressed by conventional notions of femininity, such as passivity or weakness. And Dagny did strike me as an exciting projection of woman at her highest possibility, in effect as a kind of goddess of the Industrial Revolution, a supremely American kind of woman.

Just as the characters in *The Fountainhead* were completely real to me and were the true companions of my adolescence, so the characters in the new novel instantly became important figures in my life, to be discussed as one would discuss intimate friends. Barbara, Ayn, and Frank spoke of them in the same way. Our "family" now consisted of not only Ayn, Frank, Barbara, and me but also Dagny Taggart, Francisco d'Anconia, Hank Rearden, John Galt, and the others. When Barbara and I met for a meal or went for an ocean drive or, on rare occasions, went to a nightclub, we talked about Ayn's characters as though they were people we would be getting together with on Saturday night.

Throughout most of the novel, until Galt enters the story, I could not decide whether Francisco d'Anconia or Hank Rearden were my favorite character. I kept switching back and forth, as did Barbara. "Rearden is definitely my favorite," Barbara would laugh, voicing my own reaction, "until Francisco enters the story. Then Francisco is my favorite—until the next scene with Rearden." But certainly Francisco, Galt's closest friend, is the most colorful figure Ayn ever created.

A brilliant intellect, a financial and productive genius, Francisco is a man whose personal theme is pure gaiety and an unclouded capacity to enjoy life. He is the first person to join Galt in the strike, and Francisco assumes the persona of an irresponsible woman-chaser, indifferent to achievement and to d'Anconia Copper, so that the world will not know that he is deliberately and systematically destroying his fortune and all his industrial properties.

"In a sense," Ayn remarked, "I created Francisco in the tradition of the Scarlet Pimpernel—or Zorro." Part of what she meant by the "stunt" aspect of *Atlas Shrugged,* which delighted her so much, was just this adaptation of elements from popular literature, even from Saturday afternoon serials, recast in high intellectual and literary form.

Ayn remarked, "Francisco is the philosophical expression—the concretization in a human character—of what I heard in the operetta music I fell in love with in my childhood. Francisco symbolizes the enjoyment of life on earth." She went on to say that the drama of his character is that he experiences the most terrible losses—he loses Dagny and he destroys d'Anconia Copper—as the cost of fighting his battle and of masquerading as his exact opposite, and yet his sense of life remains untouched by tragedy. "I suppose Francisco is about as un-Russian as you can get," I remarked. "Exactly," Ayn said, beaming. For me personally, Francisco was an inspiration, a role model, a source of spiritual fuel.

In the character of Hank Rearden, the leading industrialist in the novel and the highest representative of the kind of person Galt and Francisco wish to avenge and liberate, Ayn created a hero who is different from her other heroes in that he struggles with inner conflicts. All other Ayn Rand heroes appear to have sprung from the brow of Jupiter, fully grown and formed. "What I like about Rearden as a character," said Barbara, "is that he is not perfect. He makes terrible mistakes. You see him anguished, bewildered, torn, divided against himself—trying to understand what is right. He's a human being. And in the end, in spite of his mistakes, he is not defeated—he does triumph." Out of a misguided sense of duty and honor, Rearden chooses to remain married to a woman he does not love or respect. Out of a failure to understand his own sexuality as an expression of his mind, spirit, and values, and out of a belief that it represents the dark side of his nature, he condemns himself for his passion for Dagny, who is the first and only woman he has ever loved. Out of naïveté and mistaken generosity, he remains blindly tolerant of people who are plotting his destruction. His personal integrity, sometimes at the cost of his own agony, is absolute. "Rearden is meant to be the American businessman at his best," Ayn said. "Self-made, inventive, resourceful, unselfpitying—and much too innocent for his own good."

The plot developments in the first two-thirds of the novel are integrated around the relationship of Dagny and Rearden. We see through their actions the kind of intelligence, courage, and integrity that underlies industrial innovation and achievement. We see the heroism of that achievement, as well as its spiritual foundations. We see their impossible battle against power-hungry bureaucrats and envious, fascist business rivals who seek to defeat them (or harness them) by means of government decrees and regulations. We see, one by one, the brains of the country quitting and disappearing: industrialists, engineers, scientists, artists, philosophers, and people who have one attribute in common—ability. The gates of factories are closing, conveyor belts are stopping, roads are growing empty, buildings are crumbling, and weeds are climbing over the abandoned ruins of great industries. Dagny and Rearden fight to preserve a world that no longer exists. They are too much in love with their work and possess too much strength and endurance to accept the perspective that Francisco is slowly disclosing to them. They are unready and unwilling to "shrug" and go on strike.

Rearden is Ayn's most detailed study of masculine psychology, and I marveled at her insight, especially about sexual issues—not so much Rearden's sexual conflicts as the healthy and dominant side of his passion. "How do you know all that?" I once asked her, and she answered, "It's simple. I know what I want as a woman, and I believe that a woman's desires and a man's are complementary; it's a rational universe. So I created Rearden and my other heroes out of what I want to feel, see, and experience as a woman." She added, "You're mistaken if you think that every man would respond to Rearden's psychology as you do."

The conversation about Rearden, like most of our conversations, took place in the presence of Barbara and Frank. If there was a subtext to the discussion that had to do with building bridges of sexual understanding between Ayn and me, none of us perceived it.

In retrospect, it strikes me as obvious that through discussions of her novel, I was disclosing more and more intimate details about my own emotions to Ayn and at the same time revealing my understanding of her psychology, while Ayn was doing the same with me. Those discussions continued the courtship we had begun the first night we met, in a way that was safe, legitimate, and invisible, even to ourselves.

In the fall of 1950, when Barbara and I were reading the novel as Ayn was writing it, Galt had not yet appeared in the story. Early in our reading, I spotted his unidentified presence, to Ayn's astonishment and delight. The scene involves one of the lesser characters. Eddie Willers is Dagny's childhood friend and personal assistant. He is meant to represent the best of the average man; he is honest, conscientious, hardworking, and bewildered by the irrationality of the world around him. Eddie, the "feudal serf of Taggart Transcontinental" (which is a title he adopts proudly when it is flung at him as an insult), often takes his meals in the employees' cafeteria. There, he has acquired the habit of sitting with a nameless worker who seems to share Eddie's intense interest in the railroad. We never hear this worker speak; he is merely a silent presence with whom Eddie thinks aloud and shares his concerns. In their first scene together, I felt an odd chill run through me when I read these lines:

"Yes, we have Diesels on order, at the United Locomotive Works, but we've waited for them for two years. I don't know whether we'll ever get them or not. . . . God, do we need them! Motive power—you can't imagine how important that is. That's the heart of everything. . . . What are you smiling at? . . . Well, as I was saying, it's bad."

I stopped, read these lines again, then looked up at Ayn and announced, "The worker Eddie is talking to is John Galt."

Ayn almost screamed with excitement: "How did you know?"

I grinned. "I know you," I answered. "I know the way your mind works. It was the juxtaposition of Eddie's statement about the importance of motive power with his question to the worker, 'What are you smiling at?'"

"My god!" Ayn exclaimed. "You really do know me! No one is intended to guess this soon in the book. Galt works at Taggart Transcontinental—that's one of the ways he keeps track of what's happening in the economy and also how he acquires information about Dagny. At this point, the reader is intended to think the worker is just a literary device to facilitate exposition, not an integral part of the plot."

"You wouldn't use a literary device just for that purpose. It would be too ordinary, too unimaginative."

"You understand that, too?"

It was such moments, multiplied many times by similar incidents, that tightened the bonds between us.

Bonds were also tightening between Barbara and me. "There's no one else I can talk to as I talk to you," she said many times. "That never changes."

Neither Barbara nor I especially liked Los Angeles. I found the place too vacationlike, too lacking in energy. It was not, in my eyes, a "serious" city. I wanted to live in New York. I had not yet visited there—Barbara had— but Ayn's writings had made it the focus of my dreams. Barbara had fallen in love with New York from reading Thomas Wolfe. In my mind, moving there became associated with taking a final step into adulthood, as if New York were the "real" world.

Ayn herself spoke of longing to move back to the East. She had lived in California since her return to Hollywood in 1943, when the film production of *The Fountainhead* was delayed. Then, settled in at the ranch, she did not want to interrupt the writing of her new novel with another move. She would return to New York, she said, the minute the novel was completed. "New York is the only city," she told us.

I wondered if Frank would miss the ranch. I watched his face while Ayn was speaking; it revealed nothing. Frank, too, hated the West Coast, Ayn assured me. "Frank is as eager to return to New York as I am." He listened but did not comment.

One day, Ayn took Barbara and me into her study to show us some of the notes she had made in preparation for writing her novels. I was excited at the prospect of such intellectual intimacy. Ayn's notes on *The Fountainhead* revealed a portrait of Roark that struck me as highly spiritual. I had not yet become acquainted with Zen Buddhism and therefore did not consider how Zen-like this portrait was.

I wondered if I would ever attain the kind of serenity Ayn was describing. But right now, that did not seem important. Not when it was possible to feel this alive, not when I was standing in Ayn Rand's study being given a guided tour of her writer's mind.

I was reading, in her sharp, angular, European handwriting, some of her notes for the new novel. She believed that her most important task as a novelist was to develop an all-encompassing "rational morality." I remarked that by the time she had written this, she must have gone beyond her original notion of simply writing an action novel to dramatize the importance of political and economic freedom to the creative mind. She agreed and said that she had seen that in order to tell the story properly, she was obliged to work out her moral philosophy in comprehensive detail on the one hand and, on the other, to create a plot that would properly dramatize it.

In a novel, she said, nothing is more important than the plot, and in a philosophical novel nothing is more important than the way ideas and actions are integrated. "I despise novels like Thomas Mann's *Magic Mountain,* in which characters merely sit around and philosophize about life. And that's why I admire Dostoyevsky so much, in spite of his mysticism and his malevolence; he's a master of integrating philosophy, psychology, and action. There's no one better at it. Read *The Possessed*—it's a masterpiece. If you want to write philosophical novels, your events really have to dramatize and illustrate your ideas. Integration is everything, just as a rational human being is integrated, just as mind and body, theory and practice, need to be integrated in a proper existence."

I had not yet realized that one of the characteristics of nineteenth-century Russian novelists was to create characters on the basis of an individual's ideas—in contrast, for instance, with English novelists, who tended to characterize on the basis of social class considerations. And so I did not yet recognize how typically Russian Ayn was in this aspect of her literary approach. She told me explicitly that she created characters out of philosophical abstractions, and neither of us was aware of the psychological limitations this imposed. But I was aware of her animus against treating her heroes from a developmental perspective when I read her notes for the character of John Galt:

> No progression here. . . . He is what he is from the beginning—integrated . . . and perfect. No change in him, because he has no intellectual contradictions and, therefore, no inner conflict. . . . His important qualities (to bring out): Joy in living—the peculiar, deeply natural, serene, all-pervading joy in living which he alone possesses so completely in the story (the other strikers have it in lesser degree, almost as reflections of that which, in him, is the source); all-pervading in the sense that it underlies all his actions and emotions, it is an intrinsic, inseparable part of his nature. . . . It is present even when he suffers. . . . [I want to show] the worship of joy as against the worship of suffering, [and his] magnificent innocence—the untroubled purity—a pride which is serene, not aggressive— "the first man of ability who refused to feel guilty."

Growing up, I was bewildered by the unhappiness of most people. It had never been acceptable to me or logical that such could be the nature of life. Ayn's emphasis on joy had powerful meaning for me. I stood at her desk, looking down at these notes, with her on one side of me and Barbara on the other. I was at the center of a universe from which pain had entirely disappeared.

"Tolstoy," Ayn remarked during one of our many discussions about literature, "said that a good writer, after watching a street fight, should be able to describe a military battle. I've had to do a lot of research for this novel but perhaps not as much as you might think. It's an issue of grasping the essence, of observing the street fight. Of course, Tolstoy is not my kind of writer, although I can appreciate his skill. He's too much of a naturalist, or a 'realist.'"

"I wouldn't exactly call Dostoyevsky a romantic," I commented. By now, I had read most of his novels. "Unless you want to invent a special category, a 'negative romanticist,' who focuses on what might be and ought not to be."

"True. He writes with magnificent contempt and indignation about human irrationality. You would never call him a naturalist; he has too passionate a moral vision, even if it's one we wouldn't agree with."

There was no theme to the discussion, we were merely drifting, almost associationally, Ayn stretched out at one end of the enormous sofa and I stretched out at the other. Barbara was sitting opposite, her eyes glowing as if she were a child in a roomful of toys, and I imagined that Winnipeg felt far away to her. Coffee and pastry, served as usual by Frank, rested on the low table in front of the sofa.

I was content to listen silently while Barbara began voicing her impressions of a Dostoyevsky novel she had recently read. "The sheer intelligence of the man, never mind his neuroses, the sheer intelligence of his observations of people, of human psychology . . . and then his unexpected humor, his irony . . . and the way he takes you inside the mind of irrationalism, makes you feel it, gives you that perspective . . . It's wonderfully lucid and insane all at once." My glance swung between the two women, as if contemplating a scene that I had staged.

Occasionally, Frank and I would smile at each other in unspoken understanding.

Ayn asked if we had ever read Henryk Sienkiewicz's novel *Quo Vadis?* We hadn't. She began to extol its virtues, describing it as perhaps the finest historical novel ever written, "from the point of view of the integration of plot and theme. It deals with the moral bankruptcy of the declining years of the Roman Empire, when Christianity is first emerging. The recreation of the period, the development of the plot, the way all the elements are tied together, are magnificent. Of course Petronius, 'the arbiter of elegance,' is my favorite character."

We talked about Victor Hugo, the novelist she admired above all others, whom she had discovered as a young girl in Russia. "It was the grandeur of his vision that inspired me." She was captivated by his larger-than-life characters, the extraordinary inventiveness and imaginativeness of his plots, and his superlative sense of drama. The first Hugo novel she read was *L'Homme qui rit,* followed by *Les Misérables,* then everything of his she could find. She was fascinated by his sense of life—the vision of human existence as supremely important and the vision of man as a hero. "Even his villains are heroic. Hugo couldn't create a true villain without stature. Which I think says something about his own psychology. He was a giant."

She went on to talk about her favorite play, Rostand's *Cyrano de Bergerac,* again stressing the plot, the dramatic inventiveness, the beauty of the writing. "That is theater," she said, "which is why I can't stand to look at the junk they put on today. It's one world or the other."

When she told us that she had cried the first time she read *Cyrano,* I wondered if her dislike of her own appearance caused her to identify with the hero. I agreed with her about the play's greatness.

We eagerly consumed whatever books or plays she recommended and enjoyed them so thoroughly that if it had occurred to us that we were in any sense being tested for the purity of our premises, we would have dismissed the thought as irrelevant. What did we care? Were we not all becoming closer and closer soul mates?

Evenings such as these were fairly typical. But occasionally a note of tension would enter our discussions, when it seemed to Ayn that Barbara or I was being seduced or deluded by "alien values." In the case of Barbara, a focus of Ayn's concern was Barbara's enjoyment of Thomas Wolfe, whose novels Ayn thought to be without literary value.

First, Ayn elicited Barbara's agreement that the essential elements of a novel were plot, theme, characterization, and style. Ayn did this in the flat, unrevealing manner of a district attorney leading a witness to an inexorable conclusion. Then she began reading from *Look Homeward, Angel,* analyzing Wolfe's defects in virtually every key area of fiction. "It's all adjectives and overblown emotion," Ayn pronounced.

I felt torn. On the one hand, I agreed with Ayn. She had helped me articulate many of my own misgivings about Wolfe; aside from his literary inadequacies, I found him intellectually and spiritually empty. On the other hand, beneath Barbara's quietly gentle exterior, I knew she was suffering and that something was being dimmed within her.

To me, Ayn said, "I give Barbara enormous credit because of how much reason means to her. But her sense of life is touched by pain." She mentioned, as evidence, Barbara's enthusiasm for *Tristan and Isolde.* "She won't be at her best until she frees herself of that touch of tragedy."

I had a similar experience with Ayn regarding *Jean-Christophe,* but it was a good deal milder for three reasons: first, I was already disenchanted with Rolland; second, Ayn's assault was more philosophical than literary, and I experienced no conflict in agreeing with her; and finally, she was more easygoing about *Jean-Christophe* and did not press with the quiet, deadly ferocity she had brought to the novels of Thomas Wolfe. Still, I felt pushed along a particular path faster than I would have moved at my own speed. I did have moments of resentment at the pressure she could generate to win my agreement. But, like Barbara, I told myself that Ayn was in the right. Such moments seemed a small price to pay for the benefits of the relationship.

On the UCLA campus, through the fall of 1950 into the winter and spring of 1951, there was increasing talk of Red-baiting, hysteria about communism (would anyone have complained of "hysteria" about fascism?), and the persecution of professors with liberal or left-wing politics. This last puzzled me a good deal, because in my classes on government, economics, political philosophy, ethics, or indeed on any other subject, I heard much abuse of capitalism, the free market, the American political system, and American culture in general.

The professor who had mocked me for being "prejudiced against dictatorships" continued to make sarcastic comments about business, businessmen, and anyone misguided enough to speak in their defense. An economics professor was so openly contemptuous of anyone who did not share Keynesian premises that I was compelled to stand up one day in class and ask him point-blank, "Is it possible for a student who believes in laissez-faire to pass your course?" A professor of art history spoke glowingly of the "idealism" of Soviet Russia, as contrasted with the "materialism" of America. A psychology professor blithely announced that anyone who was not a socialist was suffering, intellectually and morally, from arrested development. Students who had never read a word of Karl Marx were spouting Marxist platitudes. And in classrooms, in the university cafeteria, on campus lawns, Barbara and I were encountering every kind of vituperation, every kind of hostility, from students who believed that we thought well of capitalism.

We did encounter conservatives on campus, and we liked them, as a group, no better than the liberals. We shuddered when we heard the expression "atheistic communism," as if the worst thing to be said about communists was that they did not believe in God. "We're atheists," we announced cheerfully, and laughed at the question, "Then why aren't you communists?" Atheism, we would say, is not grounds to condemn communism, and "loyalty to the faith of our fathers" is not grounds to champion capitalism.

Our dominant impression of liberals was of sanctimonious self-righteousness, fanatical hostility to anyone who did not agree with them, ignorance of economics, and lack of respect for a rational argument. Our dominant impression of conservatives was of moral weakness and confusion, fear of intellectuals, fanatical hostility to anyone who did not agree with them, and lack of respect for a rational argument. Both sides said, "What? You don't believe in minimum wage laws? Or protective tariffs? Or military conscription? You don't even believe that the telephone company should be a legally enforced monopoly?"

"Boy, is our work cut out for us," Barbara said gleefully.

It seemed to me that at such moments, her eyes said we were indeed meant to be together, comrades in arms, fighting for the glory of man, for the supremacy of reason, and for the sanctity of an individual life.

As time went by, we delighted more and more in mastering the intellectual arguments and communication skills that made it possible to turn around an adversary's thinking, so that that person ended up as a friend. One such person was a young businessman named Harry Kalberman who, some years later in New York, married my sister Elayne.

Through Ayn, I had discovered the works of Ludwig von Mises. One of the founders of the Austrian school of economics, he was a brilliant scholar, a lucid thinker, and an intransigent defender of capitalism. Highly esteemed in Europe, he was at that time still relatively unknown in America. I began studying his books, such as *Socialism* and the recently published *Human Action,* with great enthusiasm. I also read *The Road to Serfdom* by Friedrich von Hayek, von Mises's student, who would later be awarded a Nobel Prize for his work in economics. I was astonished to learn how thoroughly the case for socialism had been refuted—and how ignorant just about everyone on campus seemed to be of that fact.

"Of course, part of the problem you're fighting is the current intellectual fashion," Ayn said to me, "but the problem goes deeper than that. What you're really fighting, darling, is a thousands-of-years-old tradition that equates morality with self-sacrifice. That means you're fighting altruism. According to altruism, man has no right to exist for his own sake, and his prime duty is to place others above the self, sacrificing his interests for someone's idea of 'the common good.' Altruism and capitalism are incompatible. Capitalism rests on the recognition of individual rights. If man has no rights, if his life belongs to others, if self-interest and the profit motive are evil, then capitalism is evil, never mind how productive it is, and communism is noble, never mind how much blood it spills. The battle for capitalism can't be won by proving its practicality; that's been done. What the world needs—and what capitalism deserves—is a moral defense."

I said to Ayn, "When I tell people I'm opposed to altruism, they go crazy. They think it means I'm opposed to kindness, charity, benevolence, and respect for the rights of others—and yet *altruism* means none of those things. What people miss is what it actually does mean. Just the same, at a deeper level, they accept its premise—self-sacrifice to others as the highest good."

"Which is precisely the idea Auguste Comte intended when he coined the term. *Altruism* means others above self. Comte was a total collectivist, a total advocate of dictatorship. That's why the basic issue is an individual's right to his own life. That's where the battle has to be fought."

Early in 1951, I went to meet Barbara for lunch in Westwood, at a restaurant near UCLA. Barbara and I were now seeing more of each other and were closer than we had been at any time since our first months in Winnipeg.

She sat down, looked straight into my eyes, and said, "Will you marry me?"

I felt almost annoyed, as if my feelings were being toyed with out of some incomprehensible whim. To leap from our context, with all its conflicts, to a proposal of marriage? I immediately answered, "No," then added, a little more gently, "Come on. What is this about?"

"I'm afraid," Barbara said, and I saw there were tears in her eyes. "I'm afraid of what's happening to me." I knew that she meant the other men in her life, her concern about her choices, and that I represented some kind of anchor. She added, "I know you're the person I belong with. In my heart I love you. You know that."

We talked for a long time. Part of me thought, "Don't be a fool. Don't wait. Marry her now." But another part knew that would be shortsighted and self-destructive. If we were to be married, it had to be real. It had to be because Barbara loved me—not because, through me, she might "save" herself.

We agreed that we would commit ourselves to a relationship; we would see if we could make it work. Anyway, we were too young to get married now, we said. We would resume our affair. We promised sexual exclusivity. Barbara wanted to know if I would demand that she cease seeing her male friends, with whom she was not sexually involved, she assured me. No, I would not demand it.

There was little elation or joy in this discussion. It was earnest, intense, muted. I only sensed the possibility of future joy—against a background of uneasiness and agitation.

I wondered about Ayn's influence in bringing Barbara to this moment. By now, we had read nearly two-thirds of the new novel and were thoroughly acquainted with her theory of sex, which she had sketched at our early meetings. We had read the incredible scene between Francisco d'Anconia and Hank Rearden, in which neither man knows the role that the other plays in Dagny Taggart's life. Francisco says:

> A man's sexual choice is the result and the sum of his fundamental convictions. Tell me what a man finds sexually attractive and I will tell you his entire philosophy of life. Show me the woman he sleeps with and I will tell you his valuation of himself. . . . He will always be attracted to the woman who reflects his deepest vision of himself, the

woman whose surrender permits him to experience—or to fake—a
sense of self-esteem. The man who is proudly certain of his own value
will want the highest type of woman he can find, the woman he
admires, the strongest, the hardest to conquer—because only the possession of a heroine will give him the sense of an achievement, not the
possession of a brainless slut. . . . There is no conflict between the standards of his mind and the desires of his body. . . . Love is our response
to our highest value—and can be nothing else.

I found this a provocative and exciting idea. If it represented an over-
simplification of a complex psychological issue, I was not yet aware of it.
Nor was Barbara. She and Ayn had a number of private discussions about
love, sex, and relationships. For Barbara, Ayn's theory was a trap she felt
compelled to enter. Barbara would have said that she was entering in the
name of reason, in the name of self-esteem. It would be many years before
I would have the perspective, understanding, and compassion to think,
What chance could Barbara have against Ayn Rand?

One night we lay in bed together after we had made love; the lovemaking
was intense on my part, compliant on Barbara's. We were silent for a while,
and I did not know whether Barbara was still awake. Dropping the discipline I usually felt compelled to maintain with her, I surrendered to a feeling of unbearable loneliness. Too often, when we were together, I felt myself
fighting ghosts. Barbara would look at me with half-closed eyes, mysteriously remote one moment, warmly affectionate the next, but rarely straightforward about her inner experience. "I love you," she would say, but it was
not a kind of love I understood. It was not the kind of love I wanted. I
stirred in the half-darkness and Barbara turned to me. "What's the matter?"
she asked urgently, in response to whatever she saw on my face.
    "Sometimes," I whispered, choking, "this whole situation is very, very
hard." She did not say anything, just took my hand and pressed it. After
a while, she began talking about how upsetting it was for her to see me
in pain. "I always think of you as being able to handle anything. I know
this is terribly unfair, but when you look like you're suffering, I take that
to mean weakness. When there are tears in your eyes, I don't know what
to do. I want to run, and I know that's not right. It's ridiculous to expect
you not to have feelings. But if I'm honest, I would have to admit I lose
respect for you."
    I could not speak. I felt an icy sense of withdrawal. She's a child,
I thought. She's a child. Then what are you doing with her? Get out.
Get out.

I did not know what Barbara was aware of in that moment, or what she sensed from me, but she threw her arms around me and clung tightly. Feeling the warmth of her body and the hunger of my flesh for contact and some stubborn refusal to lose the hardest battle I had ever fought, I heard myself answering, Get out? What are you thinking? You've got to give her time.

The thoughts I had tried to dispel in that moment had not been extinguished; they had merely been submerged. They had gone underground until a time when I would be ready to hear them. By then, we would be married.

April 9, 1951, was my twenty-first birthday, and Barbara and I were invited to spend the day at the ranch on the following Sunday. Since Ayn usually wrote seven days a week, often from early morning until well into the evening, we did not spend many full days with her. "I'm taking the day off in honor of your birthday," she announced.

When we arrived, I could see that she and Frank were smiling in some special way, as if about to spring a surprise. After we were seated, they disappeared into Ayn's study and returned a moment later with their arms full of books, which they proceeded to spread out on the coffee table. It was a beautiful leather-bound set of Ibsen's complete works, red, gray, and gold, and I was stunned into speechlessness. "Happy birthday, darling!" Ayn said brightly and kissed my cheek. Frank stepped forward, put his hand on my shoulder, and said with surprising feeling, "Happy birthday, Nathan."

I was moved beyond my power to explain. I reacted as if I had never before received a gift from anyone. I felt lifted out of myself in gratitude and euphoria.

Later, the four us went for a walk. Seeing how affected I was by the gift, Ayn smiled, "What's the matter? Didn't you really believe we were friends?"

"I never before felt I belonged anywhere," I said. "I would have said it didn't bother me, either. Now I know it must have—because of what I'm feeling right now. I don't remember ever being this happy."

"Frank likes you very much. He likes you both. That's unusual for him—he doesn't like most people. If Frank hadn't felt there was something special about your letter, we wouldn't have met. I would have felt, Why bother? I've had too many bad experiences. But this only proves why one shouldn't make collective judgments."

Later, when Barbara was walking with Ayn, and I with Frank, I said to him, "This is really so wonderful of you both."

"You don't know what you're doing for Ayn," he answered.

"You don't know what Ayn is doing for me."

"Oh, yes, I do," Frank said, suddenly wise and assured. "When you're young, you can't know what you are yet. Not fully. You can't know what you've got. But an older person can see it and help you to see it. Ayn gives you that. She helps you to appreciate yourself. She can see your future."

For a few minutes we walked in silence. Then, unexpectedly, he remarked, "You and Barbara will work things out."

"Do you think so?"

"She's a good girl. And Ayn will help you."

We decided to move to New York to continue our education. A conflict between Barbara and a socialist professor made this seem necessary, when he told her that she would do well to seek her graduate degree elsewhere because he could not imagine any thesis she might write that could elicit his approval.

"By all means go to New York," said Ayn. "Barbara can't possibly remain at UCLA. Not after what that bastard told her. And you two shouldn't be apart, not now. But god, I'll miss you both! Terribly!"

It was not an easy decision. When I thought of being in New York with Barbara, making a fresh start together, not knowing anyone there, not having any of her old boyfriends to contend with, I felt optimistic, excited, and confident that the last barriers between us would dissolve. When I thought of separating from Ayn and Frank, I felt pain—more than I expressed to anyone.

Barbara was two years ahead of me in college; she had already earned her bachelor's degree and would be working toward her master's in philosophy at New York University while I completed my undergraduate degree. In retrospect, it is not easy for me to re-create the context in which moving to New York—leaving Ayn—seemed an appropriate action to take. Looking back, I find my own decision astonishing. It only underscores for me how desperately I wanted my relationship with Barbara to succeed.

We all consoled one another by talking about exchanging letters, making phone calls, even visiting each other. "And, anyway," said Ayn, "the moment the novel is finished, Frank and I will move back to New York." She had now been at work on the book for six years. "It will only be a year or two. Two at the most. I don't dare interrupt the work sooner. I'm coming to the chapter where John Galt enters the story!"

On an afternoon near the end of June, we drove to the ranch for the last time. Barbara seemed sad to leave but not as sad as I. Many years later, she would acknowledge that part of her was eager to be away from this environment, away from Ayn's influence, free and on her own.

Ayn and Frank seemed so unhappy to see us go that I found it difficult to stay connected with my own feelings. I concentrated on projecting an air of calm and restrained cheerfulness, seeking to dispel any hint of tragedy.

When we embraced good-bye, all four of us had tears in our eyes. We wiped them away, grinning, trying to cheer one another up.

"It's only for a little while," said Frank, echoing Ayn. I thought of Frank's having told me that the best years of his life were those he had spent on the ranch.

In spite of my sadness and my hesitancy about leaving, I felt the exhilaration of embarking on a new adventure. I was going to New York—the greatest city in the world, the center of *The Fountainhead* and of the new novel, the heartbeat of Western civilization, a place of drama and challenge and unlimited possibilities. Through Ayn's writing, and through my relationship with her, I had fallen in love with America. I felt connected to this country as I had never felt connected to the country of my birth. Ayn had a European's appreciation of the United States and a keen understanding of its historical uniqueness, and she had transmitted her vision to me. Now I was moving to the city that was, for the entire world, the symbol of America.

We drove up the long driveway to the road that would lead us through Chatsworth, back to Los Angeles. I stopped to wave good-bye one last time. We were too far away to see their faces clearly. I would not know until a long time afterward that as they waved to us, tears were streaming down Ayn's face.

6

THE FIRST FEW MONTHS in New York turned into a nightmare. Later, I would wonder why Ayn was so intent on saving my relationship with Barbara, given the nature of Barbara's and my problems. If someone had asked me that question then, I would have answered that surely it was because Ayn knew the relationship was important to me. Only much later did an additional explanation occur to me.

On leaving California, Barbara had spent a couple of weeks with me in Toronto and had then gone on to Winnipeg. We planned to meet later in the summer in New York. We were not yet engaged, but we were "engaged to be engaged."

I was uneasy over the separation. Our relationship was tenuous. I did not know whom Barbara might meet or what former boyfriend might reenter her life. I knew only that no foundation of confidence had been built between us yet.

We remained in constant contact by letter and telephone. When we spoke, I heard a disquieting mixture of warmth, strain, intimacy, distance, affection, elusiveness, and anxiety. But a phone call or two later, she would be loving and euphoric, eager for our future together, and I would tell myself not to be "malevolent."

The uncomplicated happiness of my relationship with Ayn stood in sharp contrast, even though I defined the relationship as being of a different order. With Ayn, everything was simple, natural, and easy. I wrote to her every three or four days, sharing my experiences in Toronto: my efforts to convert my family to our philosophy, my struggles to write a novel, an unexpected series of encounters with my cousin Allan Blumenthal, and my concerns about Barbara.

Writing those letters gave me a sense of being connected to a living intelligence I could trust—and to a rational universe. I was not alone in the world. Barbara might be problematic, but Ayn was as firm and reliable as the law of gravity.

I wrote to Ayn about my political and philosophical arguments with people and my often unsuccessful efforts to remain calm in political discussions—especially with my sister Florence and her husband, Hans Hirschfeld, a businessman, both of whom I was intent on converting.

Florence, now twenty-eight, and Hans, thirty-eight, were initially rather adversarial, especially about issues pertaining to political economy. Gradually, however, they began to give way. But the process of conversion would nonetheless take years. I do not think it was complete until they read *Atlas Shrugged*.

Elayne and Reva, now twenty-six and twenty-five, respectively, had no particular interest in politics. They were relatively receptive to my ideas about reason, individualism, enlightened self-interest, capitalism, and romantic realism in art.

I wrote to Ayn and Frank about Reva's returning from her honeymoon with her new husband, Sholey Fox, an architect, and about Reva's desire that I "educate" him, as she was ahead of him in her acceptance of Ayn's ideas.

It would not have occurred to me to mention to Ayn that I was pleased that these intellectual discussions allowed me to connect with my sisters and, in the case of Reva and Florence, with their husbands. I would not have acknowledged this thought even to myself. What did *family* have to do with the great issues of life?

I sent Ayn and Frank one postcard from New York City, where I went for an interview at New York University. I was seeing the city for the first time, and I thought of Ayn's description of Roark's walk through these same streets. Dreams and reality flowed into each other. The postcard contained a magnificent photograph of the skyline. My whole message read, "Good God!"

A few weeks later, in a letter dated August 19, 1951, I wrote as if trying to break a barrier: "I miss you terribly and think of you always. The one consolation to the fact that we may not see each other for a year is that with both of us in the East, we'll have the rest of our lives together to solve the mysteries of the universe." The letter began, "Dear Ayn and Frank," but it read like a letter written solely to Ayn.

Again, in a letter dated August 21, I wrote: "Ayn, I don't know whether it's love or what—but as each day goes by and I look at your picture on the mantelpiece near my typewriter, you seem immeasurably better looking." And as an aside to Frank, I wrote, "Frank, my offer is still open to trade the picture for the real thing. I've got the best picture of Ayn framed in a leather case and placed on the mantelpiece of my study—but I could easily mail you the leather case and put Ayn on the mantelpiece. What do you say?"

I thought I was being funny.

During that same summer, I resumed my friendship with Allan Blumenthal. He was now twenty-three years old, of medium height and slight build, with light hair and blue eyes. He was a bit inhibited perhaps, in the manner of an English schoolboy—as "correct" as ever in demeanor.

He was curious about Ayn Rand and was obviously impressed that I knew her. He wanted to know what she and Frank were like, where they lived, what we all talked about, and whether she really meant the things she had written in *The Fountainhead*. Looking at me as if he had never quite seen me before, he said, "And you've become a friend of hers? Who would have thought?"

When I visited him a few days later, he began talking with a kind of driven candor about some painful personal problems. I was on fire with the notion that ideas were able to explain emotions and behavior—and with the possibility of changing emotions and behavior by changing the ideas that gave rise to them. I was able to help him, for which he thanked me earnestly. He stunned me by saying, "You might have saved my life."

Allan still dreamed of being a concert pianist. I urged him not to relinquish this aspiration. "Who cares what your family wants? It's what you want that's important." Then I added, "You see? This is why Ayn Rand stresses that to be selfish in the rational sense, as contrasted with the petty sense, takes courage and integrity. It's anything but easy. Never mind what people tell us."

In late August, Barbara and I met in New York to register at New York University and to begin a new life together.

Barbara moved into a modest walk-up on Twenty-Ninth Street, a few yards from Fifth Avenue, and I took a room in the Carteret Hotel on Twenty-Third, two blocks west of Fifth.

Our favorite activity was walking, looking at buildings, and watching people and automobiles streaming past, the sights and sounds merging with everything we had ever read about New York. We told each other that Ayn was right, that this was the only city, the center of the universe, and wouldn't life be perfect when Ayn and Frank were here with us?

On another September evening, I answered the telephone to hear Ayn's exuberant voice. "Well, darling, how would you like to see us? I can't stand California any longer. We're moving back to New York. We'll be there in three weeks."

I would not let her off the phone. "Wait a minute! This is wonderful. But how come? What changed your mind?"

"When I finished the chapter in Atlantis, when Dagny meets Galt and discovers the secret of the strike, I thought, Why am I sentencing myself to exile? Who knows how long I will need to finish the book? I want to be in New York. And naturally, darling, I miss the two of you. Anyway, that's my explanation. Frank would answer a little differently." She chuckled. "I don't know if I should tell you what he said." Her voice sounded abnormally alive. "He says I've become a hopeless dependent and can't live without you!"

I laughed in answer. "I like Frank's version better."

When I ran to Barbara's apartment to share the news, she seemed as happy and excited as I was.

There was a quality of intellectual seriousness about the professors at NYU that somehow seemed different from what, for the most part, I had experienced at UCLA. I even liked the fact that NYU at Washington Square had no real campus but consisted of a group of structures that looked like rather old office buildings. The atmosphere was almost grim: no lawns, no playing fields, no terraced banks of flowers, nothing to distract from the life of the mind. There were bookstores everywhere—in the streets surrounding the university and scattered throughout Greenwich Village—and I spent hours in them, drunk on how much was there for me to learn. I wrote about this to Ayn and Frank, as I wrote about everything important in my life. Each letter ended with "Hurry up!" or "Why aren't you here yet?"

During the third week of October, Ayn and Frank arrived in New York and moved into an apartment their lawyer had arranged—at 36 East Thirty-Sixth Street. "Easy walking distance from my hotel!" I shouted to Barbara on the telephone.

And then the four of us were together again, in Ayn and Frank's apartment, talking about "Atlantis," the chapter Ayn had recently finished. Barbara and I were laughing and interrupting each other, and Ayn was saying to me, "Nathan, you're impossible. Please let me finish a sentence." Such interruptions were her biggest complaint about me in the first year or two of our friendship.

Ayn appeared vibrant, intense, inexhaustible, as if introducing Galt and establishing his character in the story had renewed her vitality. When she spoke of him, her eyes glowed with love. Frank and she had driven from Los Angeles to New York, and Frank, who of course had done all the driving, looked happy and pleasantly tired. "It's good to see you two," he smiled. Barbara, too, looked happy, with only the faintest reflection of anxious tension in her eyes, and I brushed my awareness of it aside, because I did not want it to be part of this occasion.

As we sat around talking about Ayn's new chapter—Barbara and I had insisted on reading it that night—John Galt felt present among us, a spiritual presence of overwhelming reality.

We talked about how Ayn saw Galt, relative to her other two heroes in the novel, Rearden and Francisco, and Ayn said that she did not intend Galt to be perceived as their superior in any important way. He is "merely more serene within himself, and of course free of any conflict." Rearden has conflicts, she said, but at his core he is on the same level as the other two men. Francisco, she declared, is totally on Galt's level; he, too, has no internal conflicts, and the differences between them are ones of style, not essence. Dagny falls in love with Galt, she explained, because in form he is a more complete embodiment of her personal values. Did we think readers would find that difficult to understand? Ayn wanted to know. "I don't find it difficult to understand," Barbara stated, "but I think readers might." We talked about what might be said in the novel to make the issue clearer, but our efforts trailed off inconclusively.

The next evening, after rereading the chapter, I suggested that perhaps Galt, as presented, was a bit abstract and needed a few more personal touches, more indications of his feelings at a simple human level. Ayn agreed. In the final version of his characterization, Ayn added "humanizing" elements not present in the first draft we read. When, for example, Ayn showed me a reference that Galt makes to his pain about abandoning the motor he has invented, she announced, "I put that line in for you, darling." Galt remains, however, the most abstract of her heroes. Ayn offered this explanation for her characterization of him: "One does not approach a god too closely. One does not get too intimate with him. One maintains a respectful distance from his inner life."

Atlas Shrugged has about it the quality of a great myth—all the characters, major and minor alike, are touched by this quality. But in her portrayal of Galt, Ayn shifted to the highest level of abstraction, perhaps because in him she wished to focus most clearly on the underlying spirituality of her vision of the human ideal. "Galt," she once said to me, "is definitely presented as man seen as a god. To some extent, that's true of all my heroes, but in Galt it's most pronounced." I added, "In essence, we see him only as Dagny sees him. He's written exclusively from an external perspective, from the perspective of woman as man worshiper." Somewhere, dimly, it occurred to me that Ayn's approach to the characterization of her heroes—Galt, in particular—would have to exact a cost in diminished psychological realism. At the time, the thought did not really register.

One evening when the two of us were together, Barbara cheerfully announced, "I've solved the problem of who is my favorite—Rearden or Francisco." "How?" I asked. She answered, "Galt is my favorite."

My joy at Ayn and Frank's return to New York lasted about two or three weeks.

The three of us were sitting in Ayn's apartment—Ayn, Barbara, and I. Frank had gone off somewhere. Barbara and Ayn sat at one end of the room and I at the other. I stayed apart to stress my nonparticipation; I thought this might make talking easier for Barbara. She was conveying to Ayn some of her confusion about the realm of emotion, about love, sex, and human relationships. And she spoke about her feelings of anxiety.

My mind was half-drifting when, to my surprise, in a quietly purposeful voice, Ayn asked Barbara if she had slept with a young man while she and I were purportedly "committed." He was someone with whom she had claimed to have a warm but platonic relationship. Barbara's answer was vague but gave me the impression that she had not. Then, a few minutes later, in the same tone, Ayn asked the question again. I was puzzled. What was the matter with Ayn? Barbara had already answered that question. Had I missed something? Then, in a low, husky voice, Barbara answered yes.

I sat without moving, trying to force my brain to absorb this new information. The sound of their quiet voices continued, a distant background to the turmoil that was tearing at my insides, flinging me into a state like none I had ever experienced before. The pain felt physical, and it was excruciating. I reproached myself for my reaction. What right did I have to be shocked now? All I could think was, I tried to trust, and I was proven wrong. Her protestations of love meant nothing. I no longer knew what was real and what was unreal.

Looking back, I have thought many times that that was the night our relationship should have ended (if not much earlier). In continuing, I was ignoring too much evidence that we were poorly suited for each other. But she had become the repository of too many of my projections and dreams. I loved her, or at any rate I felt bonded to her. And there were times when I was incredibly happy with her. And the wrong kind of ego involvement forbade me to acknowledge defeat and walk away. And I'm sure I had rescuer fantasies. And then there was Ayn's strange, unexpected response.

There was no sound of reproach in Ayn's voice, just a gentle, persistent probing, encouraging Barbara to explore and voice her feelings. I could not stand to listen. I needed to escape, to be alone. I got up and went into the bathroom. It was as if there were some great pressure building up internally, pushing against the wall of my chest and stomach. I bent over, holding myself. I fought not to cry out. I finally regained sufficient calmness to return to the living room.

Ayn's benevolence and warmth toward Barbara confused me. Given the moral ruthlessness that was more typical of Ayn, this was unusual. She stressed that although she did not approve of what Barbara had done, she continued to believe in her goodness. I felt almost angry, as if Ayn were unconcerned about the impact that Barbara's actions had on me. As if she could read my thoughts, she turned and said to me, "I know this is terribly hard for you, Nathan. But everything is going to be all right. We're going to solve this, once and for all." Her tranquility in that moment projected an almost supernatural certainty.

Later, when Barbara was out of the room for a moment, Ayn said—and the look on her face told me how foolish I had been to imagine that she was unconcerned about my feelings—"You went into the bathroom so you could be alone with your suffering." I nodded, and she went on. "Darling, I'm so sorry. This is terrible for you."

"What made you think of asking about that fellow?"

Ayn smiled. "What else would Barbara have to be so anxious about?"

The next day, when we were having lunch, Barbara returned to the subject. With a trembling voice and the look of a frightened child facing an angry parent, she said, "That's not all. There's more." She proceeded to recount two additional affairs.

I must assume that she was hungry for some form of love and acceptance—without being judged—that she did not experience with me. That is what she said to me years later. But at the time, I felt bewildered and devastated. What had been the most vulnerable part of me was turning to ice.

Ayn continued to be warmly supportive of both of us, undisturbed by Barbara's revelations, compassionate toward me, and almost incomprehensibly serene.

Sometimes my anger was ungovernable. Once, in my hotel room, I spent half an hour shouting insults at Barbara, driven to greater and greater fury by the sight of her nodding her head, agreeing with everything I said, as if she were welcoming the abuse. In a complex mixture of rage, pain, hatred, and desire, I initiated "lovemaking" very aggressively and was astonished by the intensity of her responsiveness.

Barbara and I became reconnected sexually, and I determined anew to persevere in my struggles to rescue our relationship. I was not ready to face the effect that continuing the relationship would have on my self-esteem.

"What you are doing is not easy," Ayn said to me one evening. "I admire your strength. If you believe she's the woman for you, you don't let go."

"I'm afraid," I answered, not certain of how to explain what I meant. "I'm afraid of what's happening inside, to me, while all this is going on. Something is happening—something is going wrong with me—and I don't know how to tell you what it is."

Ayn looked perplexed. "But surely it will pass, and none of it will matter if you succeed, if Barbara comes around."

I did not fight harder to make myself understood. I told myself, Ayn is right. Don't dramatize. And so I sank deeper into emotional repression.

"You could do me one favor," I said to Ayn. "You talk to Barbara. You try to help her."

"Of course I will, darling."

We continued to read—and reread—the new novel. We even had a small influence on its content, beyond my suggestions about the characterization of Galt.

One of the most imaginative lesser characters in *Atlas Shrugged* is that of Ragnar Danneskjold, the philosopher turned pirate. He, Galt, and Francisco are close friends, and when Ragnar lands his plane in the hidden valley of the strikers, he briefly greets his wife, whom he has not seen in eleven months, then departs for breakfast with his two friends. "Ayn," I protested, "this is impossible. I don't care how close the three men are—or how important their ritual breakfast is on June 1 of every year. Any man in his right mind, and certainly any hero of yours, is going to make his wife his first priority. Otherwise, it would be damned strange." Ayn sighed and said a little reluctantly, "I suppose you're right."

It was Barbara who was responsible for Ragnar's being married. For certain literary and philosophical reasons, Ayn had made Ragnar shockingly beautiful. When Ayn mentioned a minor character in the story, Kay Ludlow, an exquisitely beautiful actress who joins the strike, Barbara suggested that two such individuals aesthetically belonged together. Ayn chuckled—and agreed.

"It looks," I was now saying to Ayn, "like you haven't fully accepted that you married those two characters." She asked, "Suppose I have Ragnar arrive in the valley the night before. Would you then accept that he was gone for an hour in the morning for breakfast?" And that is the way the final version of the novel reads. Ayn joked, "Barbara saw to it that Ragnar got married, and Nathan saw to it that he was a good husband."

Kay Ludlow has only a walk-on role. I once teased Ayn about the absence of significant female characters in her novel, with the exception of Rearden's wife, Lillian, who is thoroughly despicable. Ayn's eyes sparkled with gaiety, and she answered, "This is my fantasy. What do I need other women for?" Then she added, "I suppose, as a writer, I'm not really interested in women, except in relationship to the men. It's man I wanted to write about—the ideal." I responded, "What about woman—the ideal?" This was an old argument between us. She said, "Dagny is that." I persisted, "But you show several versions of the male ideal, not merely one." She shrugged, "*You* write about women. It doesn't interest me." I would not let the subject go. "But Ayn, you're a woman." Again, her eyes sparkled with amusement. "And glad of it, too. I've never wanted to be a man, not for a moment. Do you know why? Because then I'd have to be in love with a woman." I gave up. I did not know how seriously to take Ayn's antiwoman remarks. Her earnestness and her humor both seemed authentic. I wondered what any of this meant in terms of her own self-concept. I did not realize that it would have been worth my while to have pursued this issue more vigorously.

The writing of the novel was proceeding more slowly than Ayn had anticipated. She worked long hours every day, pushing herself to the point of exhaustion and beyond it, and although she was happy with the final result, she was not happy with the time needed to achieve it. "If only I wrote more 'inspirationally.' But, you know, with me everything has to be conscious. That's why the work is so laborious. Of course, I use my subconscious—one has to—but part of me resents that, fights it, and my resistance slows me down."

Some evenings I sat in Ayn's living room, waiting for her to emerge from her study, and through her open door I would hear her reading her work aloud, seeking the smallest failure of rhythm or balance, or an inexact word, or a missing adjective. She demanded of every sentence and every paragraph the perfection of poetry. When I observed that there was something profoundly musical in her writing that I did not quite know how to identify, she answered, "*The Fountainhead* was written in notes. This book is written in chords. Much harder. Much more demanding. Sometimes I feel my brain is going to crack open." She often complained of excruciating tension in her neck and shoulders.

We would talk about my favorite passages: Dagny's and Rearden's train ride on the "John Galt Line" in Part One, which climaxes with the start of their affair, or Dagny's airplane pursuit of John Galt at the climax of Part Two. We spoke of Ayn's extraordinary ability to communicate the sensory reality of motion, or her ability to shift between descriptions of physical action, inner emotional experience, and broad philosophical meanings, or her artistry at manipulating implication and indirection to evoke the most profound feelings in the reader.

"If you want to obtain the strongest emotional response," she told Barbara and me one evening, "then you write between the lines, never on the line. You write around the feeling. You don't spell it out explicitly." Barbara had some resistance to this idea; she seemed to prefer a more Wagnerian approach to writing. "What's wrong with stating the emotion or whatever directly? What's wrong with being explicit?" Ayn answered, "Because if you tell the reader everything, if you don't leave spaces for his mind to fill in, if you don't engage his consciousness by giving him something to do, if you try to do it all for him, then you leave the reader passive. His consciousness is not engaged as it could be, so he's not that involved emotionally. In this issue, Thomas Wolfe is my exact literary opposite. He thinks if he shouts his feelings at you, that will make you feel something. It doesn't work that way." Barbara sighed. "It works for me," she said. For the flash of an instant, I saw anger in Ayn's eyes. "Well, darling," she replied in a gentle, satin-and-steel voice, "it's just not good writing."

The sessions between Barbara and Ayn continued, and Barbara and I slowly, tentatively, grew closer and happier. Once mysterious and elusive, Barbara shifted radically in the opposite direction; she now reported to me the smallest details of her activities, far beyond anything I had requested. When I asked her why she felt the need to give me such specifics, she answered, "I don't want any more lies between us, or any omissions, not even over unimportant things. Whenever I say anything that isn't quite exact, my anxiety flares up." I felt sadly touched by this, and grateful, because whatever her motives were, her compulsive honesty was healing for us.

I felt at times that Ayn and I were placing Barbara in a humiliating position to which no one should be subjected. Yet, under the circumstances, I could not envision an alternative. It is easy enough now to see that the kindest and most rational thing I could have done was to wish Barbara well and suggest that we go our separate ways. How much suffering I would have spared us both!

There were occasions when I grilled her unmercifully about past activities, driven by my own terror of losing her to "an alien world." We were two hurt and damaged people, hurting and damaging each other, and not knowing what to do about it. We looked to Ayn for a miracle.

"Barbara," Ayn told me, "has a genuine longing for integrity. She was not really meant to have made the kind of mistakes she made." She said it with the authority of royalty. When she spoke this way, I felt torn. Part of me wanted only to believe Ayn, and another part felt uncomfortable about her way of putting things—as if she were the supreme arbiter in all matters pertaining to the condition of a human soul.

Whatever this way of speaking signaled, I was already beginning to hear it in myself when I handed down my own opinions and moral judgments. With Barbara, my pain and anger were slowly surfacing in the form of condescension and arrogance. This made everything worse. It is painful for me to remember that.

An unquestioned absolute during this difficult time was Barbara's enthusiasm for Ayn's work and devotion to Ayn herself. "This is important," Ayn said more than once. "It shows her basic character." I heard nothing strange in this observation; it sounded utterly reasonable.

The idea of marriage became increasingly appealing. Marriage was a lifetime commitment. I imagined that it would give Barbara and me the structure and security to protect and nurture our growing closeness. Our respective families were providing us with a monthly allowance—$250 each—and they both agreed to maintain it until we graduated and became self-supporting. We did not ask for or expect more than that; neither of us believed it was anyone's obligation to subsidize the marriage. If our families expressed any negative reaction, it was only about our lack of interest in having children. Both of us liked children, but neither of us wished to be parents; we wanted a life organized around our work.

We continued to enjoy NYU more than UCLA. We felt intellectually stimulated and challenged. I think, for example, of two philosophy professors—Sidney Hook, a pragmatist and a socialist, and William Barrett, an existentialist—who were poles apart from each other and still farther apart, intellectually, from us. Barbara took several courses with Hook; I had one or two with Barrett. We laughed at our classroom discussions, our fights, the statements our professors uttered that we thought preposterous, the questions hurled at us that sent us searching for answers, and we would interrupt each other as we told our stories to Ayn and Frank.

Usually, we talked philosophy with them, in part because that was the topic on which Ayn had most to say. Sometimes she would remark, "I really don't know much about psychology. I leave that sewer to you, Nathan."

She was constructing a philosophical system and yet, by her own statement, she knew almost nothing about psychology. It did not occur to me that this deficit was dangerous to her intellectual efforts, as well as to Barbara and me personally. Her attitude was, in effect, that rational minds do not require psychology. Philosophy is enough. Psychology is essentially for pathology—that is, for the irrational in people. I argued with her about this, and she would always concede that I was right: "Yes, of course, Nathan, we all have a psychology, and the operations of the mind do need to be studied, but . . ." And a week or two later she would say, "Oh, how I hate your profession, Nathan. How I hate the irrational. How I hate having to deal with it or to struggle to understand it."

Sometimes Barbara and I played hooky from school, went to Times Square, and, moving from theater to theater, saw perhaps four films in a single day. It was our favorite form of recreation. In the darkness of the theater, we held hands.

But Barbara was shyly reluctant to hold hands on the street, especially if we were anywhere near NYU. "What would Plato think?" she would say jokingly. I found this shyness utterly mystifying. She was willing to challenge the beliefs of the whole world, yet she worried what people would think if they saw us holding hands? I interpreted this as some strange remnant of conventionality that would surely pass.

I was reluctant to discuss with Ayn one problem that persisted—the disparity in Barbara's and my desire to make love. Barbara said no at least as often as she said yes. I naïvely imagined that this was a problem that marriage would somehow solve.

I had not been able to maintain my decision to leave psychology out of my dealings with Barbara. Discussions of our relationship overlapped inescapably with discussions of her problems. "I'm caught in a trap," I complained to Ayn. "To involve myself at the psychotherapeutic level seems wrong, and not to involve myself seems wrong." But whatever we were doing, the strategy seemed to be working. Barbara looked happier, said she was happier, spoke more of loving me, and spoke less of having feelings pull her in other directions.

I was becoming progressively more interested in psychotherapy as a profession. I saw it as a doorway through which to enter and explore the human psyche. But writing remained the deepest and most enduring of all my career goals. Nothing seemed more natural or compelling than the process of taking whatever most mattered to me and making it real by putting words to paper. "That's one thing we agree on for sure," said Barbara.

In the summer of 1952, Barbara and I decided that the time had come. We set a wedding date for the following January.

"What would I have done," I said to Ayn, "if you had not been here to help?"

Nathaniel and Barbara's wedding, Rand looking on, 1953

She answered, "You're going to have a happy life together, and both of you will have earned it."

Limousines carried Barbara and me and our family members to the home of Barbara's aunt and uncle in White Plains, New York. I remember almost nothing of the final months leading up to this event, except that there were doubts, insecurities, and conflicts, almost to the end.

I remember the sound of the tires rolling over the snow and ice as we moved like a caravan through a night filled with stars. Mist rose from the car windows, and icicles hung from tree branches, reflecting the gleam of our headlights.

I was now twenty-two years old. The challenges of my career still lay ahead, but tonight was my celebration of a battle fought and won.

With Ayn and Frank standing behind us as matron of honor and best man, their eyes and faces glowing with a happiness that was like a blessing on this event, Barbara and I took our vows. I felt powerful, effective, sure of myself. I loved Barbara. I did not think to ask myself whether that meant we were well suited for each other.

There was a dinner party after the ceremony. Scattered throughout the room, in addition to family, there were a few friends. The nucleus of a group we had just begun to form, they were young people who admired Ayn's work and who were keenly interested in her philosophy.

Later that night, we returned to our apartment—a single room on East Thirty-Fifth Street—to find that Frank had decorated it with flowers in a stunningly imaginative way, transforming it into the intimate setting of a beautiful country inn. I was touched by his thought and effort—and by his superlative artistry. His dramatic floral arrangements had the impact of sculpture. I had not been aware of this side of him before.

Then Barbara was standing before me, wearing a pale nightgown that stressed the slenderness of her body. She smiled at me in the half-darkness, her blond hair fell to her shoulders, and her green eyes projected a kind of innocent vulnerability that promised total surrender.

This was my wedding night. This was my wife. Tonight there could be no question about whether or not we would make love. With that thought as reassurance, I took her in my arms.

7

<hr>

"WHEN YOU WERE COMING to meet me for the first time," Ayn asked me one evening that spring, "were you at all concerned that I might disappoint you? That I might not live up to your expectations?"

I was sitting on her living room floor, playing with the gray-and-white kitten she and Frank had brought with them from California. He was named Frisco, after Francisco d'Anconia. Ayn could not look at him without smiling affectionately. She would stroke him, talk to him, whisper words of adoration. It was as if he tapped into the softest, most nurturing side of her nature.

"No, I wasn't concerned at all," I told her. "I didn't even consider it. I knew that the author of *The Fountainhead* was not going to be something less in person. And I was right, wasn't I?"

She seemed pleased. "Amazing. I would have been so afraid of disappointment if our roles had been reversed."

"How can you know? You've never met anyone who wrote a book like *The Fountainhead*."

"True. Everything I've liked has had some inconsistencies, some contradictions. *The Fountainhead* doesn't have any." This was said impersonally, with no implication of boasting, but merely as a self-evident fact. I had grown accustomed to hearing her discuss herself and her work this way. "Still," she went on, "I admire your benevolence. You know, my biggest goal is not to let any disappointment or setback affect my sense of life. I hate bitterness. Do you see any bitterness in me?"

"No," I said, looking at the mouth I had seen twisted in anger many times when discussing other people's "irrationality." I wondered what the truth about that bitterness was and if she really wanted to hear it and whether I would ever have the courage to speak of it to her. I was vaguely aware that there were signs of the most terrible bitterness, but superimposed on them were images of her eyes laughing when she was happy with the day's writing or of her face softening when she held her head against Frank's chest or of her dancing around the room to her tiddlywink music. I told myself that this was her core, that this was her essence, and that nothing else mattered.

Expressing a concern she often had, she said, "I don't want to be touched by any malevolence." She began to speak about early experiences that had hurt or disappointed her—from her rejection by Leo to her failure to get writing jobs in Hollywood to her experiences with publishing *We the Living, Anthem,* and *The Fountainhead.*

I was surprised that Leo was still so important to her. I assumed that if one were happily in love, old romantic wounds automatically faded away, which was naïve of me. She spoke of her pain over Leo as if it were brand new, and there was an edge to her voice that did not fit my view of her. Perhaps what made me uncomfortable was not the hurt but the hint of anger after so many years.

Speaking of her experiences in Hollywood, she seemed much more detached; this part of her life did seem to be truly behind her. When she spoke of the career struggles involving her novels, she projected a strange kind of pride, as if to say that she had personally suffered almost everything she had ever written about. This evoked empathy and protectiveness in me.

I was keenly interested in her reminiscences and never tired of them, even when I had heard many of the stories before. Every word she uttered was important to me, because I wished to penetrate every corner of her consciousness, to absorb everything, to know her, and to be connected with her in that special way that is sometimes true of identical twins. This was tied in my mind to the process of thoroughly grasping her way of seeing and apprehending the world—of understanding everything within her from which *The Fountainhead* and *Atlas Shrugged* had sprung. I wanted to know her secrets, her uniqueness.

"You know," she said, "when I'm writing, I'm living in the world of the novel, not 'ordinary reality,' and there's always that sense of shock when I come back to the world at the end—when the job is finished. I was not fully satisfied literarily with *We the Living*—I was not yet in control of my style—but I was completely satisfied with the plot, with the structure, and with the climax. I can't tell you exactly how many publishers rejected the book, but there were a great many. The chief criticism was that I was too intellectual, too concerned with ideas. Then there was the opposition from all the people who were indignant because I criticized Soviet Russia. I wasn't 'open-minded' enough, I wasn't 'tolerant,' I didn't appreciate the 'noble experiment.' It was hard. There were times Frank and I had almost nothing to eat. Finally, Macmillan accepted the book—against the violent objections of Granville Hicks, an editor there, and also a member of the Communist Party and an editor of *New Masses.*

"The book was not supported by Macmillan—not in ads, not in any way. They did nothing for it. I expected attacks from the critics, of course, and there were plenty. Political much more than literary. Literary criticism would have been much easier to take at that time. There was no way for the book to find its readers. It did not do well, and then Macmillan destroyed the plates and let it go out of print just when it was beginning to catch on, just when readers were beginning to discover it. It was a terrible blow. I cried a good deal during those years. I tried to get work as a screenwriter, and it should have been possible, because *Night of January 16th* had a good run on Broadway, I had published a novel, and I was becoming known. But my agent could get me nothing, and the word coming back from Hollywood was that no one wanted to get involved with someone so outspoken about Soviet Russia. I was blacklisted."

As I listened, I tried to imagine what it would have been like to live through the early years of Ayn's struggles, when she could not have known how it was all going to work out. I wondered if I could have matched her perseverance. Any obstacle I had ever had to deal with seemed embarrassingly trivial by comparison. I felt privileged to be a witness to what I regarded as a heroic journey.

I wanted to offer some kind of comfort or protection but did not know what to say. Frisco watched us attentively, almost as if he were following the conversation. Trying to strike a lighter note, I said, "Do you realize that Frisco can't understand any of this? Can't conceive of it?"

She smiled. "Yes, and that's what I love about him. I said that about Wynand's cat in *The Fountainhead*—the purity of a consciousness incapable of grasping human irrationality or evil."

We began talking about *Anthem*. I expressed dismay that she had been unable, prior to 1946, to find an American publisher for this marvelous work. It's so much more lyrical than any of her other writings, by far the most abstract in its method of stylization. It had been written in the summer of 1937, while Ayn was still struggling with the plot of *The Fountainhead*. She had not yet devised the climax that would pull all the elements of the story together. Exhausted by her efforts, she stopped long enough to "rest" and write *Anthem.*

"When I found that novella in the Toronto Public Library," I told her, "I learned it was out of print and not available for purchase anywhere, so I stole the library copy." Many years later, addressing a conference of librarians, I had the pleasure of making this confession publicly. I sent the library a new copy of the book. Now I chuckled and asked Ayn, "What philosophical stand do you want to take about my stealing your book because I absolutely had to own it?" She waved her cigarette holder and said gaily, "I give you a special papal dispensation."

"But you know," she went on, "the struggle with *The Fountainhead* really sums everything else up. Twelve publishers rejected it as too intellectual, too noncommercial. Later, I learned that some of the editors who rejected it thought it was a great book. Can you understand what it means to be rejected not because you're not good enough but because *you're too good?* That's the worst horror."

Bobbs-Merrill was the thirteenth house to whom the novel was submitted. The novel was recommended there by Ayn's boss at Paramount, the story editor Richard Mealand; he was enthusiastic about the project and offered to help.

Archie Ogden was a new editor at Bobbs-Merrill, and when Ayn first met him she didn't expect him to like the book. "He seemed like an overly friendly Peter Keating." Archie loved the book. "His admiration for it and his understanding of what I was doing literarily were everything a writer could dream of asking for." He recommended that Bobbs-Merrill acquire the book, but his superiors turned him down. "At that time, Archie was new at that firm, but he staked his job on his independent judgment, and I will always be grateful for that. He wired his boss, 'If this is not the book for you, then I am not the editor for you.' Can you imagine such a thing? He got a return wire saying, 'Far be it from me to dampen such enthusiasm. Sign the contract. But the book better be good.' Now, do you want to hear something funny? On a previous job he had turned down Dale Carnegie's *How to Win Friends and Influence People.* How's that for a logical universe? Archie would smile and say that he was proud of his judgment both times. Thanks to the enthusiasm and integrity of Richard Mealand and Archie Ogden, *The Fountainhead* got its chance. Of course, the battle was not over. Bobbs-Merrill ran a couple of fairly meaningless ads that did not state what the book was about, and sales began slowly. I was terrified it was going to be *We the Living* all over again. Bobbs-Merrill was very passive about the book. I was desperate, and there was nothing I could do."

The book's success was made entirely by word of mouth. The first three months were slow, then sales began to rise, and then they exploded. It stayed on the best-seller list for a long time and went back on when the movie came out. "But, you know, the people at Bobbs-Merrill then were really dreadful. It was wartime, and there was a paper shortage, and they kept letting the book go out of print in spite of incredible sales. It was a nightmare. Finally, they subcontracted to another company that had a large stock of paper, and after that the book stayed in print. But nothing, absolutely nothing, came easily."

Ayn talked about all the hostile reviews and the failure of even the sympathetic reviewers to communicate the novel's view of individualism. One exception was Lorine Pruette in the *New York Times Book Review*. She identified individualism as the novel's theme and wrote, "Ayn Rand is a writer of great power. She has a subtle and ingenious mind and the capacity of writing brilliantly, beautifully, bitterly. . . . Good novels of ideas are rare at any time. This is the only novel of ideas written by an American woman that I can recall. . . . You will not be able to read this masterful work without thinking through some of the basic concepts of our times." Ayn remarked, "Coming when it did, in the midst of all the attacks, the review really lifted my spirits. It gave me the sense of a human world out there."

A rift between Ayn and Isabel Paterson, whom she had once liked more than any other woman she had met (notwithstanding the fact that they disagreed about religion), deepened over the issue of the book's review. In *The God of the Machine*, Paterson's chapter "The Humanitarian with the Guillotine" was pure Ayn Rand, but she did not acknowledge her indebtedness to Ayn's ideas. Strangely, Ayn did not seem resentful as she told me this; she was very mild on the subject. She was less mild about the fact that Paterson, who professed love and admiration for Ayn, declined an opportunity to review *The Fountainhead* for the *Herald Tribune* when Irita van Doren, head of the book section, proposed it. In the early months of the novel's struggle, a favorable review by Isabel Paterson could have helped enormously. Ayn learned of the refusal sometime later. Paterson explained that she had been reluctant to air in print certain of their differences.

"Our differences," Ayn said to me, "involved religion and, though we didn't discuss this, our sense of life. The romantic spirit of the writing would have antagonized her. And she would not have liked my treatment of sex. She would see it as unchristian." Ayn added, "Still, at the time we were friends. She expressed devotion to my work, and she knew the kind of battle I was fighting and what I was up against." Ayn waved her hand in a characteristic gesture of dismissal. "But that was not why our relationship ended. I was disgusted with her, but I had promised to introduce her to some conservative friends when she visited California. Paterson's own life had not gone well, and she was becoming increasingly belligerent toward everyone. She spoke as if no one was really fighting for capitalism except her. Everyone else was a coward or a hypocrite, she was saying, not really willing to commit themselves uncompromisingly. She insulted some of the best supporters of capitalism I knew. In California, she became totally irrational. She could be brilliant, as you can see from her book, but that was the end between us. And she was the one woman with a mind I respected."

We returned to the subject of the book's reception; the distortions of Ayn's ideas in the press; and the strange phenomenon of being world famous, widely read, and simultaneously grossly misrepresented and misperceived. We spoke of other innovators who had similar experiences.

Wishing to address the happier side of her life, I said, "In the end, you won."

"Yes and no. Professionally, I did; I don't have to worry about money anymore or about finding a publisher for my next novel. But personally? My biggest disappointment was and is people. I thought that somewhere in the world there were giants—my kind of men—and that when *The Fountainhead* was published, everything would change; I would find them. That's not what happened. But I'll never give up believing it's possible."

"And yet, look at the amount of fan mail you get, even after all these years."

"Bobbs-Merrill says it's unprecedented, in its experience, for a novelist to receive the huge amount of mail that comes in for *The Fountainhead*. But still . . ." She began to soften only at this point. "Shall I tell you what I regard as my greatest personal reward for *The Fountainhead*? You. You are the kind of reader I always dreamed of finding. You're the proof that what I write about is possible."

When I heard these words, a part of me felt a twist of pain. I thought that life should have had more to offer her as a reward than a young man who had not yet accomplished anything. She deserved a contemporary, an equal in achievement and experience. And part of me felt elated, buoyant, powerful beyond imagination. I had never gotten used to the compliments she consistently paid me, and it was impossible not be affected by them.

Lying flat on my back on the floor, holding Frisco above my head, I felt free of everything but a confidently untroubled serenity. It was great to be alive.

"Well, Frisco," I said, "I guess it's up to you and me."

The first year of my marriage to Barbara was, from my perspective, the best in our entire relationship. Her loyalty now seemed absolute. We were going to school, planning the future, and building a life together. "I really am happy," she said to me with glowing eyes, and I believed her. We shared our classroom experiences; critiqued each other's school papers;

laughed about the intellectual fights we got into with fellow students; talked endlessly about Galt, Rearden, Francisco, and Dagny; held hands in the darkness of movie theaters; visited Ayn and Frank and read the latest pages of Ayn's novel; and felt bonded by our participation in a special world.

"I am so proud of you," Barbara would sometimes say after a visit with Ayn and Frank or after reading a paper I had written for a psychology or philosophy course. "I really do love you," she would say. "I love you," I would answer.

I told Barbara that I loved her many times. But I never told her I was proud of her, although there were certainly times when I was. I regret that omission to this day, not because I believe that it alone could have made things right between us but because I know what it would have meant to her to hear me say it—and because she deserved it.

She was now relatively free of anxiety. But I observed that she continued her policy of meticulous truth telling about the smallest details of her actions, in spite of my assurances that it wasn't necessary.

But our sexual problems remained unsolved, and they threatened to keep the past alive and virulent. Often, I was aware of being accommodated. I fought not to let it matter too much. I told myself that everything else was getting better and that a day would come when Barbara's desires would match mine. But sometimes I would erupt over her passivity in bed and her periods of moody withdrawal.

I am sure that I contributed to our problems, although I did not know in what way. Perhaps I was not empathic or kind enough. Or perhaps it was no one's fault—just that we were not right for each other. That last perspective is how I see it today. Just as we cannot command love, so we cannot command sexual desire.

There were occasions when Barbara made love with seemingly unreserved enthusiasm. Then I would feel that the breakthrough had finally happened. But it did not last.

Sometimes we had strange clashes that neither of us quite understood. I found her excessively sentimental, even maudlin at times. Her feelings could be hurt over what I regarded as trivia. Her quality of wistful sadness could be irritating and frustrating, and I might lose control and say so. She often found me abrupt, impatient, insensitive, judgmental, and arrogant.

In my own eyes, my impatience was my worst trait. "You can be so kind when you want to be," she would say to me. "Why are you sometimes so unfeeling?" Finding myself agreeing, I would feel miserable.

My frame of reference for understanding people was how they viewed reason and reality and their degree of personal autonomy or independence. These were the criteria by which I assessed healthy psychological development. My efforts to understand certain phenomena in people led me to write a paper, for my own mental clarity, on what I called "social metaphysics." A number of interrelated observations led me down this road.

In my philosophical and political discussions with people, I was struck again and again by how difficult it was for many of them to grasp, let alone accept, unfamiliar ideas that went against the mainstream "received wisdom." Reason, logic, and factual demonstration seemed to have so little impact when the ideas I presented collided with more conventional belief systems. The world that others perceived seemed to many to be the only world that mattered, the only world that was real. I could understand it if they disagreed with my viewpoint based on clear-cut premises, but the opposition I encountered was of a different kind, often consisting of statements like "But this is not the way people think!" "But *everybody knows* that self-interest is not a moral motive!" "Who else thinks of reason the way you and Ayn Rand do?" "If what you're saying is true, it would be taught in universities." There was nothing to fight, nothing to engage—only a person's fantasies about the ideas inside another person's mind. To such persons, thinking about a new idea meant bouncing it off the opinions of "significant others." "Where is their sense of reality?" I wondered aloud to Ayn. "Where is their concern with objective truth?"

Two people who had entered our lives in New York helped me focus my thinking on this issue further. Both were to become members of our intimate circle.

One was a childhood friend of Barbara's. Joan Mitchell, an aspiring painter and a student of art history, was twenty-three years old, blonde, petite, nervously arrogant one moment, and shyly reticent the next. Joan struck me as affected, mannered, and overly concerned with her image— and yet undeniably intelligent. I wanted to like her not only because Barbara loved her but also because she did seem enthusiastic about *The Fountainhead* and wanted to learn about Ayn's philosophy. I wanted to expand our circle and viewed her as a promising convert. Moreover, I sensed in her that one important trait—a deep dissatisfaction with "things as they were," a longing, however inarticulate, for something "more," perhaps for ecstasy. "Joan," Barbara said to me, "is a much better person than she has ever let herself be—or perhaps than she herself knows." I liked Joan yet remained puzzled that a woman could simultaneously see herself as an advocate of reason, individualism, and independence and still

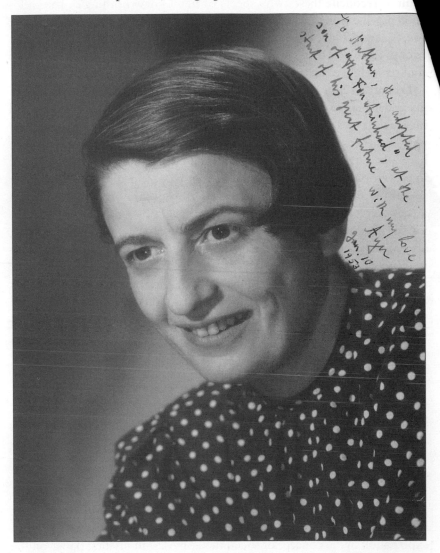

pation with impressing other people. I found it dif-
...ese two aspects of her. I knew nothing of the child-
...ds that must have laid the foundation for this problem;
...ad little empathy. Nevertheless, I grew fonder of Joan as
...ner better and ultimately came to see her basically as a good
...ng earnestly to develop herself and noble in her aspirations.
...d Peikoff, Barbara's cousin, represented a far greater challenge to
...erstanding. He had visited us in New York a number of times, and
...ptember 1953 he moved there with the intention of studying philoso-
...for a year, after which he would decide whether he wished to return to
...is premed studies in Winnipeg or remain in New York and pursue a career
in philosophy. He was now twenty years old, of medium height, with a
somewhat frail build and a coltish way of walking. When he spoke, his
voice often had a nervous, nearly hysterical quality. Leonard cared for nothing but philosophy, and for this I warmed to him. But I could see almost
immediately that in his consciousness there was very little "objective reality," no sense of reality *as such*, apart from what anyone thought or
believed. There were only Ayn's ideas and the ideas of his professors. When
Ayn was talking, he couldn't retain the viewpoint of his professors, and
when his professors were talking, he couldn't retain the perspective he had
learned from Ayn. I watched him, observed his struggles, tried to help him,
and tried to understand how someone so intelligent could be so lacking in
independence.

The ease with which Leonard could be "brainwashed" at school was
bewildering and disturbing to Ayn, Barbara, and me. I said to Ayn, "He
has the rationality and independence to select your ideas, even if they keep
slipping between his fingers. I mean, if it isn't rationality and independence,
what is it? But then why is he so easily overwhelmed? Where is his judgment? Why can't he retain anything from one conversation to the next?"

I was struggling to understand people who seemed to have little independent contact with reality apart from what others thought, felt, or
believed. Then, late in the year, I believed I found the beginning of an
explanation in the concept of social metaphysics. In my first paper on the
subject, I wrote: "As always, the question is: what does this person think,
feel, believe 'reality' is—and my answer is: other people [for almost all
practical purposes, if not literally]. The ultimate reality here, the ultimate
frame of reference—this is why I call it a 'metaphysics'—is the consciousness, beliefs, values, perceptions of various other people."

Over the next decade, I developed and amplified the idea of social
metaphysics. I conceived of a variety of social metaphysical types with significant psychological differences. I explained how this orientation could

coexist in some individuals with isolated areas of high independence
in the case of great scientists who were able to challenge their colleag
assumptions about the nature of the universe yet were frightened to
lenge the values of the folks next door.

In rereading my treatment of this subject in *The Psychology of
Esteem,* which was published in 1969, I regret the lack of compassic
the inappropriate moralism underlying my entire discussion. They
rather than illuminate. Unfortunately, these attitudes were typica
thinking of the period. I also regret that I did not approach the
from a more developmental perspective. My approach is badly
plified. I wish I said more about how the problem is to be solved
take up the theme of social metaphysics again in a book pub
1996, *Taking Responsibility,* in which my present views are m
rately reflected.

When I made my first notes on social metaphysics, I did not
Ayn would leap on the idea with almost savage eagerness—
offered her not a means of better understanding human beh
sword to be brandished in the battle against irrationality. People who did
not think for themselves or who did not uphold independent convictions
or who unthinkingly accepted ideas and values that Ayn regarded as evil
were "social metaphysicians." Because many people do not think for
themselves, it was not difficult to find evidence of the syndrome everywhere. A high level of autonomy, especially in moral issues, is the exception, not the norm.

"You've gone far deeper than my idea of the second-hander in *The
Fountainhead,*" Ayn exclaimed. "You've really gone into the root of
human rottenness." Turning to Barbara, she said, "Now you see why I say
Nathan is no longer simply my student. Now I am his student, as well."
Soon, I too was brandishing the concept as an intellectual weapon—and
causing a great deal of suffering among our friends and acquaintances.

Today, I would never suggest to anyone that he or she was a "social
metaphysician" because, in the words of my friend the late child psychologist Haim Ginott, "labeling is disabling." It is far more helpful to
focus on "growing in autonomy and self-trust."

One of the most interesting people to join our circle was a man to whom
Ayn initially took a strong disliking.

He was an economic analyst, employed by the National Industrial Conference Board. For nine months, he was married to Joan Mitchell, which
was how we got to know him. He was tall and solidly built, with black
hair, dark horn-rim glasses, and a propensity for dark, funereal suits. At

, as
ues'
·hal-

Self-
n and
istract
of my
roblem
versim-
I would
lished in
ore accu-

oresee that
as if I had
avior but a
...was worried...

as somberness incarnate, looking chronically weary,
v. Barbara, Ayn, Frank, and I once encountered him
ming out of an elevator. "He looks like an under-
. The man's name was Alan Greenspan.

t a champion of laissez-faire, but he was very pro-
also a logical positivist, which meant that he was
to know anything with certainty. He announced
e senses were untrustworthy, and that degrees
ssible. "I *think* I exist," he stated, "but I can't
rtain that anything exists."

ad and displayed a strong interest in our
uncing that I enjoyed talking to him. I
buried deep in his psyche and was con-
n, his philosophy notwithstanding. He
len side that drew me to him, and he
nded emotionally to something heroic
nself for his impracticality.

stand talking to him?" Ayn demanded. I answered, "I'm
going to bring him around intellectually." This was one of the rare occasions when I thoroughly enjoyed disagreeing with Ayn; in matters of
psychological judgment, I deferred to no one. "Never!" she declared. "A
logical positivist? I'm not even certain it's moral to deal with him at all."
I smiled. "Wait and see."

Barbara, not I, accomplished one of the most hilarious aspects of Alan's
conversion. The four of us were in Winnipeg, Barbara visiting her family
and Joan visiting hers. At a party there, I spied Barbara and Alan talking
intently in a corner, their heads close together. A long time later, they
emerged, and Barbara pulled me aside to declare gleefully, "Guess what.
I got him to admit that banks should be operated entirely privately, that
there should be no government-chartered banks."

I laughed incredulously. "How?" I asked. "How did you do it? I didn't
know you even knew what a chartered bank was."

She grinned triumphantly. "I didn't. But somehow we got to talking
about them. So I led him into explaining what they were and why they
were considered necessary—as if I were checking on *his* understanding.
Then I persuaded him that government shouldn't be involved, that a free
market in banking is preferable. I sold him on the merits of a completely
unregulated banking system. Just by arguing on the basis of the information he provided."

I shook my head in admiration. We had acquired a grasp of economic
and political issues that did not make this kind of "conversion" entirely

unusual. We knew the fundamentals, and we knew how to reason
them, even when we lacked specific knowledge. We had been expe
trained. Back in New York, I loved telling the story of Barbara's vict
over chartered banks.

Persuading Alan on economic matters was not too difficult. It wa
apparent that he had an extraordinarily lucid understanding of how mar
kets functioned—a fact that would be almost universally acknowledged
by his colleagues years later when he became economic adviser to two
presidents and then chairman of the Federal Reserve Board. Persuading
Alan on philosophical issues was much harder. His attachment to uncertainty was tenacious. "How's the undertaker?" Ayn would ask. "Has he
decided he exists yet?"

"Probability is all that is possible," he would say to me, not only about
economic forecasting but about everything. And I would answer, "Without something of which you're certain, how can you judge probability?"
"Can you prove you exist?" he would ask, and I would respond, "Shall I
send you my answer from nonexistence?" "Validate the laws of logic," he
would insist, and I would reply, "'Validate' is a concept that presupposes
your acceptance of logic. Otherwise, what does it mean?"

This went on for some months, while Ayn watched from the sidelines,
mildly disapproving but disarmed by my optimism. One evening I grinned
and asked her, "Guess who exists." "What?" she exclaimed. "You've
done it? He's decided he exists?" I nodded triumphantly. "You'll have to
stop calling Alan 'the undertaker' now. He's really an unusual person.
You're going to like him."

Ayn duly noted his enthusiasm about *The Fountainhead*. When, after
a number of meetings with her, he was invited to read *Atlas Shrugged* as
it was being written, he came alive with an excitement that no one had
ever seen in him before. Shyly and reluctantly, he began to yield to the
romantic side of his nature; he fell in love with Ayn's portrayal of business and industry. Ayn compared him to a "sleeping giant" who was
slowly waking up. She grew progressively fonder of him. In fact, he
became a particular favorite. "You were right," she said to me. "He has
a first-rate mind."

I visited my family in Toronto, and my cousin Allan Blumenthal and I
continued our talks. One of the main issues we discussed was his coming
to New York to study music at Juilliard.

One day I was at his home, and we were telling his mother about his
dislike of medicine. She protested that her son was losing his mind, because medicine offered such a respectable way to earn a living. "But he's

rom
rtly
ry

s

interjected, when I saw Allan's expression of for-
mother looked at me as if I had said something
shrugged. "So who's happy?"

house, I asked him, "Do you understand what your
what it means? Allan, in any sane world, it matters
you're happy. This is the time to fight for your life."

ng become a physician, Allan came to New York, began
Juilliard, and became a member of our circle. "The class of
began to call us, because that was the year *The Fountainhead*
lished.

sister Elayne moved to New York, and she, too, became an enthu-
ic member of our group. She required no urging. Although we had
red an apartment in California, it was only now that I began to expe-
ience her as a friend. Our relationship had become philosophical. Nonphilosophical relationships had no serious status in my mind. I did not
believe in the kinship of blood, only of ideas.

The core group of Ayn's admirers, the inner circle of the Ayn Rand
world that formed prior to the publication of *Atlas* in 1957, eventually
included Barbara and me; Barbara's cousin Leonard Peikoff; her childhood friend Joan Mitchell; Allan Blumenthal; Alan Greenspan; Elayne;
Harry Kalberman; and Mary Ann Rukavina, an art historian introduced
to us by Joan. As she saw the group growing, Ayn said to me, "You're creating our own society."

We met at Ayn's every Saturday evening to read and reread the new
novel; to talk about philosophy, psychology, political economy, literature,
and art; and to have our own experience of family and community. At
some point, it amused Ayn to call our group the "Collective"; such a
name suggested our exact opposite, because we saw ourselves as highly
evolved individualists. We all thought the name was funny and quickly
adopted it. The joke was on us, because we were in fact a collective in
ways that none of us was able to appreciate yet.

Frank had lost his healthy-looking ranch tan, and his movements were
fractionally slower. The inactivity of his first year in New York had aged
him. He would sit through long, silent hours while Ayn worked or while
Ayn, Barbara, and I talked. No one knew the contents of his inner life.
Nor did we inquire. He projected a diffuse goodwill that was like a protective barrier around himself.

In the spring of 1953, he found work making arrangements for a Park
Avenue florist, and in some cases selling his arrangements to buildings for
their lobbies. He did not make a great deal of money, but the work gave

him a purpose, and the income gave him some small sense of financial independence. Aside from that, Ayn was his sole means of support.

I was taken by the self-assertive imaginativeness of his arrangements; they disclosed a powerful artistic force. "Is this what's inside you?" I asked him once. As if it were the most obvious thing in the world, he answered naturally, "Oh, yes." I wanted to say, "How come you don't express it in some more serious way?" but I knew that would be condescending, pompous, and totally inappropriate. Instead, I said, "There's more to you than meets the eye," oblivious to the fact that this, too, was condescending and pompous. He answered, with his special quality of gentle humor, "There's more to everyone than meets the eye, Nathan."

I gathered from Ayn that they had not talked about intellectual matters for years, not since the beginning of their relationship. Now, they talked less than ever. Ayn's intellectual needs were being met by Barbara and me and by the Collective. During our evening sessions, Frank's role became more and more ornamental.

And yet even when he was sitting silently, there was often something subtly life-affirming in his demeanor. He projected the most extraordinary benevolence. The whole group was fond of him, and I think he sensed that. Barbara felt especially close to him; she identified with him, and I think he sensed that, too.

When my sister Florence, curious about our life in New York, asked, "But what exactly does Frank *do*?" I knew that most people were puzzled by Ayn and Frank's relationship, and I could not blame them. Nonetheless, I loved him.

At Ayn and Frank's apartment, Barbara and I again met Henry and Frances Hazlitt. I regretted that Ayn did not see more of them because I would have liked to know them better. It did not occur to me to seek them out on my own, because they were so much older.

Progressively, Ayn was withdrawing from former friends—from anyone who did not intimately share the world she was writing about. "After working on the book all day," she said, "it's agony to switch my consciousness to the outside world. Discussions with the Collective are almost the only form of social life I can bear, because it's the same universe as the book."

Notwithstanding Ayn's withdrawal, we did meet Professor Ludwig von Mises and his wife, Margit. This was exciting for me because, having studied many of his books, I thought he had one of the outstanding minds of the century. He was then in his seventies—witty, brilliant, and almost impishly charming.

Ayn's attitude toward von Mises was puzzling. I never saw her be anything but friendly, respectful, and admiring, although I had heard stories about their clashing once, rather heatedly, over questions of ethics. Ayn was almost girlish in the way she complimented him on his momentous achievements, and he seemed to find her delightful and stimulating. I was therefore shocked when, looking through her copy of von Mises's *Human Action,* I saw marginal notes that used frank language to condemn many of his statements. Ayn was particularly offended when he attempted to defend capitalism without referring to moral principles or when he seemed to support Kantian epistemology (which to Ayn was a disaster). The margins were filled with abusive comments. It was not her disagreement that disturbed me but the savagery of her attacks. The only way I could rationalize it was by considering Ayn's passion for ideas, which sometimes allowed normal human considerations to fall by the wayside.

"Do you really think of him as a bastard?" I asked Ayn. "I can't believe that." She looked thoughtful for a moment, then answered, "As a total person, no, I suppose I don't. But if I focus on that aspect of him, where he goes irrational, yes, I do." What I interpreted this statement to mean was, von Mises is brilliant, his contribution is enormous, he is wonderful, but he is still "of the world"; he is not one of us. I recognized some of Ayn's psychology in myself.

I was troubled by the disparity between Ayn's behavior toward von Mises and her comments in the margins of his books. To accuse Ayn of hypocrisy would not have occurred to me. But I recall discussing my confusion with Barbara, who shared my reaction. We let the matter go, assuming that one day we would understand—and that *of course* Ayn would have perfectly good reasons for her behavior.

Several years later, when he read *Atlas Shrugged,* von Mises was profoundly enthusiastic and complimentary, although I had the impression that ethics as an intellectual discipline did not particularly interest him and that he did not see its urgent relevance to his own work.

He paid Ayn one compliment she treasured, which Henry Hazlitt related to her. Hazlitt told her, "Lu Mises called you 'the most courageous man in America.'" "Did he say *man?*" Ayn asked, and Hazlitt replied yes. Recounting the incident to Barbara and me, she said, "Isn't that *wonderful?*"

Ayn thought more highly of Hazlitt and von Mises than of any other conservatives she knew. (Today, they would not be called conservatives but libertarians.) Clearly, von Mises was a giant, their disagreements about epistemology or anything else notwithstanding. She was aware that Hazlitt was sympathetic to altruism and pragmatism, but she thought him a brilliant economic writer and, like von Mises, an uncompromising advocate of freedom. Nonetheless, she was withdrawing from conservatives in general, not only because of her preoccupation with the novel but also because she saw herself as having less and less in common with them.

"I am not *primarily* an advocate of capitalism," she would write in *The Objectivist* in September 1971, "but of egoism; and I am not primarily an advocate of egoism, but of reason." In the 1950s, many of the conservatives opposed communism more than they favored free enterprise. "Anticommunism by itself is almost meaningless," Ayn would say. "That's one of the things wrong with McCarthy. You can't fight communism effectively unless you're for something better. A lot of those people don't know what in the hell they're for." Some of these conservatives favored certain forms of censorship, so as to protect "public morality"; many favored military conscription. "They're not defenders of individual rights," Ayn would say scornfully. Many attempted to justify capitalism through appeals to religion, "which amounts," Ayn would say, "to conceding reason and science to the enemy." Many of them were hopelessly nonintellectual; when Ayn attempted to explain that the battle was ultimately philosophical, their eyes glazed over.

For a long time, I had been arguing that we had to find some other name for ourselves, politically. "We're not conservatives," I said. "There's no tradition left for us to conserve. Government intervention in the economy has been the status quo since the nineteenth century. What we stand for is actually radical."

Ayn detested Eisenhower, who was then president; she had supported Taft, with reservations. To her, Eisenhower was the epitome of the compromising, unprincipled conservative. I recall her indignation, several years later, when she showed me a *Time* magazine article, dated July 29, 1957. "Here," she said, "is proof of everything I ever said about Eisenhower—and why I hate the typical conservative mentality."

Recalling his tortuous postwar discussions with Zhukov—a "confirmed Communist" but an "honest man"—Dwight Eisenhower went on: "One evening we had a three-hour conversation. We tried to explain to the other just what our systems meant . . . to the individual, and I was very hard put to it when he insisted that their system appealed to the idealistic and we completely to the materialistic, and I had a very tough time defending our position because he said: 'You tell a person he can do as he pleases, he can act as he pleases, he can do anything. Everything that is selfish in man you appeal to him, and we tell him that he must sacrifice for the state. . . .'"

Asked by the New York *Times*'s James Reston if he meant to imply that democracy was more difficult to defend than Communism, the President patiently explained: "Look, Mr. Reston, I think you could run into people you have a hard time convincing that the sun is hot and the earth is round. . . . Against that kind of belief you run against arguments that almost leave you breathless. You don't know how to meet them."

When I looked up from the article, Ayn exclaimed, "Is that a sickening evasion, or isn't it? That abysmal bastard *could not answer Zhukov.* A representative of the bloodiest dictatorship in history is boasting of his country's moral superiority—and the president of the United States, the greatest, noblest, freest country in the history of the world, *does not know what to say.* That's the intellectual paralysis produced by altruism. That's why, without a morality of rational self-interest, capitalism can't be defended."

By the time this article appeared, we had long since ceased to call ourselves conservatives. Early in 1954, Ayn said to me, "You're right. We're not conservatives. We're radicals for capitalism."

We had discarded the label of "conservative" and chosen a new designation for ourselves. In a more personal area, I made another such change. I had disliked my name for a long time. "Nathan Blumenthal" did not feel like me, and I wanted a name that did, especially because I was going to be a writer. This was typical of how I thought, in that I had strong preferences about everything: books, movies, automobiles, clothes, even colors—everything was "me" or "not me." Moreover, I wanted a name that I had chosen myself—not one that had been decided for me by someone else. As in so many other issues, *choice* was supremely important to me. Barbara felt exactly as I did. We were not yet aware that in many spiritual traditions, it is quite common for an individual to adopt a new name following a major personal transformation.

"Why should we be stuck with someone else's choice of name?" we said to Ayn. "A name is a very personal thing," Ayn agreed, and wanted to know what names we had considered. I hadn't thought of any as yet, except that I wanted to keep my initials. Ayn chuckled and said, "All writers and criminals do that when they change their name. I did."

A few weeks later I announced, "The first name is easy. It's Nathaniel. It's the last name I'm stuck on. Barbara and I will try looking through the B's in the phone book; maybe something will strike us."

In the spring of 1954, I said to Ayn and Frank, "How do you like 'Nathaniel Branden' and 'Barbara Branden'?" Barbara said, "Better than 'Barbara Buttercup,' don't you think?"

Many years later, Nora Ephron, a journalist who was later to become a screenwriter and director, insisted that it was significant that the name Branden contained "rand" (a fact I had never thought about until I read her article) and that a translation from Hebrew (based on a rearrangement of Branden to form *ben Rand*) disclosed the meaning "son of Rand." I think this was intended to support her charge of cultism. Given my absolute ignorance of Hebrew, I found her suggestion amusing, not to say plain silly. However, I disliked the implication that I wished to conceal my Jewishness, since I had always been outspoken about it. Ephron appeared eager to attack Ayn Rand and was reaching for any ammunition that was handy. Later, some other writer carried Ephron's speculations one step further: Could it be "mere coincidence," he wondered, that *Atlas Shrugged* was published by *Rand*om House?

I became Nathaniel Branden legally in September of that year—a few days before all our lives were to change forever.

It began with the way I greeted Ayn when I arrived in her apartment and the way I said good-bye when I left. When I embraced her, either on arriving or on departing, I began to make the moment last longer than necessary for a casual greeting or farewell, and then longer still. When we kissed, the earlier sense of family affection had vanished and was replaced by the faintest suggestion of sensuality. We said nothing about this. I was aware of this change on both our parts, and I knew that she was aware. I did not think about what this meant or where it might be leading. I did not suppose it was leading anywhere.

With each passing month, we became closer. At some imperceptible point in our relationship, our awareness of being male and female had shifted into sharper focus. An invisible energy charged the atmosphere. In her presence, I experienced an enhanced sense of masculine power, and I knew that she felt a heightened awareness of herself as a woman. I liked knowing that I was the cause of what she was feeling.

There was an element of danger, and I liked that, too. I felt almost reckless about it. Safety lay in the fact that we were each married and in the fact that I was twenty-four and she was forty-nine. An affair was unthinkable.

On an afternoon in late June, I visited Ayn alone. Frank was out, and Barbara was working on an assignment for school. I felt restless, bored with my studies, and delighted that Ayn was willing to abandon her writing for a daytime meeting. There was an odd lack of direction to our conversation, as if I had infected Ayn with my restlessness. It seemed like we were both waiting, neither of us knowing how to proceed.

Finally, Ayn asked, "How are you and Barbara doing?"

Barbara and I had been married for a year and a half. Our marriage seemed more or less harmonious. Most of the time, my spirits were high. Many years in the future, long after our divorce, Barbara would inform me that during this period she had been miserable much of the time. If this was true, I was not aware of it. Oblivious to my own emotions much of the time, I was no less oblivious to hers. But I knew that something was lacking in my life, and I tried to convey this to Ayn.

"It's not easy to answer you. Barbara and I are OK, I guess. We have our frictions, naturally, and sex still isn't right, but there's something more basic that's frustrating and not what I had hoped for. I can't imagine life without Barbara; I feel we're connected in some profound way, something deeper than I can explain even to myself. All of us have a sense of our own emotional capacity . . . a sense of what we're capable of feeling . . . and . . . there's a part of me that's not in the marriage at all, a part that wants . . . I don't know . . . something I've never felt, something more, something incredible. . . . Do you have any idea of what I'm talking about? There's something inside me that hasn't been touched yet, a capacity, a passion totally outside the universe I share with Barbara."

If I had begun my answer in a state of innocence, I was not innocent now. I knew precisely what Ayn would hear in my words and how she would be affected. An answer begun in pain became an act of seduction. Not a seduction aimed at Ayn's body—there was no thought of anything that tangible—but at her mind. Everything I was saying was true; what made it an act of seduction was the knowledge that I was speaking for both of us, that she could have described her own marriage in similar terms.

"Do you remember the scene in the novel," I went on, "when Dagny is working in that old office building across the street from Taggart Transcontinental? And she's thinking about her life and about how the world she finds as an adult is not the world she expected and hoped for. . . . It's so much less. . . . And she thinks of Francisco and Hank Rearden and is aware of some emotional capacity beyond what she feels for either man . . . something greater . . . And of course that's what she'll feel one day for John Galt, but she doesn't know that yet . . . so there's just this longing."

Ayn's head had dropped, her eyes were closed, and her hands were covering her face. She sat at the edge of the sofa, and I sat a few feet away by the window, watching her. She was wearing a green short-sleeved blouse, and I looked at her bare arms, suddenly aware of her vulnerability.

"What are you doing?" a voice within demanded angrily, and another voice responded, "It's all right. This is only a dream. In a few minutes you'll both go back to reality. But you can at least permit yourself this."

Lifting her head, Ayn answered with a voice weighted with emotion, "I understand you fully. I understand you better than I care to say."

We looked at each other through a long, tortured moment of silence. Neither of us was willing to venture further. I imagined what might be taking place in her mind, and she imagined what might be taking place in mine. For the moment, we had reached the limit of acceptable self-disclosure.

A few minutes later, Frank returned home, and Ayn rushed to embrace him.

"Hello, Fluff," he said gaily, using his pet name for her.

"Hello, Cubbyhole," she whispered, using her favorite term of endearment for him.

When she turned back to the room, I imagined I saw something in her eyes that I had never seen before—the faintest suggestion of guilt.

In September of that year, 1954, Barbara and I visited with my family in Toronto. Elayne was also there. Ayn and Frank delighted us by deciding to drive from New York to Toronto to spend time with us and meet my family. Ayn was afraid of flying, although later in life she did occasionally travel by air. This trip to Canada would be the first time she had left the United States since her arrival, except for a brief trip to Mexico.

The first time she was alone with me, after spending several hours in the company of my mother, Ayn whispered as we walked down the steps of my parents' home, "How did you *survive?*" I laughed.

One afternoon during the visit, in the home of Florence and Hans, Ayn and I sat facing a group of people who had wanted to meet the author of *The Fountainhead* and to ask questions about her philosophy. Ayn had insisted that I join her for the question-and-answer session. We fielded questions almost playfully, moving effortlessly from ethics to political economy to aesthetics to epistemology to current events. We sometimes elaborated on each other's answers, sometimes beginning the same sentence in the same instant, sometimes inserting parenthetical comments within the other's response, laughing openly in the pleasure of our intellectual comradeship and experiencing a level of fusion that was intoxicating.

The sense of intoxication remained the next day when Ayn, Frank, Barbara, Elayne, and I drove back to New York. In the first part of the trip, Barbara and Elayne sat in the back seat, and Frank, Ayn, and I sat in the front. Frank drove.

Ayn was on a talking jag and could not seem to contain herself. "Wasn't yesterday wonderful? That question-and-answer session yesterday afternoon—we were like Siamese twins. Our minds work exactly the same way. Your answers were models of precision. I didn't even have to be there—you could have represented me flawlessly. I couldn't have imagined quite such integration with another person. Frank, just think—Nathan is twenty-four, and look what he's accomplished already. His psychological theories, helping Allan with his music, his work with the others in the Collective. . . . Elayne, did you know you had such a remarkable brother?"

"Well, Ayn," Elayne began, amused. "That's a long story."

I laughed and protested, "Ayn, I'm becoming shy. Please stop. And besides, you never ask a sister what she thinks about her kid brother."

"I guess you're all right," said Elayne in her flat, good-natured way.

For the next several hours, Ayn would not stop. With occasional excursions into other subjects, she kept bringing the subject back to me, insisting that I was a genius, a great psychologist, a man of destiny. At some point, I began answering in kind, praising her writing, speaking of what she had given me intellectually and inspirationally, predicting her future impact on Western civilization.

Then it was evening. Ayn and I were now sitting in the backseat. Her head was resting on my shoulder, and she was saying, "I really don't know how to identify our relationship. It's not exactly friendship, as I've ever thought about friendship. It's much more than that. I certainly don't feel maternal. I have never thought of you as my son. You're way beyond being a student. You're much more than a fellow fighter. You're just . . . Nathan. That's the only way I can think of you—you're just Nathan."

"That's how I feel about you," I said softly, my arm around her, "You're just . . . Ayn." I began speaking of my appreciation of her more intimately and more personally than I had ever permitted myself before. "I can no longer imagine what life would have been like if we hadn't met."

I heard the huskiness in her voice and in my own. I was not ready to know what it meant. I listened as she went on talking, as my words mingled with hers, and I was vaguely aware of feeling irresponsible, unaccountable, but indifferent to the fact. Indifferent to the awareness that the meaning of what we were saying would eventually catch up with us.

I felt that Ayn was taking the initiative in leading us where we were going but that her conscious mind was a few steps behind mine in grasping the implications. In retrospect, I think I was naïve in that assumption.

In the front seat, Frank, Elayne, and Barbara were silent. It did not occur to me to wonder what they were thinking. They were somewhere far away.

"Just . . . Nathan," Ayn was saying, and then her eyes widened as if awareness had finally come. She looked at me almost for reassurance, as if she were uncertain of the reality of what was happening. Recklessly oblivious to what we were setting in motion, I smiled arrogantly, intimately, tenderly.

We stopped for the night at a motel. When we went to our separate rooms and I was alone with Barbara, I felt oddly suspended, fragmented, disoriented.

While I was familiar with the concept of *dissociation,* a psychological state in which the thoughts and feelings of the moment do not connect to one's wider context and do not connect to reality, I did not identify my own condition as dissociation. I merely experienced myself as moving through a void with no assessment of what that signified.

Reality came back, demanding integration, when I faced Barbara, saw the pain and rage on her face, and heard her say to me, "Do you know what it's like to be trapped in a car for all those hours and have to listen to your husband make love to another woman?"

I froze. Cut off from my own knowledge, suspended in a kind of emotional vacuum, I wondered what Barbara was talking about. I had had no time to grasp, let alone assimilate, the significance of what had happened in the car. I did not yet know whether anything of enduring consequence had really taken place. I did not want to know. Not yet. Not until I had some opportunity to meditate and reflect. I tried to answer Barbara, but I was not too articulate. I struggled for a mental focus that eluded me. I cannot recall precisely what I said, but it must have been, in effect, that she was out of her mind. Not a courageous response.

"You two are in love with each other!" she shouted. "My god, don't you know?"

I could not force my mind to work. I had left the context I shared with Ayn and was trying to reenter the one I shared with Barbara. I felt suspended between the two. I needed time to be alone, to think, to digest what had happened, but there was no time. My wife was standing in front of me, demanding answers to which she was entitled, and I had nothing to offer.

One thing was urgent and immediate—I saw Barbara's pain, and I wanted desperately to heal it, to put her mind at rest. I muttered something that was meant to be reassuring.

"Don't try to tell me I wasn't hearing what I was hearing!" Barbara cried. "I know what I know!"

Drawing on every resource I could summon, fighting for calm, I said, "Barbara, come on now. Ayn is twenty-five years older than I am." The phrase wasn't used back then, but today one would say I was totally "in denial."

"What has that got to do with what you two were saying to each other? Obviously the age barrier is not a barrier!"

"But . . . but, you know how Ayn and I are, how we've always been. We're a mutual admiration society. We even joke about it. Perhaps in the car we got carried away, but can you tell me you heard anything new, in principle, that you haven't heard us say before?"

Later, I learned that Elayne had perceived the conversation precisely as I was now explaining it. She did not think anything unusual had happened in the car.

This perspective seemed to quiet Barbara a bit. "No," she conceded thoughtfully, "but still . . ."

I had no sense of lying to Barbara. In the cold, clear light of ordinary reality, what she was suggesting truly struck me as unthinkable. My mind had slammed tightly shut against it; all I desired was a return to the "normalcy" of yesterday. What had happened in the car now felt like a hallucination. Whatever it had been, I knew beyond any doubt that I had no desire to leave Barbara for Ayn. I told her that.

"That may be true," she said, "but that's not the issue."

We agreed to try to sleep. It was a confused and anguished night for both of us.

The next morning, we all met for breakfast, and while Frank and Elayne appeared relaxed, Ayn, Barbara, and I were strained and quiet. Early that afternoon, we arrived back in Manhattan. Our good-byes were muted.

Barbara and I did not pursue the subject further. We moved through the rest of the day almost with resignation, as if we knew that another shoe was yet to drop (this would happen in my next talk with Ayn) and that until then, discussion was useless.

The next day, I walked from our apartment on Thirty-Fifth Street to Ayn's on Thirty-Sixth, thinking that we might have a long, intimate conversation about what had happened in the car or that we might not speak of it at all. I could not have said which I hoped for.

Frank was working at the florist shop, and Ayn was alone in the apartment when I arrived. At first, she seemed relaxed, and I thought, "Everything is going to be all right. We're not going to talk about what happened. We have simply reached a deeper level of intimacy, and now life can continue as before—only better."

For about an hour, we talked about everything except our feelings for each other. I did not realize, but should have, that Ayn was waiting for me to speak first. Finally she said, in a note of gentle urgency, "Now, then, we really must talk about what happened in the car. You know what I mean, of course?"

In such moments, one does not hesitate; one does not falter. I felt the spotlight fall on me, and the moves had to be impeccable. When we were alone together and connected in our special way, we created a universe that was uniquely ours. I would not fail it—or her.

"Of course I know what you mean," I smiled in a manner of total and absolute assurance.

"Well," Ayn went on, "don't you want to say something?"

With the sense of moving across a minefield, I answered, "I wasn't certain if I should . . . or whether it was better just to leave the situation . . . to our understanding . . ."

She looked at me as if what I had just said was incomprehensible.

"In the car," she persisted, "what we said to each other . . . what you said to me. . . it sounded like love." She pronounced this last word in a hushed voice. "Or have I misunderstood everything?"

I was aware of feeling pressured, pulled at a speed that I had not chosen. I knew her well enough to recognize the meaning of her intensity; her dark, luminous eyes searched my face for possible signs of betrayal. I could almost read the question in her mind: "Will Nathan be another Leo?" If she were merely inquiring about my feelings, if she were not struggling with her own feelings of love, she would have been much lighter in her approach. The quiet urgency of her questioning said everything. I looked at the woman who had been my idol since I was fourteen years old— looked at the author of *The Fountainhead* and *Atlas Shrugged*—and saw her struggling to contain emotions she could not express until and unless I allowed her to do so.

Suddenly, I had the sense that everything I had ever done, every choice I ever made, had led me to this moment. Part of me wanted to escape, to fly back to life as it had been before. But the more dominant part said, "Leap!"

"Ayn, you misunderstood nothing. *Of course* I am in love with you."

PART TWO

8

"OF COURSE I AM in love with you."

As I said those words, I knew that my life had changed irrevocably. I did not yet know precisely what I was committing myself to, but I knew I was making a commitment of enormous consequence. I thought, Whatever is to happen now, I can deal with it. I am ready. I felt expectant and energized as we looked at each other through a moment of exquisitely charged silence.

Then her expression changed, and she stared at me almost as if her intention were to intimidate. "Do you understand what you are saying?" she whispered. "This is not an impulse? You are not being capricious?"

I shook my head as if to say, You know better than that.

Her words were like steps across a tightrope high in space: "If I love . . . if I give myself emotionally . . . it's such an exception for me. . . . The man has to understand . . . what he's undertaking. . . ."

I felt a rising euphoria that clashed with the tense solemnity of her manner, and I had to fight a desire to laugh exuberantly. I could see the cautious older woman struggling for control over the young girl within her who wanted only to surrender to the moment. Her expression shifted from eagerness to caution and back again. The ferocity of her struggle unnerved me a little, but even my apprehension contributed to my buoyancy. This was life as it was meant to be lived, filled with danger and ecstasy and unimagined possibilities. I felt as if I had broken free of a whole network of constraints, had shattered the ordinary framework of existence, and that I, Nathaniel Branden, had taken Nathan Blumenthal by the hand and led him into a context uniquely his own, where he could be fully himself. "Do you really understand," she was saying almost ominously, "what you would be undertaking?"

"I love you," I said, feeling it with the power of absolute certainty and implying that nothing else needed to be said.

She went on questioning me. Was I prepared to make the emotional commitment implied by my declaration? I was not entirely sure what this meant; nonetheless, I nodded confidently. It occurred to me that she was seeking to draw me out while she had as yet made no declaration of her own; she wanted the initial risks to be mine. I thought, a little impatiently, that she always needed to be in control, the master of any encounter, but I did not mind too much because her feelings were so transparent. It was obvious that she wanted to stop talking and to embrace and that she would not permit herself to do so. She did not look formidable; she looked uncertain and vulnerable.

She said, with a touching quality of almost youthful honesty, "I know . . . in a novel . . . it wouldn't happen quite this way. . . . The woman wouldn't be interrogating the man. . . . But please understand and . . ."

Disarmed by her words and manner, feeling intensely how precious she was to me, I assured her that I understood completely.

"*What* do you understand?" she asked.

"I understand that, in some sense, you see yourself as putting your emotional life in my hands."

"Exactly. That doesn't frighten you?"

"No."

"If this is a mistake," she said, "I have more to lose than you do, if only because I'm older."

I accepted her statement without pointing out that the risks for me were hardly negligible, even though she seemed oblivious to them.

"I don't know what we're going to do," I said, "but this is not a mistake."

"This changes nothing about how I feel about Frank or how you feel about Barbara," she said, confident of her right to speak for both of us.

I found her statement only slightly doubtful; I did not yet know what the truth was. I told myself, "Ayn surely knows; she seems so certain."

"It changes nothing," I affirmed.

"I do love you," she confided almost shyly. "There, I've said it." Then, with more certainty, she said it again: "I love you."

Wanting to put us both at greater ease, I answered in a lightly mocking tone, "I was wondering when you were going to get around to it."

"Please don't joke. Not now."

She lifted her face to mine, and we kissed and held each other in a way that was new for both of us, and it felt natural and normal and inevitable.

She kissed as she did everything, with absolute and total commitment, which I thought wonderful. For me, the moment was exquisitely erotic. We trembled with excitement. I knew that in this arena, her deepest desire was not to control but to drop any semblance of control, to melt and yield and respond.

Ayn whispered, her eyes sparkling with humor, "What's the matter with me? This is what should have happened the moment you walked in the door today."

"This is the difference between art and life," I said chuckling.

She laughed in agreement. We were both still a little nervous, and that, too, was enjoyable, as if sharing nervousness was itself an act of deepening intimacy.

Any thought or feeling, any confusion or uncertainty that might have clashed with the happiness of the moment seemed unimportant. I identified the impulse that drew me into this new relationship with Ayn as the voice of reason, the voice of my highest self, to which any other internal voice would have to give way. I was dimly aware that in some compartment of my consciousness, there was agitation and protest, an alarm signal too faint to have an impact. I had committed myself. I felt love, excitement, dismay, and disorientation; I felt alive.

"We must do nothing to hurt Frank or Barbara," Ayn uttered suddenly and firmly.

I did not know how we could avoid it, but I agreed that we would do everything we could to protect our respective marriages. It occurred to me that we were already contradicting that agreement by the nature of our discussion, but was there any other sane way to proceed?

"We won't have an actual affair," she said. "The romance will be nonsexual, in the ultimate sense."

Part of me felt relieved by this statement; another, more dominant part felt disappointed.

"You mean it will be sexual in everything but fact," I answered.

She nodded.

"We must do nothing to cause them discomfort publicly," I declared.

Again she nodded and said that we would do our best to respect their feelings in every way we reasonably could. We discussed this a long while, and then she declared, "We will ask them if they object to our meeting alone once or twice a week, just to talk."

"We meet by ourselves occasionally anyway."

"But now it will be a regular and integral part of our lives."

"That would be wonderful."

"I'm sure they'll agree to that," Ayn said. "We have a right to something."

There was an edge of anger in her voice, directed against Frank and Barbara. Intuitively, I felt I knew the source of that anger; in this moment and context, they were impediments. Whatever the reasons, we felt that they did not match us in energy, initiative, strength, ambition, or passion, although we did not explicitly acknowledge this. These were matters we talked around, rather than addressed head-on. Now, in Ayn's voice, the unexpressed had risen to the surface for the briefest flash of an instant. It was not named, but it was felt, and it was in our eyes as we looked at each other in silent understanding—we would not be stopped.

Then the conversation switched back to our importance to each other and how each made the other feel uniquely understood. And as we talked, Ayn continued to shift between two different aspects of her personality: one moment, happy, vulnerable, and open; the next, guarded, detached, and stern.

"I've never given anyone but Frank this kind of power," she said, almost as a warning.

I wondered about the nature of Frank's "power" and what it meant practically. From the way she looked at me, I believed that she was continuing to wonder, Am I seeing him objectively? Is this encounter really what it seems? Can I trust him? I thought that, given the extraordinary and unexpected nature of what was occurring, her response was entirely understandable; did she not have every right to her concerns?

I was aware that an adjustment was taking place deep within me. I had often felt that I had to be older than my chronological age with Ayn and that the younger parts of me had no place in our relationship; that feeling had now increased to an unprecedented degree. I felt that I had to be the man she had never had in her life but had urgently needed and deserved—a contemporary who could match her strength and give her the kind of support she said she had never experienced. I now required of myself that I be a fifty-year-old man.

In the excitement of facing this challenge, I was aware of something powerful emerging within me, an indomitable and inexhaustible force.

I was less aware that something else, more delicate, was dying—the joy of being twenty-four. If there were cries of protest from that disowned self, I chose not to hear them.

I was Nathaniel Branden, and I could do anything. That is what I told myself.

If ever a decision had multiple motivations, it was the decision to become romantically involved with Ayn. I loved her, but there was also the matter of ego. The challenge was exhilarating. She had a stupendous mind and an electrifying personality—and when I looked into her eyes, I saw admiration. It was inevitable. Too great an electric charge had built up between us. She was a passionate woman, I was a passionate young man. It was drama, it was theater, it was an adventure, it was idealism, it was vanity, and it was madness.

We decided it was time to bring Barbara into the discussion, and I telephoned and asked her to come to Ayn's apartment. Nonetheless, when the doorbell rang, I was unprepared. I did not think to ask Ayn to let me talk with Barbara by myself. Ayn conveyed an urgency about informing Barbara of the facts at once. In retrospect, the way we proceeded strikes me as barbaric.

Almost immediately, Ayn said, in a compassionately gentle voice, "Well, Barbara, it must have been difficult for you since the car ride, and you've probably been wondering what Nathan and I have been saying to each other today."

Barbara nodded her head numbly. Her face disclosed no discernible emotion beyond a tinge of apprehension. It was as if she already knew everything. As if no transitions, no explanations, were really needed. As if, in her own mind, she had heard everything Ayn and I had just said to each other and as if what she was hearing now were only a confirmation.

I stood by silently, disconnected from all emotion, as Ayn explained that the shift in our relationship had been coming for a long time and probably should have been obvious to us all. She said it was logical and normal and quite unastonishing, if one thought about it, that she and I would love each other not just as friends but as man and woman.

"We're not Platonists," Ayn said. "We don't hold our values in some other realm, unrelated to the realm in which we live our lives. If Nathan and I are who we are, if we see what we see in each other, if we truly hold the values we profess, how can we not be in love?"

As I listened, the image of Ayn as matron of honor at Barbara's and my wedding came flashing through my mind, and for one instant I felt horror. Then the image and the horror were gone, like a fading fragment of a dream. Ayn went on talking for a long time, amplifying her argument in such a way that the validity of what she was saying seemed more and more self-evident. She was a sorceress of reason.

Barbara kept nodding her head, like someone in a trance. I felt a sudden surge of agonized protectiveness, but stood frozen and did not move toward her.

"This does not mean that Nathan does not love you," Ayn went on, "just as I love Frank. You must understand that."

I thought irritably, Why is Ayn speaking for me?

"I know Nathan loves me," Barbara said, with a dignity I found immensely attractive. I walked over and took her hand.

"Barbara," I said softly, "what's happened between Ayn and me had to happen. It changes nothing about how I feel about you." I meant it.

"You have nothing to fear," Ayn said. Even in that moment, I knew that statement was preposterous, notwithstanding what I had said to Barbara. Ayn went on, "He's your husband, and nothing will change that. Look at the age difference between Nathan and me. We have no future, except as friends. I'm not going to make myself ludicrous with a younger man. All we would like is time to be alone together, one afternoon and one evening a week. . . ."

While Barbara sat in a visibly dazed state, Frank came home. It was clear from their exchange in the first moments of his arrival that he and Ayn had already had some preliminary discussion. He looked as if the entire situation were already known to him—as if he, too, had been present in the room all afternoon. His face seemed paler than usual and more drawn. I thought I saw a hint of anger in his eyes, but not when he looked at me, only when he looked at Ayn.

With the persistence of a drill cutting through granite, Ayn proceeded to repeat what she had said to Barbara, now going into many more details about her feelings, about her intellectual loneliness, about what I had given her and how she saw me, about the uniqueness of our relationship. "Frank, you yourself have spoken of how much you love Nathan, of what he's brought to our lives. You've seen the whole struggle of my career, so you know what it means to have found a mind and a character like his. He gives me a kind of understanding I thought impossible. He's my future. He's the one who will carry the work forward. Only he exists now. He's here in our lives now. Frank, in a way you saw what was coming before I did. It was you who said Nathan was the reason I came back from California when I did. It's a rational universe—this *had to happen*."

"I can't stand this!" Barbara cried, then slowly melted in surrender to the sounds of Ayn's hypnotic voice. "I won't put up with this. It's outrageous!" Frank shouted, then relapsed into passivity and impotence even before Ayn could complete her response.

After Barbara and then Frank flared up in angry protest, Ayn became still warmer, gentler, and more implacable. She acknowledged their feelings, conveyed compassion for their pain, and tried to make them accept the situation with the single-mindedness of a military commander who, looking neither to the right nor to the left, marches relentlessly forward.

I was silent. I was almost fascinated by the artistry of her persuasiveness, feeling more like a spectator than a protagonist in the drama. I did eventually say to Barbara and Frank, "This is something apart from our normal, everyday lives. But it's not really all that new, if we're honest about it. Ayn and I have always had a special connection. Both of you have known that. And I never felt that either one of you resented it or was jealous."

"It's not as if we were proposing a sexual relationship," Ayn added.

I found myself wondering why we were not proposing an affair and whether Barbara would really care; I could not imagine her feeling sexual jealousy where I was concerned. Now, I nodded in support of Ayn's statement.

Ayn asked Frank and Barbara, "Do you want to leave us because of Nathan's and my feelings for each other?"

The answer was a hesitant and reluctant no. They acknowledged— yielding slowly and fighting unspoken resistance—that they understood and in fact respected those feelings.

Ayn persisted, "Then do you want us to go on as before, pretending that our feelings do not exist?"

That did not seem reasonable either, Frank and Barbara conceded, looking more and more defeated. They were not fighters, not in this context, not against Ayn and me. They had no chance.

"Faking reality does not work," Ayn declared. "What realistic alternative is there to what we're proposing?"

Some part of me was carried along by sheer excitement, some by Ayn's certainty, and some by an accumulation of pain and rage at Barbara that now made me indifferent to her suffering.

"There isn't an alternative," Frank said in response to Ayn's question. He did not say it happily. Barbara's expression had an unself-pitying austerity when she nodded her head in acquiescence.

Ayn's manipulative dishonesty, and my own complicity in it (which is so obvious to me in retrospect), seemed in that moment like "rationality" and "realism."

When Barbara and I said good-bye to Ayn and Frank, we all hugged one another. We were attempting to create a spirit of love, a spirit of transcendence and of triumph over unworthy fears. I felt pain at any suffering I might be causing and, at the same time, I felt exultation, as if we had all reached a height none of us had conceived before.

Later that night, back in our own apartment, Barbara said to me, "I love Ayn so much. And it's no mystery to me why she's in love with you.

You're the kind of man she should have. I want to see her happy." There were tears in her eyes, and I held her close, stroking her hair, not knowing what to think, say, or do. She whispered, "I want to see you happy. I know what I've never given you. Both of you deserve more than you've ever had. I want you to have it. I mean this selfishly. This is not self-sacrifice."

We made love that night. Barbara, for once, took the lead with more feeling than she had brought to our bed for a long time

Ayn's and my sexual affair began five months later, in January 1955.

I was clearly the initiator, much more so than I had been previously. In my private afternoon and evening meetings with Ayn, I became aware of my impact as a man in a way I had not experienced before. When Ayn looked at me, I saw what I had always longed to see on a woman's face—appreciation that combined the sexual and the spiritual. Her admiration did not remain abstract or divorced from her body; it was immediately translated into physical terms. Her mind and her sexuality were integrated. This was the kind of woman I could understand.

Ayn frightened most people who were in awe of her authority and intellect. What she wanted was a man whose esteem would take the form of reducing her to a sex object. This seemed so simple and natural to me. All I could think was that, in this arena, I was at last free to be uninhibitedly myself—to release an energy that had very little outlet in my marriage.

"I don't want a Platonic relationship," I announced to Ayn. "Not in any sense whatsoever. With you, I want to experience everything."

I felt a new and deeper level of confidence, certainty, and knowledge of female sexuality that seemed to have materialized out of nowhere. I discovered that whereas I could falter in the emotional realm, I felt as secure in the arena of sex as I did in the arena of intellect.

"I'm afraid of what's happening," Ayn confided. "This could change our lives in a far more radical way than we had thought. Are you sure—are you absolutely sure—you want to proceed?"

"Absolutely."

I had lost all sense of restraints or barriers. There was only what I wanted. I did not think about how either Ayn's marriage or mine would be affected. I still wondered if Barbara really cared if I slept with Ayn. If she did suffer, part of me was comfortable with that—the part of me that felt wounded and unforgiving.

Ayn had spoken more than once of her admiration for the tale of Siegfried and Brunhild. Brunhild could defeat any suitor in combat, and she surrendered only when Siegfried—passing through one obstacle after another, including a ring of fire—conquered her with his sword. She fell worshipfully at his feet. "That is my metaphor," Ayn had said, "for my favorite image of ideal love. Or at least the beginning—the 'courtship.'"

She *wanted* to be a little frightened of taking the final step, and she *wanted* me to persevere, to overcome her fears and blast through her objections. She wanted to care about Frank's feelings, and she wanted me not to care at all. As to Barbara's feelings, I doubt if Ayn seriously considered them. She wanted me to override two marriages, the age difference, and every kind of conventional objection—and I did so.

I was sometimes astonished by the degree of my ease and comfort in getting what I wanted, the sense of operating in a context where mastery was effortless. Looking back several decades later, I am still somewhat amazed and unable to explain my certainty in an area where my previous experience had been so limited.

When we discussed our desires with Barbara and Frank, it was clear that they had expected us to become involved sexually.

Ayn asserted, as she had asserted five months earlier, that nothing need change, that we each loved our spouses as much as we ever had, that we were an indestructible foursome.

Her primary focus, however, was on her own emotional needs. "You both know how little I've had in my life by way of personal reward," she would say to Frank and Barbara. I shuddered when I heard this; could Ayn be unaware that she had slapped Frank's face? But Frank displayed no visible reaction. "And you two understand, as perhaps no one else could, what Nathan is to me . . . the realization of everything I write about . . . and what it means to have him in reality, on earth, not just in my writing or in my mind." I felt uncomfortable but took my reaction as a sign of immaturity. "If the four of us were of lesser stature, this would not have happened, and if it somehow had, you would not accept it. But it is the logic of who we are that led us to this. It's completely rational that Nathan and I should feel as we do toward each other. It's totally rational, given our premises, that our feelings would include the sexual." I relaxed; this perspective sounded valid. "If he and I were the same age, the problem would be entirely different. But we're not the same age. So what we're talking about, at most, is a year or two. Can either of you see me as an older woman, a few years from now, pursuing a younger man? It would be contemptible. This is the last period in my life when I can think about or permit myself this—I'm a realist about age. What we're asking for is temporary . . . just to have had it . . . for a little while. . . . I think we are all great enough to handle this without tragedy for anyone."

This conversation took place in November 1954. By December, after several more discussions, we all knew that sometime soon the affair would begin.

Ayn's and my cruelty did not lie in falling in love or even, primarily, in pursuing an affair. The cruelty lay in how we dealt with the matter: our lack of genuine compassion for Frank's and Barbara's predicament; our lack of contact with them at the level of genuine human feeling, as contrasted with the rarefied atmosphere of philosophical abstraction; our failure to relate on a simple husband-and-wife plane, rather than as storybook characters. Ayn and I prided ourselves on our rationality and realism, and yet these were precisely the traits we failed to offer Frank and Barbara or to bring to our emotional life. In retrospect, I am horrified by our irresponsible unconsciousness.

Oddly enough, Barbara and I grew closer during this period. We shared a special kind of affection and caring that were insufficient for the intensity of romantic love but that were real and valuable nonetheless. "I want you both to be happy," Barbara said often, with desperate, even heartbreaking, earnestness.

It was obvious that some part of her motivation in agreeing to the affair was expiation for not loving me more. "I want you to have everything you deserve," she said. "And Frank has said in so many words that you are the kind of man Ayn deserves." When I heard the pain in her voice, I felt tormented, torn, confused. She said, "If I had the power to push a button so that none of this would have happened, I would not push it. I don't want to live in a world in which you and Ayn could never find each other as man and woman. I can't wish that for either one of you. I want a world in which such things can and do happen, because it's right, it's what I want to see in life . . . even if, in this case, it's hard for me. . . . I know you're concerned for me. You don't want to hurt me. I can see what this is costing you. It will be all right; it will really be all right." Whatever it was that held Barbara and me together—and made it so hard for us to let go of each other—was strengthened by such moments.

In her words I heard loneliness, longing, even despair. I also heard her struggle to be brave, to say and do what she believed the situation required, to fulfill her own vision of a heroine. She is a giant, I told myself. Never mind the things we sometimes fight about. She is an incredible human being; her values really matter to her.

At no time did Barbara ever hint at leaving me. In fact, she would say with childlike solemnity, "When it comes to marriage, we're like Catholics, right? We don't believe in divorce?" And I would answer, no less seriously, "When it comes to marriage, we're like Catholics." Because each of us knew that the other approved of divorce in principle, this was our way of stressing that, whatever our problems, our commitment was for life.

"A year or two," Barbara said, "and then you and Ayn can be just friends again, and by then I'll be fully ready to be your wife." She spoke as if one day our sexual difficulties, and any other conflicts we might have, would be resolved, would be behind us, and as if our love would fulfill what it had once promised to be when we walked through the snow in Winnipeg, on fire with the discovery of each other. How this was to happen, neither of us knew.

Some months after the affair had begun, I asked Ayn how Frank was taking it. She smiled enigmatically and answered, "Sometimes he finds it a sexual inspiration. He looks at it as a wonderful adventure of which he's a part."

"Barbara also enjoys the situation sometimes, maybe just a little, as if our relationship makes her own life more glamorous, more exciting." This is what I thought at the time; later I would learn from Barbara that I had been entirely mistaken.

Ayn smiled. "You see? We'll have our year or two together—and there will be no victims, no tragedy."

Because Ayn and I had become increasingly intimate prior to the start of the affair, with the intensity of our embraces building for months, the "first time" did not entirely feel like the "first time" but rather like the culmination of many sexual encounters, beginning with our return from Toronto.

In the realm of sex, I knew her as thoroughly as someone I had been intimately involved with for years. I had penetrated her consciousness in every way I possibly could since first reading *The Fountainhead,* so the actual act of sex felt almost like a continuation of the same endeavor. The desire to "know" her in all conceivable senses was central to my interactions with her. It was as if we had been engaged in foreplay for four years—since the evening in March 1950 when we first met. Later, Ayn told me that was exactly how she felt.

I was conscious of two different responses to our first sexual experience. My body felt completely unastonished, completely serene, as if what was now happening was the most natural thing in the world. My mind, in contrast, had flashes of amazement and disorientation at the thought "I am now *sleeping with Ayn.*" The two perspectives were like musical themes running in counterpoint, yielding a result more thrilling than either could produce by itself—a high level of excitement devoid of any trace of tension or anxiety. I believed I did see a touch of apprehension in Ayn, but it was a kind one welcomes because it makes one feel more alive, makes the moment more momentous.

She made love with the same single-tracked concentration with which she did everything else; nothing existed but the moment, our bodies, this sensation, and then the next. What was electrifying was that in her gentlest, most sensual touch, I could feel the full force of her personality, as if the voltage of her mind and the voltage of her flesh were one.

Watching her eyes watching me was aphrodisiacal. I knew that what she wanted most was not my tenderness but my aggressiveness, my willingness to do anything I felt like doing, without asking and without hesitating. She wanted me to be a master, to use her language, exercising his rights over his property. This, and this alone, allowed the female in her to emerge fully. Because I had no unusual sexual predilections and no interest in giving or receiving pain and every interest in giving and receiving pleasure, our lovemaking was uncomplicated happiness.

That I could bring such joy to a woman twenty-five years my senior, a woman I admired so passionately, nourished my sexual self-esteem. That she could evoke an intense response in a man so many years younger, a man she perceived as the incarnation of her values, nourished hers.

A year or two. That is how I thought about it in the beginning. Safe, time limited, not a way of life. And the first few months of the affair brought me a joy that could not be extinguished by anything that happened later.

In the bedroom there was no split between the novelist and the woman. She was sensual, passionate, uninhibited, aggressive, submissive, strong, helpless, and magnificently greedy. She made it abundantly clear that her most ardent desire was to be reduced to a state of total surrender, which meant that I was free to release my own aggressive energy. We were like two prisoners let loose.

Nothing we could say or do could frighten or overwhelm the other. Nothing was too much. Whatever one gave, the other welcomed. Whatever one wanted, the other provided. We embraced sex as a person embraces oxygen after being underwater for too long.

"What's happening to me?" Ayn would say. "You're turning me into an animal." And I would grin mockingly and answer, "Really? What were you before?" "A mind," she would say. And I would reply, "Really? Do you have a mind? Who ever told you that?"

Sometimes I would arrive in the afternoon and ask how the writing was going. And she would answer wryly, "What writing? I've been sitting at my desk for the past three hours, unable to concentrate on anything except . . . I don't know myself anymore; I can't believe this is me. Have you been sent by the enemy to prevent me from finishing this book?"

She was in the midst of writing the most difficult part of the novel—Galt's radio speech to the world in which he explains the reasons for the strike, exposes the philosophical ideas that have brought the world to destruction, and expounds the new moral vision needed to redeem civilization. Her challenge was to present the essence of a new philosophical system and to do so in the dramatic style appropriate not for a treatise but for a novel. We spent many hours discussing the smallest details of her formulations. These hours were exhilarating for me but often tense and stressful for Ayn. I was in awe of her achievement. The sixty-page speech took her two years to write. Those were the two hardest years of her career. It was not merely the difficulty of the project that made the writing take that long; her mind and time were divided between the novel and our relationship.

"I'm proud of the fact," she said to me, "that I'm willing to set aside the most important project of my life so that I can spend time on us, either with you or else alone, thinking about you. I'm proud of the fact that love matters to me this much. I'm almost ashamed to admit that what I'm experiencing now, I have never experienced before. I have never permitted Frank to be a distraction from my work. I feel disloyal even telling you this."

I replied that, given the greatness of the novel and what I knew it meant to her, I found it incomprehensible that she was so often willing to set it aside—for anyone or anything.

She smiled. "Then you don't really understand what you are to me."

I did not want to think that I loved less than she did. Yet I was concerned that if she was willing to set aside everything for our relationship, I would be expected to do the same. I reproached myself for this reaction and told myself that I had failed to understand her. Was she not the high priestess of creative work? Had she not spoken more than once of her scorn for novels that centered on love, as contrasted with novels in which love was integrated with the character's pursuit of other goals?

I asked her, "You don't mean that love as a way of life comes ahead of work?" And she replied, "No, of course not. The two are equal in importance. But for me, now, this relationship will be given everything it needs. Don't you feel the same way?" I answered yes—what else could I say?—and felt somewhat relieved. But a sense of obligation that would not yet come into focus remained. I knew that love versus work was not really the issue; the issue had more to do with what precisely was involved in loving Ayn. Was there an implicit commitment to make every other value and interest in my life, including my marriage, subordinate to her needs? Ayn had actually given me clear signals to this effect. I suddenly felt plunged into agitation and chaos, which must have been apparent to Ayn, who asked a little sharply, "What's the matter? Where have you gone to? You've disappeared."

She loved to talk, for hours, about the emotional meaning of our relationship. Intellectualizing made feelings acceptable. I felt awkward in these discussions. Whereas the age difference did not seem important in intellectual or sexual contexts, it became confusingly important to me when the primary focus was on emotion. Philosophical discussions were by nature abstract. Sex, too, was abstract in our case, existing in a private world of its own, cut off from the normal flow of daily living. In the worlds of philosophy and sex, we were not so much persons as forces achieving union in a unique dimension created anew at each meeting. But when it came to emotion, I confronted the fact that I was twenty-five, she was fifty, both of us were married, and we were at different developmental stages. Because I was constantly striving to adjust to Ayn's level rather than she to mine, she saw no problem in any of this. And I did not know how to explain my reticence, neither to myself nor to her. "I know that the average woman finds it easier than the average man to talk about love, relationships, and emotions," she said to me, "but you're not the average man. What's the matter with you? Are you repressed?"

In fact, self-liberation and self-alienation were proceeding simultaneously along different tracks of my personality. While I was becoming freer in important areas, I was becoming more repressed in others. I now know that emotional repression is a defense, a survival strategy, but I did not yet recognize what I was defending against or why.

I did believe that I was more troubled than Ayn over the pain we were causing Barbara and Frank. When I raised the issue, her manner often became subtly impatient, as if to say, Why talk about it? It can't be helped. I faulted my inability to match her ruthlessness; I had flattered myself in imagining a toughness I now seemed to lack. I thought she was more realistic than I was.

When I told her I felt awkward, embarrassed, and miserable about forcing Frank out of his own apartment twice a week, she suggested renting a small apartment in the same building. It would be exclusively ours. I was enthusiastic and implored her to do so, since I could not have afforded the new apartment. But she kept putting it off, saying, "Suppose someone found out what it was for?" She was obsessed with keeping our affair a secret. "Can you imagine how our relationship could be twisted and used against me by malicious gossipmongers? I am proud of everything I have done in my life, and I am certainly proud of what we are to each other, but you know how it would be interpreted by conventional standards. And why should I have to justify myself or explain anything to anyone?" All four of us had agreed that no one else was ever to know. This meant that the relationship was to be kept secret not only from the world but also from our closest friends. Ayn had begun to lay the foundation for a life of lies and deception. Earlier, there had been the lie to Barbara and Frank that "nothing will change," and now we were lying to everyone in our circle. But, of course, *lie* was a word we never used. We didn't have to. We had a philosophical explanation for everything.

Often, Frank would be leaving as I arrived. We would shake hands, Ayn would kiss him good-bye, and he would depart. She could not understand why this sometimes left me strained and on edge for the next hour or two. "What's the matter with you today?" she would ask, and when I would explain, she would say, "Well, I don't like it either, but reality is reality."

What neither of us suspected, and what I would not learn until Barbara told me many years later, was that Frank's usual destination when he left the apartment was a nearby bar. He was becoming an alcoholic.

Ayn was oblivious to the enormity of his suffering, just as she was oblivious to the tension she sometimes brought to our meetings—the tension of wrestling with the challenges of Galt's speech, along with her own nervous irritability. If I tried to describe its impact on me, she would apologize. Then she would wonder why her apology didn't instantly put me at ease.

The magnitude of these problems became evident only much later. In the first few months, our sexual relationship was at its peak, and no small frictions or strains or tensions or periods when I seemed to pull back were assigned any importance. There was too much to be happy about. I told myself that whatever wasn't yet quite right merely had to do with the early stages of a relationship. Nonetheless, Ayn began to ask me more and more often, "What's the matter with you?" That challenge was the first crack in the structure of our serenity, a crack that eventually would become an abyss. All my life, I had been relatively unconcerned with the opinions of others, but I could not be unconcerned with the judgment of my idol. Her rebukes were painful to me, and they were coming with increasing frequency.

However, we did typically get over our moments of tension quickly, and Ayn continued to compare me to her heroes and to wonder aloud how she could survive without me. And when Frank and Barbara were present to hear such statements, they smiled in acquiescence.

"I felt that Ayn *couldn't* live without you, for all practical purposes," Barbara said to me many years later. "But if I had dared to suggest that that was a trap not only for Frank and me but also for you, you would have been outraged and indignant."

I sighed and answered, "True."

"In a sense, you were as much a victim as Frank and I."

"No," I said. "There were no victims. I don't believe in victims in situations of that kind. There was ignorance, confusion, and misguided idealism if you like, but there were also payoffs. There were benefits for each one of us, and until we can be honest about that, we can never come to grips with what happened." This was a conversation we had many times.

A few months after the affair began, Barbara awakened one night in a state of panic, her heart beating wildly. Concerned that she might be having a heart attack, we summoned Allan Blumenthal. It was not her heart but her mind and emotions that had been stricken. She was having an anxiety attack—one far worse than anything she had experienced at the time of her "confessions."

"What's happening to me?" Barbara cried in bewilderment. The essence of an anxiety disorder is that one feels assailed by feelings of dread that do not connect to any concrete, tangible threat. Barbara's whole system was flung into emergency alert—except that there was no discernible emergency.

I was familiar with the phenomenon of anxiety disorders, but I proceeded to read everything I could find on the subject and to question my psychology professors at NYU. Nothing I learned seemed useful; I had no idea what would help. Someone suggested that perhaps Barbara should enter psychoanalysis, which, after several years of treatment, might alleviate her suffering; I thought this suggestion absurd. No one proposed medication, and I was not yet aware of the early tranquilizers that existed. I felt that it was my duty to produce a solution, and I did not know what to do.

Barbara's anxiety began to flow into different spheres of her life in the form of phobias. Suddenly, air travel terrified her, then heights, then elevators. I watched with agony and with admiration her desperate battle not to surrender. She forced herself to do everything she was afraid of doing. She rode an elevator to the top of the Empire State Building, as if by sheer dint of will and courage she could defeat her demons. I was often impressed by her perseverance and bravery. For about eighteen months, her terror was relentless. Then, mysteriously, it began to fade away.

Eager for an explanation, Ayn began to speculate that Barbara's anxiety resulted from her overreliance on feeling as a guide to action, which was how we both tended to see Barbara, even as she struggled during this period to be ruled by "reason" irrespective of the cost to her emotional life. Ayn wrote a psychological paper on the subject of Barbara's "emotionalism." Meanwhile, I asked myself, If we live by emotion rather than reason, is it not inevitable that we will feel increasingly out of control, and increasingly apprehensive that disaster, or retribution, is imminent? My point seemed valid, but it added to, rather than diminished, Barbara's suffering. The idea was provocative theoretically but in no way immediately helpful therapeutically. Also, it did not address the question of why the attack should come now—at a time when Barbara was living more "rationally" than she ever had before. Neither Barbara nor Ayn nor I raised the possibility that there might be some connection to Ayn's and my affair. None of us was willing to deal with that.

Sometimes when I arrived at Ayn's apartment, I was clearly agitated over Barbara's condition. The truth was, I felt I should be home by Barbara's side. If I did not become cheerful and loving within a few minutes, Ayn would reproach me for my sentimentality, my lack of concern for *her* feelings, and my failure to appreciate that, whatever was wrong, Barbara had almost certainly brought it on herself.

"Why should I be victimized," Ayn demanded, "for Barbara's problems?" The fact that Barbara was my wife lost all reality for her. Confused and horrified, I had to keep reminding her of this reality. I thought of the contrast between Ayn's attitude now that her own interests were involved and her compassion when Barbara had begun to disclose her infidelities several years earlier.

The more Ayn criticized Barbara to me, the more protective of Barbara I became. Once Ayn said, her voice hushed and trembling with intensity, "Do you think there's some other man in Barbara's life *now?* Could that be the cause of her anxiety?" I was stunned by the violence of my anger, and I answered in a toneless voice, "Absolutely not." I was certain of my judgment then, and I never had grounds to doubt it later.

During one of our private meetings, Barbara telephoned Ayn—something she normally would never do when I was there. She explained tearfully that her panic was reaching new and unbearable heights and pleaded for permission to come over so she could talk to us. I listened in horror as Ayn began to reproach her in a loud voice, saying things like "How *dare* you invade my time with Nathan?" and "Are you indifferent to *my* context?" and "No one ever helped *me* when I needed it! You'll always be unhappy until you learn to stand on your own feet!" Ayn came back into the living room, raving against Barbara and then against me when she saw the stricken expression on my face, and for the next hour I listened to harangues about my "irrationalism." She cried, "Is this what your love for me means? Why do you allow Barbara to manipulate you? What happened to your mind and values?"

The only thing worse than feeling trapped in a nightmare is forbidding oneself to *know* that one feels trapped in a nightmare. I tried to attribute Ayn's behavior to her unbearable tension over her difficulties with Galt's speech, the great pressure she was under, and her fear that what we had together would somehow be taken away. I would not permit myself to think that Ayn's behavior was sick or evil. I tried to feel compassion for the distress she had to be experiencing. Sensing this attitude in me, she gradually became calmer, even mellow. I made love to her somehow, and afterward, she began speaking of Barbara with care and concern.

The next time I saw Ayn and Barbara together, they were both warm, affectionate, and relaxed, as if the blowup had never happened. Ayn conveyed that she wanted to do everything in her power to help Barbara. They had many long discussions in which Ayn was totally supportive. But Barbara's anxiety raged on, unabated. And Ayn's bouts of suspicious disapproval returned, alternating with times of benevolence. Watching this, I fought feelings of anger and despair and told myself that it would all pass and that all of us would be happy again.

I was now in graduate school and had officially begun the practice of psychotherapy. For some years past, I had been a psychological consultant to some of our friends, who had mentioned their experiences to other friends and acquaintances. Soon, people were calling to request appointments. The fact that I was not yet a professional psychotherapist did not deter them; I felt flattered and more than a little excited. At first, I did not charge for my time, welcoming the opportunity to try out my ideas and to learn. But by the spring of 1955, as the requests for therapy continued, I decided to make my work official, and I announced a ten-dollar fee for a two-hour session. Still, a question taunted me: If I am able to be effective with other people, why can't I help my own wife? Another question that I should have asked myself was, If I am able to bring sanity into the lives of other people, why can't I bring it into my own?

I had begun to appreciate how widespread the problem of anxiety was, and I was evolving a theory about it. I was impressed by Freud's contention that virtually all neurotic problems could be understood as direct expressions of anxiety or of the defenses erected by its sufferers. But in his account of the causes of anxiety, I thought he was making an unwarranted generalization. Freud had decided, in the final version of his theory, that anxiety is triggered by forbidden sexual desires that break through the barrier of repression and cause the ego to feel threatened and overwhelmed. Decades later, Karen Horney countered that this may have been true in the Victorian age but that in our day the source of anxiety is the emergence of *hostile* impulses. I could not see why Freud and Horney confined the problem to one particular impulse—*any* feeling that was experienced as overwhelming and as threatening to ego control could activate anxiety. And then I wondered, Is it only *impulses* that the ego experiences as dangerous? What about . . . ? I began to make notes.

I learned about the work of Kurt Goldstein, who studied the anxiety suffered by brain-injured veterans. These men were comfortable only in rigidly organized environments. If, for instance, a nurse moved a hairbrush a few inches from where the patient had placed it, the patient panicked. The mind, I reasoned, is our basic means of survival. These men are impaired at the cognitive level. They are impaired in their ability to cope with the environment. Impaired in their fitness for survival. How logical that they would suffer anxiety.

When the ego feels in danger of being overwhelmed, when it is rendered unable to function appropriately—by the emergence of unacceptable feelings or impulses, for instance—might this not be a problem parallel to that of Goldstein's veterans? *Any* threat to a person's ego, I decided, anything that he or she experiences as a threat to the mind's efficacy and control, is a potential source of pathological anxiety.

When I had developed the first general sketch of my theory of anxiety, I proposed it to John Tietz, my adviser at NYU, as the subject of my master's thesis. He said it was much too ambitious for a master's project but that I should go ahead and do it anyway; he would protect me from anyone's objections. As I was quite outspoken in class and often challenged my instructors, he knew I might need a defender. He and I had hit it off from the moment when he announced, in mockery of the behaviorists, "Ladies and gentlemen, I shall conduct this class on the assumption that you are all conscious." I had burst out laughing in appreciation, and he and I had grinned at each other. Now he said to me, "I think you're on to something important."

But the early versions of my theory were so abstract, more philosophical than psychological, that I could not make my ideas useful to Barbara. I did not yet know how to translate my ideas into therapeutic tools.

During this same period, I was onto an idea that would affect my entire professional future, influencing my work in psychology for the next three decades.

As clients came for consultations, I looked for a common denominator among their complaints and problems—for some underlying principle or principles that could illuminate the various forms of their unhappiness.

All of my philosophical training with Ayn led me to look for fundamentals, for essences, not to see only concretes and particulars.

Before long, I was struck by the thought that the underlying problem is faulty self-esteem—a flawed self-concept, intellectual self-doubt, a sense of unworthiness or guilt, an experience of inadequacy, a feeling that "something is wrong with me" or that "I am not enough."

I went to the university library to read the literature on self-esteem and was astonished to learn that almost nothing had been written on the subject—not by that name, at any rate, and not as the concept was forming in my mind. Some psychoanalysts were writing about it but in terms foreign to what I sought.

One day, alone in the apartment, I paced the floor, trying to find words for ideas that were still vague and unformed. On an impulse, I telephoned Ayn, apologized for the interruption, and asked, "Can I think aloud with you for a few minutes?" I had evidently caught her at a fortunate moment, because she answered cheerfully, "Sure."

"I have been thinking about something I've noticed in all the people I work with—something they have in common. And if I'm right, this issue is really at the root of everything. And what I'm after is terribly important—it will explain a lot. I think the basic problem with people is poor self-esteem."

Ayn began to laugh.

"What's the matter?" I asked.

"Wait until you read what I'm writing in Galt's speech about self-esteem!" she announced. "Just a few sentences really, but it's important. . . . Go ahead—tell me what you wanted to say." She sounded warm and receptive, like a full participant in my process.

I was in a fever of excitement. "I can't stand this. Can I come over?"

When she opened the door to me a few minutes later, I noticed that she did not look strained but refreshed and relaxed. "How did you get here so fast?"

"I ran."

She settled down on the sofa, inserted a fresh cigarette into her holder, and said, her eyes bright with amusement, "You might as well speak first, because if I try to talk before you've told me whatever is on your mind, you'll interrupt and not let me finish anyway."

I began to pace again, stopping to face her, then erratically moving on. "Now listen," I said. "Suppose we discover that just about every psychological problem can be traced to faulty self-esteem—that is, can be understood either as a direct expression of poor self-esteem or as an expression of what people do to escape facing the problem, or to compensate for it, or to prove to themselves and others that no problem exists. Do you appreciate how much this would explain? OK, so we have to know, What is self-esteem? I've looked, and I can't find a decent definition anywhere."

I could see that Ayn's eyes were looking at me with good-natured mockery and that she was forcing herself not to speak. I held up my hands as if to keep her at bay and rushed on: "What's tricky about self-esteem is that it contains two separate but intimately related ideas: *efficacy* and *worth*." Ayn leaned forward eagerly. Why was she grinning? "Either one alone is not yet full self-esteem. If you feel efficacious but unworthy, you don't enjoy good self-esteem, and if you feel worthy but not efficacious, you don't enjoy good self-esteem."

Ayn was now nodding and beaming, as if she were anticipating my next steps. "By *efficacious,* I mean intellectually self-confident and self-reliant, and by *worthy,* I mean entitled to assert your own interests and needs. Something like that. And if this is what self-esteem is, then it has survival value. Self-esteem is a powerful need, maybe our most basic need. And when, for whatever reason, the need is unmet and unfulfilled, then the consequence is what we call 'neurosis'! Why are you looking at me as if you love me?"

"Because I do." She laughed happily. "Now then, may I speak?"

"Speak!" I shouted exuberantly. In the rigid, overintellectualized structure of our lives, there was not much room for playfulness, except in exchanges like this.

"In Galt's speech, you'll see that I describe self-esteem as one of the three cardinal values of my moral code. I define it as the conviction that you are competent to live and worthy of living."

"That's a brilliant way to say it."

"It's the same idea as what you're groping for—efficacy and worth. I'm not writing psychologically. I'm writing philosophically about the importance of self-esteem for a rational life and about the danger of tying your self-esteem to the wrong values. Look how rational minds arrive at the same point. Are we or are we not brain mates? Wasn't our romance inevitable?"

I was not to be distracted by this line of talk. I did not want the focus to be on our relationship. I told her about my efforts to find discussions of self-esteem in the psychological literature. "Would you believe," I said, "that you can go through book after book and not even find *self-esteem* in the index? I can't understand it. What do they think is important if not this?"

"I'm amazed that you have the patience to read all those books."

I knew by now that Ayn read very little, which astonished me. During this period of her life, she occasionally read mysteries or thrillers but little else except the *New York Times*.

"Freud doesn't write about self-esteem as such," I said, "but do you know what he says about the feeling of inferiority? He says its roots are a child's discovery that he—or she—can't have sex with the opposite-gender parent! Hence the feeling that 'I can't do anything'! And Alfred Adler claims that the origin of feelings of inferiority are the infant's experience of being smaller and weaker than everyone else! Plus, he claims, everyone comes into this world with one kind or another of 'organ inferiority.' And the rest of our life can be understood as our struggle to compensate for our original deficiencies. Our tragedy, in other words, is that we're not born as fully empowered adults. And people take this seriously. . . . I can't wait to graduate. Most of the time, school drives me nuts."

"Well, darling, your work in psychology is cut out for you. You're beginning from scratch."

"No, that's not true," I answered quickly, uneasy about her penchant for dismissing the work of thinkers she had not read. I began defending Freud and Adler, explaining the importance of some of their ideas. "Only, what I'm after is something else—something they're not talking about."

Ayn began to lecture me on my generosity to other writers—how could I claim to find anything valuable in Freud?—and she insisted that I was crediting them with insights of my own.

Whatever Ayn's intention, I did not feel complimented; I felt reduced. Somehow, Ayn's praise always took the form of reasserting her own authority. And at the moment, I was not interested in the direction she was pursuing; I wanted to talk about self-esteem.

We did return to the subject of my interest, but the slightest part of my happiness was gone until I succeeded in enrolling Ayn in my enthusiasm again.

Perhaps I recall this encounter with particular clarity because of the importance the study of self-esteem was to have for me. Perhaps it has remained so vivid because of the pleasure I felt in sharing my discovery with Ayn. And perhaps it is because Ayn once recounted this incident, with great delight, in the question-and-answer period after a lecture. But I think there is another reason, and this pertains to my thoughts while walking home, which in their own quiet way were ominous and terrifying.

I was grinning happily as I bounced along the street, until I heard an inner voice saying, This is what you want from Ayn. This is the kind of relationship with her that you find fulfilling.

I knew that my mind was light-years away from any thought of sex or romance during this meeting and that I did not welcome Ayn's overtures. I was horrified by the sudden feeling that I did not want our relationship cluttered by such an intrusion. I loved the lightness and freedom of our intellectual relationship. In this arena, there were no rebukes, no emotional demands, and no conflicts with any other loyalty.

As I recalled the car ride from Toronto to New York, as I replayed the conversation in Ayn's apartment the day we declared our love for each other, as I contemplated the chain of events I had set in motion, changing all four of our lives forever, the voice began to pound louder and louder in my head: What have you done? What have you done? What have you done?

9

"THIS IS GENIUS," I said to Ayn. It was a Saturday evening in the spring of 1956. Galt's speech was finished, and I was reading it for the fifth or sixth time.

Scattered throughout the living room of Ayn's apartment were the various members of the Collective, each of them reading a different chapter of *Atlas Shrugged*—Barbara, Alan Greenspan, Leonard Peikoff, Allan Blumenthal, Joan Mitchell (who was to marry Allan); my sister Elayne and her new husband, Harry Kalberman; and Joan's friend Mary Ann Rukavina. As usual, Frank was half-sitting, half-lying, sprawled out like a cat, neither reading nor speaking but gazing around the room tranquilly and distantly.

Ayn's entire social existence was now confined—almost without exception—to the people in this room. The oldest person present, apart from Frank, was more than twenty years her junior. But we all had one attribute in common—absolute devotion to Ayn and her work. As she entered the final stages of writing *Atlas Shrugged,* she had almost no capacity for any other kind of relationship. The Collective both served as her fortress and inhabited her fortress.

Ayn and I were sitting together at the dinner table, apart from the others. We kept our voices low so as not to disturb anyone. Pointing to the pages of Galt's speech, I said, "I can hardly believe what you've managed to cover, to condense, and yet to keep lucid and convey in an exciting and dramatic form."

"Galt doesn't sound like he's arguing or debating, does he?" She had asked this before. "His speech must never convey that, and yet I have to provide the reasons and proofs for all of his statements."

"You've succeeded."

"The publisher will tell me the speech is too long, of course. Not that that matters. It's the length it has to be."

"Yes, of course. To hell with that. It is the length it has to be." I turned the pages of the chapter. "Listen, I've been studying the section where you demonstrate why Man's Life is the proper standard of morality, and the economy and clarity of your explanation, to say nothing of the central concept itself, are awesome. You've addressed one of the most challenging problems in philosophy, the derivation of an ethical standard, and you've provided the answer—*in a novel!*"

Ayn replied, "Philosophers say you can't derive an 'ought' from an 'is'—you can't derive a code of ethics from the facts of reality—but Galt does just that."

"It's so funny to hear you talk about what Galt does. You did it. You've given morality a nonmystical foundation. You've shown that a morality of reason is possible."

I felt unconflicted love and admiration. At such moments, it was impossible to believe that there could be any discord in our relationship. The terrible thought What have I done? and everything that the question implied now seemed infinitely distant. But that question arose unpredictably in other contexts, then quickly receded again into the dimness of an almost forgotten unpleasant dream.

These shifts of perspective had become habitual. When one was dominant, the other was barely real. There were times with Ayn when I felt utterly and totally fulfilled, as if I were where I was meant to be, but there were other times when I felt only a numb detachment and the sense of being trapped in a role I did not wish to play. At times, I could speak happily and passionately of my feelings for her, and at other times, I could hardly speak at all, and whatever I said sounded hopelessly stilted and awkward.

When I was caught in this latter state and could not free myself, Ayn would sometimes become angry. "I felt more as if I were a person to you, and not just a mind, before our affair began. Now, if I want us to talk intimately, you keep running away into philosophical abstractions. Instead of feeling more visible than before, I feel less visible." She said this at times when she wanted to talk about love and I wanted to talk about philosophy or psychology or *anything* that would remove me from the realm of the personal.

Looking back, I cannot help thinking that another woman, more experienced and less self-alienated than Ayn, would have grasped rather quickly the essence of the problem—that there was no way for a young man, even a precocious one, to maintain a romance with someone twenty-five years older, especially one of Ayn's character and personality, without sooner or later displaying erratic behavior. Add to that the fact that we were both married and that the affair was a secret from even our closest friends. And although it was easy enough to insist that we did not "owe" our friends the truth, that did not alter the experience of living in a network of lies and deception, which Ayn insisted on.

At the time, however, I shared Ayn's conviction that a romantic relationship between us *should* be possible and that if it were not working, the problem was some defect of mine. What sustained this conviction was that, at times, I felt and acted like a man in love. Then, we were both ecstatic. I often paced the streets, struggling to think my way through this dilemma. But I rarely confronted the fact that I most enjoyed our relationship not in romantic moments but in moments when our focus was more intellectual or literary: when we were sharing the world of *Atlas Shrugged*, discussing ideas, and answering philosophical or psychological questions raised by members of our group. As an intellectual companion, Ayn fulfilled more than I had ever dreamed of, but for a romantic companion I wanted a woman of my own age. I could hear Ayn's voice asking what woman my age could conceivably compete with her in *any* department. And to this I had no answer.

As we sat facing each other across the dinner table, Ayn was radiating a happiness that I thought would be obvious to everyone in the room. I was often amazed that our friends were so oblivious to what Ayn's and my relationship had become. It was as if they had a particular image of us and our relationship and they could not think beyond it or even notice conflicting evidence. At this moment, the sexuality in her glance was as loud as a shout; how was it possible that no one else in the room could hear it? Many years later, Barbara would tell me that the one person with suspicions was Joan. Tonight I dared to join Ayn's mood and genuinely to experience love, desire, playfulness, and romantic exhilaration. It felt exciting and a little dangerous to match her signal with my own glance, in defiance of everyone else present. I simultaneously wanted to enjoy our secrecy and to proclaim the truth to the room and the world.

"So what were you saying about Galt's discussion of the foundation of ethics?" she asked me playfully.

As usual, she was smoking. Her long cigarette holder, a gift from Barbara and me, was sterling silver, engraved with the names Galt, Francisco, Rearden, and Dagny. She had abandoned her usual uniform of skirt and blouse in favor of a gray silk dress; I reached over to brush ashes off her sleeve, my fingertips pressing her arm for an instant.

Laughing silently, and trying to ignore the open eroticism of her manner, I struggled to organize my thoughts. "What I think is so important," I said, "is your approach to the whole subject of ethics. You don't begin by taking the phenomenon of values as a given. You don't begin by merely observing that men pursue various values and by assuming that the first question of ethics is, What values should man pursue? In Galt's speech, you go to a much deeper level, asking, What are values, and why does man need them? Your approach is not statistical, sociological, or historical—it's metaphysical. Your starting point is, What are the facts of reality—the facts of existence and of man's nature—that necessitate and give rise to values? And this is where a true science of ethics should begin—and, in the history of philosophy, never has."

I should mention that in 1956, it would not have occurred to us to question the use of the word *man* to denote both sexes. Unfortunately, even today no one has proposed an entirely satisfactory alternative. Ayn, of course, would have been vigorously opposed to the search for a better word.

We talked about her concept of value as that which one acts to gain or to keep. A value was the object of an action. In Galt's speech, she had written, "'Value' presupposes an answer to the question: of value to whom and for what? 'Value' presupposes a standard, a purpose and the necessity of action in the face of an alternative. Where there are no alternatives, no values are possible."

I understood this to mean that if an entity, by its nature, had no purposes to achieve and no goals to reach, it could have no values and no need of values. There would be no "for what." And an entity incapable of initiating action, or for whom the consequences would always be the same, *regardless* of its actions—an entity not confronted with alternatives—could have no purposes, no goals, and hence no values. Only the existence of alternatives could make purpose—and therefore values—possible and necessary.

Having established this progression of thought in Galt's speech, Ayn went on to one of the most important philosophical statements in all of her writing:

> There is only one fundamental alternative in the universe: existence or non-existence—and it pertains to a single class of entities: to living organisms. The existence of inanimate matter is unconditional, the existence of life is not: it depends on a specific course of action. Matter is indestructible, it changes its forms, but it cannot cease to exist. It is only a living organism that faces a constant alternative: the issue

of life or death. Life is a process of self-sustaining and self-generated action. If an organism fails in that action, it dies; its chemical elements remain, but its life goes out of existence. It is only the concept of "Life" that makes the concept of "Value" possible. It is only to a living entity that things can be good or evil.

Given the appropriate conditions, the appropriate physical environment, all living organisms—with one exception—are set by their nature to originate automatically the actions required to sustain their survival. The exception is man.

"Do you think people will understand this idea?" Ayn asked. I knew that she meant not just one idea but the whole argument, including her derivation of the concept of value from the concept of life.

"To me, the idea seems simple, and I think your presentation is totally clear."

"That one paragraph would really need to be a whole chapter in a non-fiction treatise, but of course one can't do that in a novel. I kept condensing and condensing, boiling the argument down, to the briefest, clearest statement I could achieve. A good mind will know how to fill in what I've left out."

I nodded in agreement.

Only a living entity could have needs, goals, and values—and only a living entity could generate the actions necessary to achieve them. This was an idea of the most momentous consequences, and I thought that if philosophers understood it and its implications, it could radically benefit the field of ethics, demolishing religious and tribal notions of morality, and linking ethics to man's needs as a living organism.

Barbara and I had spent many hours retracing Ayn's argument in our own words, as if we were explaining it to a third party. I felt a warm sense of connection when I looked at her across the room; she was reading some chapter of the novel intently, and her face had an expression I loved—that of a fully focused consciousness enjoying its own function. I thought how fortunate I was to have two such women in my life.

Then my mind returned to the steps of Ayn's progression, as to a pleasure from which I could not tear myself. I thought, Man, like a plant or an animal, must act in order to live, must gain the values his life requires. But man does not function solely by automatic chemical reactions or automatic sensory reactions; the method of survival possible for plants and animals is not possible for humans. There is no physical environment on earth in which man can survive by the guidance of nothing but involuntary sensations. And being born with no innate knowledge of what is true or false, he can have no innate knowledge of what is good or evil. For man, survival is a question—a problem to be solved. The perceptual level of his consciousness—the level of sensory awareness he shares with animals—is inadequate to solve it. To remain alive, man must think—which means he must exercise the faculty of forming abstractions, of *conceptualizing*. The *conceptual* level of consciousness is the human level. It is upon his ability to think that Man's Life depends.

But thinking, Ayn had written in Galt's speech, is an act of choice. In contrast to the functioning of the stomach, lungs, or heart, which is automatic, the functioning of the mind is not. Man is a being of volitional consciousness.

"The implications of this idea for psychology are enormous," I said to Ayn. "Nothing is more important for understanding the behavior of an organism than understanding its unique and distinctive means of survival."

The undertone of erotic playfulness had faded as we became caught up in the intensity of the issues we were discussing. Ayn belonged in the company of giants, I told myself. The best minds in the country should be sitting in this living room—philosophers, scientists, writers—not this group of young people. They were all devoted to her and her work, true enough, but they had yet to accomplish anything significant of their own.

Shrugging off the wave of sadness that was now more pronounced, I flung myself back into the progression of Ayn's thought in Galt's speech. A being of volitional consciousness, a being without innate ideas must discover through a process of reasoning the goals, actions, and values on which his life and well-being depend. He must discover what will further his true interests and what will subvert them. If he acts against the facts of reality, he will fail, suffer, and perish. If he is to sustain his existence successfully, he must discover the principles of action required to guide him in dealing with nature and with other human beings. In needing these principles, he needs a code of values. Galt states, "A code of values accepted by choice is a code of morality."

The reason, then, for man's *need* for morality determines the *purpose* of morality as well as the *standard* by which he selects moral values. Man needs a moral code in order to live. That is the purpose of morality—for every person as an individual. And different species achieve their survival in different ways. The course of action proper to the survival of a fish or an animal would not be appropriate to the survival of man. Man must choose his values by the standard of what is required for the life of a human being—which means he must hold Man's Life (man's survival as man, that is, qua rational being) as his standard of value. In summary of this point, Galt states, "All that which is proper to the life of a rational being is the good; all that which destroys it is the evil."

Later in the speech he says, "To live, man must hold three things as the supreme and ruling values of his life: Reason—Purpose—Self-esteem. Reason, as his only tool of knowledge—Purpose, as his choice of the happiness which that tool must proceed to achieve—Self-esteem, as his inviolate certainty that his mind is competent to think and his person is worthy of happiness, which means: is worthy of living."

This is what I wanted to fight for. I recalled a discussion with Florence when I was sixteen about a crusade that would mean something, a battle that would be worthwhile. What I had been struggling for then, I told myself, was this vision of the good. Now, I thought, I want to be the champion of man's self-esteem. I want to tell people, "Your life matters. Your life is important."

I did not recognize that in the lesson I wanted to teach others, there were vital elements that I myself still needed to learn. I was not honoring my own life as I needed to; I had submerged too much of it in Ayn. I was not sufficiently loyal to my own perception of reality; I had allowed it to be confused by my admiration for Ayn and my desire for her esteem. But I was not thinking about myself that night; I was thinking about Galt's speech and the intensity of my admiration for its author.

The group went on reading, and Ayn and I went on talking. "For some reason I cannot understand," she whispered, "Leonard cannot seem to hold the argument for life as the standard; he keeps losing it and asking me to reexplain it."

Watching him, I wondered how Leonard could manage to look nervous even while sitting perfectly still reading a manuscript. He had a quality of fragility about him, combined with a high level of excitability and a boundless enthusiasm for the enterprise of philosophy. He often tended to make me feel protective; others in our group responded similarly. He was wildly enthusiastic about Ayn's work as well as about Ayn personally. One felt certain that he would happily die for her—he had that air about him. Toward me, he also projected a feverish kind of hero worship. "You're what he would like to become," Ayn once said to me, approvingly.

Of our entire group, he was the only one who planned to make philosophy his profession. He saw his role as especially important in propagating Ayn's work, a viewpoint Ayn and I shared. Some of his problems at school were particularly embarrassing to him and mystifying to the rest of us. If, for example, he was studying the philosophy of John Dewey, he could easily fall into Dewey's perspective without noticing it, accept the premises of

Dewey that he in fact knew to be mistaken, and then proceed to panic. This might happen with any philosopher, from Plato to Wittgenstein. Leonard would sense that he had been had but not know how to think his way out, and he would come to Ayn or me in a state of intellectual chaos, desperate for an answer to Dewey or Bertrand Russell or A. J. Ayer.

More than once, Ayn had said to me, "Without the concept of social metaphysics, I would be totally at a loss to make sense of Leonard's behavior. Still, I don't understand psychology, not really. I hate your profession. How can you stand it? Without you, how would I understand anyone?"

I could not escape the sense that Ayn took pride in her ignorance, and I cordoned off this thought as something I did not understand and would reconsider someday.

My glance swung across the room from Leonard to Alan Greenspan—or "A. G.," as we called him, to distinguish him from "A. B.," Allan Blumenthal.

Aside from Barbara and me, A. G. and Leonard were Ayn's favorites, and she kept changing her mind about which one she liked most. One month Leonard was in and A. G. had the number two spot, but a month later their positions would be reversed. What she enjoyed in Leonard was his loyalty, his passion for philosophy, and what she regarded as his idealism. What she enjoyed in A. G. was his greater sense of practical reality, his passion for the world of business and industry, his appreciation of Ayn's portrayal of this world in her novel, and his greater maturity.

When Leonard was number one and A. G. was in second place, she would say, "Not counting you and Barbara, of course, Leonard is the most idealistic member of the Collective, and the most philosophical. A. G. is too 'worldly,' too impressed by success. The trouble with A. G. is, he thinks Henry Luce is important." When she changed her preference, she would say, "What I like about A. G. is that basically he has his feet on the ground. I love his love for life on earth. He really is a passionate person in his own quiet way. Leonard is too hysterical, too scattered and disorganized."

Once I teased her about her proclivity for switching favorites. "Can't you just accept that you really like both of them and that both have traits that sometimes annoy you?"

She shook her head. "You know me. I've got to have favorites. I always think hierarchically. In the Collective, first there's you—you stand alone on your own level. Next, there's Barbara. Then, on still another level down, there's Leonard and A. G. Then all the rest. I exempt Frank from this, of course, because he's in a unique category of his own. These are the terms in which I think. And observe—everyone knows it and accepts it."

Now, looking at A. G., I wondered to what extent he was aware of Ayn's opinions. He rarely voiced his feelings about anything of a personal nature, and his language tended to be detached and passive. Complimenting Ayn on some passage in the novel, he might say, "On reading this . . . one tends to feel . . . exhilarated." Or "The reader is really inspired here." But occasionally he would break down and exclaim, "Ayn, this is *incredible*. No one has ever dramatized what industrial achievement actually means as you have. What you've written is a hymn to human intelligence. *This is fantastic*." Because he was not given to such outbursts, when they erupted they especially endeared him to Ayn—and to me.

The first love of A. G.'s life was music. When he was nineteen years old, he played the saxophone in a swing band—a picture I absolutely could not integrate with the somber figure I knew. Sometimes when we had lunch together, I would kid him about his "nonphilosophical past." I also asked him many questions about economic theory and about how an economy actually functions, and I enjoyed learning from him.

A number of our talks centered on the Federal Reserve Board's role in influencing the economy by manipulating the money supply. We talked about the Fed's destructive contribution to the Great Depression. He spoke with vigor and intensity about a totally free banking system. In 1987, when A. G. was appointed chairman of the Federal Reserve Board, where he proceeded to do a brilliant job, it was odd to recall those discussions. I should add that in 1998, he announced publicly that his political convictions had not changed and that in an ideal world there would be no Fed.

A. G. had worked at the National Industrial Conference Board when I met him, until he accepted an invitation from bond trader William Townsend to form a business consulting firm—Townsend Greenspan & Company. We had spent many hours discussing the pros and cons of Townsend's offer, because A. G. feared the loss of security associated with the change. "I don't know if I have the talent to make this thing work," he said to me. I answered, "You're still in your twenties. How can you be worried about security now? Take the leap. You can do it. And if it doesn't work out for any reason, so what? You'll do something else. Anyway, this is nonsense, because you're not going to fail—not with your brains. You just don't appreciate how good you are."

A. G. had taken the leap—and was succeeding spectacularly. He was acquiring a reputation as an outstanding economic analyst who could find significance in figures that no one else could.

In 1958, Townsend died. The company, 99 percent A. G.'s, climbed to higher and higher levels of success, making A. G. a wealthy man. "You believed in me," he said, shaking his head wonderingly. "How could you be sure? I would never be sure of such a thing."

I said, "What difference does it make? You've done it."

None of us found it strange that A. G., Joan, and A. B. should be friends. The fact that for nine months Joan and A. G. had been married now seemed irrelevant. The relationships that counted in this room, we said, were philosophical. In the outside world, we had all seen ourselves as loners, even aliens. Here, we were family—by virtue of the philosophical understanding we shared.

Although he admired A. B.'s playing, A. G. had difficulty understanding A. B.'s pursuit of a musical career. "The odds are against it," was A. G.'s comment. Moreover, it was not clear that A. B. had the self-assertiveness and tenacity that a musical career demanded; few people do. I felt enormous sympathy for the difficulty of A. B.'s struggle. Without considerable endurance, he could not have held on as long as he did. He began to discuss with me the possibility of practicing psychiatry. I volunteered to assist him in any way I could.

Looking around the room at everyone, I realized that the magnitude of my secret about my affair with Ayn made close friendship with any of them impossible. I was aware of the strain between us, but I shrugged it off. What difference did it make? I was most comfortable with intellectual friendships, anyway. I did not admit to my feelings of isolation and loneliness. I did not have a single relationship in which I felt fully free to share my thoughts and feelings in a spirit of true intimacy and trust. That was painful, if I allowed myself to think about it.

On the sofa, three members of our group were reading. Two days earlier, Ayn and I had lain there, embracing. I looked at Ayn and enjoyed thinking, in this moment, in this setting, that I knew every detail of the body underneath her dress.

In one corner, Joan and Frank were whispering and laughing. "Joan," Ayn said, "has justified her existence by introducing Frank to drawing and painting. I mean it. He's become a new man. It's magnificent to see what's happening to him." Ayn was profoundly happy over this development— and grateful to Joan. In fact, we all were.

It had begun one evening when the Collective was discussing painting, and Barbara had said that she was so lacking in the premises and orientation of a visual artist that she could not possibly learn to draw. Other members of our group made similar remarks about themselves. Joan insisted that any intelligent person, properly taught, could learn to draw competently, and she offered to conduct a class to prove her point. Frank was among those who agreed to try.

It was as if a new world had suddenly opened to him. All his life, his primary orientation had been visual, and now he had an outlet. From his first sketch, he shot ahead of everyone else in the class. He began to draw constantly. Then he began working in pastels. His sense of drama and composition was there from the beginning. We were all stunned by the sensuality and theatricality of his work and by its imaginativeness. Soon he was enrolled in the Art Students League on Fifty-Seventh Street. At the age of fifty-eight, he was a man on fire, alive as none of us had ever seen him alive before, totally dedicated to the work that would consume him until, years later, his declining faculties would make work impossible.

Among Frank's teachers at the Art Students League was Robert Brackman, a member of the National Academy of Design and a highly respected painter. From the beginning, he decided that Frank had an unusual talent, and he supported Frank enthusiastically. With everything Frank had to learn, Brackman said, he brought to painting an individuality and expressiveness that many artists try for all their lives.

Unfortunately, Frank had two weaknesses that he never resolved: perspective or anatomy. He lacked the patience and discipline to study them as consistently and thoroughly as he needed to. Or perhaps he was rebelling against Ayn's invasions of his most precious territory. When she attempted to reach him on this subject, he sometimes growled back with the irritability of a teenager at a domineering mother. She might speak gently, so as not to antagonize him, and he sometimes professed to agree with her, but the conversations never led to a fundamental change in his attitude.

In the spring of 1956, when Frank's new work was just beginning, none of us foresaw that he would carry his limitations as a painter unchallenged until the end. We saw only his electrifying talent.

My private impression was that he had now become almost indifferent to my relationship with Ayn, except perhaps for feeling a sense of relief that I had lifted a burden from his shoulders. Ayn seemed to be placing fewer emotional demands on him. I did not yet know about his drinking.

The person in our group I knew least well was Mary Ann Rukavina. She was a student of art history, as Joan had been. Quiet, a little pedantic, and a little mischievous, she had an impish smile that lent a note of charm to her formal, somewhat stilted, yet almost regal manner. Some years later, she married one of Ayn's admirers, a lawyer named Charles Sures. She was a member of our inner circle, and our relations were always friendly but never close.

I felt a special kind of affection for Elayne and Harry. Harry Kalberman had left Nazi Germany with his family at age thirteen. Like Ayn, he had a European's enthusiasm for America. Harry was in business, and Elayne was an operating room nurse. I felt affection for Harry, in part because I perceived him as more manly than the other men in our circle; he had a quality of street toughness I liked. He and Elayne seemed unusually well matched. When their daughter was born, they named her Kira, after the heroine of *We the Living*. Harry became a vice president at Merrill Lynch.

Growing up, Elayne and I had not been close. Now she showed a fondness that was new to our relationship. We had come from a family in which affection was almost never expressed, and although we were able to show it in our own private spheres, we remained a little stiff with each other. Our warmth almost always came packaged in humor.

Except for Ayn and Frank, who were in their fifties, none of us at that time was older than thirty. Not yet twenty-six, I was the next to youngest in our group. I remember telling Ayn, "I'm not in full control of my life. I've still got too many jagged edges to me. I think by thirty I'll come properly into my own."

I was eager to complete graduate school and earn my own living. I wanted to continue practicing psychotherapy, to learn more about the human mind and the process of change and growth, and to write books— that was to be my future. However, the idea for yet another career activity was already germinating.

It was sparked by the enormous amount of fan mail Ayn was still receiving from readers of *The Fountainhead*. Men and women wrote glowingly of the ways the book had changed their lives, given them courage, shown them a new perspective, and projected new possibilities. Ayn read me letters written by soldiers in World War II about how the novel had given them a vision worth fighting for. It had made them determined to survive the war, come home, and work toward that vision in their own lives. The letters came by the thousands. Many of the writers asked philosophical questions about ethics, politics, art, and epistemology. "If this is the kind of interest *The Fountainhead* stimulates," I had said to Ayn a few weeks earlier, "can you imagine the response the new novel—which is so much more philosophical—is going to evoke? You're going to be bombarded. We ought to have a school of some kind." "A school?" Ayn had said. "What kind of school?"

The Collective at the wedding of Branden's sister Elayne to
Harry Kalberman, 1955. *From left*: Joan Mitchell, Alan Greenspan,
Nathaniel, Barbara, Leonard Peikoff, Elayne Kalberman,
Harry Kalberman, Ayn, Frank, and Allan Blumenthal

Now, sitting at the dinner table, I broached the subject again. "A school
is too grand, too ambitious. I have something simpler in mind. Suppose I
create a course of lectures—say, twenty lectures—that would distill the
essence of your philosophy—epistemology, metaphysics, ethics, political
economy, literary aesthetics, and perhaps some of my work in psychology—and suppose I offer this to people?"

"Offer it? Offer it how? To whom?"

"Well, I haven't thought this out clearly yet, but let's say I offer it to
people within commuting distance of New York who have written you
fan letters, and we can see what happens."

Ayn looked faintly uncertain. "I don't know." I decided to reflect on
the idea further before raising it again.

One by one, the members of the group finished their reading for the evening and began talking among themselves. Ayn and I returned to the living room, where she sat beaming with pleasure as everyone spoke with high-spirited appreciation. It was as if her novel had brought out whatever was most alive and vibrant in each one of them, and I thought about the unique power of art to evoke such responses.

Someone said to Ayn, "There is so much passion in your writing, so much deep, intense feeling. How can people say we're anti-emotion?"

"Because we're pro-reason," someone else responded.

"They assume that there's a dichotomy," said a third voice.

"Exactly," said Ayn. "They assume that if one is an advocate of reason and has no tolerance for the irrational, this means one is against feelings and emotions—because they equate feelings and emotions with mindlessness."

All of us had encountered the accusation that we were "antifeeling." All of us felt misperceived and misunderstood—and we looked with scorn on people who could not grasp the relationship between reason and emotion as we conceived it. Reason and emotion were not two contradictory or mutually inimical faculties, we insisted, but their functions were not interchangeable. *Emotions were not tools of cognition.* What one *feels* in regard to any fact or issue was irrelevant to the question of whether one's judgment of it was true or false, right or wrong. It was not by means of one's feelings that one perceived reality.

"If a person tells you that he regards reason and emotion as antagonists," Ayn declared, "he is telling you that *his* emotions are irrational and that he wants to get away with something dishonest."

We had grown accustomed to hearing Ayn not merely dispute an idea she regarded as mistaken but also provide a psychological interpretation of her opponent's motivation. Most of her later nonfiction writings reflected her penchant for this kind of psychologizing, in spite of her repeated insistence that she knew nothing about psychology. Much later, I realized that I rarely agreed with her psychological interpretations.

As our group went on talking about reason and emotion, agreeing that one must be guided by the conscious mind in all matters, that one must not follow emotions blindly—who could dispute that to have emotions lead the way was undesirable and dangerous?—no one suggested that to live by such a rule might not always be as simple as it sounded. No one pointed out that feelings or emotions might sometimes reflect a more accurate assessment of reality than conscious beliefs. In other words, nobody asserted that the subconscious mind might be right while the conscious mind was mistaken.

And yet, ironically, Ayn was not unaware of this phenomenon; she made it central to the evolution of Hank Rearden. He ruthlessly suppresses his feelings, always at his own expense, giving others the benefit of a doubt they do not deserve. He tragically reproaches himself for his passion for Dagny and his indifference toward his wife. His liberation is tied to appreciating finally the rightness of the feelings he has been struggling to repudiate. The message was not lost on us, however, that Rearden's error is treated in heroic terms. He does the right thing, in his own conscientious, tortured way, within the limits of his knowledge. He is not like the villains who follow their emotions blindly. He makes errors of judgment but never of morality. Francisco d'Anconia, seeking to help Rearden, cautions him against being so quick to sacrifice his emotions and advises him to "examine" them. But Ayn stopped there. And I have no recollection of her ever giving even this much pro-emotion advice to any of us.

What we are not shown in the novel is a character who knows how to listen to feelings, reflect on them, and perhaps gain new insights and modify conscious thinking accordingly—without following emotions blindly. Other than suppression or repression, encouraged by highly intellectualized kinds of "analysis," we had learned no real strategy for dealing with "reason versus emotion" conflicts; nor did we grasp the need for such a strategy.

What people call a clash between mind and emotion, or reason and feeling, is a clash between two assessments, two thoughts or judgments, one of which is conscious, the other of which might not be. It is not inevitable that the conscious judgment is superior to the subconscious one; that needs to be determined. We do not follow the voice of emotion unthinkingly; we try to understand what the voice may be trying to tell us. We do not simply suppress or repress; we try to resolve the conflict without assuming in advance that we know where the error lies. Sometimes our conscious mind is right and our feelings do reflect a mistake or confusion; sometimes the reverse is true.

What I did not understand back then—what none of us understood—is that we must be open to exploring, open to finding out. In the meantime, we must treat *all* of our experiences with respect. We need to strive for balance, harmony, and integration, rather than simply slashing away the pieces of ourselves that do not fit our official notion of the good or the right or the rational.

It would be fifteen years before I understood this fully. In 1971, I presented my own perspective in *The Disowned Self*. If our group had understood and practiced what healthy self-acceptance truly means, if we had been willing to acknowledge and own all the disowned parts of ourselves, our whole world would have blown apart.

"No one can fail to understand this book," A. G. declared solemnly. "Ayn, your celebration of intelligence, ability, and achievement is so clear, so powerful, so unanswerable . . . your demonstration of what human life depends on is so radiantly exact . . . so precise . . . that a person would have to do strange things to his mind to blank it out."

"No one will hate this book as much as the Catholic Church," Ayn announced. "Not even the communists."

"That's right," I agreed. "In its glorification of life on earth, in its man worship the novel is antireligious in the most profound sense. It's pro-self and antiguilt. It's pro-happiness."

"It *spiritualizes* the secular," said Ayn. "That's what mystics and religionists won't forgive."

Someone in the group that night asked Ayn about the evolution of her concept of the ideal man that animated and inspired all of her writing. This was a favorite subject of Ayn's, and her voice became bright and eager. "Philosophy," she said, "is only a means to an end. But man is the end. And for me, in fiction, the projection of the ideal man is the end. Everything else in my writing exists for the purpose of creating Galt, Rearden, Francisco—or earlier, Roark—all the philosophy and all the events."

Then Ayn began speaking of the first literary love of her life, a hero she had encountered long ago in a boy's adventure magazine. His name was Cyrus, and his story, "The Mysterious Valley," dealt with a villainous raja who kidnapped a group of British officers in a plot to overthrow British rule. Cyrus was the officer who defied his captors; laughed at threats of torture; led the escape; rescued the heroine, a beautiful, blond English girl; and led everyone to safety.

To Ayn, he was a breath-stopping representation of the virtues of independence, audacity, and courage—the ultimate man of action. "Physically, Cyrus was the model for all my heroes: tall, slender, long legs, hair falling down over one eye. . . . I was only nine years old, but I was in love. I mean this seriously. I was in love then—and still am. What I felt for Cyrus then is the essence of what I feel for all my heroes, for *all* my values."

In 1914, the year Ayn discovered Cyrus, her family vacationed in Switzerland. Ayn described it as the happiest summer of her life, climbing mountain trails with a boy she had met and liked. But while she and her family were traveling to Paris, war broke out. They hurried on to London, in search of a ship that would carry them back to Russia.

"I could not know how much was going to end that summer, not only for me but for the world. Not yet understanding what it all meant, I was happy. It was in London that I decided to become a writer. Of course, I was already inventing stories, and I loved telling them to my sisters. But, you know, I had not yet grasped that writing stories could be a profession. I was walking with my governess through the streets of London, and we saw posters for some musical revue that showed attractive blond women with bobbed hair. And when I got back to my hotel room, I began inventing stories about these women. And then suddenly I realized that this was what writers do—writing was an occupation. Very seriously, very decisively, I told myself, 'I am going to be a writer.' I hated the sentimentality of Russian children's stories and the tragic sense of life. I wanted what 'The Mysterious Valley' stood for in my mind. Purposeful people fighting for important goals—*and succeeding.*"

I watched Barbara watching Ayn, and the expression on her face was one of complete, undivided love. Barbara was about a month away from turning twenty-seven. Tonight, she showed no discernible trace of anxiety or pain. It was as if she were receiving some kind of spiritual transfusion from Ayn's words.

Yet the conflicts and frictions between them were real. Ayn's condemnations of Barbara's "emotionalism" and "value confusions" continued unabated. They were mixed, though, with affection, support, and even nurturing. Barbara's pain over Ayn's and my affair was also real, her idealistic acceptance notwithstanding.

And my own conflicts were no less real. My erotic love for Ayn was real, and so was my desire for a nonromantic friendship. My love for Barbara was real, and so was my estrangement. My desire to have an exclusive relationship with each of them was real, and so was my awareness that each relationship helped make the frustrations in the other more bearable. My sense of profound connection and affinity with each of them was real, and so was my sense that neither of them was truly the woman I wanted. I could not find a single perspective that resolved the conflicts and ambivalences with which I lived. I could only swing between one state of consciousness and another, wait for the bad periods to pass, and be grateful for times such as tonight when all my values seemed to be in relatively benign balance.

Whatever I might have been confused about, I knew that I admired Ayn more than anyone I had ever met. But one question rose up at unpredictable moments to torture me: Why, then, should the age difference sometimes matter so much that it nullified all the values in our relationship? Should not a mind such as mine be able to transcend such a consideration? And then there were more difficult questions: Was I absolutely certain that age was the core problem? Could there be other, as yet unrecognized incompatibilities? And how was it possible that there were times when I felt so serenely and happily in love?

Many months ago, I had attempted to tell Ayn of my struggle over these issues. Instantly, I saw her transformed into a distant, icy rage. She became more than a stranger; she became an adversary. "Do you wish me to understand that this has all been a mistake?" She launched into an attack on my values as if we had no history and no context. I could not bear losing her and assured her that I did not doubt my love for her. I was afraid of failing my own standards and expectations. I also feared losing Ayn's esteem. I told myself that this was a conflict I would have to work through alone—and that I must be the one not to fail her, not to cause her suffering.

There were other blows that wounded our relationship. Most of the time, I told myself that they were senseless and insignificant. If Ayn had fought with Frank, if she were bothered by some throwaway remark of mine, if she had spoken lovingly to me and I had been a little distant or too light in my response or had shifted to some unrelated philosophical issue, if she had telephoned when I was out with Barbara, then the next time Ayn and I spoke, her voice would convey the unmistakable message that I had failed her in some way. Given that I was married, I would remind myself, was she not entitled to some feelings of insecurity? Confused and self-reproachful, I would be extra-attentive until she relented. But first, there would be a detailed, often hours-long, analysis of what had taken place—until she was satisfied that I understood why she was upset and did not think her unfair or irrational. It was intolerable to Ayn that someone important to her should ever think her irrational.

Sometimes our blowups were even more intense. Once when I telephoned her from a restaurant just to say hello, she was troubled about something and wanted to talk. I found her demanding tone abrasive and unpleasant and explained that I needed to go to a class. When I hung up, I felt so irritated that I took Barbara to a movie instead. Barbara later happened to mention to Ayn where we had gone. This led to an all-night session between Ayn and me in which she proceeded to explore the possible significance of my lie. If I could deceive her about this, might I not deceive her about other things?

My confused feelings made me particularly vulnerable to this line of attack, and I probably projected a guilt that served only to worsen her suspicions. She proceeded to remind me of every instance that she could recall of elusive or inappropriate behavior on my part, which made it

Ayn Rand and Nathaniel Branden at the height of their affair, 1957

harder for me to think clearly about the immediate issue. She wondered whether I might not be an admittedly brilliant but nonetheless diabolically manipulative person who was not at all what he represented himself to be. Her speculations grew worse and worse and more removed from reality. I felt traumatized. And the rage that paralyzed me into silence made me a poor spokesman in my own defense. I told myself, You have no right to be angry. She's not entirely wrong, after all, even if she's grossly exaggerating. She senses that something is off, and some of the time, she's right. I struggled to remain calm, to show compassion for her anguish, and to stay undefensively open to whatever she wished to say. Eventually, she decided that she had overreacted, and by dawn she was arguing on my behalf against her own accusations. Not knowing what truth, honor, or sanity, meant anymore, I was simultaneously miserable and relieved.

At home, when she learned of these attacks, Barbara's typical response was protective indignation. "What does Ayn *expect* of you?" I admitted that everyone in our group was always on trial with Ayn. She gave her unconditional acceptance to no one. At any time, in response to some dubious behavior—such as liking a movie or a piece of music Ayn disapproved of, or dropping a facetious, irreverent remark about her work, or being too pleasant to the "enemy"—she might begin to wonder aloud if that Collective member were basically "a Peter Keating" or "an Ellsworth Toohey," "a whim worshiper" or "a mystic." I cannot recall a single instance when any of us questioned aloud Ayn's behavior. Only Barbara and Frank knew how many hours I spent defending one of our friends to Ayn, who speculated about his or her basic character or "sense of life." On the other hand, there were times when I was fully as guilty as Ayn of such tantrums. Was I not her alter ego?

However, in the spring of 1956, riding on the euphoric energy of writing the concluding chapters of *Atlas Shrugged*, Ayn seemed more easygoing and less inclined to criticize. She even reveled in having a "family" with which to share the most important creative experience of her life.

This Saturday evening I looked around the living room at our family. Frank and Joan were once again locked in private conversation—about art, I assumed—and Ayn said to me, "I don't want to disturb Frank. Let's you and I get the coffee and pastry. Will you help me?" When we were alone in the kitchen, Ayn turned and whispered, "Isn't it wonderful, darling?" I knew that she meant all the elements of her life at present: our affair, Frank's discovery of painting, the Collective's response to the novel, and the emotional vibrations of joy and excitement in the room tonight.

"Yes," I said, meaning it. "It's wonderful."

For a brief instant, she stepped forward, pressing against me and smiling like a schoolgirl who was delighted by her own daring. I responded by holding her ferociously, moving my hand along her thigh. I felt desire—and a tenderness that was almost painful.

She began to tell me that the Collective was only an extension of me. That without me, it wouldn't exist. That none of them would have pursued her and begun a relationship with her on their own. "You were and are the prime mover."

I felt grateful for this acknowledgment, but I wondered what was coming next.

"Without you," she said, "none of them would mean to me what they do. If you admire *The Fountainhead*, if you admire the new novel—well, darling, you'll understand what I am telling you. You are my reward. You are my reward for everything—for my work, for my life."

I closed my eyes, allowing the boy of fourteen who fell in love with *The Fountainhead* to hear what Ayn Rand had just said to him. I was not thinking of it in the same terms she used, but I felt an emotional equivalent—the sense of a reward, an answer, a vindication, a miracle extended back through time.

"Darling," she said, "there's something I think I was wrong about."

"Impossible," said the adult Nathaniel firmly. "What could you be wrong about?"

"About our future together. Why did I say the affair could only last a year or two? Can you think of any good reason why we can't go on this way forever?"

If my emotions could have shrieked out, passed the barrier of my internal censor, I would have cried that it suddenly seemed that a gun was pointed at my temple. But I had no illusions, then or later, about who pulled the trigger. I pulled it when I answered, "No. I can't."

10

AFTER AYN COMPLETED Galt's speech, one of the most important professional developments for her was selecting a publisher for *Atlas Shrugged*. At this point, only a few chapters remained to be written.

Ayn knew she would not allow *Atlas* to be published by Bobbs-Merrill, although her contract required that she submit the book there first. "Not after their rotten treatment of *The Fountainhead*," she declared. I asked, "But suppose Bobbs-Merrill wants the new book, as they almost certainly will?" She answered, "I'll set terms they'll never agree to."

Through her literary agent, Alan Collins, who was head of Curtis Brown, Ayn submitted the manuscript without Galt's speech (she would show that only to the book's ultimate publisher) to Bobbs-Merrill. Ross Baker, the New York representative of that house, proposed that Ayn and Collins join him for dinner to discuss the cuts and changes *Atlas* would require. Ayn was adamant that the novel be published exactly as she had written it. Baker's insistence on cuts provided just the solution she wanted. When he declared that the book was unsalable and unpublishable in its present form, Ayn remained intransigent and thus freed herself of Bobbs-Merrill.

The word spread that Ayn was in the market for a publisher, and most of the major houses approached Alan Collins. "What is it you want in a publisher?" I asked Ayn, and she answered, "Not agreement with my ideas necessarily; that's not the issue. But I do want understanding of the ideas—and the courage to stand by the book, to fight for it, not to be cowed into silence and passivity by the antagonism of critics. And imagination in promoting it."

The four houses that Ayn and Alan Collins selected for serious consideration were Viking, where Archie Ogden now worked; Knopf; McGraw-Hill; and Random House. On her own, Ayn would not have included

Random House, because she thought its editorial policy left-wing. But Hiram Haydn, editor in chief at Random House, had been an editor at Bobbs-Merrill and had maintained contact with Ayn across the years, always inquiring about her new work. She thought Haydn was a reasonable person with whom she could work. Haydn told Ayn that Random House had changed politically, pointing to its publication of Whittaker Chambers's anticommunist *Witness* as evidence, and Ayn agreed that she and Collins would lunch with the owners, Bennett Cerf and Donald Klopfer, so she could judge for herself.

When I visited Ayn after this meeting, she was enthusiastic. She liked both men immediately, she said. She found them open, straightforward, fair-minded, and intellectual. She was impressed by Bennett Cerf's proposal that she submit the book to all four publishers simultaneously, staging a kind of contest, not to increase the advance but to discover whose approach to the book she liked most. This was the kind of unconventionality Ayn admired.

Although she did not tell Cerf then, his suggestion virtually won her over. Donald Klopfer impressed her in a different and no less important way. When Ayn outlined the general philosophical stance of the novel and stated that it offered a *moral* defense of capitalism, Klopfer stunned and delighted her by replying, "If it is a *moral* defense of capitalism, wouldn't it have to clash with the entire tradition of Judeo-Christian ethics?" Ayn told me excitedly, "He *understood* the clash between religion and capitalism. And I think he's a liberal, politically. And most defenders of capitalism don't understand the issue." I asked, "Does he agree with you?" She replied, "I didn't ask him, and I don't care. It's such a pleasure to talk to a publisher *who can think*."

Ayn met with representatives of the other three firms, all of whom compared unfavorably, in different ways, with Random House. None had as intellectual an approach, and none thought much of Bennett Cerf's proposal, which persuaded Ayn that the idea had already accomplished its purpose. Random House was given the first, exclusive submission, and Cerf, Klopfer, and Haydn read the manuscript.

One day Ayn telephoned, her voice radiant. "I have a great story to tell you and Barbara. Can you come over?" When we arrived, Ayn looked exuberant. "Alan Collins and I went to Cerf's office. We weren't given any advance notice of anyone's reaction to the novel. Bennett stood at his desk very formally. Didn't even say hello. Just opened the meeting by saying, 'It's a great book. Name your own terms.'" She spread her arms wide and announced, "This is life as it might be and ought to be—and, for once, is."

In the weeks and months that followed, each time Ayn had a meeting with any of the three men, she would tell us about it in detail. Although none of them professed to be a convert to her ideas, all spoke repeatedly of the impact her thinking had on them. Donald Klopfer spoke of becoming more comfortable with his success, more respectful of earned wealth. Bennett Cerf spoke of being forced to rethink his views of the government's role in human affairs and, like Klopfer, of being less apologetic about success. Hiram Haydn, who was perhaps the most uncomfortable with Ayn's philosophy—and, in my judgment, the least independent of the three—spoke of feeling that everything he had ever thought or believed had somehow been turned upside-down, leaving him more than a little shaken up. All three professed great admiration for Ayn as a person.

Later, when I met them, they would shake their head in wonder at Ayn's ability to make them doubt their most cherished beliefs and would praise her brilliance, her courage, and her integrity. One of them said to me, "Whether you agree or disagree, nothing in the way you look at the world is ever quite the same after you've spent time with Ayn."

Bennett was the most effusive. "Ayn's ideas will be discussed and debated in Congress!" he announced. It was with Bennett that Ayn eventually formed the closest friendship. She found him witty, charming, optimistic. "Of course he's a social metaphysician," she said, "much too concerned with being liked, but he's intelligent, fair, and honest. I can deal with him."

For six years, since Barbara and I had met Ayn and Frank, the four of us had lived in an essentially private world, which had expanded to include the Collective. Now, with the completion of the novel in sight, it seemed that our period of social isolation was approaching an end. The Collective looked to publication day—and beyond—with euphoria. So did I, for the most part, although sometimes I was uneasy. I anticipated dark events, knowing how foreign Ayn's vision was to the culture in which we lived. But uneasiness was not my predominant feeling. Mostly, I felt the solemnity and excitement of a warrior on the eve of a battle that it is his dream and destiny to fight, combined with the eagerness of a child who believes he is about to see the world transformed into a place where battles are no longer necessary.

Not long after the signing of the Random House contract, Ayn and I were dining at the Russian Tea Room on one of our evenings alone together. Her writing was going well, our relationship was going well, and the results showed on her face. She was wearing a dark blue blouse with a huge bow; she looked foreign, exotic, intense. She had the look of a woman at home in the world, and it gave me pleasure to see her this way.

She contemplated me with an expression of special tenderness and said, "I want to dedicate the new novel to you."

The restaurant was crowded and fairly noisy, but it was as if suddenly there was total stillness, as if all sound had vanished, and as if there was only the meaning of her statement. I reached across the table and crushed her hand in mine. I could not speak. I could only look at her. "Oh, Ayn," I finally whispered. I experienced pride, gratitude, euphoria, and solemnity.

"Thank you for your reaction, darling," she said.

"There are no words to say what this means to me. I feel as if I've been hit over the head—with something so wonderful I need time to absorb it."

"I've been thinking about it for a long time. I haven't wanted to say anything until I was certain. I want to dedicate the book to Frank as well, of course. It will be 'To Frank O'Connor and Nathaniel Branden.' That is, if you accept."

"If I accept?" I asked incredulously. "Are you joking? If I accept the greatest honor anyone could ever bestow on me?"

"Think about it," Ayn said to me. "Don't be so quick to say yes. It's going to be the most controversial book of this century. I'm going to be hated, vilified, lied about, smeared in every possible way. If your name is in the book, if I acknowledge you publicly, you'll be a marked man. The attacks on me will also be directed at you. You have your own future and your own career to think about. Do you wish to be saddled with such an impediment?"

"Impediment?" I repeated, still astonished. "Please don't talk nonsense. Impediment? It's a badge of honor."

Once again she thanked me for my reaction, her face glowing with earnestness and happiness.

As if reading the page, I said, "*Atlas Shrugged*—to Frank O'Connor and Nathaniel Branden." I wondered about Frank's reaction to the dedication, but Ayn did not speak of that, and I did not ask.

"The title sounds right, doesn't it?" Ayn asked.

"Atlas Shrugged" had been the title of the chapter in which Hank Rearden finally goes on strike. One day, Frank had suggested—to Ayn's enthusiastic agreement—that it would work well for the novel as a whole.

"I think the title is perfect," I said.

As she returned to the subject of the attacks, with her usual persistence, my joy and exhilaration made it almost impossible to concentrate on her words. Why was she asking me to think about the world or about what the world thought about anything? I wondered if she felt the need to test me, even now.

Seeing my reaction, she chuckled with satisfaction, her eyes bright. "All right. I give up." Contemplating the intensity of my happiness, she asked, almost mockingly, "Are you pleased?"

"The idea of the greatest literary masterpiece I've ever read being dedicated to me is almost more than I can hold in my brain. I'm thrilled, I'm honored, I'm overwhelmed. I feel like I'm in the midst of the most marvelous dream. I'm speechless. I don't know what to say."

"You've said it," she answered. She looked at me appraisingly. "Oh, I think we both have tears in our eyes. Not quite, but almost. It's out of character for both of us, but perfectly in character for this occasion, perfectly proper." Then she added, "Sometimes you're a disappearing professor. You go off—inside your mind, or somewhere—and I can't reach you. But when it counts, you come through."

"Oh, I hope so!"

Her statement had lifted me still higher. I thought, If only I could always feel with Ayn as I do this evening. If only I could always be worthy of what she has given me. I want that more than I want anything else in this world.

"*Tonight*, darling," said Ayn, as if reading my thoughts, "is reality. Not the things I sometimes get upset with you about. Right now, none of that seems real, does it?"

She was as happy as I had ever seen her. One moment childlike and cheerful; the next moment adult, sensual, seductive; the next moment rubbing her foot against my leg under the table while looking around the room with an impish grin on her face. "Do you ever wonder what people think when they look at us?" she asked.

I answered, "No, I don't have to. I know what they think. They think you're my daughter." She laughed.

As we walked along Fifty-Seventh Street toward Park Avenue, her arm through mine, Ayn declared that if we were not having an affair, if we had remained only friends, she would not have chosen to dedicate *Atlas* to me.

"A dedication in *this* book could only be for a supreme value of mine, not just a 'friend.' I wonder if anyone will be smart enough to figure that out."

"I love you," I said, "and right now I do not give a good goddamn what anyone knows or thinks or figures out about anything."

"Well, Mr. Nathan Blumenthal of Brampton, Ontario," she said, stopping and smiling up at me.

Brampton—a small town near Toronto where I had been born and spent the first six years of my life. I thought of the road from that beginning to this night. I felt the presence in my body of some force that had no name but that had driven every step I had taken. I wondered why it sometimes felt that that force, whatever it was, separated me from other people, from everyone I had ever met except Ayn. And I wondered how something could be a source of both loneliness and joy.

Now, suddenly, I wanted to talk. I wanted Ayn to understand something. I wanted to understand it myself, and perhaps her input would help. We continued walking.

"Funny you should mention Brampton. It's strange, the memories that pop up at odd moments, like now. I remember one time, I was about five years old. I was wearing a yellow sunsuit and riding my tricycle up the street. It had been raining, and the ground was wet. I saw three boys my age playing in the mud, making mud castles, and they waved to me, but I just kept riding my tricycle up and down the street. I remember the feelings I had, but not the words; I can't quite imagine what the words would have been for someone that age. I looked at the boys; I looked up at the sky. I had some sense of the immensity of things that evoked in me an odd, painful kind of longing. I looked back at the boys, then up at the sky again—and if I could have expressed what I was experiencing, the words would have been, 'There's something more. More than playing in the mud. More than what they're seeing. More than anyone sees. More than this life around me. And something inside me is reaching for it.' This memory has haunted and intrigued me all my life."

We walked, and Ayn listened attentively, without speaking, knowing there was more that I wanted to say. "As to my parents and the other adults I encountered, I was already feeling—again, without these words, obviously—that I had been born into a lunatic asylum. Everyone seemed out of control. No one really knew why they did anything. I had the most overwhelming sense of human irrationality. Grown-ups said one thing and did another. They claimed to be feeling one emotion but plainly were feeling something different. They changed the rules and expectations every other hour. They lied to the children and to one another all the time. They were generous and kind one day and mean the next. As if they were possessed by demons. And everyone looked unhappy. And I could not understand why. I told myself I must not be afraid, that I must learn to understand all this and never, ever be like these people."

"That's what saved you," Ayn said.

What was I struggling to say—or not to say? I experienced a kind of static in my brain, like a radio signal that could not break through.

"To me," I said, "and I think to all of us in the Collective, you represent everything we did not have when we were young—sanity."

She answered, "That's what I want to be. To you, above all. There's no higher compliment you can pay me. I love you."

The next morning over breakfast, I told Barbara about the dedication. I expected her to be stunned. Instead, it was I who was stunned by the wise smile that greeted my announcement.

"I thought Ayn would do that. It's wonderful. I'm proud of you."

We wondered what Frank would feel, and we both immediately agreed that he would find the dedication entirely natural and appropriate, just as Barbara did. There was an easygoing sense of relaxed harmony between us, as there usually was when we weren't focused on our relationship.

Barbara was my first friend, as well as my first lover. She made me feel visible. In spite of our conflicts, she inspired a sense of connectedness between us that was untouched by her pain or mine.

We had moved from our studio apartment into a one-bedroom apartment on East Thirty-Fifth Street. Our bed folded up into a sofa, and the bedroom became my office, where I studied, wrote, and saw clients. My practice was growing steadily. Our dining room table folded into a desk for Barbara. She had earned her master's degree in philosophy and had written her thesis on free will at this table, where we were now drinking our morning coffee.

Barbara was working first as a receptionist and then as an editorial assistant at *Woman's Day* magazine—her first job after graduating. Soon, she would land a job teaching philosophy, only to discover that she preferred publishing to academia. The job she would enjoy the most, and the one where she would remain the longest, was in the editorial department of St. Martin's Press.

After breakfast, she hurried off to *Woman's Day,* and I to New York University for an appointment with my faculty adviser, John Tietz. When I arrived at his office, he informed me that he was retiring. This was unexpected, and I wondered if he was ill, but I did not think it appropriate to ask. I had begun to work with him on my master's thesis, which was to present my theory of anxiety. Now he repeated his opinion that my subject was too ambitious, even for a doctoral dissertation.

"Without me here to stand by you and defend you," he said pleasantly yet matter-of-factly, "you'll never get what you're trying to do through the committee. You'll be fighting them for the next three years. If you want my advice, you need to get out into the world and on your own. That's where you'll learn the things you want to learn—not in this school or any other. So here's what I propose—and I can take care of this before

I go, so there'll be no question of your graduating. Instead of writing a thesis, *any* thesis, you'll take extra coursework, which will be a thesis equivalent. I can arrange that. It'll be neat, clean, uncomplicated—and you'll be on your way. What do you think?"

I was delighted and instantly agreed.

"Now then," he went on, "were you planning to continue on for a doctorate?"

I said I had not yet decided but that I did not think so, not for the time being.

"Well, it's your decision. For some people, a Ph.D. would be important. But again, if you want my opinion, not for you. You're going to be an outsider no matter what credentials you acquire."

I thought that one day I would return to school for my doctorate—which I did, years later in Los Angeles—but for now the thought of being out of school, free to learn, study, and grow on my own, and to earn my own living, sent me sailing out of the building and across the street to a pay phone. I wanted to tell Barbara the news.

Knowing my impatience with school, she was pleased that I could graduate without stress or complications. But she said, a little regretfully, "It would have been a good thesis."

I assured her that I had every intention of writing it, not as a thesis but as a work to be published. "This will be my first book," I announced confidently (and mistakenly).

Now, walking home from Washington Square in a state of excitement, I wondered when Barbara would begin to write a book of her own. She continued to speak of her ambition to write fiction, and I could not understand what was standing in the way. As I saw it, she had the greatest teacher—and model—in the world, she had support and encouragement, and still all she seemed to do was yearn. She *talked* about writing. Once, when I asked her about her difficulties, she said, "I'm not happy enough to write."

"Not happy enough? I would think that one of the ways we *make* ourselves happy is by writing."

She sighed. "Perhaps for some people. Not for me. When I'm not happy—this is the only way I can explain it—I don't feel worthy enough to write."

Actually, Barbara was working such long hours on her job that writing a novel would have been challenging even under more benign circumstances. However, apart from that, today I can see how extraordinarily difficult it would be for any young person just starting out to write a novel in the environment in which we lived, given Ayn's repressive judgment and intimidating personality. As Barbara would observe to me in later years, it was not an environment in which to discover one's own voice.

I knew Barbara was not entirely comfortable with Ayn's insistence on the importance of plot. Ayn had defined *plot* as "a purposeful progression of logically connected events leading to the resolution of a climax." In 1968, in an article titled "Basic Principles of Literature," which was reprinted in her book on the aesthetics of literature, *The Romantic Manifesto,* she wrote:

> Since a novel is a re-creation of reality, its theme has to be dramatized, i.e., presented in terms of action. . . . A story in which nothing happens is not a story. A story whose events are haphazard and accidental is either an inept conglomeration or, at best, a chronicle, a memoir, a reportorial recording, not a novel. . . . Contrary to the prevalent literary doctrines of today, it is *realism* that demands a plot structure in a novel. All human actions are goal-directed, consciously or subconsciously; purposelessness is contrary to man's nature. . . . Therefore, if one is to present man *as he is* . . . one has to present him in goal-directed action.

Barbara explored ideas such as these endlessly, and she clearly loved Ayn's discussions of writing and found her analyses of different novels and styles illuminating and inspiring. But her intellectual agreement with the importance of plot was greater than her emotional acceptance. "My mind just doesn't seem to work that way," she complained.

If I had had the wisdom then to see that it would have been extraordinarily difficult, if not impossible, for Barbara or anyone else to write fiction in so threatening an atmosphere, I would have had the wisdom to see a great many other things as well.

I wanted to see Barbara happy, I thought that writing could make her happy, and almost everything I said on the subject was wrong.

By the fall of 1956, Barbara's anxiety had largely subsided. The worst storm of her life—in terms of immediate emotional anguish—appeared to have passed. Whatever internal struggles she was having in terms of Ayn and me, she did not choose to talk about, and I do not know how receptive I would have been. We communicated well about everything except the things between us that mattered most.

She frequently rejected my sexual advances, but that was true even before the affair with Ayn. Whatever was wrong between us had been so almost from the beginning. Unfortunately for me, my desire for Barbara had not abated. I regarded any night I could go to sleep without reaching out to touch her as being a victory of self-discipline, and I congratulated myself.

Paradoxically and bewilderingly, Barbara professed to love me, more than ever before. She often spoke as if she shared Ayn's view of me. Riding down the elevator of our building on one of our evenings out, she would look up at me tenderly, even erotically, and say something complimentary about my appearance. This made the mystery—and the agony— worse. I did not know what to say when she would declare, just when I was about to explode with exasperation, "One day everything will be as we both want it to be. You'll see."

Strangely, I was inclined to believe her. My confidence seemed to stem from two elements. One was some indestructible optimism that rendered me incapable of believing that my life could be tragic. The other was a deep sense that it was natural for Barbara to desire me as I desired her, that one day she would reciprocate my feelings, and that whatever was wrong now was a senseless mistake that would be resolved at any moment. Had my problems with Barbara seemed more real to me, I might have seen my life more clearly, acted more decisively, and spared both of us a good deal of suffering. As it was, I left too much unsaid and unchallenged too long.

But perhaps the status quo suited me. Although I would never have permitted myself this thought at the time, in retrospect it seems obvious that Barbara was my protection against Ayn, just as Ayn was my protection against Barbara. My relationship with each woman imposed restrictions and limitations on the demands that the other could make. And then there was the matter of ego gratification—I was the emotional center of two women's worlds. I suffered from the delusion that two incomplete loves could make one whole one.

Barbara, of course, had her own reasons for enduring her pain. Although there was a subtle note of tension in her relationship with Ayn, their friendship in many ways was becoming more affectionate. Her enthusiasm for Ayn's work was boundless, and the intelligence and sensitivity that Barbara brought to the novel, in her understanding of what Ayn was doing, inspired Ayn to speak of her as a soul mate. Barbara was the only person in our group besides me who could give Ayn the highly detailed literary feedback that she treasured. I do not doubt that what I often saw in their eyes when they were talking together was love.

But Barbara's support did not prevent Ayn from making overly critical remarks from time to time. "Barbara is not purposeful enough in her own

Nathaniel and Barbara Branden
holding newly published *Atlas Shrugged*, 1957

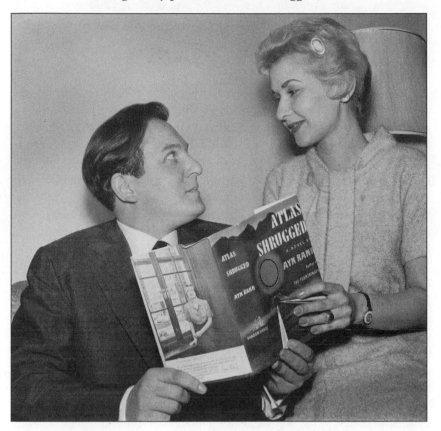

life. Didn't you tell me she likes to bask for days on the beach? That's why the importance of purposefulness in writing, both in the sense of plot and in the sense of goal-directed characters, isn't fully real to her." I had made statements much like that, which were just as silly, but I did not like hearing them from Ayn.

I could not arrive at a balanced perspective on Ayn and Barbara's relationship, just as I could not reach a balanced perspective on any of our relationships. Incongruity and ambivalence were the norm. Yet I lived in a world in which incongruity and ambivalence were presumed hardly to exist, either in our behavior or among ourselves. Were we not all apostles of reason? Did we not live in the kingdom of sanity?

The night Ayn and I had walked from the Russian Tea Room along Fifty-Seventh Street, what had I been trying to say? On a subconscious level, I was looking for a link between the world of my childhood and the world we all shared in New York. And if there was a connection, wasn't it that the world I had found with Ayn was the exact opposite of the world I had come from? It was inconceivable to me that, as an adult, I might be participating in a nightmare worse than that of my childhood.

Now, striding up Lexington Avenue toward home, I thought, I don't care about any problems right now. I was happy and excited. I was riding a current of inexhaustible energy. I was an unconquerable force. Whatever was wrong, solutions would be found. In less than a year, I would graduate. In less than a year, *Atlas* would be finished and on its way to publication. And in scarcely more than a year, I would be ready to begin writing my first book. It would be a critique of major existing theories of pathological anxiety—those of Freud, Adler, Horney, Fromm, and Sullivan—and an exposition of my own theory. To hell with everything else, I thought joyfully, without specifying what I meant by "everything else."

One of the safest and most interesting topics of discussion between Barbara and me was our admiration for Ayn. Exploring this issue intensified our bond. We agreed that Ayn was extraordinarily independent. She appeared to be absolutely firsthand in her approach to everything. It was as if she were the first person born on earth, a person who had no choice but to look at life through her own eyes. This was the trait that had so impressed me in Howard Roark.

"The difference between me and other people," Ayn liked to say, "is that I am more honest." She was speaking of intellectual honesty. I would laugh and ask her if she thought anyone else we knew, if completely honest, could have produced *Atlas Shrugged*. She resisted the idea that her powerful intelligence was at least as important as her honesty. In retrospect, it seems clear that she not only lacked insight about her faults but also often lacked insight about her strengths.

And yet, if one understood what she meant by "honesty," she was not entirely wrong, either. With the exception of certain personal areas where she could be appallingly unconscious, she had the most profound and passionate respect for facts. For her, such respect was the essence of morality, the foundation of all the other virtues. In reading *Atlas*, I was impressed by the virtuosity with which she developed the idea of respect for reality, taking what could be cold and abstract and making it living drama. She projected that same attitude in her person, and to some extent she inspired it in our whole group. "What you're teaching," I once said to her, "is that respect for reality is the ultimate virtue." "Well, of course," she answered, as if I were stating the self-evident. She conveyed to us that this attitude was intimately bound up with the heroic. She made it basic to the characterization of John Galt.

Today, it seems painfully obvious that if respect for reality was the ultimate Objectivist virtue, it was not one we practiced consistently, and it was inevitable that one day reality would present a bill for collection.

Ayn was convinced that ideas ruled the world and that, consciously or subconsciously, they ruled the life of every individual. Barbara and I absorbed this viewpoint completely. When meeting a new person, Ayn would sometimes say, "Tell me your premises," which, to most people, is a puzzling and disorienting question. Ideas *mattered* to her. If someone did not understand her conviction about the supreme importance of philosophy, that person could not understand her. If, for example, she heard a statement to the effect that man has no right to exist for his own sake but exists only to serve society (or the state or the race or the planet) or that reason is impotent to know reality or that all value judgments are ultimately arbitrary or that notions of good and evil are merely expressions of subjective emotion, then she saw, concretely and specifically, the oceans of human blood that were spilled as a consequence of such beliefs. She saw Nazi Germany and Soviet Russia—and she reacted accordingly.

This conviction about the importance of ideas could lend her enormous patience in intellectual discussions. If anyone in our group was confused about some issue, Ayn would sit down with him for eight or nine hours, if that was how long it took, until he was intellectually satisfied. She conveyed that what we thought—about the most abstract issues in philosophy or about today's headline or about a movie we had seen—was of the highest importance. Ayn took us seriously in an unprecedented, profoundly nurturing way.

I witnessed this nurturing process even with people who disagreed with Ayn violently. I sat in on many conversations with men and women who shared almost none of her principles yet who would say, "Why do I feel so inspired talking to you?" or "Why do I feel like a better person—or more alive—or as if my life matters more—when I'm with you?"

Ayn thought in terms of principles. This was evident almost immediately to anyone who spoke with her. It was one of her most striking characteristics. When she asked me, at our first meeting, if I accepted the principle that man has a right to exist, she expected me to understand that this meant that his life did not belong to others, that the government had no right to set the price at which he would offer his goods or services, and that his fellow citizens had no moral entitlement to vote his freedom away.

"If you understand a man's right to his own life," she said to me, "you understand the moral base of capitalism."

In discussions with adversaries, she always challenged them to "name your principles," by which she meant to name the premises underlying their utterances. "If you believe in military conscription, you believe that man's life belongs to the tribe." "If you believe that man's mind cannot know existence 'as it really is,' then you support irrationalism, because we have to act on the basis of *some* ideas or beliefs, and you have ruled out reason." "If you believe that certain sexual practices between consenting adults should be forbidden by law, you believe that some persons have a moral right to impose on others, at the point of a gun, their notions of appropriate sexual behavior." "By what right?" she would demand. "By what standard? Name your principles."

Because most people do not know how to name the implicit principles behind the positions they take, or sometimes do not care to, her request often evoked considerable discomfort and hostility.

"I never had to teach Barbara or you the importance of principles," she said to me more than once. "You both understand their *practical* necessity. That's one of the things I love about both of you." In the Collective, a standard joke was about the mentality of the person who, having been convinced that the government should not nationalize the steel industry, then asks, "But what about the coal industry?"

Ayn also had a great talent for establishing intellectual rapport with "ordinary people"—a cleaning woman, a taxi driver, a telephone installer. She was proud of the fact that in conversation, she could make her ideas clear to almost anyone—"except," we would sometimes joke, "a professional intellectual."

In reflecting on the traits that made Ayn so exhilarating to talk to and be with—the traits that I myself wanted to master—I was often impressed by her ability to reduce any issue to its essentials, not to get waylaid by details and not to accept uncritically someone else's definition. For example, she would say, "Don't be tricked into believing the choice is between sacrificing yourself to others or others to yourself. That's the trap you're intended to fall into by those preaching altruism. The choice is between recognizing that a human being is an end in himself—not a means to the ends of others—and practicing human sacrifices. This is what I meant in *The Fountainhead* when Roark said the choice is between independence and dependence. You wouldn't accept it if someone told you your only choice were between sadism and masochism, would you? The same principle applies here."

Once, a young physicist named Russell Targ protested against our conviction that governments should not coerce taxpayers into financing scientific research and demanded, "What do you want us to do? Go to private citizens, businesses, or institutions for our money, hat in hand?" Ayn replied, "Yes, I do. That's morally preferable to going gun in hand."

In epistemology, she rejected the notion that "rationalism" and "empiricism" were one's only choices. She argued that both doctrines were flawed and that they offered a false alternative. On similar grounds, she rejected both "idealism" and "materialism" in metaphysics. In ethics, she rejected notions of "intrinsic good" and "subjective preference" as equally irrational. "In an intellectual debate," she would say, "don't be misled into accepting your opponent's definition of the problem. Go for the essential, go to the root of the issue, which may be completely outside his premises and frame of reference."

Apart from Barbara, the person with whom I was most likely to discuss Ayn was Leonard. I enjoyed thinking aloud with him about her most interesting and admirable traits, even though he was still frozen in awe of her and did not perceive her as fully human. "That's bad for Ayn and bad for you," I would tell him. "Bad for Ayn because she won't feel completely visible with you if you can't see her as a real, living person. Bad for you because you won't understand that what you admire in her, you can emulate. You can learn to make part of yourself." Leonard would typically answer, worshipfully, "Ayn is so lucky to have you in her life. How lonely she would be otherwise!" And I would be left suspended between appreciation and frustration.

There were aspects of Ayn's psychology that I did not discuss with anyone. They had to do with her attitudes as a woman. "I never wanted to be a general," she would say, "let alone a commander in chief. My dream has always been to be the ideal lieutenant—to my kind of man." When I heard this, I thought, "I wish I were Ayn's age." It was almost as if, in being so much younger and therefore unable to give her the experience she wanted, I had somehow failed her.

At the same time, I wondered about her need for control. Given that it was so powerful, could she really surrender it in any context other than sex? And in sex, I sometimes found the ideas of control and surrender far from transparent. Once, I said to her, laughing, "Your sexual slave will now proceed to dominate you." She smiled but did not find this as amusing as I did. She was profoundly invested in the concept of male domination.

And yet she was scornful of those who, based on a reading of the love scenes in her novels, wondered if her psychology was touched by sadomasochistic impulses. I never read her this way or found this attitude present in her personal behavior, not to the smallest extent. Her heroines were not passive "clinging vines" any more than she was. A good many self-confident women seem to find the metaphor or fantasy of male dominance and female submission appealing (in certain carefully limited contexts); so do many nonchauvinistic men. Regarding the "rape scene" in *The Fountainhead*, Ayn would say, "If that was rape, it was by engraved invitation. Literal rape would be contemptible and disgusting and unthinkable to any hero of mine."

Ayn and I met privately twice a week, once in the afternoon and once in the evening, a pattern that we established at the start of the affair.

One afternoon, walking from my apartment to hers, I hoped Frank would be gone by the time I got there. I found it awkward and embarrassing when he greeted me at the door or when I stood in his living room, trying to look normal, while he smiled and kissed Ayn good-bye and left, a husband exiled by his wife's lover.

I had reluctantly accepted that Ayn and I would not have an apartment of our own. A resistance I did not understand prevented her from leasing an "office" in the same building where she lived. It would have been simple for her to do, and my presence would have aroused no questions. I had given up pressing her on this issue, but I knew that displacing Frank from his own home during our meetings was barbaric.

As I approached their apartment, my positive spirits vanished, my perspective on our handling of the affair shifted (as happened from time to time), and it seemed to me that Ayn and I were cold, uncaring persons, blind to the devastation we were causing, even though neither Frank nor Barbara complained.

But then I told myself, You're not thinking clearly; you've slipped into conventionality. I was capable of cruelty, I thought, knowing that at times I could be single-tracked, insensitive, and self-absorbed. But not Ayn. She loved Frank. If what we were doing were wrong, surely she would know and would propose a better course of action. I fought down my own agitation and told myself I was "being rational" in doing so. It did not occur to me that I might be committing the very mistake we fiercely inveighed against, that of placing someone else's moral judgment—Ayn's—above my own.

But I had begun this day feeling buoyant, and somehow that mood returned in full force, sweeping everything else aside. It was easy to forget my reluctance, easy to shake off my sense of doing something unconscionable. I felt energized, optimistic, sexual—insulated by the ruthlessness that happiness sometimes inspires.

Once, when I wondered aloud if we had chosen the right course in having an affair, Ayn said, "This relationship is sexual or it's nothing. If we are not a man and woman to each other, in the full sense—if we are merely disembodied minds—our philosophy is meaningless."

I knocked at the door of Ayn and Frank's apartment.

"Hi, Nathan!" Frank said brightly and warmly, opening the apartment door and gesturing me into the living room.

"We're having a quarrel," Ayn announced, her voice sharp. I quickly gathered that Frank's cheery greeting signaled relief at the interruption.

My arrival did not bring their discussion to an end. Instead, Ayn chose to involve me, as she had done several times before to my acute discomfort. I felt my good mood melting into numbness.

Ayn wanted to know why Frank did not take her shopping and advise her on what to wear, as I did. I could not afford to buy her clothes, but I did like to take her to stores and offer suggestions. Left to her own devices, she was more or less unconcerned with what she wore; her writing, she said, "leaves no space in my brain for such things." A young man of twenty-six, she told Frank, had the initiative to ignore her protests, drag her out of the apartment, and force her to buy new outfits. His attitude inspired her to want to do so. Why was her husband, more than twice Nathan's age, so passive, so unwilling to put more into their marriage?

I could not understand how Ayn could subject Frank to this. I could not understand how she could subject me to it. Did she not realize how inappropriate it was to compare us? Why did she do such things? There was so much rage in her today, as if a lifetime of frustration was erupting over the issue of clothes, this issue becoming the focus and symbol of everything she wanted and did not get from a husband. It was painful to see Frank so pathetic: helpless, guilty, angry and afraid to show it, empathic toward Ayn, and simultaneously detached, almost dissociated.

I thought of how little I really understood about their marriage. Ayn spoke of Frank as her hero. She always seemed loving and affectionate with him. She complimented him constantly. She insisted on cooking him dinner, no matter how exhausted she was. "A wife's job," she said. "And if I don't force him, he never eats enough."

Her attitude about cooking Frank's dinner was a prime example of what puzzled me. Sometimes she did not stop writing and begin cooking until eleven or twelve o'clock at night, and she asked him to wait for her, saying that she felt guilty when he prepared his own dinner. By the time dinner was ready, Frank was often too tired to touch his food, which precipitated a lecture on his poor eating habits. Ayn's motive was clearly *her* self-image, not his welfare.

More than once, I tried to cajole her, humorously, into grasping the impracticality of her behavior, and she kept promising to serve dinner earlier, but the problem remained unchanged. She had a highly valued picture in her mind—she would cook dinner, then she and Frank would eat together. This had to be preserved, regardless of what it meant in terms of actual reality. The *form* of romantic love had to be maintained, for herself and for others, but it seemed to be imposed on a set of facts that did not match it.

Standing awkwardly in their living room, I now wondered what Ayn could want me to do or say to Frank. Couldn't she see how many advantages I had, how much easier my role was than Frank's? If he were passive to begin with, could he be anything but more passive in the present circumstances? I felt cast, ludicrously, in the role of umpire or marriage counselor. Yet I was not an outsider. I was one of the participants. The image of being five years old and sitting at the kitchen table, listening to my mother complain to me about my father, flashed through my brain.

It's so easy for childhood history to repeat itself. Both in Ayn's childhood home and in Frank's, the mother was the dominant force and the father was relatively more passive. Precisely the same was true in Barbara's home and mine. In this sense, we had all grown up with similar role models. No doubt, this prepared us for perceiving Ayn and Frank's relationship as "normal."

Now, when Frank looked at me, he showed no sign of resentment; on the contrary, he had the man-to-man look of an ally who counted on me to understand everything that could not be said. It was as if he saw me, too, as needing a defender. There were times when my father had looked at me the same way.

All I could think of saying to Frank, gently and almost diffidently, was that this conflict demonstrated how important he was to Ayn and that whatever Ayn had needed from him, she still needed—which meant, "I have not replaced you." I sounded stupid to myself as I spoke. Yet my statement served its purpose; it seemed to have a tranquilizing effect on them both. And when Frank got up to leave, they were affectionate, the quarrel already fading into unreality.

I tried to communicate the difficulty of Frank's position, and she quickly agreed, pleased that I was sticking up for him. She walked toward me, and we embraced. But the mood in which I had arrived was gone. "Shall we get something to eat?" I said.

Over lunch at a neighborhood restaurant, she spoke enthusiastically about the progress of her writing. She was nearing the end of the novel and felt an almost feverish need to talk about it. "The philosophical part is now done. From here to the end of the story, it's pure action. The final big event is Galt's rescue from the torture chamber by Dagny, Rearden, Francisco, and Ragnar. Now I'm free to enjoy myself. No more explaining to do. Just an exciting rescue scene. That's what I'd like to write next—a novel that would be pure action and drama with no new philosophical ideas. A novel about a man who has mastered the enjoyment of life—perhaps an adventurer of some kind—something in the spirit of Francisco d'Anconia—but no philosophical speeches. What a relief that would be!"

I sensed some residual tension in her, which I related to the incident with Frank, and I asked her if she wanted to talk about it. She answered, her voice like iron, that we had only a few hours together and that they were not to be wasted. "Priorities, darling," she said sternly. "Priorities."

She went on to talk with excitement about how *Atlas Shrugged* would end. She now seemed genuinely cheerful. She was saying, "All the key strikers are now in the valley, and the battle is essentially finished. The government has collapsed. It is night, and Galt and Dagny are walking in the mountains, high above the valley's lights. Looking out over the world, Galt says, 'The road is cleared. We are going back to the world.' And then here is the last line of the book: 'He raised his hand and over the desolate earth he traced in space the sign of the dollar.' The dollar sign is the symbol of the free mind and of free trade. Of course I'll be denounced for that—for the deliberately religious implication. They'll blank out what Galt's gesture means in the context of the story."

I thought the ending magnificent and told her so. I added, "Not just the ending but the whole treatment of Galt in the story has an almost religious feeling—perhaps I should say 'spiritual.' I think that will be a source of the book's inspirational power."

Our discussion of *Atlas* had drawn us into our own world, as it always did. As we walked back to the apartment, I told Ayn I was impatient to make love. Looking around as if committing a daring act, she pulled my arms around her body. Once inside, we went directly to the bedroom.

That we made love in Ayn and Frank's bedroom was sometimes hard to bear. And yet it remained the symbol of our relationship at its most harmonious. I cannot recall a single conflict in that setting. It stood in my mind as a place of unique safety, almost a sanctuary.

Entering it now, I was aware of the special quality of earnestness that Ayn always brought to the act of sex. She was intense as a human being and never more so than in this realm. She was everything I could wish, except playful. Nothing was casual or frivolous. When she attempted lightness, the seriousness of her attempt made me smile. I liked it more when she was her naturally earnest self. She could abandon herself. She could surrender fully to the experience,

Yet I was always aware of the powerful presence of her searchlight consciousness—of those eyes that missed nothing. When I mentioned this to her once, she told me that I projected the same quality. "We are not people whom sex makes unconscious," she said.

It was always important to me that she feel desirable, sexual, physically fulfilled. I wanted to give her that—for selfish reasons. I believed that if two people truly cared for each other, they not only wanted the other to be sexually satisfied but they also wished to strengthen and reinforce the other's sexual self-esteem, the other's sense of self as a woman or a man. This was what Barbara and I were unable to give each other.

Even in surrendering, Ayn manifested her unique kind of power. She had the most extraordinary presence, her eyes, her voice, and her gestures all asserting existence, all asserting confidence in every expression. It is said that many women find power in a man an aphrodisiac; I found Ayn's personal power no less erotic.

Whatever this relationship is ultimately about, I told myself, wherever we're headed, this is what one lives for.

There are rituals in sex, not only physical ones but also verbal ones—things couples take pleasure in saying again and again. "With you," she said, "I am totally and absolutely a woman. You've accomplished that."

"And with you," I answered, "I feel totally and absolutely fulfilled as a man. I feel as if the kind of man I am is what you want. That's what you've given me. We've always had an incredible intellectual relationship. We're so intimately connected, at times it feels supernatural. We've always had an incredible spiritual relationship. We truly are soul mates—we think and feel about so many things in an identical way. And not to have to explain or discuss or defend or hold back, after what I've experienced before. . . ."

She raised one naked foot high in the air. "Don't you think I have good legs?"

"Yes, I do."

"We would have made a good team," she said reflectively, "if we had met at the same age."

"We make a good team now."

"Yes, but that would truly have been an explosion—in a good sense. Can you just imagine what it would have been like?"

I had imagined it many times and told her so. I thought of it now, both of us in our twenties, learning and growing together.

"It would have been ideal," I said, meaning it. If I had been with her since her twenties, I flattered myself, the traits in her personality that I sometimes found difficult would not exist. She would be more serene. Free of anger, suspicion, and bitterness. Lighter. She had had to carry too much alone.

We talked about the fact that our relationship felt like a marriage—"a spiritual marriage"—occupying a separate universe of its own. "With no disloyalty to Frank or Barbara," Ayn often hastened to add.

We lay in bed for a long while without speaking, holding each other. The clock on the bureau across the room assured me that Frank would not be home for at least two more hours. Suddenly, Ayn was smiling impishly.

"'Woman is clay, longing to become mire,'" she said, quoting a line she knew I would recognize from Victor Hugo's novel *The Man Who Laughs*.

"What made you think of that?"

"Guess."

"Well, have you satisfied your longing to become mire?" I asked.

"The line is right, if one knows how to understand it. Poor Hugo. The pagan and the Christian fought within him constantly. He gave his best line about sex to a woman we're supposed to think of as immoral. But as one writer reading the psychology of another, I can tell you his heart was with her."

Ayn was using dialogue from Hugo to achieve a deeply personal act of self-disclosure, intending for the intellectuality of her form to mute the intimacy of her content. I could not help feeling some satisfaction in noticing that she, too, was capable of "turning philosophical" at questionable moments.

In spite of myself, I began to reflect on Hugo's line. Spoken by a woman of high self-esteem, it conveys one kind of message, a very erotic one. Spoken by a woman of low self-esteem who seeks *actual* degradation, it has an opposite meaning, a tragic one. Spoken by Ayn, it was probably intended to stress her desire to surrender to masculine strength, to give up all authority, to be treated as an instrument of the man's pleasure—provided, of course, that it was *her* man. I found her superabundant self-confidence inspiring and challenging.

"Uh-oh, where have you gone?" she asked. "Are you off somewhere thinking? It serves me right for bringing up Hugo in bed."

"I was just thinking that right now life is exactly as it should be."

I marveled that, in spite of my periodic misgivings about the affair and my sometime longing to return to the original form of our relationship, afternoons such as today were still possible. There were times when I felt that I was exactly where I wanted to be, doing exactly what I wanted to do. The unresolved problems in my relationship with Barbara were not unreal to me; they were merely filed in an entirely separate category of my consciousness, and I experienced them as totally unrelated to my relationship with Ayn. It was the unresolved problems in my relationship with Ayn that were now unreal.

One day, this afternoon would stand in my mind as a time of sunlit brilliance—among the last of my unclouded memories in the history of our relationship.

In the winter of 1956, I felt as if all of us in the Collective were on an express train that was roaring toward the completion of *Atlas Shrugged*. Exhilaration and anticipation were the dominant themes. We were profoundly convinced that Ayn was bringing an inestimable value to the world—intellectually, literarily, socially—and that it would be virtually impossible for people not to recognize this fact. It was difficult not to feel that we might actually see the beginning, in our own lifetime, of a philosophical and cultural renaissance. And that we would be part of it.

That winter, I graduated from New York University, began writing my book on anxiety (which I was never to complete), and established a fairly busy psychotherapy practice. My sense of mission regarding Ayn's philosophy was growing more urgent and powerful. Whatever my other goals, one part of my destiny was to transmit her message to the world. I had decided to give a public course of lectures on Objectivism some time soon after the publication of *Atlas*. My intention was to elucidate her positions on epistemology, metaphysics, ethics, political economy, and literary aesthetics and to introduce some of my ideas regarding self-esteem, social metaphysics, anxiety, and the foundations of a benevolent sense of life. I saw myself as a crusader with a sacred cause.

Ayn was not especially enthusiastic about the lecture project. She had misgivings about whether it could be successful financially, and she feared that I would martyr myself. But she did not oppose it. She asked me again, "Do you understand that you will be making yourself a public target?" The Collective in general was enthusiastic and always wanted to hear my latest plans, which were still in the early stages. I felt encouraged by their interest and support.

One issue with which Ayn and I had been grappling for some time was what name to give her philosophy. Finally, Ayn proposed Objectivism. The name was applicable to her theories of existence, knowledge, and values. In metaphysics, she held that reality is objective and absolute, existing independently of anyone's consciousness, perceptions, beliefs, wishes, hopes, or fears. That which is, is what it is; "existence is identity"; A is A. In epistemology, she held that man's mind is competent to achieve objectively valid knowledge of that which exists. And in ethics, she held that values appropriate to human beings are objectively demonstrable—in other words, that a rational code of morality is possible.

Ayn's opposition to contemporary epistemological theory was no less intense than her opposition to contemporary ethical and political theory, as Barbara and I had discovered during our early discussions with her in California. As Ayn saw it, the same rejection of reason that was expressed in politics in the resurgence of the rule of brute force throughout the world was also expressed in philosophy in the cult of uncertainty and epistemological agnosticism. She insisted that modern political barbarism was a product and consequence of philosophical nihilism. At a time when the need for answers to crucial questions was a matter of life and death, Ayn declared, modern philosophy had nothing to offer people but a choice of irrationalism (or, in her words, "mysticisms"). First, there was the "neo-mysticism" of pragmatism, positivism and linguistic analysis, which taught that it is meaningless to speak of "facts of reality" and futile to imagine that man can know any facts. Then, there was the old-fashioned mysticism of existentialism, which taught that man *can* know reality but not by means of reason, only through his "blood and bowels" (to quote my NYU professor William Barrett, who championed "blood and bowels" above mind). To me, Ayn's analysis of this resurgence of irrationalism, which had been growing since the time of Kant and which usually paraded as the voice of science, constituted one of the most brilliant, challenging, and illuminating aspects of Galt's speech.

Objectivism, I agreed, was the ideal name for her philosophical approach. Objectivism was the banner under which our crusade would be waged.

On a Saturday evening in March 1957, while the Collective sat in the living room waiting for her to emerge from her study, Ayn was writing the final pages of the novel.

Wondering if we should all depart and leave her undisturbed, someone tiptoed to her study door to get some sense of what to do. With her back to the door, Ayn heard the tentative step, muttered "I'll kill you," and went on writing.

An hour or so later, thirteen years after she had begun the novel, Ayn rushed out to show Frank the words THE END.

I recall little of that evening except an overwhelming sense of solemnity and joy—and a vague, distant hint of sadness, coming from the knowledge that a precious part of my life had now come to a close.

I thought then that for all these years Ayn had been obliged to immerse herself in a kind of alternate reality—the world of *Atlas Shrugged*—and that now, with her task accomplished, she was bringing her creation back to the world in which we lived. But I was wrong. The truth, which I would need some time to discover, was that Ayn had disappeared into that alternate reality and was not coming back. She was like the strikers in her own novel who, having seen John Galt's vision, give up everything and disappear, because the life they have lived is no longer acceptable to them.

The completed manuscript was now at Random House. Ayn had been open and receptive to Archie Ogden's editorial suggestions in *The Fountainhead* and had nothing but praise for his skill. She was not, however, receptive to editorial suggestions from Hiram Haydn. She now regarded herself as a master of her craft who did not need the services of an editor. And, in contrast to Ogden, who had always been keenly sensitive to her literary intentions and who had helped her realize them more effectively, Haydn displayed no comparable grasp of Ayn's work, her literary premises, or her goals. She found most of his suggestions dissonant if not offensive.

When Hiram could not prevail on her to shorten Galt's speech, Cerf promised to try. But when Ayn countered Cerf's request for cuts with the question, "Would you cut the Bible?" he knew to give up. Sometime later he said to me, "Ayn can be maddening, but I think that's part of what I love about her. She stands up for what she thinks is right." I grinned at Bennett and answered, "Besides, the speech is barely long enough."

I was joking, and at the same time I meant it. The speech *was* too long. But it fit the scale of the book. To me, it was a marvel of economy. Even today, I would argue that the speech, like the book, needs to be seen and understood in its own context, in its own terms, and not judged by an outside standard that may be thoroughly inappropriate.

Publication day was scheduled for October of that year. Barbara and I decided to give Ayn a surprise party hosted by the entire Collective for all the key people involved with her professional life: the Cerfs, the Klopfers, the Haydns, the Collinses, and the Ogdens. We held the event at the Plaza Hotel in a private dining room. Frank did the floral decorations.

The invitations informed the guests that Ayn was not to be told about the party. Ayn assumed that Frank was taking her to an elegant restaurant for a private celebration.

When Frank led her into the suite where all the guests had assembled, Ayn froze. Then she declared in a chilly voice, glancing reproachfully at Barbara and me, "I do *not* like surprises." My spirits crashed. Then I told myself that I should have expected it; Ayn could not bear to be out of control, least of all in any matter pertaining to her career. She had anticipated a different kind of evening. Now she had to adapt her expectations, and adaptations of this kind did not come easily to her.

Everyone struggled to cheer her up, and the man who succeeded best was Bennett. She was delighted by the cigarettes he had had especially made; they were stamped with a bright gold dollar sign (the strikers in *Atlas* smoked such cigarettes), and each package bore the Random House trademark and the words, "Who is John Galt? They know at Random House." She seemed genuinely pleased when the guests toasted her and talked about the importance of her work and their devotion to her as a person. Only Barbara and I could know how many times in the months and years ahead Ayn would refer to this evening chastisingly, with an appalling lack of benevolence and grace, for our daring to take any action involving her without her say-so.

Although the evening became progressively more festive as Ayn brightened up, I have no happy memories of the occasion; what I recall chiefly are Ayn's later scoldings. "The Collective," she said, "might not have known better. But Barbara and you should have—and you, above all."

On a happier note, in the weeks that followed, I loved being consulted by Ayn on the jacket material for *Atlas*, which she herself had written and which I thought superb. Phyllis Cerf, Bennett's wife, took the photograph that was to appear on the back of the jacket. Ayn gave Barbara and me a copy of this picture, in which she adapts a line from Galt's speech and parenthetically calls us her "fellow winners."

In Barbara's copy of *Atlas*, Ayn complimented her for all their shared "values." With a smile of irresistible charm, Ayn asked us, "Do I have to explain what I mean by 'all' in that sentence?" With a smile of equally irresistible love, Barbara responded, "No, Ayn, you don't."

In my copy, Ayn noted dates of importance, such as the day we met and the day of the car ride from Toronto to New York: "To Nathan—for what you were at fourteen—for what you were on March 2, 1950—for what you were on September 13, 1954—for what you are now—and forever—Ayn."

Not long after the novel's publication, a journalist who was interviewing Ayn asked her what she meant when she wrote of me as her "intellectual heir." Ayn replied, "It means Mr. Branden is the most consistent embodiment of what I write about, that he understands my philosophy better than anyone, and that he represents the next generation who will carry my work further." It was not particularly easy to look poised and nonchalant at that moment; the truth is, I felt foolish. And yet, I wanted desperately to be worthy of Ayn's confidence.

Ayn was not pleased with Random House's ads; she had already had her first quarrel with Bennett because of them, and she asked me to accompany her to a meeting with him. She liked my idea, which was to use the magnificent portrait of Frank I had admired on the night of our first meeting and to have the caption "This is John Galt—who said he would stop the motor of the world—*and did*. Meet him in *Atlas Shrugged*." The stylization of the painting projected a strength that would work perfectly. The final wording of this caption was both Ayn's and mine—and Bennett loved the whole concept.

One evening in early fall, Ayn, Frank, Barbara, and I went for a drive in the country to dine at a favorite restaurant. Ayn was in especially high spirits. In contrast, I was feeling uneasy. I was preoccupied with my perception of the culture at that time and my sense that *Atlas* was so profoundly radical in its basic vision and so contrary to the dominant beliefs of our age that it was inevitably going to meet with terrible hostility—more terrible than even Ayn was anticipating.

Slowly, tentatively, without knowing how much to say or how to say it, I voiced some of my concern aloud, not too clearly. Ayn startled me with her anger and impatience—not at me, exactly, but at my line of thought. "I don't want to hear about 'premonitions,'" she said. "If you can't articulate your ideas more concretely, you'd better be silent. Because if I don't break through this time—if the book doesn't get the understanding it deserves from *someone*—I mean, from some serious *minds,* not just fans—then I'm finished. Finished with this society and this century. I'll go totally on strike. You've got good instincts about the culture. You know how to read it. Is that what you're forecasting I'm going to have to do?" I assured her that I was only trying to consider every possibility. A few minutes later, she was euphoric and lighthearted again. I was not.

The Random House offices were then on Madison Avenue and Fifty-First Street. They occupied one wing of a large brownstone palazzo, the rest of which was occupied by the headquarters of the Archdiocese of New York. Important new books were usually featured in the Madison Avenue window. I was eager for the day when I might see *Atlas Shrugged* there, and one evening, a week before the publication date of October 10, 1957, Ayn, Frank, Barbara, and I drove to the publishing house to see if the novel were on display. It was—a single copy, brightly illuminated, no other author's books around it. We stood there, grinning happily. Then Barbara burst out with a statement that would long endear her to Ayn, "That's us!"

Ayn laughed, the gay, carefree laugh of a young girl, a laugh of simple delight. I would never hear that laugh from her again.

11

A FEW MONTHS BEFORE the publication of *Atlas,* Bennett Cerf invited Ayn to speak at a Random House sales conference. Everyone's expectations for the book were high, and the room was alive with excitement. A salesman asked her, jokingly, if she could summarize her philosophy while standing on one foot. This was the kind of challenge to which Ayn responded with glee. She lifted one foot in the air and answered, "Metaphysics—objective reality; epistemology—reason; ethics—self-interest; politics—capitalism." She was proud of the instant rapport she could establish in such situations. The salesmen applauded her.

When Ayn recounted the incident, I thought how exciting it was that something as explosive as *Atlas Shrugged* should be involved with a sales conference and all the other routine business of publishing. I enjoyed the sense of connection to "ordinary reality."

I did not think it strange that Ayn should choose to present to the world a new philosophical vision by means of a novel. She had said to me, "All of the world's major religions have, in effect, their own mythology—tales, parables, stories of various kinds that are intended to dramatize and illustrate abstract values and precepts. Although that is not how the novel started out in my mind, that is what it developed into—a mythology that concretizes, by means of the actions of its characters, the meaning of my philosophy."

To Barbara and me she said, "I know I am challenging the cultural tradition of two and a half thousand years." She said it to the whole Collective and to Bennett Cerf and Donald Klopfer. She warned them that they should not expect—should not count on—any favorable reviews. I do not think they fully believed her; I do not think she fully believed it herself.

The *New York Times* assigned the review of *Atlas Shrugged* to Granville Hicks, an ex-member of the Communist Party and an ex-apologist for Stalinism. He was the same editor who, years earlier at Macmillan, had opposed the publication of *We the Living*.

The article appeared in the October 13 issue of the Sunday *Book Review*. When I saw Hicks's name, I was shocked. I thought that such a choice was the depth of irrationality and injustice; I didn't yet know how typical this was of the *Times*. Few reviewers feel morally obliged to communicate clearly what a book is about before proceeding to evaluate it. I didn't know that at the time, either.

"This gargantuan book," wrote Hicks, "comes among us as a demonstrative rather than as a literary work. . . . Not in any literary sense a serious novel . . . this book is written out of hate." The review attacked the novel on every possible level. I recall, as clearly as if it were ten minutes ago, my stunned inability to grasp how anyone, even a Granville Hicks, could permit himself such dishonesty and such a lack of intellectual scruples.

Ayn appeared almost indifferent to the review. I had the impression she barely read it. When she saw shock and anguish in Barbara's eyes, she said, gently, "Darling, what would you expect from a collectivist? You mustn't let such things hurt you. Worse is ahead."

She was right in her prediction. "Galt is really arguing for a dictatorship," declared Robert R. Kirsch in the *Los Angeles Times*. "The destruction of the weak to the advantage of the strong is applauded," wrote Patricia Donegan in the *Commonweal*. The philosophy advocated in *Atlas Shrugged,* said a reviewer in another New York newspaper, "makes well-poisoning seem like one of the kindlier arts." A few writers thought this line especially clever, because it began appearing, without acknowledgment, in other reviews.

Although Ayn read very few of these pieces, I made myself read every one of them, telling myself, "This is the world in which you are living. Learn to understand it. Fully face the nature of the battle you have to fight."

"Execrable claptrap," I read in one review. "Crackbrained ratiocination," I read in another. "Terrible writing," I read in a third.

"Of course political liberals and left-wing intellectuals will hate the book," Ayn told us many times, "but wait. The worst attacks will come from the religionists." Again she was right. Of all the hostile reviews I saw, none quite matched the ferocity of Whittaker Chambers's in William Buckley's conservative magazine, the *National Review*.

Ayn had met Buckley sometime earlier; he had invited her to tea. With characteristic bluntness, she had asked this practicing Catholic, "Tell me, how can an intelligent young man like you believe in God?" Later, when she reported to Barbara and me on this meeting, she summed Buckley up as follows: "Clever, but an intellectual lightweight. An opportunist. Very 'social'; not genuinely interested in ideas. And potentially dangerous if he acquires an influence, because he tells people that the foundation of capitalism is religious faith, which implies that reason and science are on the side of the collectivists."

Whittaker Chambers was a former confessed communist spy turned religionist. To expect him to review with integrity a book whose values were the antithesis of his own in every essential respect was like asking him to step outside of his own soul—like asking Satan to review the Bible. He accused the novel of advocating crude materialism and dictatorship; he implicitly equated its ideas with Nazism. "The Dollar Sign," he wrote, "is not merely provocative. . . . It is meant to seal the fact that mankind is ready to submit abjectly to an elite of technocrats. . . . From almost any page of *Atlas Shrugged*, a voice can be heard, from painful necessity, commanding: 'To a gas chamber—go!'"

I do not know if Ayn ever read the review in its entirety; she said she did not. Her voice was like ice when she told the Collective, "If Buckley's goal is to establish himself publicly as the champion of capitalism—God help the country!—then I am the one person he and his gang have to try to discredit and destroy."

Ayn remained typically indifferent to Chambers. It was Buckley whom she condemned, because he portrayed himself publicly as a champion of capitalism and freedom. She knew he was not, pointing out that he merely favored different political controls from his liberal adversaries. He favored censorship, for one thing, to protect "public morality," and military conscription, for another. "He's a champion of property but not of human life," she said with disgust. Soon her disdain for him became widely known; she would not sit on any platform with him and would not remain seated at any social or political event where he stood up to speak.

I recall visiting Ayn a year or two after the publication of Chambers's review and seeing a postcard Buckley had written her from a New York restaurant, wanting to know why they could not be friends. Ayn speculated that he must have been drunk when he wrote it. On another occasion, I was present when he telephoned her, teasing her about her animosity and suggesting that they "make up." Again she commented, "He sounded as if he'd been drinking."

There were many enthusiastic reviews of *Atlas Shrugged*, but most of these appeared in publications outside New York City. However, there were two exceptions. In the *Mirror*, Ruth Alexander wrote, "Ayn Rand is destined to rank in history as the outstanding novelist and profound philosopher of the twentieth century." In the *Herald Tribune*, John Chamberlain wrote a long and passionately complimentary review in which he praised *Atlas* as an artistic masterpiece with a magnificently uplifting vision; only in the concluding paragraph did he express dissatisfaction that Ayn had chosen to "re-write" the Sermon on the Mount, that is, to challenge Christian morality. Although she appreciated the practical value of his review, in terms of selling books, his remark about the Sermon on the Mount effectively destroyed any personal meaning his praise could have for her. Also, she was angry that Chamberlain referred to the novel as an allegory. "My characters are *not* symbols," she declared. As I reflected on the novel later, her reaction puzzled me, because even though her characters are not symbols literarily, neither can they be taken as fully realistic. In retrospect, I am convinced that the book can best be appreciated as a unique blend of the romantic, the realistic, and the allegorical and that Chamberlain was more right than wrong in this regard.

Reviews that came in from around the country often hailed the book's literary quality. Ayn was praised as a great stylist, a master of plot construction, an expert at orchestrating ideas, action, and suspense. The book's themes were described as "challenging," "daring," "exciting," "provocative," "stimulating," and "revolutionary."

However, the attacks significantly outnumbered the raves. The negative reviews echoed the same kind of ferocious animosity I had seen in the New York publications, sometimes using the same language. It was as if there were an invisible network, and every wire was transmitting the same message: "Stop Ayn Rand. Say whatever is necessary to discredit her."

I had foreseen disagreement; I had not foreseen the violence of the hostility, the quality of enraged hysteria. I especially had not foreseen the widespread misrepresentation of Ayn's ideas. To me, her opponents were debating with straw men. They equated her philosophy with that of Herbert Spencer or Nietzsche or Spinoza or Hobbes, thereby revealing their philosophical illiteracy. What they did not do was identify accurately and then challenge the ideas for which Ayn in fact stood. No one wrote, "Ayn Rand holds that man must choose his values and actions by reason; that the individual has a right to exist for his own sake, neither sacrificing self to others nor others to self; that no one has the right to seek values from others by physical force or impose ideas on others by physical force; and she considers such ideas wrong, evil, and socially dangerous."

I was prepared to hear them say, "In advocating freedom and individual rights, Ayn Rand goes too far." Nothing could have prepared me for the accusation that she was advocating dictatorship—nothing I had previously read or seen, nothing Ayn had warned me of, nothing in my darkest prepublication premonitions.

Now is not the time to feel, I told myself, fighting a sense of being engulfed in madness. Now is the time to try to understand.

Ayn acted equally indifferent to praise and criticism. The gaiety had largely disappeared from her manner, and she conveyed the stony calm of someone in a fortress who is settling in for a long siege. "It's earlier than you think," she said to all of us. "Historically speaking, even earlier than I had imagined. It's not the attacks that are depressing—I expected that. It's the absence of any good mind with a significant reputation who has come forward to say publicly what *Atlas* actually is. Someone with the power to make himself heard. I had counted on *some* kind of better understanding."

The advance sales for the book had been high. Then, presumably in response to the negative reviews, sales began to drop. But as more and more readers began to share their own reactions, sales began to climb and went on climbing; the novel stayed near the top of the *New York Times* best-seller list for a long time. Later, when it was obvious that the book was on its way to becoming a classic and that nothing and no one was going to stop it, Bennett Cerf remarked, "In all my years of publishing, I've never seen anything like it. To break through against such enormous opposition!"

Nonetheless, I saw a change in Bennett's attitude. It was obvious that he himself had been affected by the countless denunciations—not only in books and articles but also at dinner and cocktail parties, in literary circles, in every corner of the world in which he moved. He faced rebukes from friends and associates for having published *Atlas*. He spoke less and less of being personally influenced by the book's ideas; he went out of his way to stress his disagreements.

I was not surprised. I remembered a conversation he and I had had in which he had said to me, "I think Ayn is right about a lot of things. Her respect for personal achievement, for one. Her opposition to the welfare state, or much of it, for another. But one mustn't say that. You have to throw welfare programs at people—like throwing meat to a pack of wolves—even if the programs don't accomplish their alleged purpose and even if they're morally wrong."

"Why?" I asked.

Bennett leaned forward and whispered in the manner of sharing a confidence, "Because otherwise they'll kill you. The masses. They hate intelligence. They're envious of ability. They resent wealth. You've got to throw them something so they'll let us live."

I answered, "It looks like we respect human beings more than you do." This was not a man, I knew in that moment, who was likely to weather the storm that was coming.

We had all thought that the success of *The Fountainhead* had sufficiently established Ayn so that *Atlas Shrugged* would be recognized and appreciated more readily, in spite of the inevitable attacks. "We were wrong," said Ayn. "It's *The Fountainhead* all over again. *Atlas* will have to make its way by word of mouth, against every kind of public opposition. Only I'm more well known now, so it may happen faster."

Today, both books have sold many millions of copies, and they continue to sell actively in hardcover and paperback. Combined sales of all her titles have topped twenty million.

Not long after *Atlas's* publication, Ayn appeared on Mike Wallace's television show, *Night Beat*. Wallace asked her how she felt about the torrent of attacks against her. She answered by citing her favorite poem, Rudyard Kipling's "If": "'If you can bear to hear the truth you've spoken twisted by knaves to make a trap for fools . . .'" Then she said, "I can bear it. It's not fools that I seek to address." The station received a great number of wildly enthusiastic calls and letters, as would always happen when she appeared on television.

She and Mike Wallace became friends. Like Bennett Cerf, Wallace seemed to be liberal. Nonetheless, Ayn found him both intelligent and courageous; she referred to him as a prime example of why she often found liberals easier to talk to than conservatives. "One can *reason* with Mike," she said. Because of his fascination with her ideas, notwithstanding many disagreements, she labeled him, jokingly, "an Objectivist fellow traveler." I liked Mike, as I liked Bennett, but I was more cautious than Ayn, feeling fiercely protective of her; I knew that neither of these men, in the ultimate sense, was an ally. "And in a war," I thought, "that is the standard by which one judges people."

What Ayn wanted most of all was to find *minds*—men and women of the kind she wrote about. She had imagined, when she sent *Atlas Shrugged* out into the world, that she would find them. In a twist on George Washington's famous statement, "Let us raise a standard to which the wise and honest can repair," she said, "I have raised a standard, but the wise and honest have not repaired to it." She appreciated, in a perfunctory sort of way, the praise *Atlas* received, and she was happy about the book's sales, but on a deeper level she was bitterly disappointed. She was mainly unimpressed by the intellectual caliber of those who wrote about her favorably. She had expected to receive from someone in the culture—someone who was a public figure and who had an influence—a more profound kind of understanding.

We in the Collective were, in effect, "family," insiders who had been brought up by her. What she longed for now was an outsider, someone she had not educated, a contemporary with eyes that could see and a voice that could speak. No such person appeared.

"How is Ayn taking the reception of *Atlas?*" the various Collective members would ask me, and I would answer, "It's tough. Very tough." I would try to convey Ayn's point of view to them. "Isn't she happy about the sales?" they would say, and I would respond, "Sure. But more is involved than sales. She wants something more personal." They talked about their own disappointment and bewilderment only with one another. With Ayn, they felt obliged to put on an air of detachment and confidence, not to pass to her the burden of whatever hurt they might be experiencing.

"How is the Collective taking the reception of *Atlas?*" Ayn would ask me. I would shrug and say, "Well, you know. Pretty stunned, I guess." She would smile sadly and say, "I can't help them. Not this time. Not with this. Can I leave it to you to teach them the proper philosophical perspective?" I assured her that she could. On many occasions, she did lecture them on the state of the culture in an effort to lift their spirits and, no doubt, her own.

Only with Barbara could I be fully open about my own pain, as she could about hers. "What kind of world is this?" I would say. And with her mouth pulled tight in her own quiet anguish, she would nod her head knowingly, and sometimes we would embrace each other in mutual support and comfort. "It's our turn now," I said to her. "Ayn has done enough. She's entitled to rest. It's we who have to carry the work forward." We stood in the midst of a battlefield, bonded together more powerfully than ever by a shared cause, a shared vision, and a shared suffering. I thought that Barbara and I might yet create a true marriage—a marriage of fellow warriors. Some dreams take a long time to die.

In January 1958, a few months after the publication of *Atlas Shrugged,* I initiated a lecture course titled "Basic Principles of Objectivism," which was a systematic presentation of Ayn's philosophy, including aspects she had not covered in her writings, as well as material from my work in psychology. "I hope you won't be hurt," Ayn said to me.

I knew nothing about the business of offering public lectures and had asked Ayn if she could put me in contact with someone who might have practical advice to offer. Ayn spoke to a few people, but when they heard that a young, unknown psychologist without a university affiliation was proposing to offer lectures on philosophy in a hotel meeting room, the consensus was that the venture was inherently impractical, and they had no counsel to provide. Ayn's own skepticism and lack of enthusiasm grew as well, especially during her dark moods, which were occurring more and more frequently, in spite of the sales of *Atlas*.

I did not know whether I would succeed or fail. I knew only that I had to try—not simply because Ayn's philosophy was so important to me and because I wished to disseminate it but also because I felt a need to *do something* in the face of the animosity surrounding us. The lecture course gave me an action outlet, so I did not have to feel passive and helpless. My motive was selfish—it was *my* battle for *my* ideas.

I asked her to let me borrow all the "intelligent" letters from fans within a hundred-mile radius of New York in order to prepare a mailing list. Barbara did the typing, and I sent a letter to each of these people inviting them to take the course. There would be twenty lectures given once a week for a total of seventy dollars. I rented a room in the Sheraton-Russell Hotel on Park Avenue and Thirty-Seventh Street, two blocks from where I lived. My initial capital outlay was for stationery, stamps, and the rent on the meeting room. Ayn had no financial participation in the venture then or later; it was entirely my own project. However, she agreed to join me for the question period at the conclusion of each lecture, and her presence was enormously helpful.

In the winter and spring of 1958, when the course was first given, I had 28 students. When I offered it again that fall, 45 students attended. When I offered it a third time in February 1959, the number of students jumped to 65—and thereafter kept on climbing, eventually leveling off at about 160 per class. The course was given twice a year, and growth was stimulated by students' enthusiastic word of mouth and by the small announcements I began running in New York newspapers, chiefly the *Times*. This last was Barbara's idea, and it proved to be a brilliant one.

I originated the project under the name Nathaniel Branden Lectures; later, I incorporated as Nathaniel Branden Institute. The reason for this choice of name, rather than, say, the Objectivist Institute, was to establish a certain public distance between Ayn and myself—to communicate that as a business, I was operating entirely on my own, although I had Ayn's intellectual approval.

One of the most inspiring aspects of the project was the high intellectual caliber of many of the students—from a sixty-year-old professor of physics to a twenty-seven-year-old Ph.D. in economics to a precocious

Branden lecturing on Objectivism, age 34, 1964

sixteen-year-old girl. Students came from every sort of background and profession: businessmen, housewives, lawyers, secretaries, college students, physicians, scientists, stockbrokers, nurses, teachers, psychiatrists, and engineers. A significant number of the men and women instrumental in founding the Libertarian Party, which is the country's third largest political party today, took one or more courses at Nathaniel Branden Institute. Students soon demanded additional programs, and I next created a course titled "A Critical Analysis of Contemporary Psychology." I invited the other members of our group to join me in offering lectures. Barbara gave a course titled "Basic Principles of Efficient Thinking." It was she who originated the concept of psychoepistemology as it was to be used in Objectivist writings and lectures, and this course grew out of her reflections on the subject. Leonard offered "A Critical History of Philosophy," Mary Ann gave "The Aesthetics of the Visual Arts," and Alan Greenspan taught "The Economics of a Free Society." In later years, other courses were added, including ones in which I presented my evolving psychological theories.

In the beginning, all I was aware of doing was offering a structured, nonfictional presentation of Ayn's ideas, into which I had incorporated some of my own. I did not know that I was in the process of launching a philosophical movement.

Later, when Ayn pointed out what I had accomplished, I protested, saying that it was her novels that had launched the movement. "No," she answered. "My novels created readers. Nathaniel Branden Institute created the movement. Until NBI, there was no public focus for my ideas— no place where people could study my philosophy systematically, meet one another, form groups, and coordinate efforts to spread the ideas further. All that began with your lectures. You made the name Objectivism famous."

By the fall of 1958, it was apparent that Ayn was sinking into a deep and tenacious depression. Not the sales of her novel or the torrent of fan mail or any of the interesting people we were meeting seemed to cheer her for more than a few hours or evoke in her any desire to write again. The thought of another project—*any* other project—exhausted her. Every day, she sat long hours at her desk playing solitaire, the game becoming a metaphor for her sense of her position in the world. She did not read. She left her correspondence largely unanswered. Her body ached with numerous tension pains. She had written a novel about a man who stops the motor of the world; now it was as if her motor had stopped.

She saw herself as trapped in a swamp of mediocrity, malice, and cowardice. She had found admirers but no champions. She saw herself lied about, misrepresented, dismissed, or trivialized, while thinkers and writers she regarded as third-raters were hailed as "serious," "significant," "profound." She gave interviews to journalists who came earnestly, respectfully, and benevolently, or so it seemed, and then went off to write a hash that twisted and distorted every thought she had tried to convey. She heard herself labeled a "fascist" by totalitarian utopians and authoritarian liberals, because of her ferocious opposition to collectivism. She heard herself praised by enthusiasts whose understanding of her work was often superficial, off-center, and even frivolous. She felt, she complained, like an adult sentenced to live in a world of children, some of whom might be "nice" but who were children nonetheless.

I did not grasp the severity of her state, at first. I thought she was experiencing a delayed letdown after thirteen years of high emotional intensity while writing *Atlas* full-time. Ordinary living could hardly compete. In many of our discussions, from the summer of 1958 and for the next two years, she would begin to cry while describing her perception of the world and her own place in it, and she confided that she cried almost every day. This struck me as shockingly out of character, and I realized that I had underestimated the depth of Ayn's struggle, with which I felt enormous and painful empathy.

We had long conversations on the telephone every day. I visited her two or three evenings a week, sometimes alone, sometimes with Barbara, so we could discuss how we might better interpret the events that were such blows to Ayn's ambition, energy, and enthusiasm. These sessions typically lasted until five or six in the morning.

Her suffering was devastating to watch. I knew that what I needed to project most, in her presence, was calm, serenity, and my own belief that answers could and would be found. It was hard at times to fight my own feelings of despair. My tendency toward emotional repression grew much worse during this period.

The Collective was hit badly. "How is it possible," they would ask on Saturday evenings, "that we can be accused of advocating the complete opposite, politically, of what we stand for?"

"It's an aberration that will pass," I would say, simultaneously trying to bring sanity to my friends and to fill Ayn with hope. "Look at our historical and social context. This country was born in rebellion against European aristocracy, so there's a tradition of animosity toward anything that even remotely sounds like elitism. Yet Jefferson himself spoke of

America as a home for a 'natural aristocracy'—not the aristocracy of inherited privilege but an aristocracy of ability—and of course *Atlas* supports that idea. After all, some individuals achieve more, create more, and contribute more than others. All men are equal before the law, or should be, but all men are *not* equal in intelligence, talent, and productiveness. But we're living in a century when this fact is not supposed to be acknowledged. We're living in the midst of a tidal wave of egalitarianism, and God help someone who says, for instance, that Thomas Edison is in any sense superior to the village idiot. *Atlas* says the distinction between the earned and the unearned, and between the competent and the incompetent, is a difference worth respecting, and the enemy says, 'How cruel, how undemocratic, how antisocial!' And then, finally, don't forget how hard the Left has worked to sell the idea that anyone opposed to socialism or communism must be a fascist—an idea which the liberals have bought totally, adapting it to read, 'Anyone opposed to the welfare state is a fascist.'"

"But Ayn," someone in the Collective would protest, "is the most ferocious opponent of fascism—and every other kind of statism—in history. *Can't people read?*"

"Never mind that," Ayn would interject. "The Left doesn't care to know what I have said; they're consciously dishonest. The question is, What of the people I am defending, the men of ability? Where are they? Why don't they come forward? Why don't they speak up?"

I would shrug and grow silent, because to these questions I had no answer.

I began to hear a statement from Ayn that I would hear again and again over the years. "You are my lifeline to reality. Without you, I would not know how to exist in this world." It did not occur to me in the beginning that this statement could become a burden of steadily increasing weight because of the responsibility it entailed. Hearing it then, I felt only pride and pain—pride that I was able to give so much to Ayn, and pain that it should be needed.

Sometimes I would say to Ayn, "Everything negative you say about the world is true. And yet, to be honest with you, there are times when I think, 'You wrote *Atlas Shrugged*. And in the face of that fact, how can anything else be important? How can any pain get to you? How can it matter?'" And Ayn would smile sadly and answer, "Sometimes I tell myself that, too. I tell myself that's the way I should feel. That's how I imagine Galt would feel. If I am making a mistake, if there is something I'm not seeing, I don't know what it is. That's why I drive you crazy, night after night, looking for answers. I'm not passive; I'm not just resigning myself like the sort of people I despise. I don't stop thinking. Thinking is all I do."

She complained that she had lost all sense of whom she was addressing when she wrote, "The state of the culture is far worse than I imagined." She said that she could not fight lice, could not fight when all she felt for the adversary was contempt. "So what is the sense of continuing to write? For whom?" She said that she was not an altruist, that she did not work merely to serve others, and that she had no interest in having monuments erected in her honor after she was dead. "I want some meaningful reward for my work now."

When I asked if the writing itself were not a reward, she smiled bitterly and replied, "It used to be. When I was younger. But with *Atlas Shrugged,* I've said what I wanted to say and needed to say. There's no reason to say or do more. Not without something coming back to me that I didn't generate."

On one occasion I said, "Look, I loved *The Fountainhead,* but it never would have occurred to me that you needed anything from me, that I would have anything to offer you. Right now, there are good people reading *Atlas* who lead private lives of their own, who wouldn't think of trying to contact you, who wouldn't think there's anything they ought to be doing except reading you, appreciating you, talking about your work in their own circle—which they're obviously doing, because it's got to be word of mouth that is responsible for the terrific sales of the book." And Ayn would answer, "True. Those people are not the problem. I appreciate them. The problem is that not one first-class brain has stood up in public to defend me—to give me some sense that there's a human race out there and that the struggle is worth it."

That was part of the truth but not all of it. The darker, and now dominant, side of her emotional life had been present long before the publication of *Atlas.* Certainly, she had always felt profoundly alone. Perhaps it was the penalty of genius, I told myself, thinking of all the great minds in history who had been tortured by bouts of depression. Perhaps the real root of her anguish is the simple fact that one gets tired of being able to see farther and more clearly than anyone else. 'Genius means isolation,' I thought. But if this were true, what could I possibly say that would be helpful?

The bitterness that had always been part of her makeup was becoming more pronounced. She was impatient, irritable, angry, and quick to condemn—Frank, me, Barbara, Leonard, anyone in the Collective who said or did anything even slightly ambiguous or questionable. If some of Joan's paintings were dark or grim (I no longer can say whether they actually were or not), Ayn would wonder aloud about Joan's "malevolent sense of life." If Allan Blumenthal expressed enjoyment in listening to Beethoven or Mozart, both of whom Ayn disliked, she would say (although not to him directly, because musical standards could not yet be "proven"), "That's why there will always be a wall between us. Our souls are essentially different." If Alan Greenspan mentioned a social event he had attended, Ayn would speculate about his fundamental seriousness or lack of it: "Do you think Alan might basically be a social climber?" If Leonard were too friendly to one of his professors or insufficiently outspoken on Ayn's behalf, he more than once had to face Ayn's accusation of treason: "If I can't count on you to recognize the enemy, who can I count on?" Sometimes I defended the Collective against Ayn, often I joined her.

Ayn vacillated constantly. She could be withdrawn and unfriendly toward one or another of them at one meeting, then warm and affectionate at the next. Thoroughly caught up in Ayn's emotional world, I often manifested the same vacillation, as my feelings of isolation continued to deepen.

During this period, Frank had never seemed so helpless. He looked on in mute despair, participating in Ayn's suffering, the gaunt planes of his face occasionally broken by flashes of angry indignation on her behalf. Much of the time, he disappeared into the private world of his painting, where not even Ayn could reach him. Once, when I asked him how he felt about the reception of *Atlas,* he answered bitterly, "People are swine."

"Frank," I said urgently, "you mustn't abandon Ayn now."

"Thank God she has you," he answered.

I blamed the world for being irrational. I blamed myself for not knowing how to bring Ayn back to life. I blamed the Collective for not supporting Ayn's work more creatively and aggressively. The one person I did not blame was Ayn. If her reactions were excessive at times, if she could even be cruel, didn't she deserve our understanding and compassion? I did not want to hear that anyone's feelings had been hurt by Ayn. As I saw it then, no one else's feelings mattered, including my own. Only hers did.

I communicated this viewpoint to our friends. I was Ayn's bodyguard, her protector and defender. I could make myself as ruthlessly implacable as she. I had always sought to participate in her inner world, to join with her intellectually and spiritually. Now I chose to enter the dark perspective that was swallowing her; I would follow her anywhere to maintain our connection. I, too, became impatient, irritable, and harsh in my judgments, leaving behind more and more of my humanity while telling myself that this was what it meant to live one's idealism in the world. To some extent, Barbara did the same. I saw this and approved. Barbara often tempered her severity with some measure of warmth; paradoxically, I approved of that, too.

Ayn's depression persisted relentlessly. "I'm ashamed of myself for crying so much," Ayn said one evening. "The Collective would be shocked if they knew. You don't tell them, do you?" I told her I did not. "Galt would handle all this differently. Somehow, he would be more untouched by it. More realistic. But I don't know how or in what way. I would hate for him to see me like this. I would feel unworthy, as if I had let him down." I was used to hearing her discuss Galt as if he were a real person; all of us did that. I said, "I look at it differently. If I were knocked down and hurt badly by something that had happened to me, so that I was crying a lot or devastated or whatever, I think I would say, 'All right, look at me. I'm in a bad way. So what? In a little while, I'll pick myself up again. Meanwhile, this is reality. Why pretend it isn't?'" She chuckled unhappily. "You're quoting my own philosophy back to me. Only, for once, I can't seem to apply it."

Meanwhile, the response to the lecture courses was growing. We were now receiving inquiries from all over the country, as well as from Canada, Europe, India, and Australia. An enormous demand was mounting for our courses and for more information about Objectivism.

"This is the one bright spot in my life," Ayn said, "so far as my view of the culture is concerned. I could not have imagined this. Ideas *do* matter to some people. I see it in your students. From week to week, they're changing. Because of your lectures, all of them are becoming better human beings."

She could extravagantly praise my students one moment, then be furiously impatient with them the next. In the question periods following my lectures, she often became angry with any question she felt should not have been asked, perhaps because it had been answered in *Atlas Shrugged* or perhaps because she believed that any honest person would figure it out for himself. Most of our students seemed to love her, but sometimes she could be terrifying.

Once, a man with a thick Hungarian accent began his question, "In his speech, Galt contends that . . ." He never got any further because Ayn exploded. "Galt does not *contend*," she shouted. "If you have read *Atlas Shrugged,* if you profess to be an admirer of mine, then you should know that Galt does not 'strive,' 'debate,' 'argue,' or 'contend.'" The man looked stricken. He pleaded, "But Miss Rand, all I meant was . . ." Ayn thundered back at him, "If you wish to speak to me, first learn to remember to whom and about what you are speaking!" Ayn was obsessed with clarity and precision in speaking and writing. It was a passion I generally shared. Certainly, we trained the Collective to achieve high standards in this regard. But I did not feel sympathy for the passion in this instance; I thought it totally misapplied. The man sank back into his chair, embarrassed and defeated. I felt concerned for him, appalled by Ayn, and annoyed with myself for not speaking up on the spot. Later, when I was alone with Ayn, I pointed out that the man had a foreign accent and probably was not aware of the nuances contained in the word *contend.* "I never thought of that," Ayn replied with a look of astonished, childlike innocence. I noticed, sadly, that the man never came back. I can still see the expression of hurt and shock on his face.

There were, of course, question-and-answer sessions when Ayn was warm, friendly, benevolent, and charming. Once, when a student apologized for the naïveté of some question, she told him encouragingly, "There are no stupid questions, only stupid answers." Yet the rage was always there, lingering in the background of her consciousness, and it could be activated anytime she felt that a student had brought the perspective of "the world" into the lecture room by asking a question that hinted too loudly at alien influences. Sometimes, Ayn would apologize to me later for her outbursts. "I'm not promising it won't happen again," she always added.

Mostly, the students idolized her. They were thrilled by the opportunity to have such direct access to her. If she occasionally lost her temper, most of them seemed to think, What of it? As one former NBI student put it, when I interviewed him two decades later, "Look how much she had to offer! Look how much I was learning! If she got a little berserk now and again, so what?" The students were participants in a marvelous intellectual adventure. For one evening a week, they were in a world of unlimited possibilities. They were acutely conscious of what she gave them.

She offered them a comprehensive and intelligible view of human existence. She offered them a frame of reference by which they could understand the society around them. She was not only a superb dramatist who created vivid and inspiring heroes and heroines but also a philosophical system builder—during a century when system builders were out of fashion and almost impossible to find. She provided students with a vision of what life on this planet is essentially about. She offered a unique vision of human nature and of human relationships. And today, reflecting back on those years, I see clearly that what matters is not whether her vision was correct in all respects—I know now that it wasn't—but that she *had* a

Rand portrait, 1957

vision. It was a highly developed one that promised comprehensiveness, intelligibility, and clarity. It provided answers to some of the most important questions of life. And human beings long for that; I did, and our students did.

We need to feel that we understand the world in which we live. We need to make sense out of our experience. We need some persuasive portrait of who we are as human beings and what our lives are or should be about. In short, we need a philosophical vision of reality. I knew that twentieth-century philosophy had almost totally abandoned the responsibility of offering such a vision or addressing itself to the kind of questions men and women struggle with in the course of their existence. Twentieth-century philosophers typically scorn system builders. The problems to which they address themselves grow smaller and smaller and increasingly remote from human experience. In their journals and at their conventions, they explicitly acknowledge that they have nothing of practical value to offer anyone. And during the past few centuries, orthodox religion has lost more and more of its hold over people's minds and lives. It has been perceived as having diminishing relevance. Its demise as a cultural force began with the Renaissance, and it has been waning ever since.

Yet the need for answers has not vanished. The need for values by which to guide our lives, I knew, was as urgent as ever. The world around us seemed to be growing more and more confusing—and threatening. The need to comprehend cried out in desperation. This was the need to which Ayn was speaking.

She had an extraordinary vision to offer, a radiantly rational one, I believed then. Today I am convinced there are errors in that vision, elements that need to be changed, eliminated, modified, added, or amplified. But I am still convinced there is much in that vision that will stand.

We did not tell our students that the mind is impotent. We did not tell them that they were rotten or powerless. We did not tell them that life is futile or that they were doomed or that existence is meaningless. We told them just the opposite. We told them that their main problem was that they had not learned to understand the nature of their power—therefore, of their own possibilities. We told them that their mind was and could be efficacious, that they *were* competent to understand, that genuine knowledge was attainable, and that achievement and happiness were possible. We told them that life was not about dread, defeat, and anguish but about struggle, triumph, and exaltation.

This message ran counter to the dominant religious and philosophical teachings to which most of them were exposed. No less important, it ran counter to the teachings of most of their parents, who said, "So who's happy?" and "Pride goeth before a fall" and "Adventure is for the comic strips; who do you think you are, Buck Rogers?" and "Real life is learning to make your peace with boredom" and "Life is not about exaltation; life is about duty."

And then along came Ayn Rand who said, "Oh, really?" and proceeded to create characters who did not live in the Middle Ages or in outer space but who were of our times and of this earth. Characters who work, struggle, pursue difficult career goals, fall in love, participate in intensely emotional relationships, and experience life as a great adventure because they have made it so. Characters who face opposition, endure hardships, suffer, struggle, persevere—and who, predominantly, win.

This was a major reason her books were having such an impact on young people. It influenced those still fighting to protect themselves and their own souls against the world of adults, against the cynicism and despair of their elders. It affected those fighting to hang on to the conviction that they could do better, could rise higher, could make more of their lives than those who went before them.

As Ayn's impact became more visible, as she saw what happened at the lectures, her spirits began to lift. It happened slowly. For two years, she lived a good deal of the time in hell, and I lived there with her.

Barbara remained the only person to whom I could speak candidly about what this period was like for me. "I'm proud of the lectures and what we're accomplishing, but some part of me feels much as Ayn does. I feel as if, in some profound way, this world has died for me—that the world has become an essentially boring place to live. With all the good things that are happening, the new people we're meeting, all of it, I feel more alienated than I did as a teenager. If this is what happens to Ayn at the triumph of her career, what's the point?"

Every Sunday morning, I had a ritual: I forced myself to read the *New York Times Book Review* from cover to cover. This section became the symbol of everything I loathed. Reading what was praised and taken seriously was torture; I felt blinding rage and indignation. I thought of the treatment accorded *Atlas Shrugged,* and I saw the kind of fiction that was saluted as great literature, and at times my pain was unbearable. I told myself that I would read the *Book Review* every Sunday, no matter how long it took, until I could do so indifferently, until "the culture" no longer had the power to hurt me. It was almost a form of meditation, to look into the darkest face of social reality as I perceived it then and to await the arrival of equanimity. It was a spiritual rite of passage that took nearly two years. In part, I regarded this training as preparation for my own future as a writer.

Now and again Ayn would say to me, "Sometimes my point of view changes, and then I wonder why I'm feeling so sorry for myself. I detest viewing myself as a martyr. And besides, who ever heard of a martyr on the best-seller list? Maybe I need to get back to work and stop thinking about the culture so much." I would try to encourage this. For a few days, her spirits would brighten, and I would think the worst was over, but these good moods would not last. One day she would awaken, and the despair would be back.

I was always in search of new hypotheses to account for her depression. I thought that for all the years of writing the novel, Ayn had lived with Dagny, Rearden, Francisco, and Galt as her daily companions. They were more real to her than almost anyone she knew. When the book was finished, they remained in her mind as the "friends" with whom any new acquaintance would be compared, and what actual human being could compare favorably? "Are you accusing me of being that unrealistic?" Ayn asked angrily when I told her my idea. But an hour later, with one of her typical mood switches, she said, "I think you're right." Then, a while later, "*Of course* you're right." I knew that my idea was almost as applicable to me as to Ayn and that it would continue to create frustration for me in my relationships. But neither of us pursued the subject; it remained a dead end beyond which we could not travel.

As 1959 approached, I found myself entertaining a different hypothesis about Ayn's depression. "Do you know what I think a major part of the problem really is?" I said to her. "I think that you are one of those people who, in effect, had a mission in life—and that was to write *Atlas Shrugged*. I think everything that happened earlier was just preparing you for that assignment. By a 'mission,' I mean a task logically and psychologically entailed by your deepest essence, by who you are at your core, so that its actualization leaves you thinking, 'This is what I was born for. This is what I came on earth to do.'"

Ayn nodded her head eagerly. "That's exactly how I feel about *Atlas*," she said.

"The problem is," I continued, "what do you do now? The mission has been accomplished, and you're only in your fifties and in good health. You've got to find a new challenge. That might be tough, no matter how people responded to *Atlas*."

Ayn was now happily excited. "Absolutely true," she declared.

"Well, if it is, then talking about the world is beside the point. Irrelevant. Because we're not addressing the real issue."

Ayn threw her arms around me and announced, "I have not felt this hopeful since *Atlas* was published! This is the right track, darling. This is the right track!" Thereafter, she referred to this idea as the "mission theory." It did not end her depression, but it helped.

When Barbara and I were visiting one evening, she said to Barbara, almost as if I were not present, "It's Nathan who's saving my life, because of my conversations with him and his sense of the culture, his understanding of how to fight this battle. The success of his lectures gave me hope and a new sense of what's possible. Seeing Nathan start on a shoestring, with the whole intellectual atmosphere against him, standing totally alone and establishing an institution—that was an enormously crucial, concrete example of what can be done."

To me alone, she said, "Whatever I have given you, you have given an equivalent back to me. Consider us even."

In the two years following the publication of *Atlas Shrugged,* Ayn and I made love less than a dozen times. The joy and excitement between us had vanished. Our meetings predominantly were spent discussing the issue and events I have described. Our affair died not by conscious decision but by default, as a casualty of Ayn's depression.

"I have nothing to bring to the realm of sex," Ayn said sadly. "Perhaps, one day in the future, when I'm alive again. But now all we can be is friends."

I did not argue. I was relieved. I did not want the burden of a "romance" for which I no longer had genuine enthusiasm. I needed all of my resources to continue functioning. I had a private practice and was developing the lecture series. In addition, I was pursuing my studies in psychology and philosophy; evolving my ideas about self-esteem, social metaphysics, and motivation in general; writing the book on anxiety; operating as Ayn's emotional support system; thinking constantly about how to advance Objectivism in the culture; and trying to find some joy in a marriage that had become more and more cerebral.

Barbara and I accused each other of coldness; we were both right. And yet there continued to be times of warmth and affection. We were not passionate as husband and wife, but we were often passionate friends.

I was grateful that at last my sexual interest in her had begun to decline. There had been too many nights of lying in bed fighting my desire, too many rejections, alternating with occasional lovemaking sessions that were mechanical and soulless. She was becoming a fantasy figure, an abstraction called "my wife" for whom I felt a sadly detached kind of love. But it was a love that remained important. She was a friend as no one else in my world was. I did not think of divorcing her. She was my wife, and she would remain my wife, and I told myself that someday, somehow, we would find a way to be happy together. I would not, or could not, concede defeat.

Barbara was as emotionally unfulfilled as I, but she never spoke of divorce either. She, too, did not want to fail. When she referred to our future, it was with optimism. "We have been through so much together," she said tenderly. "The worst is behind us. We'll be together for life." I drew a kind of nourishment from hearing her say this. It was as if she had said, "Not everything is falling apart. There are some things you will always be able to count on. I am one of them." Years later, she would tell me that she had felt unbearably lonely at that time, and I would tell her the same about myself.

I never thought of seeking companionship with another woman. I did not flirt, did not look around for attractive females, did not respond when other women attempted to flirt with me. In fact, I rarely noticed that that was happening, unless Barbara pointed it out, as she did from time to time.

My affair with Ayn notwithstanding, I regarded myself as a man committed to sexual exclusivity and monogamy. Ayn was a once-in-a-lifetime exception; I did not see our affair as beginning a pattern of acceptable behavior. Barbara expressed the judgment that I was fundamentally a puritan. Once, she had said this as a criticism; now, she said it with affection.

I was sitting on the edge of a volcano. All of us were. But no one was more oblivious than I.

12

_____

"ACCEPT THE FACT that in the realm of morality nothing less than perfection will do," Ayn had written in Galt's speech. By *perfection,* she meant an "unbreached rationality"—that is, a commitment to use one's mind to the fullest of one's ability, a respect for facts, reality, and logic, and a refusal to indulge wishes by evading knowledge or evidence.

As a psychologist, I knew that at least on some occasions a denial or avoidance of some aspect of reality was inevitable—fear, pain, and desire virtually guaranteed it—and that in any event the notion of flawless consistency in this sphere was a fantasy. Philosophically, I was committed to the idea that "unbreached rationality" was not merely a powerful guiding principle, a commitment to do one's best to live honestly, congruently, and responsibly, but a practice that was within *anyone's* power to attain all of the time. That Ayn herself had achieved such a state was a not-to-be-questioned axiom.

In our world, the world of the Collective, psychology was implicitly viewed as the handmaiden of philosophy. As a result, the psychologist in me almost always yielded to the philosopher. I upheld the absolutism of "unbreached rationality" as a moral imperative at my lectures—and in my own circle of friends.

Ayn and I did not say, "Live consciously. Try to be as rational as you can be. Don't make allegations you can't support. Be on the lookout for contradictions, and work to resolve them. Do your best to face the things that need to be faced. When you act, make every effort to know what you are doing and what the consequences are likely to be. Live responsibly. Accept that sometimes you will fail; don't collapse into guilt, because that serves no useful purpose. Pick yourself up, acknowledge your error, and try to do better in the future." That would have been genuinely rational advice. What we said, in effect, was, "Be rational twenty-four hours a day and in every issue; there's no excuse not to be. The root of all evil is evasion. Value your own moral perfection above all things." These are different communications with predictably different consequences.

Among us, nothing was worse than to be accused of "evasion"—deliberate unconsciousness, willful blindness, the choice of an action known to be wrong. The prospect evoked considerable anxiety. In Galt's speech Ayn had stated, "Make every allowance for errors of knowledge; do not forgive or accept any breach of morality." One member of our group confided to me, "Every night before going to bed, I review the day to see if I have done anything immoral, if I have evaded anything, refused to consider some relevant facts properly." When I said that I found this appalling—even by my standards, this struck me as excessive—I was greeted with hurt astonishment.

Of all the accusations that critics made against our philosophy, none is more ludicrous than that we advocated hedonism. If there was anything Ayn did not teach, it was the idea that a person should do whatever he or she pleases. It would be closer to the truth to say that she viewed life as a moral tightrope and that it was easy to lose one's balance and fall into immorality. Certainly, this was the perspective that profoundly affected all of us in the Collective. We despised "whim worshipers" and looked with suspicion at anyone who seemed too interested in emotions or who said, "I feel," rather than "I think." We demanded reasons for everything.

If reason was our supreme and ruling value, it was a value to be respected scrupulously in the daily conduct of our life. The idea that ideals were to be lived, not merely espoused, was a dominant theme of Ayn's. It is obvious to me today (but not then) that if Ayn was a genius at reasoning, she was no less a genius at rationalizing.

Once she had a desire—almost any desire—she could generate a chain of reasoning to justify it. No, she did not advocate doing what one pleases—not as a general rule and not for other people—but if one considers her dealings with Frank in the context of our affair, if one considers her blithe obliviousness to the devastation being wrought, and not only upon Frank—one sees a recklessness and irresponsibility completely at odds with a life of reason. This is not a statement about the validity of Ayn's philosophy; it is a statement about her own psychology. This contradiction in values may help explain why she became so agitated if anyone dared to suggest that she was being irrational in any respect.

Our commitment to the life of reason generated many positive consequences. We thought philosophically and in terms of principles. We strove for lucidity. We were keenly concerned with precision in our thought and speech. There was a clarity and focus in our behavior. We were not blamers; we took responsibility for our actions. There was a dignity in our dealings with one another. We cared deeply about being fair and just. That which we liked or admired, we praised unstintingly and enthusiastically; we believed in supporting our values. Such was the orientation of our group at its best.

At the same time, there was a rigidity, a fear of falling into error, and, for the others, a fear of incurring Ayn's or my displeasure and critical judgment. "In the Collective," Harry Kalberman remarked to me many years later, "there was always that dread of moral condemnation from on high. I don't know if you ever really understood how bad our anxiety was." There was terrible violence done to everyone's emotional life—the repression or suppression of any feeling that clashed with what an ideal Objectivist was supposed to experience, be it a sexual impulse, an artistic preference, a longing for greater spontaneity, hurt or anger with me for my sometimes abrupt and impatient manner, or hurt at Ayn's coldness when she found some action to disparage.

"I've never had an emotion I couldn't account for," Ayn liked to announce. She could turn out explanations of her emotional life with dazzling virtuosity, and it did not occur to us that her explanations could be spurious. Ayn made many self-congratulatory statements that we accepted at face value. If any of us didn't, we remained silent about it, suppressing our misgivings.

When we had difficulty accounting for some emotion of our own, we told ourselves we had to learn to be "better introspecters." *Introspection*, at that time, meant a fairly cerebral and analytical unmasking of the "premises" generating our feelings. It had little to do with the art of self-awareness as I would describe it years later in my writings in psychology.

It's not that we were insensitive to the problem of emotional repression. We discussed it often. I talked about it as an issue to be concerned with in my lectures on Objectivism. Nonetheless, its encouragement was always subtly and insidiously present.

For some years, Ayn had contemplated writing a book about "the mind versus the heart," her thesis being the superiority of the mind and the evil of placing the heart above it. She decided against writing the book because she felt she had covered the issue adequately in *Atlas Shrugged*. The intensity of her concern with this issue, which surfaced in countless discussions, became a profound if unacknowledged message to distrust emotions. Our group experienced her preoccupation as such. This message *never*, of course, applied to Ayn's emotions, which were uncritically interpreted as manifestations of irreproachable rationality.

Our official position was that emotions are not tools of cognition, which is correct. But to disparage feelings was a favorite activity of virtually everyone in our circle, as if that were a means of establishing one's rationality. All we achieved was to drive our own feelings underground.

Along with messages to the contrary, the tendency to encourage emotional repression was present in *The Fountainhead* and *Atlas Shrugged,* although I came to see this only after my break with Ayn. Here is an example from *The Fountainhead,* a passage that inspired me at fourteen. Howard Roark is at the low point of his struggle to succeed as an architect; he is working in a granite quarry, doing grinding, mindless, and exhausting labor.

> Sometimes, not often, he sat up and did not move for a long time; then he smiled, the slow smile of an executioner watching a victim. He thought of his days going by, of the buildings he could have been doing, should have been doing and, perhaps, would never be doing again. He watched the pain's unsummoned appearance with a cold, detached curiosity; he said to himself: Well, here it is again. He waited to see how long it would last. It gave him a strange, hard pleasure to watch his fight against it, and he forgot that it was his own suffering; he could smile in contempt, not realizing that he smiled at his own agony. Such moments were rare. But when they came, he felt as he did in the quarry: that he had to drill through granite, that he had to drive a wedge and blast the thing within him which persisted in calling to his pity.

How my adolescent self longed to be capable of that! Unfortunately, by my late twenties, I had become a master at it. And I believed that everyone else in our group should do likewise. Having little patience or compassion for my own suffering, I had little for theirs. I could be supportive, affectionate, and playful, but I could also be arrogant, impatient, demanding, and capable of projecting arctic remoteness. With my staff, I could be a holy terror of high expectations and zero empathy.

In *Atlas,* there is a scene in which Hank Rearden comes to Dagny's apartment on a night when he feels revolted at the deterioration of his world, at the injustice he sees everywhere, and at the seeming helplessness of the good to combat it. He tells himself that he must not convey any of his suffering to the woman he loves: "He grasped a feeling that he had always experienced, but never identified because it had always been absolute and immediate: a feeling that forbade him ever to face her in pain.

It was much more than the pride of wishing to conceal his suffering: it was the feeling that suffering must not be granted recognition in her presence, that no form of claim between them should ever be motivated by pain and aimed at pity. It was not pity that he brought here or came here to find."

The implication here is that if ever we are honest with the person we love about our suffering, our goal is to evoke pity. Certainly, this was not Ayn's actual belief, but it is what the passage conveys. And this passage is far from being the only one of its kind in the book.

When Ayn did speak of her own suffering, she was quite concerned that she receive appropriate understanding and sympathy from the listener. I recall how miffed she could be if this response were not forthcoming. Very different from the psychology she gives her hero Rearden.

Later in the story, when Dagny quits Taggart Transcontinental as a protest against outrageous government regulations, she goes to a cabin in the country to recover emotionally, to learn how to live without the work that has been her lifelong passion. She finds the suffering of her loss to be almost beyond endurance: "She had come here with three assignments given, as orders, to herself: rest—learn how to live without the railroad—get the pain out of the way. Get it out of the way, were the words she used. She felt as if she were tied to some wounded stranger who could be stricken at any moment by an attack that would drown her in his screams. She felt no pity for the stranger, only a contemptuous impatience; she had to fight him and destroy him." Here again we are offered a heroic vision of emotional repression. This passage is more than a dramatized counsel against feeling sorry for oneself; it upholds an adversarial relationship to one's emotional life as admirable.

All of us were consciously or subconsciously influenced by this "ideal." It would take me another decade to understand fully that the denial or disowning of suffering is a major source of psychological tragedy.

In passage after passage of *Atlas,* even though passion is celebrated, repression, denial of feeling, and the sweeping aside of emotion are dramatized as strength and virtue. Concern with feeling is viewed as indulgent and irrational, indicative of weakness and immorality. Psychologists tell parents, "Your children will be influenced far more by the example you set than by your verbal pronouncements." The examples set by the behavior of Ayn's characters have an impact on the reader that is far more powerful than any explicit philosophical statement about the legitimate place of emotion in human life. I cannot think of any other book in which there are so many passages that treat emotion in a negative way. Paradoxically, this happens in a novel exploding with passion on almost every page. The temptation to apply Freud's concept of reaction formation—a behavioral tendency generated unconsciously as a defense against the direct opposite repressed impulse—is irresistible. Certainly, in the end it was Ayn's emotions that proved her undoing. Or, more accurately, it was her failure to deal with them appropriately. As is always the case, the beast she feared most lay within.

Suspicion, if not hostility, toward emotion was the message that we in the Collective absorbed from Ayn's novels and from Ayn herself. The subtle encouragement of emotional repression, and therefore the encouragement of self-alienation, was a powerful component of our world—side by side with exhortations toward greater emotional honesty and authenticity. Absorbing this dangerous message made it easier to absorb others that were equally dangerous.

There were implicit premises in our world to which everyone in our circle subscribed. We transmitted these to our students at NBI. These were the premises:

- Ayn Rand is the greatest human being who has ever lived.
- *Atlas Shrugged* is the greatest human achievement in the history of the world.
- Ayn Rand, by virtue of her philosophical genius, is the supreme arbiter in any issue pertaining to what is rational, moral, or appropriate to man's life on earth.
- Once one is acquainted with Ayn Rand and her work, the measure of one's virtue is intrinsically tied to the position that one takes regarding her and her work.
- No one who does not admire what Ayn Rand admires and condemn what Ayn Rand condemns can be a good Objectivist. No one who disagrees with Ayn Rand on any fundamental issue can be a fully consistent individualist.
- Because Ayn Rand has designated Nathaniel Branden as her "intellectual heir" and has repeatedly proclaimed him to be an ideal exponent of her philosophy, he is to be accorded only marginally less reverence than Ayn Rand herself.
- It is best not to say most of these things explicitly (excepting, perhaps, the first two items). One must always maintain that one arrives at one's beliefs solely by reason.

Perhaps we were not a cult in the literal, dictionary sense of the word, but there was certainly a cultish aspect to our world (in the same way that one might speak, in the early years of psychoanalysis, of "the cult of Sigmund Freud" or "the cult of Wilhelm Reich").We were a group organized around a charismatic leader. Our members judged one another's character chiefly by loyalty to that leader and to her ideas.

Ayn did not create this atmosphere on her own. We all actively contributed. In every respect, I was a full and willing partner to whom the rightness of what we were doing felt close to self-evident. Our entire group fed Ayn's exalted view of herself, and no one did so more fervently than I. In fact, I often argued that she underestimated her own greatness. I was absolutely convinced of it. It pleased me to believe that I was providing her with an experience of greatly enhanced self-appreciation.

It troubled me sometimes that I could not find any area, philosophically, where I thought Ayn might be wrong. Looking at the history of human thought, I knew that the greatest of geniuses made mistakes and that Ayn must be making them, too. But what were they? What was I not seeing? I knew that as a human being Ayn was not without flaws. But in terms of her abstract principles, I found nothing to object to—only ideas that might need more amplification and development or more detailed grounding.

I once asked Ayn if the possibility of error ever troubled her. "No," she replied. "Not because I think I'm incapable of error but because if reason and observation lead me to certain conclusions, what can I do except hold them as true—until and unless someone can prove I've made a mistake? What can any person do, except go by his best rational judgment and remain open to conflicting evidence when and if someone is able to present any? In the meantime, I'm not going to say 'it seems to me' about matters where I am convinced reason is on my side."

Riding on the success of *Atlas,* Random House decided to publish a new edition of *We the Living.* In December 1958, Ayn received her advance copies. She showed me the new introduction, in which she stressed that the theme is abstract. The book is about the evil of dictatorship—*any* dictatorship and *all* dictatorships—not merely the evil of Soviet Russia in the mid-1920s. "Its basic theme," she wrote, "is the sanity of human life."

In its depiction of a young woman growing up in Soviet Russia, *We the Living* is more autobiographical than anything else Ayn wrote—not in terms of its literal events but in terms of background, environment, and philosophical development. For that reason, it had always been of particular interest to me.

We the Living depicts the struggle of three young, talented people to achieve life and happiness in Soviet Russia. The book is about the manner in which the system destroys all three of them, not in spite of, but because of, their virtues. In order to obtain money to send Leo Kovalensky, the man she loves, to a tuberculosis sanatorium, Kira Argounova becomes the mistress of Andrei Taganov, an idealistic communist. Neither man knows of Kira's relationship with the other, and their hate is mutual. Leo is an aristocrat, Andrei, a member of the Soviet secret police. The idea that a woman would be forced to sleep with a man she does not love in order to save the life of the man she does love is not new; that is the situation in *Tosca*, for instance, and in many other stories.

The originality of Ayn's treatment of the subject is the way in which she intensifies the conflict and makes it more complex. In *Tosca* and stories like it, the man to whom the woman sells herself is a villain whom the woman despises; he *knows* that she is selling herself. But in *We the Living*, Andrei is not a villain. He genuinely loves Kira and believes that she is in love with him; he does not know of her love for Leo. And Kira does not despise him; increasingly, she comes to respect him. At the start of the affair, she acts in desperation, knowing that it is her only chance to save Leo and knowing that Andrei has helped to establish the system that forced this action on her. As their relationship progresses, as Andrei finds the first happiness he has ever known, he begins to understand the importance of an individual life—and begins to doubt the ideals for which he has fought. And now the two relationships are on a collision course.

In my copy of the new edition, Ayn quoted a line describing Kira—a line I had once remarked on. I had said that it conveyed something essential to what I admired in a woman—a combination of powerful innocence and a sense of purposefulness. I also said that I saw just those attributes in her. Reading Ayn's inscription, I felt a muted, distant pleasure, the kind that goes with the thought, "This would have meant a great deal to me, once."

In the period following the publication of *Atlas*, many new people entered our world, and people we had known before entered it in a new way.

One such person quickly became a member of our inner circle. Edith Efron then worked for Mike Wallace. Later she would go on to a successful journalism career, and later still she would write several books, her most important being *The Apocalyptics*, a groundbreaking study of the politics of cancer.

What made her fascinating to me, apart from her unusual intelligence and entertaining sense of humor, was that when Ayn met her, she was a committed "New York liberal" whose views on most issues were diametrically opposed to ours, especially in politics. She had been profoundly affected by *Atlas Shrugged,* and Ayn fascinated her; she had never before heard the kind of arguments and explanations Ayn offered. When, at Ayn's suggestion, she read some of the economic writings of Ludwig von Mises, as well as other members of the free-market Austrian school, she decided that she had been mistaken about most of the things she "knew" about politics and economics; she became a more conscientious student of this subject than most members of the Collective, and she became a supporter of laissez-faire capitalism. The range of her reading was enormous. A superb communicator, she proceeded to convert a number of her friends.

"I feel as if all this time I've been living under some kind of censorship," she told Ayn and me. "I'm a college graduate who discovers that she's a complete illiterate in a major area. Every book I've ever heard recommended in college or out of it has been slanted to the Left. Why don't more people know about these books you're showing me? Why have I not heard of these thinkers?"

At a dinner party, Mike Wallace chuckled at her conversion. "It's not just Edith," he said. "Ayn appears to have seduced my entire staff."

My sisters Reva and Florence and their husbands Sholey and Hans read *Atlas* and were enthusiastic. We continued to grow closer—intellectually, not personally. I was now close to no one, because I was carrying too much in my private life that I could not discuss. When they visited New York, they saw Ayn and Frank and participated in Saturday night meetings. They became part of a widening group of people who were not part of the inner circle but who were keenly interested in and supportive of our ideas and with whom we maintained friendly relations.

The real surprise to me was my father—he fell in love with *Atlas,* and this silent, reticent man became more talkative on the subject of Ayn's book than I had ever heard him on any other. "What's happened to Daddy?" my mother wanted to know. I had the impression he identified with Hank Rearden. I was no longer a disappointment who had turned his back on business to pursue some incomprehensible career in New York; I was an intellectual, doing important work that the world badly needed. *Atlas* had opened his eyes to that. I was treated with new affection and respect. When my father talked with Ayn during a visit to New York, he found her to be the essence of clear thinking and common sense. "You see?" he said to me, as if it were his own discovery. "A woman can be highly intelligent."

During this same period, the year following *Atlas*'s publication, Ayn began to receive extraordinary quantities of fan mail. One letter was from a student of Professor von Mises's, a young economist named Murray

Rothbard who would one day become prominent in the libertarian movement. The letter was movingly and beautifully written, profoundly insightful concerning what Ayn had accomplished in *Atlas,* and full of what seemed like the most genuine appreciation and admiration. It was almost the model of an ideal fan letter, at the highest intellectual level.

Murray lived in New York, and Ayn invited him to a meeting. Although he clearly had striking intellectual gifts, I felt a stab of disappointment almost from the first moment. Fear and malice seemed to leap from his face. Murray told us that he differed from us on one important intellectual issue—he was an anarchist. He was convinced that government by its nature was oppressive and evil and that our idea of a constitutionally limited government in which citizens' rights would be protected was hopelessly unachievable. Without a government, we asked, how did he propose to ensure individual rights? We thought his answer ludicrous: "Private, competing defense agencies." Ayn quickly responded, "You mean, as in civil war?"

Years later, Ayn would write about her own view of government and would criticize the anarchist position in an article titled "The Nature of Government." It first appeared in *The Objectivist Newsletter* and was reprinted in two collections of her essays, *The Virtue of Selfishness* and *Capitalism: The Unknown Ideal.*

We had a few debates with Murray about government and its necessity, and these discussions were initially calm and good-natured. One evening, he brought along his own circle of friends—young students of economics, history, and the like—all of whom were anarchists and all of whom, at least in my perception, had something of Murray's manner about them. There was something fearful and given to sarcasm and hints of unidentified superiority. In appearance and style, they were indistinguishable from any of the young socialists I had ever encountered. All conveyed admiration for *Atlas.* Murray and some of the others took my course called "Basic Principles of Objectivism." An uneasy truce was declared. But the relationship was to last a very short time.

When the explosion with Murray finally came, it happened not over anarchism but over Murray's refusal to acknowledge Ayn as his source of some of the ideas he included in a paper he was publishing. In particular, the ideas had to do with the concept of causality as it related to the issue of free will. Murray insisted to me that he got the ideas from a scholar in the Middle Ages, an Aristotelian who indeed had anticipated some of Ayn's arguments. Since I remembered Barbara's and my discussions with him and knew specifically how Murray had been introduced to the ideas he was using—even if they had been anticipated earlier—I challenged his assertion on the telephone and asked him to come over so we could discuss the situation in person. He refused angrily in a way that signaled that this matter was far more serious than I had supposed. An associate of his confided that Murray had dug up this medieval scholar as his source because Murray felt it would reflect badly on his scholarship if he credited a novelist in his writing. "Academic respectability is very important to Murray."

Following our phone call, Murray went on the attack, speaking violently against Ayn, me, and all the others in our circle, effectively saying the opposite of everything he had said in his original letter to Ayn. I did not know how to interpret his reversal except as the expression of a guilty conscience. In later years, he authored many books championing "anarcho-capitalism," and he attracted a following. He also launched a nonstop campaign of lies about us that went on for years.

In the 1970s and 1980s, Murray's following would have an unfortunate impact on the emerging Libertarian Party. Whereas the majority of those in the Libertarian Party favored limited constitutional government, a minority (with whom Murray had his influence) favored anarchism. This split significantly impeded the progress of the movement, causing it to lose some credibility. As a number of surveys established, far more persons were influenced toward libertarianism by the writings of Ayn Rand than by those of any other figure. But Murray and his friends contrived to create the illusion that *he* was "Mr. Libertarianism," a task made easier by the fact that Ayn repudiated and disassociated herself from this political movement, in part because of its tolerance of the anarchist wing.

Our experience with Murray Rothbard brought to light an element of Ayn's psychology I had not seen before. Prior to our break with him, both Ayn and I regarded Murray as highly intelligent. After the break, I still thought so. It was my view of his *character* that had changed. Ayn responded differently. She challenged not only his morals but also his mind. It seemed to me that each time she spoke of him, she thought him less intelligent than before, as if no virtue could be credited to him after his betrayal. This struck me as a rewriting of history, and when I suggested this to Ayn, she became angry and demanded, "What good are his brains if this is how he acts?" I saw that further argument was futile. I was left with more uneasiness, not about Murray but about Ayn. Like other such uneasinesses, it was swallowed up by the enormous esteem in which I continued to hold her.

We met a number of professed enthusiasts who thought that our advocacy of self-interest meant license for the smallest, pettiest kind of spur-of-the-moment indulgence. Ayn called them "Nietzschean whim worshipers." She said, "They're the people who give 'selfishness' a bad name and make our battle harder. I go to such lengths in my writing to make clear in what sense I use the word *selfishness*. I use it in the context of reason. Those people ignore my context—and pretend to agree with me. I wish they would stay away from us. For once, I feel sympathy for Marx. He said somewhere that he was not a Marxist. God protect me from Randians."

I enjoyed it when, through Ayn, I had the opportunity to meet non-Randians, such as the composer Deems Taylor, whose daughter, Joan Kennedy Taylor, was a student at NBI. I recall an especially absorbing evening at Ayn's when, sitting with me in a corner, Deems helped me understand some of the things Rachmaninoff was doing musically that I had felt but could not articulate. He also told fascinating stories about personages such as Vladimir Horowitz and Leonard Bernstein. Deems invited Ayn to his home to listen to recordings of his own compositions, and she spoke of her visits with pleasure. Frank, too, seemed to enjoy these encounters. Because of Deems's age, perhaps—he was some years older than Ayn—she seemed able to enjoy him on his own terms without requiring that he be a convert.

Another, more surprising friendship was the one that formed between Ayn and Mickey Spillane. I had discovered his early Mike Hammer stories, which I liked, and recommended them to Ayn, knowing she enjoyed detective novels. Ayn admired the "black-and-white moral absolutism" of Spillane's writing and also felt that he was underappreciated as a stylist. "Granted his writing is uneven," she said, "and some passages are crude, but his descriptions at their best are excellent. Compare his descriptions of New York City in *One Lonely Night* with Thomas Wolfe's descriptions, and you'll appreciate the difference between a writer who knows how to make you *see* and one who just throws adjectives at you." I agreed with her, at least to some extent, but I was uneasy about the degree of praise she heaped on him publicly, as if she enjoyed shocking everyone—or as if she wanted to do for him what no one had done for her. At that time, liberal reviewers went literally berserk on the subject of Mickey Spillane, vilifying him hysterically; I would not have imagined that a writer of thrillers could push so many hostile buttons.

Ayn learned that Spillane admired *Atlas Shrugged*. When they met, Ayn tried to get him to think more philosophically about his work and about life, but he only shook his head. We had the impression that he had been badly hurt by the savagery of the attacks on him, but when Ayn offered him sympathy, he insisted on displaying tough indifference. "They sure hate us, don't they?" he said wonderingly, and then he grinned. He could be amusing. He told us about a dinner party where "some literary guy" came up to him and declared, "I think it's disgraceful that of the ten best-selling novels of all time, seven were written by you." Spillane responded, "You're lucky I've written only seven books." But he stopped writing for several years, after *Kiss Me, Deadly,* and when he came back he was never as good; the energy and fire were gone. "They got to him," Ayn said. "He will never admit it, but they got to him. He won't give his best because he doesn't want to be hurt anymore."

Some years later, when they were no longer in touch, Spillane unexpectedly sent her a postcard saying, "When is *Atlas* going to start shrugging again?" by which he meant, When are you going to begin a new novel?

That was the question we all wondered about. Ayn had no answer except "Perhaps someday."

The day never came. I knew, soon after the publication of *Atlas,* that it never would.

In the spring of 1959, I turned twenty-nine. I was not a lover to Ayn or a husband to Barbara. I had little time or inclination for recreation or leisure. *Play* was an empty word to me. We had parties, and they were sometimes pleasant and yet essentially devoid of gaiety. I wrote, I thought, I studied, I lectured—I harassed my friends to read more, learn more, become more effective communicators—and I fought not to be overwhelmed by frustration and bouts of unhappiness.

My writing was proceeding slowly; the task of spreading Objectivism had replaced psychology as my central concern. Unexpectedly, the one person who tried to speak to me about this was my mother. "What is all this lecturing and talking about Ayn Rand doing for you?" she wanted to know. I tried to explain that I was not fighting for Ayn Rand; I was fighting for my own convictions. She was not impressed.

The signals I got from Ayn made me feel like I was on a perpetual roller-coaster ride. One day, I was a hero, taking on the entire culture, making a success of a venture that even she had not believed in; I was her champion, the one man able and willing to proclaim to the world who and what she was. On another day, I was a bewildering disappointment, insufficiently supportive of her suffering, uninterested in her romantically, concerned only with her mind. One day, the fact that I seemed to know how to be "in the world but not of it" was admirable, the proof of a high level of development; in this area, Ayn would say, she could learn from me. On another day, the fact that I could be relaxed and easygoing with people and that I rarely became angry—with students or interviewers, for instance, or with some of the intellectuals who visited her—she viewed with suspicion, as manifesting a possible lack of seriousness and integrity.

If I ever showed the slightest sign of impatience when she made the same complaint about "the world" for the two thousandth time, we would be up all night discussing what was wrong with my psychology. Usually I walked on ice expertly, but once I made the mistake of referring casually to the "hospital atmosphere" of her home. This was late in 1959, and the air of tragedy and crisis was present almost constantly, especially when we were alone.

"Don't you understand my context?" Ayn thundered at me and did not stop reproaching me for the rest of the night, comparing me morally to the worst of her enemies. When Frank tried to intervene in my defense, she shrieked at him, and he relapsed into withdrawn silence. I felt sorry for her, and at the same time I felt enraged. The youngest part of me, which had once felt so safe in this world, now felt flung back into the nightmare of childhood, where all grown-ups are crazy and not to be trusted. In the end, I almost always made excuses for her in my mind, but the distance between us had begun to grow, like the early fissures that will one day split apart a mountain.

Even though she did not suggest that we resume our physical relationship—she was still too troubled for that—in every other respect she clearly wanted our romance to continue, and I found this difficult. I survived much of the time by disconnecting from my feelings. The realm of emotion was dangerous to my equilibrium. I made myself increasingly cerebral as a means of preserving some kind of harmony with Ayn and as a way of suppressing awareness of how frustrating my life had become. I could give Ayn intellectual companionship. I could give her compassion, empathy, and support in her battle with the world. But I could not give her romantic passion, and I felt guilty about it. I agonized over the thought that I was doing to Ayn what Barbara was doing to me, and I found it intolerable that I could cause that kind of suffering. I contemplated the indifference of my body and searched my soul for the flaw that would explain it. I saw myself as failing my "highest value"—even if another part of me was rebelling against the burden of a duty that gave me no right to my own life.

I looked for alternative ways to reassure Ayn of my devotion. I became her "enforcer." If someone in our group did something to offend Ayn or "the cause" or was not behaving as a "good Objectivist," I would invite that person to lunch and, in a quiet but deadly voice, I would inform him or her of the nature of the transgression. If the offense was big enough— say, being friendly with someone who had been critical of Ayn, or gossiping about another Collective member—our whole group convened to hear the charges, and almost always it was I who took on the role of prosecutor. I am appalled at remembering my ruthless behavior on such occasions.

One of the worst things I had done to myself over the past several years—which became a crime against others, as well—was to disown my compassionate impulses. I came to view my capacity for empathy, sympathy, and simple kindness as a potential weakness, except when directed toward Ayn. At times, the more human side of me would break through, and I would defend someone against Ayn's condemnation, but my defense would be highly intellectualized. I knew that this was the only way to reach Ayn, because any talk of ordinary kindness would most likely be interpreted as lack of appropriate realism, or a flawed sense of justice, or "treason against the good." In Galt's speech, Ayn had stated, "Justice is the recognition . . . that to withhold your contempt from men's vices is an act of moral counterfeiting, and to withhold your admiration from their virtues is an act of moral embezzlement." Ayn was firmly convinced of the importance not only of giving support and admiration to virtue but also of projecting contempt for moral flaws (and we did not think to ask whether the communication of contempt was likely to inspire improvement in anyone's behavior).

Once or twice, Barbara feebly (since she was caught up in the same madness as I and sometimes played the role of Lord High Executioner herself) tried to speak to me of the benevolence and generosity that had once been so intrinsically a part of me. Her tone of urgent desperation reached me, past the barrier of my defenses, but I did not know how to respond. To have admitted how well I understood her would have threatened every pillar of the life I had erected. My world with Ayn was my first and only sense of "home." I was not prepared to give it up.

There were rewards for my moral ruthlessness—that is to say, rewards for my cruelty. One was Ayn's esteem. Another was the counterbalance for my own feelings of having failed her. Another was the implication of my own moral irreproachability. Yet another was having an outlet for my rage. The actual object of that rage was Ayn, which I could not admit, so I redirected it at more acceptable targets. And last but not least, there was the simple fact that most of the time, I was convinced I was doing right.

My marriage to Barbara continued as before. It was somewhat happier since I ended my affair with Ayn, but it was essentially unchanged. We had a love for each other, we frustrated each other, we criticized each other, we felt simultaneously understood by and misperceived by each other. If Barbara thought about other men, I did not know it. I did not think about other women. I tried not to suffer over the issue of sex. I repressed or channeled into work a good deal of my sexual energy.

If any other man did exist in Barbara's mind during this period, it was almost certainly Wilfred Schwartz. During her periodic visits to Winnipeg over the years to spend time with her family, she had contacted him, reported to him on her activities, and felt delighted that he had become enthralled with *Atlas Shrugged*. It gave them a new connection. He was now married and had children; nonetheless, it seemed obvious to me that he was still preoccupied with Barbara. I listened to Barbara's summaries of her activities in Winnipeg and felt only a detached, untroubled support for her desire to enlist Wilfred in our cause. She seemed to be succeeding, and I encouraged her.

She was now working as an editorial coordinator at St. Martin's Press. That she also worked with me in developing Nathaniel Branden Institute (or Nathaniel Branden Lectures, as it was still called) contributed to the closeness we did feel much of the time. We saw ourselves as comrades in battle. Over the years, she would make important contributions to NBI's growth.

Barbara drove to Philadelphia once a week to offer the class "Basic Principles of Objectivism." She also gave her own course called "Basic Principles of Efficient Thinking." Sometimes Ayn, someone else in the Collective, or I drove down with her to deliver a guest lecture. We were besieged by requests to offer our courses in other cities.

We received a letter from a young couple in Los Angeles who admired Ayn's work and who proposed that we tape-record our lectures and offer them via tape transcription. Why not do it everywhere? Barbara proposed. We would find a suitable representative in a given city, work with that representative to develop a student population, and then make our courses available at a central location where everyone would gather to hear our programs on tape. This was the concept that caused the explosive growth of NBI.

Barbara left her job at St. Martin's to work for our organization full-time; I appointed her executive director. She would be the administrator; I would be the strategist, the one responsible for creating or supervising the creation of new projects. I largely withdrew from the practice of psychotherapy. My working life was divided between lecturing and writing. In a short time, our courses were being given on a continuing basis in Los Angeles, San Francisco, Seattle, Chicago, Boston, Philadelphia, and Toronto (where my sister Florence was our representative). First, we were in ten cities, then twenty, then thirty; throughout the 1960s, the number went on climbing.

The process of our expansion was always basically the same. People would write us, asking that we offer our lectures in their city and offering to help. If they seemed appropriate to represent us, we began running newspaper ads in that city. "To Readers and Admirers of *The Fountainhead* and *Atlas Shrugged*," began the ads, going on to announce a course called "Basic Principles of Objectivism."

As a result of this strategy, Ayn's name, the titles of her two most important books, and my own name appeared in newspapers around the country on a regular basis. Because the ads spoke of "the philosophy of Ayn Rand," they contributed to the change in the public perception of who Ayn Rand was—from Ayn Rand, novelist, to Ayn Rand, novelist-philosopher. In newspaper articles and in radio and television interviews—where both Ayn and I were being featured more and more frequently—this shift of perception was amplified. People began speaking of the "Ayn Rand philosophy" and the "Ayn Rand movement." They began speaking of "Ayn Rand and Nathaniel Branden." "You're beginning to be famous," Ayn said. "How do you like it?" I answered truthfully, "I like it very much."

With the growing success of NBI, Ayn's spirits continued to lift. "You've brought me back to life," she kept saying, which helped me, if only for the moment, with my feelings of having failed her. She lost the more obvious signs of depression, but her sense of gloom never vanished completely. Her irritability and dispiritedness were there much of the time, brightened by occasional flashes when she seemed like her old self. Although these flashes never lasted, she was happier than before.

Her enthusiasm for philosophical discussion seemed to have lessened, which I regretted. When I mentioned this to her once, she denied my observation and became angry at me for daring to suggest such a thing. On the other hand, her interest in discussing the worst trends of the culture—artistic, political, sociological—struck me as obsessive; I made myself participate in her endless analyses, but I found her relentlessness exhausting. In her presence, there was less and less air to breathe.

To the Collective, she praised me constantly, sometimes to my embarrassment. Occasionally, if I tried to joke about it, she would chastise me gently as if I were a child, informing me that I should not laugh at my own "greatness." I was the standard against which everyone else was judged. I was the ideal man. Her private outbursts, when I failed to be appropriately responsive to her needs and expectations, did not cease, but they were never shared with our friends. As far as I could tell, no one but Barbara and Frank knew of them. At times, I resented the Collective's ignorance of the price I paid for my privileged status.

Having curtailed my practice, I referred many patients to Allan Blumenthal. With great pain and after considerable struggle, he had abandoned his musical ambitions and was now working as a psychiatrist. We assumed that his knowledge of Objectivism, his medical training, and the training and supervision he received from me qualified him for this profession. He continued to play the piano for his own pleasure and that of his friends. If part of him was sad over the loss of music as his central focus, another part seemed relieved. I felt respect for Allan's unself-pitying dignity; I knew how hard his decision had been to make, even though it seemed the wise one.

Although the lives of everyone in our circle seemed to be progressing in one respect or another, in the years following the publication of *Atlas,* the Collective seemed to have lost its focus. In the past, we had been bound together by the excitement of reading the novel as it was being written and of learning Objectivism; now, all purpose appeared to have vanished, and our Saturday night meetings often struck me as perfunctory and lacking in energy.

Increasingly, the energy we did muster depended on stimulation from the outside, which was provided by the continuing stream of visitors to Ayn's apartment. There were professors, writers, scientists, and businesspeople who, if not always converts, were nonetheless profoundly affected by *Atlas.* I swelled with admiration for Ayn when I saw how she functioned with visitors whose occupational specialties were remote from her own. She would question her guest about his work, draw out the information she needed, and then proceed to make connections between her guest's particular field and her philosophy, which would astound whoever was present. She would argue about physics, mathematics, evolution, biochemistry, or Einstein's theory of relativity with consummate skill, using her visitor's own statements to support her points. She had the gift of making her guests feel that they and their work were uniquely understood and appreciated.

My pleasure in this stream of visitors notwithstanding, the Collective's odd inertness with regard to Objectivism continued to frustrate me. To a lesser extent, Barbara seemed to share my feelings. For a long time, I said nothing. Then, in the late spring of 1960, shortly after my thirtieth birthday, I visited Ayn one afternoon and began almost involuntarily to ventilate my concerns.

"I feel frustrated with the Collective. There's a certain kind of passivity in them intellectually. We're all supposed to be committed to the spread of Objectivism, right? To me that means constantly perfecting my grasp of the issues, constantly studying and reading about philosophy, history, economics, and literature. It doesn't mean just saying, 'I think Ayn Rand and *Atlas Shrugged* are wonderful.' Why isn't Leonard thinking about how to evoke interest in Objectivism at meetings of the American Philosophical Association? Why isn't Allan Blumenthal attending meetings of the American Psychiatric Association and seeing what he might accomplish there? I have to hound Allan even to read books in his own field! What does A. G. do, other than praise you on Saturday nights among people who already agree? I feel as if everything rests on Barbara and me. We do everything, and the others eagerly inquire about our progress and praise us. But they don't do anything on their own, they don't work at grasping how this world works and what it would take to change it, they don't develop their skill at presenting our philosophy more effectively—they don't carry their own weight! Joan seems to think that if she acts superior to people who don't agree with Objectivism, that's her contribution to the cause. Am I missing something? Am I being unfair? What's the matter with everyone? Or am I the one who's crazy?"

"The Collective are not philosophical crusaders in the sense that you are. They will never be you, and you must accept that."

I answered that I did not think I was asking anyone to be me. I was only asking that they take more responsibility for advancing a cause to which they claimed to be devoted.

After further discussion, Ayn finally said, "You're right—they could do more than they're doing."

Then she proceeded to talk for almost an hour about her own view of the group's passivity, amplifying what I had said and reinforcing it with almost ominous gravity.

I had begun the discussion wanting clarity in my own mind more than anything else; after that, I wanted ideas about what might be done to improve the group's attitude. What our conversation had deteriorated into was simply an analysis of the "shortcomings" of our friends, which was typical of Ayn, and I became restless and irritable.

Finally, to get Ayn off this track, I laughed in exasperation. "What will we call this? The 'understanding premise'?" We had a habit of labeling certain basic attitudes as "premises," like "the benevolent universe premise" or the "pro-man premise."

"Exactly," Ayn answered. "The 'understanding premise.' The premise of seeking to understand down to the root whatever bears on your interests, purposes, and goals. I think you should have a talk with the whole Collective about this idea. It's important."

Not long thereafter, when our group was together, I laid before them the concept Ayn and I had identified. Many years later, reflecting on this period, Elayne said to me, "That was the beginning of really enormous guilt for everyone in the Collective. There was some guilt before that, of course, about not being a 'good enough Objectivist,' but now it was much worse. We told ourselves you were right, and yet we really did not have the drive or motivation to live the kind of life you and Ayn seemed to expect. I suppose most of us were not really crusaders in your sense. But we reproached ourselves and—although no one would have admitted it at the time—we resented you. You, after all, were the immediate source of the guilt. The understanding premise was devastating to our self-esteem. We all made resolutions to do better, which of course we did not carry out. So we accused ourselves and buried our negative feelings toward you."

No doubt, I should have seen that what I hoped for from my friends was totally unrealistic. They were not warriors or crusaders; they were merely people who loved Ayn and *Atlas Shrugged* and who wanted the world to feel likewise. Through the accident of knowing or being related to Barbara or me, they were brought into a world that they would not have found on their own. Still, when they arrived in this world, it engaged their souls. Objectivism was my whole life. It was not theirs, with the exception of Leonard; the others had careers and spaces in their lives that were not comparably interwoven with "the cause."

I did not see that a great explosive rage was building within each one of them, which safely held in abeyance until the day I would light the fuse.

When I think back to this period of my life and what was most important to me, I do not think of any of the external events. I think of my pursuit of a deeper understanding of romantic love—just at the time when that aspect of my personal life was at its emptiest.

"Why is love so important to human beings?" I wondered aloud with Barbara, Ayn, and Frank during one of our drives into the country for dinner. Frank smiled and remained silent. Ayn responded, "It's in our nature, metaphysically, to want to admire, to find values we can esteem."

I said, "Although admiration is essential to healthy love between adults, admiration and love are not synonymous. There are people we admire but don't love. Love is something more. And why and in what sense is the longing to admire in our nature 'metaphysically'? How would one prove that?"

I had made considerable progress during these past several years in developing my ideas about self-esteem and autonomy. Now I wanted to deepen my understanding of romantic love. I had already by this time conceived the idea of writing *The Psychology of Self-Esteem*. The next project after that, I decided, would be *The Psychology of Romantic Love*.

That we longed for that passionate experience of love seemed self-evident. What was it about us as human beings that could explain this longing? What were its roots in human nature?

Through romantic love, I announced to Ayn, Barbara, and Frank some weeks later, we experience *psychological visibility.* This is a powerful need. I had been working toward this idea for more than a year. "We perceive and experience ourselves in a unique way, through the responses of our partner."

Week by week, I kept adding details and refinements to my theory. I eagerly presented it first to the Collective and then to our students at NBI. Lecturing on romantic love, I declared:

> When we encounter a person who thinks as we do, who notices what we notice, who values the things we value, who tends to respond to different situations as we do, not only do we experience a strong sense of affinity with such a person but also we can experience our self through our perception of that person. We perceive our self through our lover's reaction. We perceive our person through its consequences in the consciousness—and, as a result, in the behavior of our partner. Here, then, we can discern one of the main roots of the human desire for companionship, for friendship, and for romantic love: the desire to perceive our self as an entity in reality, to experience the perspective of objectivity through and by means of the reactions and responses of other human beings.

When we had first met, Barbara had given me an experience of visibility greater than any I had experienced before; that made what happened later so painful. With Ayn, I was lifted to a still higher level of visibility; her understanding and appreciation of me, particularly in our early years, had been inspiring and empowering. And each woman had said I made her feel uniquely visible. Everything we said to one another on this subject was true—but it was not the whole truth.

Work had always been my refuge against pain. Now, at a time when my personal life often felt desolate, I turned to the challenge of understanding romantic love. What I could not achieve in reality I would attempt to grasp in theory—not knowing that that reality was about to come knocking at the door.

She sat in the third row, near the center aisle, and at first I did not notice her.

It was February 1961. I stood on the podium of the lecture room, preparing to welcome the new class of students to the course "Basic Principles of Objectivism." There were approximately 180 people in the room. I looked out at them, feeling relaxed, buoyant, at home in this room and in the world, as was usual for me when I was lecturing.

"Good evening, ladies and gentleman," I said. "My name is Nathaniel Branden." Barbara stood at the back of the room, leaning against a wall, smiling at me. This was *our* setting—the space she and I had created together. Moved by the pleasure that that thought evoked, I did something that was out of character for me in its informality and in what would be called male chauvinism today. Pointing to Barbara, I added, "And that blond at the back of the room is my wife, Barbara Branden."

This is the man, thought the young woman in the third row, although it would be years before she would tell me. He is the man I have wanted and waited for since I was twelve years old. But he is married. And he looks like a man in love. So he cannot be for me; he will have to remain an abstraction.

"Most of you," I said to the class, "and most of mankind believe that philosophy is some vague, abstract, esoteric science that has nothing to do with your actual life. I shall begin by stating that every one of you— and every living human being—possesses philosophical convictions; that these convictions rule every action and every moment of your life; that without these convictions, you would not be able to exist—you would not be able to cross the street, let alone cook a meal, hold a job, or get married. You have no choice about the fact that you do hold a philosophy of life. The only choice you have is whether you know it or not, whether you chose your philosophy consciously or subconsciously, whether your philosophy is true or false."

He is the one, she thought, and I will never have him. But now I know he exists.

After a while, I became aware of her watching me. A young woman in the third row. Her head raised to me. It was the intensity of her glance that arrested me—and the quality of life in her eyes. Blue eyes, very conscious, set wide apart. High cheekbones. An exquisitely sculptured face. Light hair.

I heard myself saying, "The concept of existence and the concept of identity cannot be divorced. To be aware of one is to be aware of the other. They can only enter the mind together. They are indivisible, in reality and in consciousness. To know *anything* is to know that that which is, is what it is."

How odd, I thought. There is such an expression of exaltation in her glance. Why is she looking at me like that?

PART THREE

13

IN THE BEGINNING I did not think about the young woman who always sat in the third row—or not very much.

Her glance projected such an intensity of eagerness and joy that I could not help smiling at her when our eyes met. She always smiled back. That was all. I did not approach her, did not speak to her, did not ask anyone her name. She was simply a beautiful point of focus for me sometimes when I was lecturing.

If in one sense I did not quite have a wife, in another sense I had two. There was no space in my life for a third woman. And she looked so young. The idea was inconceivable.

Usually I saw her arrive a few minutes before my lecture was to begin. She was tall and slender, and her gaze had a kind of open fearlessness—almost, I thought, like that of a young boy. In contrast to most attractive women I had observed, she did not seem preoccupied with her appearance; it was as if her looks were just a fact. I liked the way she moved, with the relaxed energy of a person thoroughly at home in her own body. There was something profoundly physical about her and at the same time something profoundly spiritual; her posture and movements suggested the first, the expression in her eyes, the second. She evoked in me a sense of lightness.

I noticed that sometimes, when talking with a group of fellow students, she would display a touch of coltish awkwardness. I liked that; it stressed her vulnerability. Perhaps I saw a touch of my own unacknowledged shyness reflected in her.

When I began lecturing, she would sit motionless, looking up at me, almost always with the gaze of someone contemplating a private vision that wiped out everything else. The expression on her face was rapture.

There was nothing expectant in her glance; it was as if she were alone with what with she was seeing and what she felt about it.

I lived in a rarefied atmosphere where the passion of pure intellect reigned supreme, or so I chose to believe. My life was organized around that conviction. I had no friendships outside our inner circle, and even within the circle the cerebral dominated. For the most part, I had little time for concerns unconnected to Objectivism. I looked at what most people filled their time with, and I believed I existed on another plane entirely. Ayn had declared me the apotheosis of her philosophy, and this concept became the means of making my isolation tolerable.

I was shocked at my reaction one Monday evening when the young woman did not appear at my lecture: I became tense and irritable. I tried to delay beginning, until my staff looked at me curiously.

The following Monday, when she entered the room, I walked over to her and said, with unexpected sharpness in my voice, "Where were you last week?"

She answered brightly, and as if my question were entirely normal, "I had to work late."

I heard the hard impersonality in my voice and felt powerless to control it. "What kind of work do you do?"

"I'm a fashion model."

"What's your name?"

"Patrecia Gullison."

"How old are you?"

"Twenty-one."

"Young," I announced, and wondered what the matter with me was.

"How old are you?" she asked gaily, with none of the formality and deference I was used to seeing in my students.

"Thirty-one."

Suddenly I felt awkward and foolish. I was behaving like a pompous teenager. A little less stiffly, I said, "Hello, Patrecia."

She grinned as if there were absolutely nothing strange in my manner. "Hello, Nathaniel. Or do people call you Nathan?"

And yet, even after that, for many months I did not think about her—not much—even though we now said "Hello" and "Good night" each week.

"Time to bring out a new book by Ayn Rand," Bennett Cerf had been declaring for the past two years. In March 1961, Random House published *For the New Intellectual,* a collection of all the philosophical passages from Ayn's four novels, plus the long title essay that she wrote specifically for this volume. It was all she could bring herself to do. She was not ready for a more ambitious project.

The essay grew out of a series of philosophical discussions in which we talked about the historical steps by which the dominant intellectual and cultural trends of the twentieth century had developed. One of my contributions was the suggestion of two metaphors or archetypes: Attila and the Witch Doctor. These represented two philosophical orientations, two psychological symbols, and two historical forces that alternately fought each other and conspired together for control over men's minds and bodies. Ayn liked the symbols and made them the centerpiece of her essay. She wrote:

> The essential characteristics of these two remain the same in all ages: *Attila,* the man who rules by brute force, acts on the range of the moment, is concerned with nothing but the physical reality immediately before him, respects nothing but man's muscles, and regards a fist, a club or a gun as the only answer to any problem [for example, Hitler]—and *the Witch Doctor,* the man who dreads physical reality, dreads the necessity of practical action, and escapes into his emotions, into visions of some mystic realm where his wishes enjoy a supernatural power unlimited by the absolute of nature [for example, Hegel, and all the irrationalist philosophers and religionists who paved the way for Hitler or who supported him].

I saw her essay as a dazzling tour de force, exciting in its historical sweep, lucid in its arguments and integrations, dramatic in its imagery, moving and inspiring in its conclusions. It called upon the "new intellectual" to take up the banner of reason and to repudiate the initiation of force as a means of achieving social goals.

A few years after the book was published, some professors of philosophy who admired her work told me that although they agreed with her conclusions in the main, they saw her treatment of historical figures such as Hume, Spencer, and Kant as oversimplified, in some respects erroneous, and gratuitously hostile in ways that did not serve the valid points she wished to make.

When they first conveyed this to me, I was unreceptive, because I believed that Ayn wrote at a level of broad essentials that they did not appreciate. Later, on further reading and reflection, I came to think they were right. If Ayn disagreed with someone, she rarely confined herself to stating her reasons; in a biting mixture of moralizing and psychologizing, she typically impugned her opponents' motives, often casting them as villains in an almost theatrical sense. Moreover, she was not a conscientious scholar of the history of philosophy. Far from it; in the eighteen years of our relationship, I cannot recall a single book on philosophy that she read from cover to cover. She skimmed; she read summaries and distillations; and she depended on the reports of her associates, such as Leonard, Barbara, and me. Progressively, Leonard became her primary resource.

"What is awesome," one professor remarked to me, "is how often she is right. She hears or reads two paragraphs—and goes right to the heart of the issue. Her intuitions are staggeringly on target, even if the word *intuition* would probably make her angry."

Sidney Hook attacked *For the New Intellectual* at length in the *New York Times Book Review,* declaring that Ayn was wrong to identify intellectual freedom with economic freedom and to insist that a free mind and a free market are corollaries, given that Socrates had a free mind in a society that did not have a free market. In view of how and why Socrates died—he was sentenced to death for teaching ideas of which his fellow citizens did not approve—I found this an astounding argument, especially from a professor of philosophy; I wondered what Hook thought "a free mind" meant. I was determined to write, and publish, a detailed rebuttal of Hook's piece. I knew it would be too long for the *Times*'s Letters to the Editor column, so I raised money from Ayn's friends and admirers and took out a full-page *Times* ad. It gave me considerable pride and satisfaction to see my answer in print.

On this occasion, I discovered anew that I found the atmosphere of intellectual combat exhilarating. Seeing this, Ayn briefly became more cheerful. "It was almost worth Hook's review," she said exuberantly, "to see you in action. You're a born crusader." I agreed happily.

Whatever the frustrations in my personal life, I enjoyed the work I was doing and the subculture in which I moved. I had created my own world socially and at NBI, and I felt proud of what I had done. Growing up, I had lacked any sense of structure; now, I had created for myself the structure I wanted and needed. My life had roots at last. It is impossible for me to overstate the importance of this fact—with regard to what was to happen later.

I was beginning to be asked to lecture at various colleges and universities. I found that I especially liked addressing audiences where there was some hostility toward my ideas, not only because I was normally surrounded by so much agreement and wanted the excitement of a different experience but also because I was stimulated by the challenge of turning adversaries around. In retrospect, I see myself at those lectures as combining an incongruous mixture of arrogance and good humor, impatience and benevolence—a blend that sometimes antagonized and sometimes impressed favorably.

Among my other activities, I was giving a series of radio talks (invited by station WBAI-FM) on "the moral revolution in *Atlas Shrugged*." Bennett Cerf was present one evening at Ayn's as we sat listening to a recorded broadcast. Afterward, when Bennett complimented me, I wondered aloud if there might be a worthwhile book in these talks, and Bennett enthusiastically said yes. Soon we were discussing the book I would write—*Who Is Ayn Rand?* My initial intention was to do three essays, one on Ayn's philosophy, one on her contribution to psychology, and one on her literary accomplishments; that was to be the entire book. But when Bennett suggested that I include a biographical essay on Ayn, I suggested that Barbara write it. It was in preparation for this essay that Barbara and I taped many hours of Ayn talking about her life and development. Barbara asked the majority of the questions, because this was her project.

The opportunity to convey in print my perception of Ayn's achievements struck me as the most thrilling way to begin my writing career. I did not hesitate to set aside the book I had been writing on anxiety. I was already growing dissatisfied with that project, anyway. I wanted to present my theory of anxiety not by itself but rather in the context of my theory of self-esteem, which I was continuing to develop, and I had begun to wonder if I should begin again from scratch with self-esteem as my central subject. For the time being, all that was put on hold in favor of *Who Is Ayn Rand?*

I welcomed the opportunity to do my own exposition of Ayn's ethics. Because Ayn had been compelled in *Atlas* to present her metaethics (her derivation of "Man's Life as the standard of value") in its barest essentials, I wanted to write a more detailed presentation. In later years, she praised my effort as being clearer than the version not only in the novel but also in her own nonfiction essays, such as "The Objectivist Ethics," which appeared in the collection *The Virtue of Selfishness*. I mention this not out of boastfulness but to stress the nature of our intellectual relationship during this period.

In writing *Who Is Ayn Rand?* I also welcomed the opportunity to express my profound admiration for her literary achievements and to give my reasons. I knew how culturally invisible Ayn felt in this regard.

As a consequence of my working on this book, Ayn and I shifted to a deeper level of harmony. Her reproaches almost entirely disappeared. She could hardly complain that I was neglecting her when her rival was this book. Our times together had a warmth and affection that allowed me to imagine, for brief moments, that our problems were behind us.

Once, when I expressed appreciation for something she had done, she replied, with the faintest edge to her voice, "That's me the mind. What of me the woman?" I felt a stab of alarm and pain. Something must have shown on my face; she touched my arm and said softly, "No, that's not right. Sorry, darling. Haven't you shown me enough? Forget I said that." But we both knew that she had said exactly what she meant; only now, because I was writing *Who Is Ayn Rand?* she did not feel entitled to reproach me. "You're my lifeline to reality," she said many times, which was both a compliment and a demand. But I lacked the wisdom or the courage to name the demand to myself or to her.

If Ayn and I grew closer during this period, Barbara and I once again began drifting apart. This pattern had been operative from the beginning; when one relationship was better, the other was worse. The three of us were part of one continually shifting system. None of the problems between Barbara and me had been resolved. The moments when I felt connected to her never lasted.

And yet Ayn seemed keenly interested in seeing my marriage to Barbara preserved, in spite of the negative observations Ayn made from time to time. It did not enter my mind that she would see Barbara as safe, as no conceivable threat to her, whereas a more happily passionate marriage would change Ayn's place in my life. Only years after the break with Ayn did I suspect that my relationship with Barbara had been convenient for Ayn. Barbara was manageable.

I had hoped that writing the biographical essay would make Barbara happier. Literarily, she had done a very good job. It did make her happier, but not much. The theme of gently muted sadness remained central to her, at least as I saw her. In retrospect, that sadness seems thoroughly understandable.

Barbara's insistence that she loved me was as fervent as ever. I was confused and paralyzed when, in the midst of an argument, she would imply that I was cruel to be so impatient with her in light of how much I meant to her. I was often left feeling speechless and guilty. *Did* she love me? Then why couldn't she show it in ways that were more recognizable and meaningful to me? She was now conveying the unmistakable message that she could not live without me; this was new. After a quarrel she would tell me, with tears streaming down her face, "I would *die* without you in my life." I would feel grateful, irritated, and remorseful.

After such episodes, I would plunge back into writing, lecturing, and studying. I would urge my friends to do more, fight harder, and lift themselves higher for Objectivism and for Ayn. I would recapture the single-tracked focus that allowed me to feel that I was an unstoppable force.

It was Ayn who sensed the danger and who tried to warn me. "You're in love with struggle," she said to me. "In some ways you romanticize it. Is that the legacy of *Jean-Christophe*? Short range, that can be a source of strength. Long range, it can hurt you—it can blind you to issues you need to resolve. You have to be willing to struggle when it's necessary. But remember, the goal is to be serene—like Galt—and to be happy."

I laughed, and answered, "Lots of time to be serene when I'm older." I knew this was not a viewpoint I could defend intellectually, but it was how I felt.

Ayn shook her head nonreproachfully. "Right now you're in love with your own energy. You're drunk on Nathaniel Branden. I understand that. It's good. But it's not the whole story. Life is more than waging a battle and being a fighter." I could see that she was thinking not of Barbara and me but of herself and me—and that she still hoped for the day when we would be together again in the full sense. She wanted more of my energy directed toward her.

"I hate bitterness," Ayn said to me. "That would be the real victory of pain that I don't want to allow—to turn bitter. I've got to keep my sense of the benevolent universe."

She made some version of this statement every few months. She was preoccupied with not being affected by pain in any fundamental way, and I always did my best to reassure her that her spirit remained untouched.

"When I sit at my desk alone, I'm happy," she went on. "I reread *Atlas*, and nothing else matters. It's when I come out of my office, above all when I have to deal with the world, that I droop. If only I didn't feel such loathing. If only there was someone to respect and admire." She continued to speak as if she were in a vacuum, as if nothing that *Atlas* and NBI were accomplishing in the culture really reached her.

About a year earlier, in 1960, she had given her first university lecture, at Yale Law School. Ayn, Frank, Barbara, and I drove to Yale together, and Ayn finished writing her talk in the car, fighting motion sickness. That she had left the preparation of her talk to the very end revealed the strength of her resistance to public speaking; this was not the last time I would see her carsick while endeavoring to finish a speech en route. Her title was "Faith and Force: The Destroyers of the Modern World." Although there had been no special advance publicity, the large auditorium was overflowing, and additional students listened to the lecture via loudspeakers in another room and from still other speakers outside the building.

Now, she was accepting more such invitations. During the early 1960s, she spoke at Harvard, Johns Hopkins, the University of Wisconsin, Hunter College, Columbia, Brooklyn College, Purdue, Massachusetts Institute of Technology, Sarah Lawrence, Brown, and the University of Michigan, among others. Invariably, she attracted enormous crowds, so much so that typically Barbara or I would call the university in advance, inquiring as to the size of the room they had scheduled and then suggesting that they get a larger one. Students came to applaud her, and a few came to hiss, but they came in enormous numbers, electrified by her clarity, unconventionality, and intransigence. One could see hostile students laughing in appreciation at some of her answers, in spite of themselves. She was provocative, challenging, sui generis—she stood before them, often wearing a black cape and a gold dollar sign pin given to her by Frank—and they responded with a passion of their own.

"She," I heard one student remark to another, "is what a teacher *should* be. She *cares* about ideas."

Ayn liked the question periods the most. She did not enjoy lecturing as such, regarding it as a duty to be done "for the sake of *Atlas*." On this subject, Barbara has quoted her (in *The Passion of Ayn Rand*) as saying:

> I didn't, and don't, want to do it. . . . I know why they need to see me in person, that seeing me gives them the reality of Objectivist ideas existing here and now, not merely in a book. If this helps to spread Objectivism, and helps the sale of my books, then it's publicity for which I'm being paid, and I'm willing to do it. I don't like the personal adulation or any of the "fan" atmosphere. It's not on my terms. I appreciate the intention in an impersonal, professional way, but it means nothing to me personally. When anyone compliments me, my first question is: What's my estimate of the source of the compliments? Is it a mind I respect? When it's a mind that understands what I've done, then it's an enormous pleasure. Anything less than that—no. I don't really want anything but the response of top minds. . . . How I would love to meet a really first-class mind, a first-class person.

I understood this perspective but did not always sympathize. I was not convinced that her meeting one or two "first-class minds" would really change anything; they would still be competing with her fictional creations. And if Ayn saw herself as a great innovator, if she believed that she saw certain issues more clearly than anyone else, I felt that there was not much sense in her complaining that the world was so slow to catch up with her.

In her own writings, she ferociously attacked the intellectual establishment, the literary-artistic establishment, the educational establishment, the religious establishment—just about every establishment I could think of. And Newton had taught us that for every action there is an equal and opposite reaction, so it could be argued that the enormity of the establishment's hysterical animosity toward her had its own logic. She knew how to reach people—above all the young—and it seemed to me that if she thought and planned long-range, she should forget about her contemporaries and realize that her most important converts were now in the universities. I continued to wish that she would complain less about the lack of "top minds" and reach out more to the young people eager to learn from her. Her public demeanor remained far too remote, moralistic, suspicious, critical, and lacking in simple human warmth. That was her way of staying in control—and of reinforcing her alienation.

In June 1961, I gave the last lecture in "Basic Principles of Objectivism." It was titled "Why Human Beings Repress and Drive Underground Not the Worst Within Them but the Best." I wanted my students to honor their own idealism, their hunger for a life superior to the one they saw around them—to have the courage to listen to their own deepest longings and highest aspirations. In some respects, this was my favorite lecture in the course, and I took great pleasure in giving it.

Tonight, there was an unexpected pang at the thought that I would not be seeing Patrecia Gullison again until—I did not know when. I had come to look forward to the sight of her face each week. For the space of an evening, my consciousness split in two; part of it gave the lecture and answered students' questions with Ayn beside me on the platform, while another part disappeared with Patrecia into some special realm where there were feelings but no words. In that dream, I was free to experience the unique sense of connection between us without having to reflect on its meaning. The thought of losing the experience felt suddenly, shockingly painful.

"Have you had a good time here this spring?" I asked her at the end of the evening, when people all around us were saying good-bye to one another. She had waited until I had said good-bye to everyone else.

"I've had a *wonderful* time," she answered radiantly. "Do you know, when I first heard about these lectures, I pictured everyone as being much older, and I imagined you as a man in your sixties. I thought I would be the only young person here." She looked at me with a kind of stunning directness, as if there were nothing between us, neither space nor air, and I thought her face went beyond any concept of purity I had ever imagined. I must have frozen, because she asked, abruptly and good-humoredly, as if there was no reason why she shouldn't ask it, "What's happened to your breathing?"

"Nothing has happened to my breathing," I insisted, feeling shy and excited at once. "Did you find my lectures clear? Do you find me easy to understand?"

"You?" she said brightly. "Oh, you're easy to understand. I guess that's a compliment to both of us, isn't it?"

"Yes, it is," I answered, happy now to be on safer ground. "I wonder if you'll be taking any more of our lectures."

"I'll be back to take this course again in the fall. And if you give any other course, I'll take that, too. I want to learn."

"Why?" I asked challengingly.

"Nothing is as important as learning," she said earnestly.

She went on to tell me that she planned to go to college; her family had not been able to send her, and she was now saving every dollar she could from her modeling to finance her education. I commented on a book she had with her, and she said that wherever she went, on any job, she always carried a book. She communicated this in one long rush, as if she wanted me to know everything about her in a single moment and, simultaneously, as if speaking were a distraction.

"What do you want to study in college?" I asked.

"I don't know. Everything. I like history. I want to understand the world and people."

Neither of us wanted to end the conversation, but when I saw Ayn and Barbara looking at me pleasantly and patiently, I held out my hand and said, "See you in the fall, Patrecia."

She shook my hand with the faintest touch of exaggerated formality, and I was amused at the thought that she was mocking me a little, impishly. I liked the touch of her skin.

"Who was the girl you were talking to?" Ayn asked as we walked out of the hotel.

"She's a model. Her name is Patrecia Gullison."

"Good appearance," she said with easy, matter-of-fact goodwill. Ayn was very aware of people's looks and was typically complimentary about any appearance she admired. Not once did I ever sense in her the slightest jealousy about anyone's attractiveness.

"She's excited about the lectures," I said.

"She has the type of looks I like—you know, long legs, very slender, high cheekbones, light eyes. She's the physical type of my heroines."

"Oh, do you think so?"

And yet, over the summer, I still did not think about Patrecia. Not very much.

That August, I proposed to Ayn that together we create an intellectual newsletter. It would be an outlet for articles we would write on a variety of subjects, as well as a means of maintaining contact with students and admirers of her work.

My intention was that Ayn and I would be the chief writers for the newsletter and that the other members of the Collective would also contribute. We worked on developing the concept all through the fall, and the first issue of *The Objectivist Newsletter* was planned for January 1962. Ayn became progressively more enthusiastic about the undertaking as the months passed.

Ayn's attorney, Paul Gitlin, drew up the papers of incorporation for the project. Ayn and I were to be equal partners with equal rights and authority in all matters pertaining to the newsletter. "What happens if you two have a falling out?" asked Paul Gitlin. "What happens if there are differences you can't resolve?" Ayn smiled and answered, "Hardly likely. Still, you're right; we must cover that. First, let's agree that nothing is published that the other opposes; each of us will have absolute veto power. Second, if our differences are basic and can't be resolved, we will terminate publication, so that neither of us will be able to profit from the work and contribution of the other."

Ayn and I were listed as publishers and editors; Barbara, as managing editor; Elayne, as circulation manager.

It was perfectly natural, I told myself as I approached the start of "Basic Principles of Objectivism" at the end of September, that I should be looking forward to seeing Patricia Gullison again. She was attractive, she had a bright kind of energy, she was enthusiastic about Objectivism—she was a thoroughly likable human being. I enjoyed looking at her and talking to her. She was practically a child, twenty-one years old, ten years my junior. Even if Barbara and Ayn were not in my life, there would be no challenge in attaining anyone that young. The frequency with which I reminded myself of her youth should have been a warning about the depth of my feeling; it wasn't.

She arrived only a few minutes before the lecture was to begin, and there was no opportunity to talk to her. When she looked at me through-out the lecture, I thought she was a little remote, a little pulled back, as if contemplating me from a greater distance. The class was unusually large, and afterward Ayn and I were surrounded by students eager to extend the question period. When I was able to look for Patrecia, she had gone. The following week she arrived early, as warm and open as she had ever been, and almost immediately we began to talk.

"You didn't wait to say good-bye last week," I said without reproach.

"I wanted to see what it would feel like not to," she answered cheer-fully, as if the issue had no charge and as if there were no reason not to be truthful. While I groped for some appropriate response, she went on, smiling, "I heard you grew up in Toronto. I was born there!"

In answer to my questions, she told me that her family had moved from Toronto to California when she was seven. She had an identical twin sis-ter, Leisha; a brother, Ralph, who was several years older; and another sister, Anne, who was older still. Her family had "pioneered" for a while in California, "in the middle of nowhere."

"The man who was supposed to build us a house and have it waiting when we arrived from Canada disappeared with our money, leaving us with this empty stretch of land. When I was twelve years old, I helped dig for water. It was so exciting!"

Her father was a hairdresser, her mother operated a nursery school in Palo Alto, and they had divorced some years ago. Patrecia and Leisha were both represented by the Eileen Ford Agency and sometimes did tele-vision commercials as twins. They had both come to New York from Palo Alto only at the beginning of the year, shortly before Patrecia came to my first lecture.

"You mean there are *two* of you," I could not help exclaiming.

She laughed. "Well—not really. Psychologically, Leisha and I are very different. I don't know if I could ever persuade Leisha to come to lectures like this. I'm going to try."

Her eyes were the most beautiful shade of blue; they had such abun-dant life in them. Her forehead was broad; I recalled a line of Victor Hugo's that Ayn had once quoted, to the effect that a lot of forehead in a face was like a lot of sky in a painting.

"Why do you like the lectures so much?" I asked her.

"It's what Miss Rand and her novels—and now you—represent to me. *Sanity.*"

Sanity. Just what I had once told Ayn she gave me.

"Patrecia, you're an interesting person."

"So are you," she announced, and I could not tell whether I saw a touch of humor in her eyes.

In November, I learned that she had begun dating a fellow NBI student, Lawrence Scott, who had heard Ayn's speech at Yale and had become interested in Objectivism. He and I exchanged a few sentences, and he struck me as a thoroughly decent and attractive man, intelligent and serious.

Still, Patrecia continued to look at me as she had always looked at me.

That fall, Ayn received an invitation to speak at Ford Hall Forum in Boston. She fell in love with this particular organization and would speak there every spring until the year of her death, except one time when illness made an appearance impossible.

At first, she had been reluctant to accept the invitation, because she associated Ford Hall Forum with the political Left, but she was treated royally by her hosts, drew enormous crowds from her first lecture onward (admirers came from all over the country to hear her there), and this prestigious institution became her favorite lecture platform.

Her first lecture, delivered on December 17, 1961, was "America's Persecuted Minority: Big Business." Early that day, to the surprise and delight of the people at Ford Hall Forum, lines formed around the block for tickets. Here is how her speech began (I quote it because it captures the typical emotional quality of an Ayn Rand lecture):

> If a small group of men were always regarded as guilty, in any clash with any other group, regardless of the issues or circumstances involved, would you call it persecution? If this group were always made to pay for the sins, errors, or failures of any other group, would you call *that* persecution? If this group had to live under a silent reign of terror, under special laws, from which all other groups were immune, laws which the accused could not grasp or define in advance and which the accuser could interpret in any way he pleased—would you call *that* persecution? If this group were penalized, not for its faults but for its virtues, not for its incompetence but for its ability, not for its failure but for its achievements—would you call *that* persecution?
>
> If your answer is yes, then ask yourself what sort of monstrous injustice you are condoning, supporting, or perpetrating. That group is the American businessman.

Most of the Collective had driven to Boston for this event, and we were all thrilled by the overflow crowd, the enthusiasm of the audience, the crackling tension of the question-and-answer period, the thunderous applause that refused to stop. To us, it was another sign that Objectivism was on the march.

In *Atlas Shrugged,* Ayn had portrayed the American businessman at his best. She had also written an indictment of the pro-statist businessman who is often mistaken for a representative of capitalism, the type who prefers government protection to free trade, political privilege to competition, and legislation that gives him special favors denied to others. This latter type is in fact the chief villain in the novel. And yet Ayn had little interest in business or businesspeople as such—"just as I had no significant interest in architecture, except as a vehicle for *The Fountainhead.*" Business was a symbol; in her writing it stood for free trade and free minds, for productive achievement, for the material means of human survival, for the glory of life on earth.

Certainly, big business did not support her or her work in any way; did not buy and distribute *Atlas* in quantity, as one might imagine it would; did not champion her publicly; did not write her letters of appreciation; did not invite her to address boards of directors. I suspected that for most businesspeople she was far too radical; she advocated *total* laissez-faire. Then there was her stand on religion. And there was the business community's fear of controversy—any kind of controversy.

My impression was that her message was better received by small-and middle-level business than by big business, which was more invested in the status quo. Taxes on corporations, for instance, tended to protect older, more established businesses against aggressive, talented newcomers for whom capital accumulation was made much more difficult. Old money rarely favored laissez-faire. Those who *consistently* support the separation of state and economics are a minority in any economic group.

I said to Ayn, "One day, I really ought to write an article titled 'Big Business Versus Capitalism.'"

"I'm afraid you're right," she answered.

"What you've given us in *Atlas is* business 'as it might be and ought to be.'"

"And sometimes *is.* What is realistic is my presentation of the *process* of industrial achievement; what is romantic is that I created characters who match that process."

Ayn's penchant for seeing life as a great novel in which good and evil are locked in combat was central to her psychology (her treatment of business was only one example). This was evident in *Atlas Shrugged* and no less evident in her personal communications. Her outlook had a strain of Manichaeism—the tendency to see good and evil as essentially separate and opposed principles and to interpret all human experience in terms of their confrontation.

My own tendency was to think more biologically—to see life as a struggle for adaptation, so that behavior was best understood in terms of survival strategies and coping processes, which may be more or less appropriate, more or less in accord with the individual's actual long-term interests. The term *biocentric* (life-centered) had not yet entered my vocabulary, but its meaning was already present in my thinking. I compared the concepts of good and evil to the concepts of health and illness. They designated what was beneficial and harmful to our physical and spiritual-psychological well-being. The notion of sin was relatively absent from my thinking, whereas in Ayn's, on some level, it was still active. When I saw behavior I did not admire, or strongly disapproved of, I was still inclined to wonder, What is this person trying to accomplish?

Of course, I pronounced moral judgments, but I was never the passionate moralist—or moralizer—that Ayn was. In retrospect, I would say that in emotional terms I had achieved far greater separation of morality from any religious connotation or influence. To me, immorality was a bad strategy chosen when one could have chosen better. It's not that Ayn would have said otherwise about the literal meaning of *immorality*, but she had a need to make severe moral pronouncements on every conceivable occasion, charged with heat and indignation. Ayn used the word *evil* frequently; I used it, too, but sparingly.

We were aware of our differences but did not attach much significance to them. Ayn was satisfied that I was passionate about my values and convictions, even if my form of expression was different from hers. "Your perspective comes from being a psychologist," she said. "It's not a fundamental difference between us."

As I reread the articles we wrote for *The Objectivist Newsletter*, this difference in our focus struck me as apparent, in spite of the inappropriate moralism sometimes present in my writing. Ayn's pieces were far more filled with the language of moral contempt. In the articles I wrote after 1964, when *The Objectivist Newsletter* became a magazine called *The Objectivist*, I see the difference as more apparent still, no doubt reflecting shifts in my thinking that were not yet fully conscious.

Nonetheless, there was a streak of Objectivist puritanism in all the Collective members that at times drove out normal human warmth. The zealous concern with being morally irreproachable, combined with a tendency toward emotional repression, often inhibited spontaneity and natural affection. My own affectionate impulses, when they were not blocked entirely, often took the form of psychological encouragement, or pats on the head, or an occasional squeeze of an arm, which rarely closed the distance between the other person and me. In other moods, I could project an austerity that could be intimidating and anxiety provoking. The paradox was that because Ayn took her irreproachability for granted, she was often the freest in communicating positive feelings toward her friends; in some moods, she was kinder and more emotionally expressive than anyone else in our circle.

The tendency to be stiff and formal was noticeable in many students of Objectivism, especially when more than two people were present. "Two Objectivists by themselves can sometimes have a good time," someone said to me, "but as soon as you add a third person, everyone gets self-conscious. And parties are often a disaster. No one wants to be thought 'mindless.'"

There were wonderful exceptions. One was a baseball game held in Central Park between the "Attilas" and the "Witch Doctors," whose members included most of the Collective, plus various NBI students. What made the event so special and so enjoyable was that all matters of intellectual rank vanished and only baseball mattered. I smile whenever I remember the unconstrained laughter of that atypical afternoon.

Many smaller Objectivist circles had formed throughout the city and throughout North America. Many friendships, marriages, love affairs, job opportunities, and business associations were born out of these meetings. Ayn and I enjoyed the idea of our own ever-expanding subculture.

Occasionally, I would hear that someone had been "excommunicated" from one of these groups because of some betrayal of Objectivist standards. It seemed to me that some of these students were more severe than Ayn or I in their condemnation of infractions. "They're more royalist than the king," Ayn would comment wryly. "I guess all intellectual movements have to cope with one aspect or another of the 'true believer syndrome,'" I remarked once. Some years earlier, Ayn had discovered Eric Hoffer's *True Believer* and had recommended it to Barbara and me. "Because of our emphasis on rationality and independence," Ayn had confidently forecast, "this won't be a problem for us." I now knew that she was overly optimistic as far as our followers were concerned; I did not yet recognize that she was mistaken even about the inner circle.

Ayn had observed that in the main the lectures on Objectivism had made "better people" of even our least promising students. If asked what she meant by "better people," she could have said correctly that they were inspired by the ideal of rationality as a way of life; inspired by the ideals of independence, honesty, justice, and productiveness; and committed to taking responsibility for themselves. All of this, we saw when reflecting on the situation, had positive consequences for their behavior.

What they would not have learned from us was the importance of listening to their own inner signals, those messages from the organism that are not encoded in conceptual language. If anything, they would have learned to be almost ritualistically suspicious of the nonverbal or the subconscious. This we did not see—or if we did, we did not perceive it as a problem. Certainly, our students would have learned nothing of the "wisdom of the body"; many of them would be reinforced in alienation from the body. We did not see this, either; we did not see that an adequate psychology had to address the entire organism, not merely the neocortex.

Neither would our students have learned anything about kindness or compassion; they learned only an intellectualized kind of "benevolence," which had little to do with real encounters between real human beings. Yet if Man's Life is the standard of value, then in a world in which accidents, misfortunes, and disasters are real and continuing possibilities, kindness and compassion have survival value. Granted, it is an error to treat them as the most important virtues, placing them above rationality or integrity (which would make suffering the most important part of life), but they *are* virtues nonetheless. I am not speaking of self-sacrifice or of "compassion" coercively engineered by a government but of private, voluntary mutual aid, generosity, and goodwill. These traits and practices are life supporting. A society whose members value them is more adaptive biologically than one whose members do not. If life is the standard of the good, then kindness, compassion, and a spirit of mutual aid are virtues to be cultivated. This was a logical implication of our own ethics that we did not grasp. Some of us were kinder and more compassionate than others, but that was, in effect, a psychological matter, not one judged to be philosophically significant.

Meanwhile, the requests for our lectures came streaming in from all over the world. We began hearing of Objectivist study groups as far away as India and Australia. We were besieged with requests for more information about the philosophy.

"I really must write a comprehensive treatise on Objectivism," Ayn said many times. I sat through hours of hearing her think aloud about this project, knowing it would never happen, because the emotional energy to do it was not there.

As planned, *The Objectivist Newsletter* began publication in January 1962. The lead article, written by Ayn, was titled "Choose Your Issues" and dealt with the importance of not allowing the enemy to choose the terms of the battle and of knowing what is essential and what is not. Here is part of that article:

> Neither a man nor a nation can have a practical policy without any basic principles to integrate it, to set its goals and guide its course. Just as the United States, having abandoned its own principles, is floundering aimlessly in international affairs, is unable to act and is merely *reacting* to the issues chosen and raised by Soviet Russia—so, in domestic affairs, the "conservatives" are unable to act and are merely *reacting* to the issues chosen and raised by the statists, thus accepting and helping to propagate the statists' premises.

Barbara wrote a review of Ludwig von Mises's *Planned Chaos,* introducing von Mises to what was to become a new and ever-widening audience. The entire Austrian school of free enterprise economics was to gain a much broader readership because of our reviews and recommendations. Alan Greenspan wrote a piece titled "The Crisis over Berlin":

> Over a piece of real estate scarcely the size of Rhode Island, the Russians have brought the world to a state of war. . . .
>
> History rarely offers so controlled an experiment in rival economic systems as has been seen in Berlin during the last decade. In the late 1940s, when the rest of Western Europe was sinking under a morass of socialistic experiments, West Germany, including West Berlin, turned instead to free enterprise (at least predominantly). The results were dramatic: from a country defeated and devastated by war, it rose to become spectacularly prosperous. Meanwhile, East Germany and East Berlin barely emerged from the rubble.

I wrote about the relationship between reason and emotion. In the months ahead, although I occasionally wrote in other fields such as ethics and economics, I tended to favor psychological themes. Leonard, Edith Efron, and Robert Hessen, a young historian who had joined our circle and worked at NBI, contributed to future issues.

Ayn began writing a weekly column for the *Los Angeles Times* and subsequently went into national syndication. Her ability to remain surprising was always in evidence. For one column she wrote an unusually moving piece on the death of Marilyn Monroe; in its sensitive appreciation of what the actress stood for in the minds of a great many people, it revealed yet another aspect of Ayn's complex personality. But a little more than a year later she abandoned this project, in part because it required too much reading of and attention to current events.

In 1962, NBI began publishing Ayn's lectures and essays, as well as Barbara's, my own, and a few other people's, in pamphlet form. An essay of Barbara's, "The Moral Antagonism of Capitalism and Socialism," was adapted from a radio talk she had given. Eventually, we established NBI Book Service to sell these pamphlets by mail along with the books we were recommending to our students. NBI had moved out of our apartment and now had regular offices, shared with *The Objectivist Newsletter* and an increasing number of employees. In this environment, Barbara seemed to flower; she became an excellent administrator and handled the daily flow of business with cheerful competence. I loved watching her in this arena; she was most alive here, and I felt validated in the sense of connection I still felt with her. Here she was a crusader, and she felt in her element. If we both had a need for a great moral adventure, which was central to our motivation during those years, it was fulfilled by Objectivism; the happiness this provided allowed many other frustrations to be tolerated far longer than they otherwise might have been.

Who Is Ayn Rand? was scheduled for publication in June 1962. I wanted Ayn to be pleased with the final result, and she said she was, but sometimes when we discussed the book I noted some reserve. When I asked her about it, she said, "The book is wonderful. But you and Barbara shouldn't have had to write it, not my own students; it's almost humiliating. It should have been written by an outsider." I quoted this to Barbara, who sighed, "I wish—just once—Ayn could be completely satisfied about something."

"There's someone at the lectures you two should get to know," Joan said to Barbara and me one evening. "Her name is Patrecia Gullison. Her boyfriend is Larry Scott. Allan and I think they're a really nice couple."

"Patrecia is a very unusual girl," Allan agreed enthusiastically.

"In what way?" I inquired carefully.

"Well, she . . ." Joan began eagerly and then broke off. "You'll have to see for yourself. She's just different. It's hard to explain."

I did not know whether Barbara noticed the looks on their faces, something young and attractively vulnerable that touched me.

"The clearest thing I can say about her," Joan added, "is that when you're with her, you like the way you feel about yourself."

"I think Patrecia and Larry are engaged," Allan remarked.

When Patrecia and Larry had coffee with Barbara and me, I consciously chose to focus most of my attention on Larry, who kept raising philosophical questions that I enjoyed answering, knowing it was Patrecia for whom I was showing off.

They informed us that they planned to be married in June. I congratulated them both, thinking idly that Larry was the same age as I, which meant he was ten years older than Patrecia. But they looked attractive together; he did not seem too old for her. If someone had asked me what I was feeling, I would have said that I was happy for them in a detached, benevolent sort of way, and I would not have found significance in the numbness that felt like a general anesthetic to my body.

One evening after a lecture, Patrecia announced in a state of high excitement, "Miss Rand invited Larry and me over for a visit!"

Later, when I asked Ayn about it, she told me she was impressed by them both; she saw them as serious and idealistic. "I think I agree with Joan; Patrecia has a lightness of spirit that's interesting, not ordinary. Of course, she's young; we'll have to see what she grows into." Then Ayn chuckled and announced, "I invited myself to their wedding. All four of us will be getting an invitation." The feeling of numbness deepened. "Terrific," I said.

Barbara and I had learned that Larry was quite a good amateur photographer, and we asked him to take our pictures for the jacket of *Who Is Ayn Rand?* He came with Patrecia to our apartment on an afternoon in May. When the photographic session was over, Larry had to leave for an appointment, and we invited Patrecia to stay on for a visit.

I wanted Barbara to like her, to appreciate her as I did. When I saw Barbara warming to Patrecia's bright energy and unself-conscious openness—as Patrecia talked about her life, about what *The Fountainhead* and *Atlas Shrugged* meant to her, about the modeling profession, about her admiration for Larry—I felt a quiet exhilaration. With great warmth, Barbara was conveying a friendliness and goodwill that matched my sense of the occasion.

Patrecia made no attempt to disguise her pleasure at being in our apartment and answering our questions and being the focus of our attention. In her eagerness to make herself known to us, her words sometimes tripped over each other, her voice rising in uncontrolled excitement: "Oh, God, listen to how loud I'm getting!" She had a youthful vulnerability that made her totally unlike anyone else we knew.

Something Patrecia said prompted Barbara to ask if she ever felt bored, for example, if she were on a date with an uninteresting man. Looking surprised at the question, Patrecia answered that she never felt bored. "I think people who get bored easily are people who are boring themselves, part dead inside and looking to others to make life interesting. There are always ways to make an evening entertaining, if you're not passive." I asked her how, and she said, "This will probably sound crazy. I don't know if I can explain it, but there's a kind of music inside of me, and I can bring that music to anything I'm doing—and sometimes I can draw music out of whoever I'm talking to, at least while I'm talking to them."

It was time to take our dog, Muttnik, for a walk, and I asked if the two women would join me. Barbara said, "I'm a little tired. I feel like reading for a while. Why don't the two of you go?"

On the street Patrecia said, "I'm afraid I don't express myself clearly sometimes. I wish I were more articulate. I think I might have been a bit intimidated by Barbara; she speaks so well." I asked her if I intimidated her. "Oh, no," she answered. "Because I always know you're going to understand me, so I'm not afraid of how I'll sound, so I speak more clearly."

I complimented her on her candor in naming her fear. She shrugged and said easily, "Why shouldn't I name it? Everyone is afraid of something, at one time or another. I'm not afraid to admit it; a lot of people are. That's not just fear; it's cowardice. I'm not a coward."

A young boy went sailing past us on his bicycle, an expression of rapture on his face. Pointing to him as he went by, Patrecia said, "Oh, look. Isn't his face perfect? There's something so innocent about a young boy. His bicycle is his spaceship."

I told her that I had felt that sometimes when I was a boy, and she answered, as if uttering an obvious truth, "One of the best things about you is that you're friendly with that side of yourself." I did not think I had a single friend who would have made that statement or even agreed with it.

I was conscious of how she moved; she had a superabundant energy that seemed to spill out of her gestures and steps like a torrent of life. This was combined with a gracefulness that at one moment made me think of the movements of a dancer and the next of an athlete. It was the gracefulness, I realized, of a person for whom the body is experienced as the primary vehicle of self-expression—the body as soul in action.

"You have a way of moving that projects a magnificent enjoyment of life," I said casually.

She received this with delight, as a precious compliment. "When I was sixteen, I wanted to be a dancer. I danced all the time." When I asked her why she didn't pursue it, she answered, "It wasn't mental enough. I knew in the end it would be frustrating. I wanted an outlet for my mind." I asked, "What might that be?" For the briefest of moments, I saw sadness touch her eyes, as she said, "I don't know yet."

Then, without transition, she began speaking of how much she liked Ayn's treatment of man in her novels: "To me, that's one of the most important things about her as a writer." I had the sense that she took some pleasure in leaping from subject to subject unexpectedly, challenging me to follow. "Can you believe there are readers who are surprised when they learn Ayn Rand is a woman? Is that stupid? Only a woman could write her novels; only a woman could have her perspective on the male characters. The passion for the shape of a man's body, for example. Her kind of man worship. When I read it, I felt, '*That's me*. That's the way I feel—about man the ideal, the abstraction.' Not most of the actual men one meets, of course. When I first read *The Fountainhead,* I was excited from the very beginning—the description of Howard Roark standing on the cliff. I was in love with Ayn's angle of vision, the way she looks at things. It felt like coming home to myself."

"I think she's a remarkable person," I said to Barbara later.

Patrecia's twin sister, Leisha, now attended my lectures. The resemblance was truly startling. At thirty feet I could still mistake one woman for the other, although Patrecia's features were slightly finer. Even close-up, some people were confused.

Leisha elicited in me none of the feelings that Patrecia inspired. Leisha conveyed anxiety and a desperate desire to please, an eagerness to be perceived as "good." She could hardly have been more conventional in her values, I thought. Whereas I saw Patrecia as active, assertive, and independent, I saw Leisha as passive, accommodating, and dependent—by conventional standards, more feminine. She had initially been reluctant to come to the lectures because Patrecia's enthusiasm had scared her a little. "In the modeling field," Patrecia mentioned once without rancor, "most people like Leisha more." Reflecting on the difference in my response to the two women, I thought how much more important the spiritual was than the physical in terms of what draws one human being to another.

I learned that Patrecia, the younger of the two, had spent the first eleven days of her life in an incubator. And yet from infancy onward, her parents perceived her as the most aggressive member of the family, the most exploratory and adventuresome. "I always felt Leisha was closer to me," her mother had told her, "because Leisha was more timid, more afraid. I could understand that. To me, you were always a teeny bit of a stranger."

One evening at NBI, I saw Patrecia talking to Joan Kennedy Taylor, and I joined them. Joan lived a considerable distance from the hotel where I lectured, and I offered to give her a lift home; I had never done this before. Casually, I said to Patrecia, "Come along with us. I'll drop you off, too."

I drove Joan home first, then headed south again, through Central Park, toward Patrecia's apartment on the East Side. It was a warm night, and the top of the convertible was down.

We did not speak. Patrecia sat with her head thrown back, her eyes closed, her face lifted to the night. The delicate, sculptured planes of her face projected not sensuality but near transcendence. She looked ecstatic.

It was the shocking suddenness of my own response that stunned me. In the next instant, I was aware only of the slenderness of her body under her summer dress, of the line of her legs and hips. And for one terrifying, intoxicating moment, I thought that my hand was going to reach down to take possession of her—simply, as a right—certain that it was what she wanted.

When she got out of the car across the street from the apartment she now shared with Larry, I called, "See you at the wedding!" and drove off.

The next time I saw her, May 31, she was walking down the aisle on her father's arm. Larry stood waiting for her, smiling proudly and happily, and Barbara sat on one side of me, Ayn and Frank on the other.

"She looks beautiful," Ayn whispered. I was unable to answer or to move, because, now, for the first time, the thought was clear and unmistakable in my mind: "I do not like this. I do not like Patrecia's marrying another man."

The intensity of my reaction was shocking. It was as if I were experiencing a personal violation, as if my most private possession were being taken from me. The questions my reactions raised were terrifying, except that I did not feel terrified. I felt excited, agitated, absorbed by my own passion.

Standing in line behind Ayn, Frank, and Barbara, waiting to congratulate the bride and groom and their families, I thought that in this context it would be permissible for me to hold her for an instant and to kiss her, and I felt reckless about what she would or would not sense in my touch.

Then we were off to the restaurant where the wedding party was being held, and I could feel nothing but the memory of her skin and her mouth. From a great distance, I was astonished to notice that I continued to talk and act normally. But inside, I was completely out of control. I moved from person to person, unable to concentrate. I chatted with Leisha and with Patrecia's parents, Elsie and Raymond. Raymond had read Ayn and admired her and tried to talk to me about it; I heard nothing. Then Patrecia broke through the crowd and asked that Ayn, Frank, Barbara, and I pose

Ayn, Barbara, and Nathaniel
at the wedding of Patrecia and Larry Scott, 1962

with Larry and her for wedding pictures. The experience was disorienting; how could she seem happily in love with Larry and at the same time look at me in that special way of hers that caused the ordinary context of my life to vanish? The next day they were scheduled to depart for a honeymoon in Europe.

Later that evening, alone with Barbara in our apartment, I told myself, "All right. Back to reality."

In early June, a few days after the wedding, Barbara and I stood together on Fifth Avenue, looking at the prominent display of *Who Is Ayn Rand?* in Brentano's window.

Since the age of fourteen, I had known I wanted to be a writer. Now, seeing a dozen or more copies of my first book in Brentano's window, I felt transported. My problems with Barbara and Ayn vanished; Patrecia was a pleasantly distant memory. Nothing existed but the books in front of me.

The expression on her face told me that Barbara felt as I did. She, too, was looking at the first concrete fulfillment of a dream held since adolescence—to be a professional writer. We held hands. We knew why we had come together as a couple and why we had remained together—for the values that had led us to this moment. We were where we belonged.

Neither Barbara nor I could imagine an alternative to the life we were living. For all practical purposes, we thought of happiness not in terms of our personal lives but in terms of the progress of Objectivism. We had been euphoric, for example, when Ayn had received a letter from L. Quincy Mumford, Librarian of Congress, in which he had written: "Among the most widely discussed philosophies of our time is that associated with your writings. In your fiction and essays you have made the Objectivist philosophy an issue affecting many levels of public discourse. When the history of our time is written, your work will have a prominent place. In order to insure that your work will be the subject of informed study, I invite you to place your manuscripts and personal papers in the Library of Congress." Our shared pleasure in events such as this was our substitute for the fulfillments of a real marriage.

Another such pleasure, in the fall of 1963, was our trip with Ayn and Frank to Lewis and Clark College in Portland, Oregon, where Ayn was to become an honorary doctor of humane letters. The entire student body and faculty was to read *Atlas Shrugged,* and there would be two days of discussions, some led by Ayn, some led by the two of us together. Ayn and Frank were in high spirits. For two days, I forgot every problem in my life and was simply and uncomplicatedly happy.

Barbara and I thought of progress in terms of the sales of Ayn's books, the lecture invitations, the radio broadcasts, the articles on Ayn's work that were now appearing with increasing frequency, the student enrollment at NBI, the number of cities across the continent where our lectures were offered, and the people who were entering our lives as a consequence of their response to *Atlas Shrugged.* We watched the flow of new people with passionate interest.

An important friendship had developed between Ayn and John Hospers, a professor of philosophy at Brooklyn College. He had heard Ayn speak there and had been greatly impressed, even though his orientation was radically different from hers in virtually every sphere. He later wrote several widely used textbooks and was destined for a distinguished career. Reading *Atlas,* he became wildly enthusiastic. He visited Ayn regularly to discuss philosophy and became a total convert politically and a partial convert ethically; their enduring differences centered on epistemology, metaphysics, and aesthetics. Hospers was more sympathetic to logical positivism and linguistic analysis, though he was not a pure exponent of either; he found many of Ayn's criticisms persuasive. More important to both of them, however, was the passion they shared for philosophy. I saw that Ayn enjoyed talking to him as she enjoyed few "outsiders"; she found him unusually intelligent and fair-minded and on more than one occasion addressed his classes.

Their friendship had come to a painful ending in October 1962 when, at Hospers's instigation, Ayn addressed the annual meeting of the American Society for Aesthetics at Harvard University. Her speech was titled "Art as Sense of Life," and Hospers was to comment on her paper. He offered to show her his comments in advance, but she declined, saying that she was confident of his friendship and his integrity and that she knew the event would be what she called "civilized." After her talk, Hospers proceeded to challenge her viewpoint, not with the good-natured demand for greater clarification or specificity she expected but with the kind of gentle sarcasm that professors take for granted and that Ayn found appalling. To her, it was an enormous, unforgivable betrayal.

When she responded to Hospers's critique with her own brand of sarcasm, I sank deeper into my seat, knowing that disaster had struck. Afterward, while Ayn went back to the hotel with the rest of our group for a party in our suite, I was assigned to bring Hospers along in a separate car and in effect to read him the riot act. I went through the motions halfheartedly, feeling thoroughly miserable.

At the party, no one acknowledged Hospers, no one spoke to him, and Ayn acted as if he were not there. I whispered to Barbara, "If Ayn is really through with him, she owes it to him to say it to his face." Barbara nodded, sharing my discomfort. But Ayn said nothing to him, and their relationship ended that night.

Years later, when he was teaching philosophy at the University of Southern California, I talked with him one evening about the meaning of Ayn in his life. He spoke of her with passionate admiration, telling me that the memory of those wonderful philosophical discussions was still precious to him as one of the highlights of his intellectual career. "You know," he said gently, "when Barbara interviewed me for *The Passion of Ayn Rand,* and I began to talk about the past, suddenly—so many years later—I found myself weeping. Isn't that remarkable?" I answered sadly, "That was how Ayn could affect people."

During this same period, I formed a friendship that was to enjoy a somewhat longer life than Ayn's and John's. Robert Efron, Edith's brother, was a research neurophysiologist at the Veterans Administration Hospital in Boston. I was greatly impressed by one statement he had made about *Atlas:* "This is the work of a great biologist." We visited each other's cities and had many long discussions about biology, psychology, and philosophy. I found him to be among the most brilliant of the new people we were meeting. I noted that, although their relations were cordial, Ayn never quite shared my enthusiasm. Like his sister Edith, Robert Efron was not a "worshiper" of the kind Ayn was used to in the Collective. He was older and more formed by the time he met Ayn; he exhibited a certain detachment that I thought made Ayn suspicious, although she never said so. She would subtly rebuke me sometimes when I told her I was going to Boston for the weekend.

"Do you really find him more worthwhile than the Collective?" she would ask.

I would answer, "He's got more to say that interests me right now; that's all I can tell you."

"What kinds of things do you talk about?"

"Oh, lots of things. Evolution, for instance."

She would shrug and drop the subject. I knew it was not the Collective she felt protective of but herself; she was jealous of any interest of mine she could not share. What went unsaid between us was that time spent with Robert Efron was time taken away from her.

I was fond of Edith, and sometimes Ayn was tense about that, too. There was an irreverence to Edith and a streak of sarcasm. I did not like the sarcasm, but I did like the irreverence.

Within a few years, Edith was excommunicated, and Barbara and I met with her alone to deliver the sentence. We would both regret our loss, agreeing that, along with her brother, she was among the best minds we had met. We reproached ourselves for our complicity in banishing her. In 1981, about a decade and a half later, I asked Barbara, "Why were we angry with Edith Efron? Why was she expelled?" Barbara sighed and answered, "I haven't the foggiest idea."

We met Henry Mark Holzer, known as Hank, and his wife, Erika—both attorneys—and Hank became the lawyer for Ayn and me, doing work for both *The Objectivist Newsletter* and NBI. Occasionally, we wanted strong letters sent to someone on our behalf, and Holzer's zeal in such matters was intense in those days. He had a style that was more than a little abrasive.

We met screenwriter Al Ramrus and television producer Ted Yates; economist Martin Anderson, later to become an adviser to two presidents; theatrical manager Ralph Roseman; drama coach and stage director

Phillip Smith; his actress wife, Kay Nolte Smith, who later became a gifted writer of psychological thrillers; Spanish artist Jose Capuletti, whose work Ayn first saw at the Hammer Gallery on Fifty-Seventh Street and greatly admired; psychologist Roger Callahan and his wife Barbara; and psychologist Lee Shulman and Lee's future wife Joyce, who would also become a psychologist. Roger, Lee, and Joyce became particular friends of mine, along with Ralph Roseman.

I met Lee and Joyce through Roger Callahan, whom I met as a consequence of his enthusiasm for the chapter on psychology in *Who Is Ayn Rand?* At that time, Roger and Lee more or less shared the ideas of psychologist Albert Ellis, and as a result of our association, they shifted their thinking in my direction—to the annoyance of Ellis who seemed to feel that Roger and Lee had been "stolen."

I had met Ellis some years earlier, in 1958, when Mike Wallace had published an interview with me in the *New York Post*. Ellis dropped me a note complimenting me on it, which led to a lunch at his institute. We soon discovered that although we both professed to be advocates of reason, agreed that irrational beliefs played a central role in emotional problems, and shared a disdain for psychoanalysis, the differences in our ideas were profound. Ellis was a materialist, an advocate of logical positivism, and a moral relativist. He was antagonistic toward any notion of certainty and was especially antagonistic to my concept of self-esteem (which he misrepresented for many years). Our relationship at that time was cordial but distant.

The parties Barbara and I threw got bigger. In addition to our new friends and acquaintances, my sisters Reva and Florence in Toronto, and their husbands, Sholey and Hans, sometimes came to New York and were included in social events. Roger, Lee, and Joyce, all of whom lived in Detroit, also visited us in New York periodically. "You have truly created your own society, darling," Ayn said to me. "With all its imperfections, it's a magnificent beginning." I knew that in another mood she could speak of our friends differently. But for the moment, I was glad to hear her say it.

One day, Joan telephoned and invited Barbara and me to a New Year's Eve party. I asked if anyone outside the Collective were coming. I did not deceive myself about why I was asking or for whose presence I was hoping. Joan answered, "Bob Efron and his wife from Boston. Al Ramrus. Larry and Patrecia Scott. Oh, I don't know who else—I'm still calling people." In that instant, Joan felt to me like an infinitely precious human being.

When Ayn, Frank, Barbara, and I arrived at the New Year's party, on December 31, 1962, we acted out our ritual. Everyone rose to greet Ayn. She turned around, like a child preening, and waited for people to admire her outfit. Praise was instantly forthcoming. Then Ayn pulled out a cigarette holder and lit up. Then the party proceeded.

Tonight, I did not pay attention to any of this. My eyes searched the room. But she had not yet arrived. I wandered around, feeling restless.

When the doorbell rang and Patrecia and Larry entered, I deliberately held back until they had said their hellos, then walked over and shook their hands warmly. They greeted me exuberantly, as if I were their closest friend.

I thought impersonally that they looked good together. Both were tall and held themselves confidently. She had blue eyes and blond hair; his eyes and hair were dark brown.

At some point, I heard Patrecia mention "the two most rational men I know," and I knew she was speaking of Larry and me. She went on, looking directly at me, "Larry is the most rational man I know." She glanced at him with great warmth and affection, then her glance swung back to me. "You're next. I live with Larry and I know him, and I don't really know what you're like on a daily basis, so you're the second most rational man I know." I saw that she was playing with me, and I was amused. She's full of herself tonight, I thought.

Larry was grinning at me with unreserved esteem. It was as if what Patrecia was saying and doing had his full understanding and blessing.

"Did I hear you call Nathan the *second* most rational man you know?" Joan asked Patrecia, chuckling.

"Uh-oh, look at his face," Patrecia said in mock fear, pointing at me. "He doesn't like that."

Suddenly, I felt shy and slightly unnerved. Another part of me enjoyed the fact that she dared to tease me. No one ever dared to tease me.

She leaned forward almost intimately and asked, "You want to be first in everything, don't you—with everyone?" Her insinuation was so flirtatious that I wondered what those standing around were thinking. Larry continued to beam. I could not help myself; I began to laugh, in self-protection.

Stepping still closer, in the manner of a detective trying to intimidate a suspect, she persisted, "Isn't that what you really want? To be number one, in every possible respect, with everyone, women in particular?"

It happened much too quickly and much too unexpectedly for me to assimilate that what she was saying was essentially true—not about women in general but certainly about her. It was a truth that was now

Patrecia, 23, two years after first meeting Nathaniel at NBI, 1963 throwing me off balance, because I had not known it or faced it until this moment—my desire to be important to her. Just the same, I felt, it was not a fact to be announced in this manner and context; her youth and her exuberance had gotten the better of her judgment. "Have you been drinking?" I joked, knowing that she did not drink.

Suddenly, the humor vanished from her face, and disappointment took its place. "You lack courage," she said wonderingly. "Nathaniel Branden lacks courage. Can this really be possible?"

I knew that, a moment earlier, she had wanted me to acknowledge unapologetically the accuracy of what she was saying, to acknowledge it and not to make a joke of it while allowing the deeper meaning of her statement to remain silently understood between us.

Although I saw objectively that she was acting inappropriately, this knowledge was swept aside by a rush of elation. She is not afraid of me! I rejoiced. In the world in which I moved, I had been elevated to a larger-than-life status. In front of all my friends, knowing my position here, she had dared to say to me, "You lack courage." She stood there gazing at me, this beautiful, electrifying person, neither child nor woman, with the smile of a young girl and eyes that had looked upon the world for a thousand years. I felt joyfully transparent. I felt overwhelmed with admiration. I felt drunk.

"Barbara!" I called at the top of my voice. "Barbara! Where are you? You've got to hear this! Patrecia says I lack courage." Habit drove me to share this moment with Barbara—habit, and the desire to avoid, until I could be alone, the deeper meaning of what had taken place. I strode into Allan's study where she was talking with a few friends. Eagerly, I tried to convey what had just happened and what had so impressed me. Barbara smiled affectionately and went on talking to our friends. Ayn, sitting next to Barbara, looked at me blankly.

When I returned to the living room, Patrecia was deep in conversation. For the rest of the evening, her eyes sparkled with humor whenever she glanced in my direction. Periodically, I would break into a laugh, unable to shake off the sense of intoxication and to return to normal consciousness.

I fell asleep thinking of Patrecia. I woke up thinking of Patrecia. All New Year's Day, I saw her face before me. That was how 1963 began.

14

"I'M COMING BACK to life," Ayn began saying with increasing frequency and urgency in the spring of 1963. "Can you imagine what these past years would have been like if you did not exist?" she asked during one of my visits, and I felt a familiar sense of heaviness. "Do you still love me?"

With only the briefest pause, I answered yes, knowing that the sense in which this was true was not the sense she meant or wanted.

It was the only answer that would not have precipitated an immediate crisis, the end point of which would have been the annihilation of our relationship. "I refuse to see myself as a nonsexual being," she had said to me. "If we're not a romance, we're nothing."

That she and I might be "nothing" was not a possibility I could accept. And in an impersonal way, I approved of the way she insisted on seeing herself—as someone I *should* find desirable. I often experienced her perspective—and her pain—as my own. That was part of the trap.

She went on, "Do you think . . . ?" There was no mystery about the meaning of the unsaid; she wanted my reassurance about the eventual resumption of our affair.

I replied, "I need time. Life at home is more and more of a shambles. I've got to find a way to pull my marriage together." Of course, this was purely an excuse, in that my marital problems had nothing to do with sexual remoteness from Ayn.

She sighed. "I don't feel fully ready yet, either. I was just testing your attitude for the future. Can I help you with Barbara?"

Neither of us found such an exchange bizarre.

Long before my encounters with Patrecia, I had begun to feel increasingly distant from Barbara. Nothing essential had improved between us. Notwithstanding her work at NBI and for *The Objectivist Newsletter,* which

I appreciated and admired, I felt progressively more estranged from her. I knew I was hurting her, and I did not know what to do.

We got on each other's nerves. Our sexual relationship fluctuated between nonexistent and uninspiring. In earlier times, in spite of our problems, there were times when our sexual encounters were somehow happy and wonderful, even if that was not often. But those times were gone. Now we were becoming increasingly critical of each other—impatient, judgmental, chastising.

I continued to be stunned by her declarations of the last two or three years that she could not live without me. I felt that I still loved her in some sense, and so I was often touched by what she said, and yet I felt no closer to understanding her responses to me than in the first years of our relationship.

And I did not fully understand myself, either. I did not understand the nature of the tie still holding me to her. It had never been easy for me to decide that I loved someone; once I did decide, once I lifted the barrier within me, it was as if I could never fully close it again. So Barbara was part of me, fused at the level of identity.

I was now thirty-three, and Barbara was thirty-four. I did not fully grasp the magnitude of her unhappiness. I did not know that in her own mind, she had decided that if she had not found a way to be happy in our world by the time she was forty, she would leave it all behind—leave me and leave Ayn if need be, leave everything, and start her life all over again. She told me that years later. When I heard it, I knew that in this respect she'd had more common sense than I.

While she allowed herself to wonder about options and alternatives, my mind was closed to other possibilities. Once, returning home from an evening of dancing in the country, she said hesitantly and tentatively, "We had a good time tonight. We enjoyed the music and dancing. It was fun. Ayn wouldn't have. She wouldn't have liked the music or anything else about tonight."

Immediately, I felt defensive about Ayn and responded, "True, it wouldn't have been her kind of evening, but . . ." I did not finish the sentence because I did not know how to.

Quietly and persistently, Barbara said, "Nathan, listen—please listen. Ayn would see a difference of this kind as a gulf between us, a gulf in our values." I did not answer. "Nathan, what does that mean?"

I sighed unhappily. "I don't know what it means." Barbara sank back into her seat and let the subject drop. I felt immense compassion for her. In remaining silent, I felt I was betraying her. If I had spoken my true feelings, I would have betrayed Ayn. Barbara was crying out for the right to have a youth, to be free and happy; I did not acknowledge that she was crying out for me to respond in that way as well.

The entire structure of my life felt precarious—all of it resting as it ultimately did on a relationship that seemed indestructible one moment and appallingly fragile the next. Deeper than any estrangement that had developed between us was my tie to Ayn at the most profound level; the thought of being without her was intolerable. I could not have said what benefits I now derived from our friendship. I was increasingly aware of feeling drained by it. Yet I could not let go. Our relationship was the rock of my life. It felt as if I had come to Ayn out of a void—and without her and the world we had created, a void was all that awaited me.

When I saw Patrecia and Larry together, they seemed harmonious. I liked the respect and esteem they conveyed to each other. With me, Patrecia was a shade more reserved than she had been in the past, which I thought appropriate. For me, the experience of New Year's Eve had been like taking a dangerously exhilarating drug; an experience enjoyed once but not to be repeated because it was too threatening to what I would have called the "rational" shape of my life. It was quite beyond my view of the universe to understand that the drug was striving to *liberate* my reason, not to overwhelm it.

When I was not thinking about my marriage or my future with Ayn, I was thinking about the book I wanted to write on self-esteem. But the chaos boiling inside me made concentration difficult. Life consisted of interruptions. If I was not having a quarrel with Barbara, I was called on some emergency by Ayn. If life was peaceful with them, I had to fly to another city to give the opening lecture in my course, "Basic Principles of Objectivism."

On one occasion, all four of us flew to San Francisco for an opening night with several hundred students, and Ayn joined me in the question period. A short time later, we topped this event with the biggest opening night in our history—eleven hundred people in Los Angeles. The overflow crowd listened to the lecture in the foyer through loudspeakers. A fire marshal came to inform me that the size of the audience was hopelessly in violation of the fire law; then he winked and told me not to worry, just to clear people out of the aisles a little. He was an admirer of Ayn Rand. His name was David Bergland, and one day he would be the Libertarian Party's presidential candidate.

If my writing was not interrupted by problems, it was interrupted by triumphs—by the growth of NBI and the demand for more personal appearances. Moreover, I had to contribute an article each month to the newsletter. Gradually, I conceived the idea of writing psychological articles that I would later adapt for my book on self-esteem. First, I prepared an outline for the book. Next, from the outline, I projected a series of articles. Then, I scrambled the order in which I wrote them. It was the only way I could think of to get the book done.

To celebrate the success of our work and to expand our vision of an Objectivist minisociety further, Barbara and I decided to hold an NBI ball. Everyone in the Collective was enthusiastic—except Ayn. "Don't you think you should have asked my opinion in the matter before you said anything to anyone?" she asked me sharply. I replied, bewildered and slightly annoyed, that I couldn't have imagined that she would disapprove. "Objectivism," she declared sternly, "is me—and I am not feeling particularly happy. A ball seems frivolous. NBI is an educational organization, not a social one." I sighed, thinking of what Barbara had tried to tell me the night we had gone dancing. I pointed out to Ayn that it was not unusual for schools and universities to hold dances; reluctantly, she agreed. Then, suppressing my anger, I asked her if she wished me to cancel the event. "No, I won't ask that. But thank you for making the offer. It was the right thing to do."

The event was black-tie. Mike Wallace and his wife sat at our table, and his presence seemed to please Ayn enormously. She joked with him, "Do you suppose you will be publicly compromised by being seen here tonight?"

I danced with Barbara. I danced with Ayn. I danced with Joan. Then I felt free to dance with Patrecia.

From the moment she came into my arms, my defenses collapsed, as did hers. We communicated through our silence. Holding her body, I felt that I knew it more intimately than I knew Barbara's or Ayn's. For the first time, I allowed myself to know fully and consciously that I wanted her. When I danced with her again at the end of the evening, I saw Ayn watching us; it seemed to me that her eyes were angry.

Preparing for bed that night, I thought that I had received a sentence with no appeal—to live with this desire, never to act on it, never to acknowledge it to anyone, and somehow to find a way to endure.

To my friends and students, I became still more aloof. There was nothing of importance within myself that I was prepared to share. I felt encased in ice.

That spring, neither Larry nor Patrecia attended any NBI lectures. They came only to a reading I had done of Ayn's three plays—*Night of January 16th*, *Ideal*, and *Think Twice*. Then they appeared at the end of the season's last lecture.

"Just dropped by to say hello," Larry said. They looked radiantly cheerful, the perfect image of a happily married couple.

"Wait a while," I said. "We'll have coffee."

A television crew was there to tape an interview with me. Larry and Patrecia stood watching and smiling. I was conscious of the energy flowing to me from her glance.

The television taping took longer than expected. They could not wait. They waved and left.

I did not see her again for nearly four months.

By fall, I had locked Patrecia away in some specially sealed compartment of my mind—like one of those anomalous facts that scientists neither deny nor affirm because it cannot be integrated into any recognized structure of knowledge and belief.

Barbara and I had moved into a new building at 120 East Thirty-Fourth Street; we had a large apartment on the twentieth floor. On the second floor of the same building were the offices of NBI and *The Objectivist Newsletter.* I had an office in our apartment; I preferred it to working below, where Barbara and our staff worked. We now had a business manager—Wilfred, Barbara's old boyfriend and sometime antagonist from Winnipeg. He had brought his family to New York in May 1963.

He himself came to New York approximately a year earlier for reasons of his own that were unrelated to Objectivism or to Barbara. At some point, he began helping NBI as an unpaid consultant. One day, Barbara came to me and proposed expanding Wilfred's role at NBI to full-time employee. The fact that we could not pay him what he was worth did not matter to him. She conveyed that he had lost enthusiasm for his Winnipeg business and wanted to involve himself more deeply in the Objectivist cause. I thought about it for a while and then said, "OK, let's give it a try."

Her face was expressionless as she answered, "Thank you."

Later, I said, "I know you and Wilfred will always care for each other. That's not a problem to me. I trust you completely."

I knew that they were spending a good deal of time together and had been for more than a year. They seemed to be getting along better than they ever had before, which in no way troubled me. I knew that Wilfred was one of the most important men in Barbara's life and always would be, and I was comfortable with that.

"Barbara has suffered so terribly over Ayn," I told myself. I wanted her to have something of her own, but not an affair. An affair struck me as invalidation of everything Barbara and I had been trying to create. In spite of all that had happened, some part of me clung to the vision of her as "my Barbara." I suspected I was being completely unreasonable yet felt incapable of thinking my way out of it. I knew that they would not have an affair in secret, without my knowledge and consent.

One afternoon in October, I met Patrecia on the street. She was carrying a huge black model's case in one hand and a handbag and book in the other. Our greeting was warm, cheerful, and unstrained. She mentioned that she was thinking of taking some classes at Hunter College. I mentioned a new course of lectures I was preparing on psychology. Then I said, "If you're ever in my neighborhood and feel like coming up for a cup of coffee, consider yourself invited." Her eyes shone with a child's excitement. "Really?"

I wondered how soon she would come. The thought of her visit flooded me with happiness.

When she entered my office, she walked carefully—almost, I thought, as if she were entering a temple. As she moved around the room, looking at objects, running her hand over a book or a vase or stack of paper, there was a suggestion of reverence in her touch. Yet her manner projected not humility but confidence and a deadly earnest joyfulness.

This was her theme, I thought as I watched her. This was her sense of life—not joy exactly but ecstasy. It shot into the world from her eyes.

"Can you believe," she said, sitting in a chair by my desk, "that when I saw you for the first time at NBI, you struck me as much older than I? I was twenty-one that night and you were thirty-one; it seemed like such a great distance. Far greater than the distance between Larry and me, though you two are the same age. And then that night we stopped by when you were being televised last June, I thought for the first time how young you look." I answered that I felt especially young whenever I talked to her and that I did not know why.

We both spoke with a kind of grim earnestness that was devoid of flirtatiousness or sexuality, as if the occasion were too solemn for any hint of lightness. Only later did we relax and begin to smile.

I sat on the sofa facing her and asked questions about her childhood, wanting to know everything I could about how she had developed. She spoke of her early years as insane. "I grew up in a totally irrational universe." Her parents were some kind of eccentric Christian mystics who believed in spirits and demons and supernatural forces, and they had terrified their children with these notions. She related a number of quite frightening experiences in her early years.

"In spite of the terrible things he did," Patrecia said, "I felt sympathy for my father. I thought my mother treated him terribly. She starved him sexually and tried to squeeze the life out of him."

I asked, "What did you learn from all that?" and Patrecia answered, "I learned, very early, that most of the terrible things people do, they do because they are afraid. No, not because they are afraid; because they won't *admit* they are afraid."

I admired the serenity with which she spoke. She did not seem eager to discuss her childhood, but she answered my questions willingly. She told me of the most appalling incidents without a trace of bitterness or self-pity; she did not see herself as anyone's victim.

"I don't like people who are bitter, do you?" she said. "They feel sorry for themselves."

She asked me if I remembered the time she had spoken of having music inside of her, and I told her I did. "The music helped me," she said. "I mean, the conviction that something better was possible."

We began to talk about *Atlas Shrugged* and *The Fountainhead* and their meaning to her. Here, my critical antenna was fully up. Her statements were impeccable; she seemed to understand the spirit and vision of those books with her whole being, even if she did not yet fully grasp some of the more technical philosophical issues.

"This is so wonderful," she said suddenly. "I am so happy to be here. I've always wanted a chance to talk to you like this."

Then she proceeded to tell me, guilelessly, that sometimes when she was alone in her apartment, she danced to me—that is, danced around the room while imagining that I was her audience and that she was speaking to me not with words but with the motions of the dance. I searched her face for any hint of seductiveness; I saw only innocence and pleasure at the memory of what she was describing. "Sometimes, when something was troubling me, you helped me." "Do you do this only when you're troubled?" I asked. "Not at all," she answered with the faintest suggestion of a smile.

Toward the end of the afternoon, she expressed concern that she had talked too much. "I think I really wanted you to know me," she said. I asked why that was important to her and she replied that perhaps she wanted validation. "From you that would mean something."

When Barbara came home, I told her about the visit, reporting a good deal of what had been said. I did not mention the part about Patrecia's dancing to me. Nor did I mention the exhilaration that was tearing through my body like fire. Having no idea of the depth or intensity of what I was feeling, Barbara projected nothing but happiness for me, total and absolute benevolence.

A week or two later, Patrecia returned. This time, she entered my office with the carefree manner of someone who has decided to be daring. She walked to the chair behind my desk and sat down. "I want to see the room from your perspective," she explained. Then she stood up. "Was that improper?"

"Absolutely not," I heard myself saying. "Please sit down again. I like seeing you there."

I felt such a rush of sexual excitement that I flung myself down on the sofa, hoping she would not notice.

We talked about philosophy, and modeling, and Leisha, and the people she had met at NBI, and why some students seem to use Objectivism in ways that enrich their lives while others merely turn into robots. She mentioned how kind Allan and Joan had been to her. "Joan once said she wanted to adopt me," Patrecia said, laughing. This was an aspect of Joan that was unknown to me, and I was intrigued. "When you're alone with Joan," Patrecia was saying, "and she relaxes, she gets open—and lovable." I was intrigued; I did not doubt that this was true.

When I went into the kitchen to make coffee, Patrecia accompanied me. I did not turn on the light, and the room was in half-shadow; light came only from the broad expanse of the living room window. She stood in the center of the room, her back to me, and I broke. I put my arms around her wordlessly, holding her as if my life depended on it, as if I were struggling in an invisible sea and her body were my only support. She leaned against me. Her head was against my cheek, and I saw that her eyes were closed. I felt despair.

After a moment, I stepped away and resumed making coffee, concentrating on keeping my movements steady. I was not prepared to speak of what had happened, and I saw her accept my decision. We returned to my office and continued our discussion, our eyes saying everything that our words did not.

I did not see her again for two weeks, until early December. It's not love, I told myself insistently. It's some kind of incredible fascination. I felt my world disintegrating.

There could be no question of confronting Barbara or Ayn with what was happening and asking them to understand what I did not understand myself. On one side, there was Barbara, my wife, my comrade-in-battle with whom I had been building a relationship for fifteen years. On the other side, there was Ayn, whom I admired more than anyone on earth and who spoke of me as her lifeline to the world without whom her existence would be unbearable. Against that, there was a twenty-three-year-old woman at a far lower level of philosophical development who earned her living as a fashion model—and with whom I felt an affinity, an aliveness, an *awakening* that was as terrifying in its intensity as it was incomprehensible to my rational mind.

I knew that the essence of my attraction to Patrecia was spiritual and that the sexual attraction, though supremely important, was only a consequence. However, I could not yet identify the content of the spiritual connection; I experienced only its overpowering presence.

I believed that, whatever my mistakes had been with Barbara or Ayn, I had always striven to conduct each relationship with honor. Was I about to forfeit my integrity for a passion I could not justify? I refused to consider an affair. Yet the idea became an obsession.

What I needed, I thought, was time. Time to sort out my feelings, to see what was happening in rational perspective—as I taught others to do. Time to cut myself free—not from Barbara or Ayn but from Patrecia.

On the day of her third visit, it was snowing. She wore a fur coat and hat and looked unbearably beautiful, the light in her eyes wiping every thought from my mind but one. I pulled her against me, her arms rose eagerly around my neck, and our mouths crushed each other as if this first kiss might also be our last. Her hat fell to the floor.

Then I stepped back, helped her take off her coat, and led her into my office. We fell into each other's arms again. Her face reflected only pure, guiltless enjoyment, with none of the pain that sometimes shadows ecstasy.

We did not have sexual intercourse. Neither of us was ready for that. So I was not yet committing myself fully; I might still find a solution that would not lead to disaster. Foolishly, this is what I told myself—not confronting the fact that it was already too late and that nothing could ever be the same again.

A long time later, when we were able to talk, she whispered, "I love you. I've loved you since I was twelve years old, when I first thought that one day I would find a man who would see in my face what I saw in his. Do you think our souls are in our faces? I do. When I was twelve I thought, 'Someday I'll be free from all this, free to find my own kind of life, my own world.'"

I was not prepared to say that I loved her. I had said those words to only two women in my life. I did not know what Patrecia was to me other than that she was oxygen and that for years I had been moving through a world without air. I held her face in my hands, breathing in her being.

I asked her why she had married Larry. She said that she had believed I was unattainable and that she had admired him more than any other man she had met. She felt that she did love him in a way. They seemed to share so many values—Ayn's world and everything it meant to both of them. Larry had wanted to get married, and although she knew she was not ready, she allowed herself to be persuaded because she did not want to lose him. "Larry was the opposite of everything I had seen as a child; he was solid and consistent. That meant a lot to me. He married me, knowing how much I care for you. He cares for you, too, deeply. That's one of the things I admire in him. You don't have to tell me that I've probably made an insane mistake. It's insane to get married when you're not one hundred percent certain. Cruel to Larry, and cruel to myself."

"Yes."

And then, overcome by the reality of our present circumstances, I said miserably, "So what are we doing now? This is completely wrong."

"Yes," she said sadly.

I saw the way she was looking at me, the trust in her eyes. "Patrecia, will you give me time to think? There are things about my life you don't know. It's all much more complicated than you can imagine."

Patrecia could never have guessed that I was thinking about Ayn. She said she knew how much I loved Barbara. That was obvious, and she expected absolutely nothing of me. Today might be the beginning and the end between us, but if we were to continue together in this manner, she would not deceive Larry. She would tell him the truth. He had a right to know the facts and to decide whether he wished to go on living with her while she worked out her relationship with me. "He does not deserve this," I agreed sadly, thinking that in whichever direction I looked, there was only suffering. I asked Patrecia if she would be willing for a while longer to say nothing to him until I had time to think the situation through more carefully, and she said yes.

Alone in my apartment, I paced the living room, swinging between feelings of exultation and torment, struggling with the question of what to do. I had once asked Barbara to endure my affair with Ayn. I could not ask her now to accept *another* woman in my life—one whose meaning to me she could not possibly accept. I knew she would be devastated. I felt that my life depended on what I was now experiencing with Patrecia—this sense of freedom and aliveness—but that I could not justify this to anyone, not in light of my other commitments and values. I told myself that I was a total scoundrel. But if I were a scoundrel, why did I feel cleaner and more like myself when I was with Patrecia than at any other time? I felt that if I confronted Barbara and Ayn with my confession, I would hurt them beyond repair—Ayn in particular, who was far from recovered—and in so doing, I would betray every value I espoused. And if I didn't confront them with the truth, I would betray myself. I saw two roads—and each seemed to lead to moral treason.

Later that week, I fought to keep my face and manner impassive when Barbara asked that I give my consent to her having an affair with Wilfred. She had been seeing a great deal of him. It would change nothing in our marriage, she said—just as Ayn had said it in another context long ago. I thought that if I gave my consent, it would be the final nail in the coffin of our marriage, my final acceptance of the death of the dream I had when I was eighteen years old. It seemed that everything was falling apart: my marriage, my relationship with Ayn, my personal integrity, my vision of what my life was to be. And in the name of the fantasy I was still trying to hang on to, I told her—irrationally, cruelly, stupidly—that I couldn't give her what she wanted. In truth, I did not care if she and Wilfred slept together; it was my *consent* I could not tolerate. If the crash were to come, it would not have my signature of assent.

I did not want to know that I was fighting a battle that had already been lost—the preservation of our marriage. I looked at her hurt face across the dinner table and thought, Now I have given you the right to despise me, because I am truly a hypocrite.

Throughout December, I visited Patrecia in her apartment and she visited me in my office. The passion went on escalating until she begged me to make love to her, saying that right and wrong and long-range consequences no longer mattered to her. I knew this was not true; I knew how proud she was of her own honesty.

I realized that to make love to her would be to embrace the greatest joy of my life and at the same time to enter a nightmare worse than any in my past. She loved me, trusted me, looked up to me, and counted on me to know what I was doing, and all I was prepared to offer were two choices of pain: the pain of our being lost to each other or the pain of being together under dishonest conditions. The third option was not one I was prepared to consider—giving up my world and walking away from Ayn (and Ayn's admiration), Barbara, and NBI. I loved the world I had created. I was proud of it. I could not abandon it. Objectivism was still the central passion of my life.

When Patrecia came to my office early in January, I took her in my arms, I kissed her eyelids, I held her tightly, and I said with agonizing happiness, "I do love you. Of course I love you." I felt as if I were holding my own soul in my arms, in the person of a woman.

"You must think carefully about what I am now going to tell you. If we are to have an affair, you must agree never to tell Larry, never to tell anyone. There are reasons, and I will tell you about them soon, but not today. You must give me your word of honor that unless a day comes when I release you from your promise, whatever happens between us will be secret."

"*Never* tell Larry?" she asked uncomprehendingly. "Never? And you're not going to tell Barbara?"

"No. But Barbara is not the primary problem." This was more bewildering still; her eyes searched my face for some indication of what I could mean. I told her that I knew what I was asking and what she would be hurting within herself. "Don't agree simply out of desire, because you'll regret it later," I said. She looked at me almost contemptuously and replied that if she agreed, it would not be out of desire but out of love.

In the second week of January 1964, knowing that I could not allow her to proceed without fuller knowledge, I met her in Central Park and told her the whole story of my relationships with Barbara and Ayn. The affair with Ayn did not surprise her. "Do you remember," she said, as we sat on a bench overlooking the half-frozen lake, "the night at NBI when, in answer to some question, Ayn said that any fully rational woman who shared her philosophy would be in love with Nathaniel Branden, if only abstractly? You looked so shy and uncomfortable standing there, trying to appear nonchalant. I wondered then, What was Ayn saying about herself?" When I went on to speak of Ayn's suffering and of her lifelong struggles, Patrecia listened with tears in her eyes.

"I cannot deliver a new blow to her," I stated. Patrecia nodded her head—whether in understanding or in agreement, I could not have said. "I can't. And I can't accept losing her, either—she's too important to me. Since I was fourteen years old, this woman has been at the center of my thoughts and my values and everything I admire. You said once I lacked courage. Maybe you're right. Certainly, I lack it in this area." Patrecia's look was silent compassion—for me, for Ayn, for all of us. Herself, as well, perhaps.

"As for Barbara," I went on, "I'm still trying to make the marriage work. Do I sound insane? I'm not ready to give up and walk away. But there's another consideration; if I tell her the truth, then I put her in the position of having to join me in lying to Ayn. Is it right to do that? The torture is, I don't know what's right any longer. That's what's killing me.

I didn't think a problem of this kind was possible. I thought I would always know what was right. I was so proud of that.

"And there are still other factors. I know Ayn. If, at this point, I were to tell her not only that my feeling for her is no longer romantic but that her rival is a girl of twenty-three, it wouldn't matter who the girl was— that would be the end not only of her and my relationship but also of NBI, *The Objectivist Newsletter,* and everything I've been trying to build since Ayn and I started. I can't let it go. I need to be honest with you. I can't let it go. I don't want to. I love it."

"Are you sure," Patrecia asked wonderingly, "that Ayn would react that violently?"

"You would see an explosion such as you cannot even begin to imagine."

She asked why she could not at least tell Larry about us, and I answered, "Because for any of this to make sense, you would have to tell him about my affair with Ayn. Ayn has said over and over again how adamant she is that no one ever know. Some part of her is still a nine-teenth-century Victorian, or the Russian equivalent. I just can't take a chance on Larry talking to somebody else, out of his own pain, perhaps. I've betrayed Ayn in enough ways already. I know what terrible burdens I'm putting on you, so, before things go further, be sure, Patrecia. Please be sure. . . ."

Looking at me as if she were still unable to absorb what I was asking of her, she said with a heartbreaking effort at clarity, "Then I guess the only choice is . . . to give each other up . . . or to take whatever we can have, for as long as we can have it, or until we find an answer. . . ."

I saw my best, highest vision of myself fading before me—and I felt a violent, desperate, rebellious rage: against Ayn, against Barbara, against my sense of invisible chains, against myself for being unable to think my way to a solution that matched my values. I told myself, Don't transfer any part of the blame to Ayn or Barbara; the guilt is yours.

I taught people that if, for any reason whatever, they placed another value higher than their self-esteem, they would pay for it—and the price could be worse than they had the power to imagine. I thought of that now, looking at Patrecia and knowing I was unwilling to give up either Patrecia or Ayn and that the cost of my deception could be terrible. And I thought, So be it.

A week or so later, I again visited her apartment—and we made love for the first time. I told myself that whatever lay ahead, whatever the cost, it would be worth it. As I held her in my arms, the happiness I experienced lifted me beyond any level of fulfillment I had ever known. It was an answer to every frustration, every heaviness, and every moment of suffering in the past fourteen years. "Patrecia and Nathan," I said to her exultantly, and she answered from somewhere inside her music, "Nathan and Patrecia."

Twelve or thirteen days later, in the first week of February, I recognized that my stand on the subject of Wilfred had become ludicrous and unconscionable, so I gave Barbara my consent to their affair. I felt uncomfortable with the credit I was given for my "generosity," because I knew that generosity had nothing to do with it and that I deserved no particular thanks, especially since I did not tell Barbara about my affair with Patrecia.

When I thought of the lies and deceptions to which I was now committed, I felt self-hatred. When I thought of the man beginning to awaken within me, I felt pride. The ascent into liberation, the descent into hell—both had begun.

15

PATRECIA AND I were driving along the Henry Hudson Parkway in the winter of 1964. I had no more passionate wish than to remain in this space forever, cut off from the past and the future, with reality reduced to the sensation of speeding motion, the sight of snow and naked trees against a slate sky, and Patrecia beside me, her face alive with excitement and happiness, her legs stretched comfortably forward, her hand resting on my thigh.

"This is the way I like to see the countryside," I said, "as a backdrop to your face."

"This is the way I like to see the world," she answered, "as a backdrop to your face and your body."

I tried to tell myself that what I was now experiencing with Patrecia was immoral. It was impossible. I could say the words, but I could not make them real. I was betraying Ayn, I was betraying Barbara, I was betraying what I taught my students—and what I was experiencing was a sense of spiritual uplift. How was it possible, I wondered, to be a liar and an adulterer and yet to feel that I was passing through some rite of purification?

I was learning to lie expertly, as I became a master at inventing reasons to be away from the office. If I had only an hour, I would drive to Patrecia's apartment, make frenzied love to her as if I were never to see her again, and leave, sometimes without our exchanging thirty sentences. She had begun to forgo work in order to be available whenever I called. We would talk endlessly on the telephone. There were days, like today, when I would steal four or five hours; sometimes we would spend them in bed in her apartment, and sometimes we would spend them driving in the country.

I existed in a constant state of joy and frustration. If we spent our time making love, I was desperate for conversation; if we spent our time talking, I resented the time taken from lovemaking. If I spoke at too great length, I was desperate for the sound of her voice, but if she spoke at great length, I felt frustrated about all the unexpressed things I wanted to tell her. I wanted to stand looking at her from a distance, to contemplate her as a being in the world apart from me—and I wanted there never to be space between her skin and mine.

Now, racing through the countryside, I remembered a shocking moment in Ayn's study a few days ago, when Ayn had shown me a photograph of Patrecia she had stowed in her desk. She had handed it to me, grinning. Straining to sound casual, I had asked, "How do you happen to have that?"

"I asked her to give it to me," Ayn had answered brightly, amused by my reaction; she always loved to shock. "I told you I like her physical type. She's very American-looking. You couldn't quite imagine her from any other country. You know, that kind of cheerful energy."

My God, there are sides to you I still do not understand, I had thought, telling myself that I was living in a world with Ayn, Patrecia, and Barbara that I would never be able to explain to anyone, including myself.

Mentioning the incident to Patrecia now, I said, "What must you have felt when Ayn asked for the photograph? It must have been awkward for you."

"It was very awkward."

Patrecia began to question me, gently and tactfully, about the evolution of my relationship with Ayn. I could see that a part of her understood perfectly how and why an affair had developed, while another part of her felt dismay at the whole situation. I thought, In her heart, she does not approve. But she squeezed my arm and said only, "The present situation has got to be hard for both of you."

She had never questioned me about my marriage to Barbara. She waited for whatever I was prepared to volunteer. And I had adopted the same policy with regard to Larry.

Nor did she ever ask me about the future. But at our last meeting, she had stunned me by saying, "I'm hoping we'll have six months." My voice strangling, I had asked, "Six months? What are you talking about?" She had answered, "The differences in where we are in life. I'm so far behind you. There's so much I have to learn. You're set on your course; I haven't even found mine yet. You think that doesn't matter, but it will, eventually." Six months—it had the sound of a death sentence.

Now, on the parkway, Patrecia said to me, "You're driving very fast. If you get a ticket, you might be asked when and where and how you got it."

I answered, "You didn't mean that, did you—about six months?"

"I don't know. At this moment, I see us going on indefinitely. When I'm alone and I think about your life and your work, I know that you have other loyalties that have to be respected. And I think of where you are and where I am. Oh, I don't know—I get confused. We'll have to wait and see what happens." Then she shook her head, as if to dispel thoughts of anything but the present moment, and smiled a brilliant smile that demolished pain. "And appreciate what we have," she said.

During one of my visits to her apartment, before the affair began, she had said to me, "There haven't been many women in your life, have there?"

"Just two," I had answered. "How did you know?"

"I knew from the beginning that you were a man who had never been promiscuous."

"But how?"

"You have a special kind of sexual intensity that one wouldn't see in a man who plays around—almost a kind of sexual fanaticism—that I associate with purity."

I had intuitively known what she meant but expressed my surprise that someone so young would know it.

She had answered, "There are certain things—if you're conscious—you just know. Experience doesn't have much to do with it."

Now, in the car, I reminded her of that conversation; I asked her what else she knew about me that she hadn't yet told me, and she answered, "I know you like a lot of distance between yourself and almost all other people, such as your students. It's almost funny, watching you come into the room at a lecture. You have a way of striding toward the platform that says to everyone, loud and clear, 'Don't approach me. Don't speak to me.' You scare people. They don't want just to learn from you. They want to feel that they're important to you, that their admiration and appreciation matter to you—and it doesn't, not in the way they would like. It reaches you, but in a fairly superficial way; you're really off somewhere else. Sometimes I think it wouldn't hurt you to be a little kinder and friendlier with them. But another part of me likes your detachment—I think I would feel a greater pressure to nurture them in some way—and I envy your lack of concern."

I told her that sometimes my sense of distance from my students bothered me, too. "Sometimes I'm more curt than I intend, and then I reproach myself later. You know, in the NBI world, I'm sort of a public person, and if you don't protect yourself, people will swallow you up—their needs don't ever stop. Everyone seems to want something, more than I've got to give. I haven't yet learned how to find the right balance." She nodded in agreement and said, "That's one of the things I think is awful about being other people's fantasy figure. When you're up on the lecture platform, you give them everything you've got. Do they have a right to expect more than that?" I did not say it then, but today I would say, "Yes, they had a right to expect my simple humanity."

"What else do you know about me?" I asked, and she answered, "I know that when we walk down the street together, and I imitate your way of walking, very aggressive, almost a kind of march, with that grim look of a professor very busy thinking about something, you like to see me do it. I make you laugh." It was true; she was an excellent mimic, and she did make me laugh.

"I love you," I said to her.

And yet a voice inside my head would not relent: Is this reality?

In the beginning, I did not know what she would come to mean to me. I thought of our relationship as an extraordinary adventure in love, a unique experience outside the normal orbit of my existence. I imagined that somehow my "normal" life would continue, essentially undisturbed. I wanted to believe that. Yet Patrecia's recent statement about our affair's lasting six months continued to nag at me.

If I'd had greater respect for my emotions, enough to have examined them more carefully—if I had lived less in a world of abstractions—I would have understood far sooner the depth and permanence of my involvement. I would have known that from the moment Patrecia came to my office, my life with Barbara and Ayn had ended, and that if I wanted roots, I would have to create them anew.

The actual end did not come quickly. It took four years and eight months from the first time we made love. Like the process of a long, protracted death, it came with agony and with periods of deluded hope and apparent remission.

It happened against the background of one advance after another in the sphere of work.

For the spread of Objectivism, the 1960s were one long rocket explosion of growth. This itself contributed to my emotional disorientation. I ran from the home I shared with Barbara to Ayn's apartment to the offices of NBI and The Objectivist Newsletter to Patrecia's apartment—while watching in astonishment the poised skill I possessed, that of an emotional juggler. While our personal lives were spinning increasingly out of control, the success of Ayn's, Barbara's, and my working lives kept gathering momentum. We were gaining adherents in escalating numbers, expanding our professional activities in all directions, and broadcasting our message to the world in ever-widening waves of impact. The structure I had wanted to create for myself was growing stronger and more deeply entrenched just at the time when I most needed to break free.

I recall my gratification as I sat in Barbara's office at NBI and listened to her report the stream of requests for our lecture series pouring in from Europe, Africa, Asia, and Australia. I loved the anecdotes she or other staff members would bring to me. An Indian psychologist came to the United States on a fellowship to complete her studies at a university in Boston. Shortly after her arrival, as one of her first questions about America, she asked her hosts, "Can you tell me, please, how to contact Nathaniel Branden Institute, so I can hear the lectures on Ayn Rand's philosophy?" Soon, she was enrolled in the Boston tape series. Incidents like this were reported to me almost every week. Writing in the leftist *New Leader* (September 26, 1960), one antagonist warned his readers, "Objectivism, unlike most other past and present right-wing movements in this country, has more of an intellectual than an emotional appeal and is consequently attracting young people to its ranks." We laughed gleefully at comments of this kind, even though we did not like the designation *right-wing* or any other designation that suggested conservatism, and even though the rest of his article was filled with inaccuracies. In another publication of a similar political persuasion, *New University Thought* (Autumn 1962), an English teacher wrote about the danger of Ayn Rand's influence on college students. Reading it, I felt immense satisfaction.

At Yeshiva University, I spoke with an English teacher, Professor Henry Grinberg, who reported the same trend. At the start of the semester, he had given his freshman English class the assignment of writing a paper on the book they had read during the past year which they had most enjoyed and which had most impressed or influenced them. "Twenty-five percent of my students wrote on one or another of Ayn Rand's novels."

Although Objectivism was attracting people of all ages and backgrounds, it was logical, I thought, that its major following should be among the younger generation, particularly among college students. This group was the one most likely to be open to new ideas; most eager for a rational, intelligible view of life; and most dissatisfied with the intellectual and cultural status quo.

The mail we received at NBI and *The Objectivist Newsletter* provided interesting insights into what was happening around the country. "I heard some people arguing about *Atlas Shrugged* at a dinner party. The book sounded interesting, so I went out and bought it." "I first read *Atlas Shrugged* because people told me it was an evil book no one should read." "After fighting with my professor for a month, I finally obtained permission to do my term paper on Objectivism." "I first discovered the works of Ayn Rand when they were recommended in a course on psychology." "At the end of the first class, my professor of philosophy suddenly announced, without explanation or context, when no reference had been made to the subject, that if anyone turned in a paper on Objectivism, that student would automatically fail." "Can you recommend additional readings to supplement our discussion of Objectivism in an ethics seminar?" "I first heard about Ayn Rand when Galt's speech was quoted in a political science class."

"When our bank mailed out a reprint of Francisco d'Anconia's speech on 'the meaning of money' from *Atlas Shrugged,* I went out and bought the book." "My psychiatrist recommended I read *The Fountainhead* and *Atlas Shrugged* as a helpful adjunct to psychotherapy." Increasingly at NBI we heard of students who had been advised to take our courses by psychiatrists and psychologists.

All through the country, Ayn Rand study clubs and Objectivist study clubs were appearing on college campuses. We had no official connection with such clubs; they arose spontaneously, on the initiative of students we did not know. Ayn was sometimes apprehensive about such groups' speaking as if they had her personal endorsement, and more than once, she had Hank Holzer write a cautionary letter. She was concerned with protecting the purity of her system against the distortions of confused or irresponsible admirers. On occasion, she shrieked about her fans' "exploiting" her work. Sometimes Barbara or I would complain to Ayn about the gratuitous severity—or hostility—of Holzer's written communications, and sometimes we succeeded in toning them down. Ayn insisted that people call themselves "students of Objectivism" rather than "Objectivists," and many strong letters were sent from our office demanding this.

As the operations of NBI continued to grow, we created a publishing division, NBI Press, which issued one of Ayn's favorite novels, released early in the century and now long out of print, *Calumet "K,"* as well as Victor Hugo's *The Man Who Laughs,* almost unknown in this country. Ayn wrote introductions for both novels. In addition to NBI Book Service, which sold our books and pamphlets to the people on our rapidly expanding mailing list, we established NBI Art Reproductions in order to sell prints of paintings by Frank, Joan, and a portrait of Ayn painted by Ilona (Ilona Royce Smithkin) that would subsequently replace photographs on the jackets of her books. "My God," said Ayn, "you really are building an empire."

Who Is Ayn Rand? was published in softcover in June 1964, with a first printing of one hundred thousand copies, and it went through several such printings throughout the balance of the decade.

A year earlier, Robert Hessen and I visited Ayn to propose that she publish in book form a collection of the essays on ethics that she had been writing for *The Objectivist Newsletter.* The idea was Robert's, so we knew Ayn would resist, because she had not come up with it first. But after some discussion, Ayn agreed, and she assembled a book titled *The Virtue of Selfishness.* First published by New American Library in softcover in 1964, its success led to a hardcover edition. It was followed in 1966 by another collection, *Capitalism: The Unknown Ideal.* I contributed a number of essays to both books, and in the second book there were also articles by Alan Greenspan and Robert Hessen.

I had urged Ayn to expand on her ethical theories when she wrote for *The Objectivist Newsletter,* instead of merely commenting on current events, as she was often inclined to do, and I was gratified to see her more philosophical essays pulled together and made available in a single volume. I was especially pleased to see in print for a wider audience the elaboration of her ideas concerning individual rights, which were the foundation of her political thinking. She included her essay on racism, a piece I had suggested for the newsletter, against her initial reluctance.

"Of course, racism is evil, but the leftists have made it their issue," she had protested.

I had argued that that was precisely why we should come out with our own analysis of the problem; we should not surrender the field to the opposition, and it was important that the piece come specifically from her. In the end, after several months of discussion, she had agreed and had written a powerful article branding racism as biological collectivism that was totally incompatible with an individualist philosophy and explaining why a free market best serves the interests of all races. She reiterated her theme that the smallest minority on earth is the individual and that the rights of minorities can have no other base.

Much as I liked *The Virtue of Selfishness* as a whole, I was uncomfortable with the first sentences of her Introduction to the book:

> The title of this book may evoke the kind of question that I hear once in a while: "Why do you use the word 'selfishness' to denote virtuous qualities of character, when the word antagonizes so many people to whom it does not mean the things you mean?"
>
> To those who ask it, my answer is: "For the reason that makes you afraid of it."

But there are others, who would not ask that question, sensing the moral cowardice it implies, yet who are unable to formulate my actual reason or to identify the profound moral issue involved. It is to them that I will give a more explicit answer.

This was a typical example of the Ayn Rand I liked least. Why begin the book with an insult? Why assume ignoble motives on the part of the questioner? What was accomplished by sounding a note of abusiveness on the first page?

This was a mild version of the angry behavior she displayed during the question-and-answer periods at my lectures, and it troubled me there, too. The result of this policy was that our students became afraid to ask her questions, alarmed at the prospect of what she might announce about their psychology or moral state. I knew that Ayn saw her position as one of moral intransigence. I had also seen it that way once. Now, I was beginning to see it as bad temper and displaced rage.

The question she addressed at the start of her Introduction was not irrational and did not necessarily come from the questioner's fear; it could just as well come from bewilderment. It would have been more appropriate and more persuasive to begin her response benevolently, especially since she had something genuinely new to teach. When I suggested this to her, she became impatient, launched into a brief lecture about not yielding an inch to the enemy, and dismissed my comment as if I had a sudden intellectual lapse, best forgotten.

As its title suggests, *Capitalism: The Unknown Ideal* discusses issues in political economy and the moral basis of a free society. Ayn was especially fond of her lead piece, "What Is Capitalism?" My own favorites were a piece called "The Roots of War," which I still wish would be required reading for anyone genuinely devoted to peace, and a devastating analysis of the student protest movement, titled "The Cashing-In: The Student Rebellion." In her critique of the current educational system, she was ahead of her time. Only in the 1980s would many of her ideas begin to be properly understood and appreciated.

It was during her work on *For the New Intellectual,* a few years earlier, that Ayn had first realized how thoroughly she enjoyed nonfiction writing. "All I have to think about is clarity and logic. The arguments don't have to be integrated with emotion, story, and suspense." Ayn lacked the motivation to write an entire book from scratch, but thanks to the newsletter and then, after 1966, to its successor, *The Objectivist,* a new collection of her essays would be published in book form every two or three years. I felt proud of my role in helping to bring this about.

Smiling one day at what must have been my grin of self-satisfaction, she chuckled. "You're an intellectual entrepreneur, and I'm one of the factors of production you're organizing. That's all right—go ahead—I don't mind." She expressed gratification at the salary she was receiving from *The Objectivist Newsletter*. "I always wanted a source of income apart from my books. Without the newsletter, I wouldn't have that, and without you, I wouldn't have the newsletter. I would never have started it on my own." I listened gratefully, wanting to believe that contributions of this kind somehow offset what I was unable to give her—and knowing I was deluding myself.

The Virtue of Selfishness and *Capitalism: The Unknown Ideal* were published by New American Library, because Ayn had broken with Bennett Cerf and Random House. She had offered Bennett a collection of her essays. The lead piece was to be "The Fascist New Frontier," based on a lecture she had given at Ford Hall Forum, in which she drew parallels between the ideology of fascism and the ideology contained in the speeches of John F. Kennedy, emphasizing the common demands for personal "sacrifice" on the altar of "public good." At first, Bennett seemed enthusiastic about the project and reported excited responses from the bookstores. Then, less happily, he began reporting opposition from his own editors. Then, finally, as if this had always been his viewpoint, he refused to publish the book unless Ayn withdrew the piece on Kennedy. Of course, Ayn would not withdraw it. From the farewell notes they exchanged, it was obvious that there was a good deal of sadness on both sides. Ayn said grimly, with a conscientiousness that touched me, "I'll always give Bennett credit for the ways in which he did support my work." She would not acknowledge how deeply hurt she was personally; her discussion of the issue was entirely philosophical. "When you deal with a person of mixed premises," she declared with stern detachment, "these things happen." One more pillar had collapsed, and the weight of my responsibility for Ayn's happiness felt correspondingly heavier.

By late 1964, NBI was offering courses in fifty-four cities. Plans were under way to offer taped programs in Munich and the Marshall Islands in the South Pacific, as well as somewhere under the Atlantic Ocean in a Polaris submarine (Barbara's project, of which she was very proud).

By the end of 1965, we were approaching eighty cities. We had been asked to make my course "Basic Principles of Objectivism" available to soldiers in Vietnam, and we were also making plans for Greenland and Pakistan. Barbara had hung a large map of the world in her office, with flags pinned to locations where the lectures were offered. She displayed it proudly for visitors.

"Do you ever feel like we're on an express train?" Barbara asked, paraphrasing a line from *Atlas,* in one of those rare moments of happy intimacy still possible between us. I grinned and nodded.

We were on an express train. But up ahead, the bridge was out.

In April 1964, near my thirty-fourth birthday, NBI held its second ball, which again led to an explosion on Ayn's part. "You have no emotional time for me or our relationship, but you do for a dance?" she shouted.

This was said during a period when I spoke to her at length every day on the telephone, still visited her twice a week, and spent at least one full afternoon or evening a week with her. What she now wanted was the resumption of our affair, and I kept inventing reasons to hold that issue at bay. Ayn was now fifty-nine. "When, if not now?" she asked.

At the ball, I danced with her a good deal. I danced with Patrecia briefly and carefully. And yet to hold her in my arms publicly, even under these circumstances, felt like a justification of the entire event. In the midst of all the important people of my life, this was the one encounter, the one interaction, that felt *right*.

"Ayn's blindness on some issues is incredible," Barbara remarked, and I froze, wondering what she meant. "Any other woman I can think of, seeing how you behave, would conclude that the fire is gone, the affair is past history, and all you can be now is friends. Watching how you are with her from the sidelines, I think it's all so obvious. How is it possible that she doesn't understand that?"

Relaxed now, I answered that I still felt a kind of love for Ayn, at times very intense, and I showed this plainly. I was therefore responsible for maintaining Ayn's confusion. "Yes and no" was Barbara's comment.

In other moods, more empathic to Ayn, she said, "You've got to find a way to help her see the truth. A way that won't devastate her. Not that Ayn would ever admit to being devastated. Poor Ayn. Poor Nathan."

In another context, she would say, "There's always been another woman in comparison to whom I've been found wanting. First, it was Ayn's heroines. Then Ayn. Now, God help me, a twenty-four-year-old *child*." This last was said in response to my evident admiration for Patrecia, which I displayed openly, although I had not yet told Barbara about the affair. I thought that her complaint was justified. I had rarely given her the experience of simple acceptance.

We continued to discuss our marriage with Ayn. It was wrong, I knew, to solicit Ayn's help while withholding information about Wilfred and Patrecia. Barbara did not seem troubled by her deception, and when I asked her about it, she announced, "Wilfred is irrelevant to our problems."

"Fine," I thought. "So is Patrecia." I knew that my resentment and guilt were speaking, not my intelligence.

I did not communicate to Ayn my growing certainty that my marriage was finished, because I knew that it would only heighten her desire for a resurrection of our romantic relationship. What I wanted was for Ayn herself to grasp that our time as lovers had passed and that now, after so many years together, we should be the best and closest of friends.

There are other bonds no less powerful than romantic love. I felt bonded to Ayn with a symbiotic intensity. A cable of steel connected our souls. Life with her was rarely happy any longer, except for brief, exhilarating flashes, but life without her continued to feel like death.

I knew that the deception I was perpetrating conflicted with my own convictions about human relationships. I paced the floor of my office for countless hours, trying to think my way toward an alternative that would not result in the total collapse of the life I had built. I could not find it. I knew that absolute truthfulness would mean the end of everything. "Check your premises," I kept repeating like a mantra, but the torment remained: *Which* premises?

I struggled with questions: Is it rational to give up Ayn and Objectivism? No. Is it rational to give up Patrecia? No. Then what does rationality consist of?

All the years of mangling, denying, and "transcending" my emotions were now taking their revenge. By too often forbidding myself to feel, I had denied myself access to much of my inner life and to many of my most intimate values. I had undermined my ability to think—in the very area where thinking was now urgently needed. My sense of helplessness kept building.

By late fall of 1964, the weight of my self-reproach was becoming excruciating, like a great rock crushing self-respect out of my body. For the first time in my life, I was experiencing a crisis of self-esteem—from which I was to learn a great deal, but slowly and agonizingly.

One day, I returned from Patrecia's to find Allan Blumenthal and Leonard Peikoff waiting for me in my apartment. Barbara had let them in, then gone downstairs to the NBI offices.

"Nathan doesn't love us anymore," Allan announced to Leonard in mock solemnity; he looked mischievously forlorn.

Bewildered, I asked, "What's this about?"

They proceeded to explain that I had become inexplicably kinder in my dealings with them. I had withdrawn all demands and expectations concerning Objectivism. I projected that I merely wanted them to enjoy life. They spoke in the exaggerated manner of describing a tragedy.

The change in me they were describing had begun almost immediately after the start of my affair with Patrecia. Some of the cause was my own happiness, some came from my feelings of guilt. "What moral right have I—now—to expect anything of anyone?" was the conscious thought in my mind.

Leonard shook his head in half-mocking, half-serious regret and declared, "You've lost respect for us; there's no other possible explanation. You've given up on us; that's why you've become so pleasant and easygoing. Since you no longer think we're able to amount to much, you figure we may as well be happy."

"I can't win with you two," I answered, feeling a mixture of amusement and sadness, feeling also that what I was saying was true.

One afternoon about a year earlier, I had dropped by Ayn's for a visit, and Leonard was there, being counseled by Ayn about a personal problem. Ayn asked him to repeat for my benefit what he had just said to her. She had been trying to raise his self-esteem, not too successfully, and he had confided in her, "Whenever I begin to feel better about myself, whenever I begin to feel pride, I see Nathan's face, and I imagine I see scorn and contempt, even though I've never actually seen that look on his face in reality, and my good feelings about myself collapse."

I was stunned. Then Ayn had protested, "But Nathan is your champion. He's the one who most often defends you when I'm angry at you." Leonard had answered miserably, "I know. I know." Ayn had gone on, "Perhaps it's the fact that I'm a woman—and you want the esteem of a man. Nathan is the man you most admire, the man you most want to be like."

Then Leonard had said, "It isn't that I feel he despises me, but that deep inside I feel he *should,* if he really knew me."

"Oh, Leonard." Ayn had sighed, while I had stood looking at the two of them, feeling as alienated as I had ever felt in my life.

Now, grinning cheerfully, Allan declared, "You're becoming mellower and gentler. Can a mellow and gentle Nathan still be Nathan?"

I knew that underneath this banter was a curiosity about what it all meant.

"Old chaps," I said, because there was nothing else to say, "you drive me nuts."

Within a year, Leonard made Ayn angrier than she had ever been with him before, and he was exiled to the University of Denver, where he had been offered a job teaching philosophy. His offense, as always, involved some failure to support and defend Ayn and her work in his dealings with other people. His assignment was to redeem himself in Ayn's eyes, to prove somehow that he could be a good Objectivist, perhaps by his proselytizing in Denver. He would accept this verdict as he accepted all of Ayn's verdicts, as reasonable and appropriate justice. I was chief prosecutor at his trial, and afterward I had a special dispensation from Ayn to be kind to him privately, within limits, so that his suffering did not drive him past a point of no return. The anxiety level of the entire Collective went up after this event. If this could happen to Leonard, it could happen to anyone, and if it did, every friend in the group would be aligned against one—as they were now aligned against Leonard.

Looking at the Collective on the night of Leonard's temporary expulsion, I thought, If I were to tell Ayn the full truth and she were to react as I know she will, is there one of you who would not fall into line behind whatever she might then choose to say about me? There was not a person in our group without above average intelligence, but in this issue, their intelligence would be useless.

People spoke to me about Patrecia as if she were their personal discovery.

In the summer of 1964, Florence's oldest son, Leonard, came to New York City for a visit. Then sixteen, with a remarkable intellectual capacity, he was tall, athletic, intellectual, and exuberant and had enough energy for three teenagers. I was very fond of him.

Leonard went with Joan and Patrecia to the New York World's Fair. He had met Joan before, but he was meeting Patrecia for the first time. Later he said to me, "Patrecia is fantastic. Has she got energy! She can keep up with me! Have you ever noticed how physically strong she is? Watch how she moves! And yet she's so slender! Isn't she *something?*" Grateful for the opportunity to talk about Patrecia with someone, I asked my nephew what else he liked about her. "When she looks at me," he answered with deep feeling, "she *sees* me. Adults don't do that with kids. She asks about my life and what I'm doing, and she's *interested*. She really listens. She makes me feel respected."

Patrecia and Edith Efron became friends. This intrigued me, because Edith, who was a few years older than I, was among the more cerebral members of our group and was usually contemptuous of nonintellectuals (as well as most intellectuals). "With Patsy I can *play*," Edith announced cheerfully. "With Patsy I can be *young*."

When Joan visited me in my office, she said earnestly, "You still don't know Patrecia well, do you? You really should take the time. I don't know anyone else like her. I don't even know how to explain this—she reaches me. That's all I can say. She reaches me. As if she looks at you and sees what no one else sees." In that moment, I wanted to embrace Joan and tell her how well I understood. Instead, I listened impassively. I said only,

"I like Patrecia very much. And I like what comes out of you when you talk about her."

I thought there was something important that Patrecia gave to people that I wanted to learn.

"It's my sense of life," Patrecia said, when I spoke to her about it.

No, I answered. It was more than that.

"Then I'll tell you what it is," she said thoughtfully. "When I'm with someone, often I don't pay much attention to the self they show the world. I always try to find their best self, even if it's buried deeply, even if they don't know about it, and I try to speak to that part of them, as if that's the only part that really matters."

"But isn't that faking reality in a way? I mean, to ignore all the rest?"

She answered that she did not ignore all the rest, that she saw it but chose not be controlled by it in her responses. "I admit I don't see everything you see. But that's one of the things I want to learn from you—how to see everything, without letting that kill my ability to respond as I do." She said many times and in many ways, "I want to learn what you know, but I don't want to lose who I am." It took me a long time to understand what she meant.

Part of what she meant, although she did not have the words to tell me then, was that she wanted to master a higher level of linear, analytical, and conceptual functioning without weakening her strongly developed intuitive capabilities. But that was not all. "Ayn's writing," she said, "makes you aware of how much evil there is in the world, how much irrationality and cruelty, and it's important to be aware of that. But a lot of NBI students—that's all they see. They may talk about a benevolent sense of life, but they're really malevolent, always looking for evidence that the world is an evil place. And when your sense of life is malevolent, you become mean and cruel yourself, never mind what you say philosophically. I wish Ayn would write more articles that stress the positive in life, like the best parts of her novels. I don't dare say this to anyone in the Collective because they would all say I was crazy—what does a twenty-four-year-old model know?—but I can say it to you. Sometimes when I'm with the Collective, I'm afraid. It's not just NBI students. It's the Collective, as well. Something has gotten to them. A deadness. I don't want it to get to me."

In October, Patrecia and Larry moved to a new, larger apartment, the penthouse of a building one block away from where Barbara and I lived. From my bedroom, I could look east on Thirty-Fourth Street and see the penthouse and imagine that behind those glass windows Patrecia was looking back at me. Almost every morning, while Barbara was still sleeping, I got up and stood looking out from our window for a long time.

"Is it possible to be in love with two people at the same time?"

This was one of the most frequently asked questions following my lectures. At first, I was surprised; I could not imagine why so many people would be interested. Gradually, I gathered that many people felt this issue touched their lives. "In the realm of human relationships," I typically answered, "I suppose we must say that almost anything is possible. Two people can each embody our values, or perhaps slightly different aspects of our values, in so profound a way that we cannot help but feel love for both of them. And yet, I have to add that sustaining a love for two persons and integrating that love into the everyday structure of one's life has got to be almost terrifyingly difficult. Sooner or later, one relationship tends to lose out to the other, and the danger is that the person who tries it will make a mess of both."

I was acutely aware of Ayn's sitting beside me as I spoke, aware of the faintly superior smile on her lips, and knowing what she would stand up and say when I had completed my answer. "It's a project that only giants can handle properly," she always added. "When average people talk about it, they mean something much more casual than love as Mr. Branden and I discuss it. If you really mean a serious passion, if you mean romantic love, the highest kind of rationality and integrity are demanded. And even then, it's a rare phenomenon, nothing that happens every day, nothing that most people even need to think about."

Another question we often heard was "Can heroes such as Miss Rand writes about actually exist?" Ayn would always insist on answering that question herself. Inwardly I would cringe, knowing what was coming. "You're looking at two of them," she would say, pointing to me and herself. Pointing to Frank and Barbara, she would add, "And there are two more." This would effectively end the discussion.

On one occasion, someone asked a question about some viewpoint of Ayn's. I launched into an answer, then stopped and apologized for speaking for her when she was present in the room. "You can speak for me anytime you wish," Ayn announced, "on any subject whatsoever." Turning to the students, she stated, "There is no subject on which Mr. Branden is not qualified to speak for me."

Notwithstanding the growing tensions between us, Ayn continued to pay me the most unreserved compliments on every possible public occasion. Feeling uncomfortable and fraudulent, I would tell her, "Ayn, I am not John Galt."

"Yes, you are," she would insist, "except for a few blemishes."

When I recall my erratic behavior with Ayn during this period, my absentmindedness, my elusiveness, my coldness—alternating, as always, with expressions of passionate devotion—I am inclined to think that at least some of it was motivated by a subconscious desire to be seen realistically, to jolt Ayn out of her fantasies, to get a message through that I was not prepared to convey in words.

At the height of my arrogance—and I have been guilty of arrogance for years—I had not imagined I was John Galt, but by the end of 1964, every time I mounted the NBI lecture platform, I felt less like Nathaniel Branden.

In 1960, I had become interested in hypnosis. I had discovered the papers of Milton Erickson, a psychotherapeutic genius, the most innovative figure in the history of hypnosis. I became keenly interested in what hypnotic phenomena could teach us about the nature of the human mind.

Over the next several years, I did hypnotic demonstrations for the Collective and various other friends—from the induction of positive and negative hallucinations, to time distortion, to posthypnotic suggestion. Ayn was suspicious and a bit hostile. "It's a fraud," she insisted initially. To her, the notion of trance seemed incompatible with her view of an ideally rational consciousness. In contrast, I saw altered states of consciousness as mental capacities that could sometimes be highly useful. Today, of course, there is much wider appreciation of the ways in which hypnosis can be helpful in all the healing professions.

One evening, I did a demonstration of age regression. I used as my subject one of our secretaries at NBI whom I knew to be an excellent hypnotic subject. I had regressed her to the age of thirteen, and she was doing splendidly, but I saw that a few of my friends, especially Ayn, continued to look skeptical. Allan Blumenthal, who was most in tune with what I was doing, got a sudden inspiration and handed me a ballpoint pen, motioning me to show it to my subject. When I did so, she frowned in unmistakably genuine puzzlement. "What is this?" she wanted to know. "It's not a pen, and it's not a pencil. What is it?" Ayn gasped as understanding hit her; when this young woman was thirteen, ballpoint pens did not exist. "You win," she muttered reluctantly at our next meeting. "I have no explanation of how it's possible, but obviously hypnosis is something real." Not three months later, I heard her announce to a visiting professor in her living room, "Hypnosis is a fraud." In response to my request for an explanation, she said only, "I'm just not convinced."

Thereafter, hypnosis occupied a strange status between us. It was neither real nor unreal, neither a fact nor a nonfact. It was just my private eccentricity that she would indulge because of who I was. I recall the disconcerted look on her face during some of our discussions, torn as she was between the impulse to declare hypnosis nonsense and her reluctance to suggest that her "intellectual heir" had lost his mind. Occasionally, she would make passing reference to this interest of mine as evidence that we were drifting apart.

Almost any new interest of mine could now lead to an unpleasant conversation. I tried to persuade her to read Arthur Koestler's superb book *The Ghost in the Machine*, explaining that although I did not agree with some of his conclusions, his treatment of evolution was brilliant and psychologically and philosophically important. When I attempted to explain non-Darwinian theories of evolution, she nodded with perfunctory interest, then quickly became impatient with me. "You have time for everything but you and me," she declared. "Hypnosis, Koestler—what next? Extrasensory perception?"

When I tried to tell her of some new research that suggested that certain kinds of depression had a biological basis, she answered angrily, "I can tell you what causes depression. I can tell you about rational depression, and I can tell you about irrational depression. The second is mostly self-pity, and in neither case does biology enter into it." I asked her how she could make a scientific statement with such certainty, given that she had never studied the field. She shrugged bitterly and snapped, "Because I know how to think."

I was astonished at how closed she typically was to any new knowledge that seemed to clash with her familiar paradigms. Outside the territory where she felt in full intellectual control, she was utterly lacking in a spirit of openness or adventure. Where my work was concerned, she made it abundantly clear that my task as a psychologist was to develop knowledge that would support her work as a philosopher. She was instantly on the attack about any line of inquiry that had even the *appearance* of challenging her notion of the "rational." She projected herself as the commander of an eternally beleaguered fortress.

In her grandiosity and suspiciousness, her behavior bordered at times on paranoia, although that is not a thought I would have permitted myself. The worst I would have accused her of were the slight excesses so often typical of genius.

I did not attach significance to the fact that, since her late twenties, she had been taking amphetamines daily for weight control, on the advice of a physician. I do not think the discovery had been yet been made that a protracted use of amphetamines can precipitate paranoiac reactions.

Nor was I aware that her single-tracked obsession with her own frame of reference and her reflexive suspiciousness of anything foreign to it almost went with the territory of being a major innovator. Such blinders often have functional utility for the creative process, whatever the cost in terms of an out-of-balance psyche. Freud and Wilhelm Reich were two examples in my own field. Milton Erickson, I would one day learn, was another; Erickson, I am told, tended to speak as if no other work in psychology but his own could possibly be worth studying.

A tendency already in evidence when I first met Ayn grew much more pronounced during the 1960s. She viewed her personal likes and dislikes in art, literature, and music as being close to laws of nature. If, for example, she regarded Rembrandt as "a talented draftsman, nothing more," if she were antagonized by Shakespeare's "fatalism," if she detested Beethoven's "malevolence," then anyone who spoke admiringly of Rembrandt, Shakespeare, or Beethoven might well be met with spoken or unspoken contempt. "Not my kind of person," she would say. "Not my sense of life." Similarly, if someone failed to enjoy Victor Hugo, or Dostoyevsky, or even Mickey Spillane, that person would be watched carefully for other signs of deficiency.

In March 1966, she wrote an article for *The Objectivist* titled "Art and Sense of Life" (subsequently reprinted in *The Romantic Manifesto* in 1969), which she concluded with these ominous words: "When one learns to translate the meaning of an art work into objective terms, one discovers that nothing is as potent as art in exposing the essence of a man's character. An artist reveals his naked soul in his work—and so, gentle reader, do you when you respond to it." The use of words like *expose, naked,* and *gentle reader* could have no other purpose than to intimidate—to scare the hell out of her audience.

To our more fanatical and conformist students, Objectivism did not signify merely the body of abstract philosophical propositions and arguments that we wrote about and taught. Its meaning was expanded to include every personal like and dislike of Ayn's. They absorbed and embraced Ayn's implicit dictum, "Objectivism, *c'est moi.*" These students proved that they were good Objectivists through their skill at mimicking Ayn's viewpoints down to the smallest detail—re-creating Ayn, as it were, within themselves. They further proved it by watching one another, suspiciously and critically, for deviations; if they could not match Ayn in intellect, they could at least match her in harshness. They scourged one another mercilessly for any signs of "social metaphysics."

Patrecia had always spoken of Ayn with great affection and regard. But one day I asked for her first impressions when she saw Ayn at my lecture, and she answered with some hesitancy, "I was disappointed. I didn't like those slashes of bitterness in her face. And her eyes, to tell you the truth . . .

now please don't become upset . . . I felt I was seeing madness there. Enormous anger. Something out of my childhood. Of course, later I came to see her as a wonderful person, but still . . ."

I took a long breath to control myself and to give me time to think. Part of me felt indignation against Patrecia—how could she say this of the author of *Atlas Shrugged*. Another part felt admiration for her courage, for the unfrightened way she looked at me as she spoke, even though she knew how her words would affect me. I heard Ayn's voice roaring in my brain: "If you are who you say you are, you will now walk away from Patrecia and never look back." I looked into the steady blue eyes watching me across the lunch table as if she could track my thoughts, her face lifted in acceptance of whatever I might now choose to say, and I knew that no power on earth could make me abandon this woman.

"Patrecia," I said, "please don't ever say this to me again. I understand that you're only describing what you felt in that first moment, but it's not something I wish to hear about Ayn Rand." She nodded gravely, without apology, and answered, "I understand." The terror at the root of my response was the not-to-be-admitted knowledge that I had seen in Ayn's eyes precisely what Patrecia had seen. To think of Ayn as mad in any respect whatsoever was to plunge my universe into chaos. If there was a streak of irrationality running through Ayn, what did this mean about my entire life? What did this mean about me?

And yet at some level, I, too, was aware of something wrong in Ayn, an explosive rage that did not fit my more exalted view of her. I wanted to get Ayn out of my question-and-answer periods, for example, because I was appalled by how she sometimes abused our students. Because Ayn did not enjoy these sessions, it was simple enough to thank her for her past help and to say that NBI was sufficiently well established that her participation on a weekly basis was not necessary. "Thank God," Barbara muttered as Ayn began to come less and less frequently.

"Larry and I are fighting a lot," Patrecia told me in the spring of 1965. "And it's not his fault. What he wants is reasonable—he wants a wife in the full sense, and he has a right to expect that. Only, I don't have it in me to give."

My own marriage was moving toward collapse. Barbara and I were quarreling almost constantly. One moment, she was violently angry toward me, the next, hurt and bewildered. One moment, I was projecting warmth and affection, the next, a deadly chilling remoteness. Most of our conflicts were over trivia, surface manifestations of the deeper unhappiness and frustrations between us. I perceived her as hypersensitive; she perceived me as hypercritical. I perceived her as often maudlin; she perceived me as often unfeeling. Nether of us felt accepted by the other for who we were. Both of us felt misunderstood.

Toward the end of summer, we agreed to a "trial separation." That was how we named it. "I can't stand how miserable we both are," Barbara said. "I can't stand fighting all the time." I do not know what she thought silently, but I felt that once I walked out the door of our apartment with my bags, once I experienced life apart from her, I would never return to our marriage. Perhaps that was why I initially resisted her tearful, angry suggestion of a separation.

I took an apartment on the third floor of our building, telling our friends that I needed the office space, not wishing to make the break public until Barbara and I definitely decided what we wished to do.

We discovered that, living apart, we could often be kinder to each other. "There might still be hope," Barbara said to me tenderly.

I asked her if she had ever thought of marrying Wilfred, in the event that he left his wife. "You don't understand," she said wistfully. "You are the only husband I ever wanted."

When I told Ayn of the decision to separate, she breathed what looked like a long-suppressed sigh of relief. "Now, darling, perhaps there will be a chance for us to be in love again."

16

"I WANT TO SEE real, living, and in the hours of my own days, that glory I create as an illusion! I want to know that there is someone, somewhere, who wants it, too! Or else what is the use of seeing it, and working, and burning for an impossible vision? A spirit, too, needs fuel. It can run dry."

These lines are spoken by Kay Gonda, the heroine of *Ideal*, a play Ayn had written in 1934 during a time of difficult professional struggle. Ayn referred to the speech often, applying it to herself. "A spirit, too, needs fuel," she would say, "and I am running dry. I am running dry."

Gonda is a beautiful actress who projects such a quality of glory that she comes to stand as a kind of symbol for the values and ideals of her admirers. Her quest in the play is to discover whether their professed worship in fact has any meaning—a theme that was a lifelong preoccupation of Ayn's. Gonda appears in the life of a number of her fans, seemingly in great danger, and they are challenged to help her, at considerable risk to themselves. Only one man, Johnny Dawes, passes her test and dies tragically and unnecessarily in order (he believes) to save her.

The play had only one small production. After Ayn's death, Leonard Peikoff published it in a collection titled *The Early Ayn Rand*. The play is bitter, anguished, and radically unlike her future works in its emotional quality, although traces of that quality are present in all her writing. It is clearly the cry of a soul that feels wounded. It illuminates an aspect of Ayn's psychology that was to become increasingly and calamitously central to our relationship.

In the story, Kay Gonda has spread the rumor that she is wanted by the police for murder and that she is trying to escape arrest. Not one of her admirers is willing to help her until she meets Johnny Dawes, a young man who is alone and utterly alienated, a man "who cannot live today." The two have the following exchange:

GONDA: What do you dream of?

JOHNNY: Nothing. Of what account are dreams?

GONDA: Of what account is life?

JOHNNY: None. But who made it so?

GONDA: Those who cannot dream.

JOHNNY: No. Those who can *only* dream.

The play was not meant to be "realistic," in that Ayn did not really believe that people should be willing to put their life on the line for an actress they loved but did not actually know. Yet in the story, Johnny does redeem Gonda's view of humanity by dying for her, and Gonda accepts his gesture when she has the power to prevent it.

There was a parallel between the play and the relationship of everyone in our circle to Ayn. What Ayn made overpoweringly clear to us was that the ultimate test and proof of one's idealism were one's loyalty to her work and to her personally. We absorbed this view profoundly. As a consequence, our self-esteem was intimately tied to our support of Ayn and to her positive regard of us.

No one can understand my motivation during this period of my life who does not grasp the extent to which I had internalized this idea.

Ayn and Frank moved from their apartment on Thirty-Sixth Street into a newer, more spacious apartment on the sixth floor of our building at 120 East Thirty-Fourth. Now we were all on different floors of one building: Ayn and Frank, Barbara, the offices of NBI and *The Objectivist Newsletter*, and I. Larry and Patrecia were a block away.

One day, Patrecia came to my apartment, obviously wanting to talk yet acting strangely shy and reticent.

Finally she declared, "I've decided what I want to do professionally. I want to be an actress." She looked at me as if she anticipated a negative reaction.

She was not entirely wrong. It was one of the rare times I did not want her to see what I was feeling.

On hearing her announcement, my spirits crashed. It was not because I doubted she could be a good actress; I knew she could be. But I regarded the profession of acting as one in which great suffering was almost inevitable. Failure bred one kind of pain, success bred another.

I felt afraid for Patrecia and afraid for our future.

"What do you think?" she asked nervously and challengingly.

It was axiomatic to me that I would give her choice my full support. "If this is what you want, what's the best way to proceed? Tell me, why are you so tense?"

"I've always disliked everything I've ever heard about acting and that whole world. I've always thought of it as phony, unreal, crazy. I thought you might think I'd lost my mind. I remember some producer saying that he had rarely known a happy actor and never a happy actress. Still, it's what I feel myself drawn to, it's what I want to do, and I believe I can be good. I've been weighing this for a long time. I know it's a horrible sort of life—probably."

I thought of my friend Ralph Roseman, who had come into my life some years ago when he wrote Ayn an enthusiastic letter about *Atlas Shrugged*. He was a successful theatrical manager and a sometime acting teacher. I proposed a meeting between them.

"I was the first person you and Patrecia spoke to about her interest in acting," Ralph would recall years later. "After working with her for a while and having many discussions about the theater and being impressed by the questions she asked, I thought her potential was enormous. She brought to her lessons qualities that actors spend years developing, such as emotional openness and a sense of daring. She took direction very well. Her one fault, which is common with talented beginners, was that she threw herself into a role with such relish that she failed to relate fully to the other actors. Later, when she studied with Rose Schulman, I saw that this trait was being corrected. Rose shared my opinion of Patrecia's potential. The one performance that I saw her in—in 1966, in Philadelphia— was Lorraine Hansberry's *Sign in Sidney Brustein's Window*. It was her first stage performance, I believe. She was marvelous. Her energy and spirit excited the audience. Her appearance, of course, was beautiful. One would never have thought this was her first job. She had something that was electrifying. Vulnerability and raw power."

In the late afternoon of November 9, 1965, the lights of New York City went out, in the famous power failure that would remind many people of *Atlas Shrugged*.

I knew that Barbara was in the NBI office and that Ayn was in her apartment. When I tried to telephone Patrecia's apartment and couldn't get through, I became alarmed, for no reason I could explain. I ran down the stairs to the street, then down the street to her apartment building. With the power out, the elevators were not working. I ran up twenty flights to the penthouse. Discovering that she was not there, I returned to the street, which was now dark, and began searching for her. Eventually, I gave up and went to Ayn's apartment.

Within a few minutes, Patrecia appeared with Frank and a flashlight. Their spirits were festive. Like a number of other people, Patrecia had been helping those on the streets or in darkened buildings find their way to their destinations. Encountering Frank, she had offered to escort him home. "Aren't you a guardian angel!" Ayn exclaimed. "Frank's rescuer! Oh, thank you, darling!" Within an hour or two, we were all there together: Ayn, Frank, Patrecia, Larry, Barbara (who stayed only briefly), and I— eating and talking and laughing by candlelight. "Isn't this like a wonderful scene in a novel?" Ayn said cheerfully. Later, I was stunned and pleased to hear her say to Patrecia, "You have such an air of benevolence; that's why I love you." I reminded myself that for Ayn, this was only a moment's mood. As absurd as it seems, that evening I felt supremely contented.

One month later, in December, Barbara and I decided to make our separation official, at least among our family and friends. We had not yet decided to initiate divorce action, but we wanted to end our pretense of being a happily married couple. Among the first people we told were Elayne and Harry, and Allan and Joan; all four took the news with considerable distress.

Not long after that, Larry and Patrecia informed Allan that they had decided to separate and divorce. He asked them to withhold a public announcement for several months—"because Barbara and Nathan are just about to announce their separation, and we don't want people thinking the two events are related. You know how gossip and rumors start." They agreed to his request.

Barbara and I denied to everyone that any other romantic interest was involved in our decision to separate. "We're just incompatible," we said. "We're just not able to be happy together." I was astonished at the suffering we caused our friends and families, for whom our marriage evidently had meant more than I had appreciated. That we chose not to take anyone into our confidence as to the real nature of our problems only increased the sense of distance that Barbara and I experienced with everyone.

I wanted to tell Barbara about Patrecia and me. There was now no reason not to—except for Ayn. To tell Barbara was to ask her to lie to Ayn, as I was doing, and I decided that this was unacceptable. Although I became progressively more open about my feelings for Patrecia, I did not yet tell Barbara the full truth. Barbara was now quite open in her agitation about Patrecia. I wondered why she cared. She kept questioning me about Patrecia's and my relationship, and I kept describing it—unconvincingly—as a friendship.

In retrospect, it is obvious to me that I was making her "crazy" with this deception. I created a conflict for her. She admired me and was convinced that I would never lie to her. Yet the things I said made her doubt her sense of reality.

Even though Barbara's and my separation was now official, and even though she and Wilfred were accordingly much freer to enjoy their affair, she continued to convey that it would somehow be a tragedy if we did not find our way back to each other. It was almost as if, psychologically, she was as bound to me as I was bound to Ayn. Occasionally, I found myself wondering if Barbara could be right, but not often. I gathered that many of the old tensions between Wilfred and her had once again begun to trouble them.

Many years later, Barbara declared in her biography of Ayn that by the summer of 1965, exhausted by our relationship and in love with another man, she was intent on obtaining a divorce. In fact, for a long time after that, she was still requesting a reconciliation. In May 1966, about eight months after I moved out, Barbara went on a world cruise "to be by myself, to think about the future and what I want out of life, perhaps to find a solution to our relationship," and she wrote several almost lyrical love letters that invariably began, "Nathan Darling" or "My Dearest Love." In one of these letters, she asked, "Did I ever tell you why I love you?" She proceeded to tell me in passionately complimentary terms and to inform me that I provided the inspiration for the hero of a novel she had begun to think about writing. In another letter she stated, to my confusion, that she now knew that everything she had ever wanted out of love was possible and that it was I who had made it so for her. "I will always love you," she wrote. I did not call the ship on her birthday, May 14, because I wanted to impress upon her the full reality of our present state. Then I proceeded to feel self-reproachful, knowing she would be hurt, and I subsequently wrote to her rather more warmly than I felt.

Commenting on these letters years later, Barbara said, "Of course I didn't *really* love you—in the full sense. But I felt I *should*."

Beginning in 1966 and continuing into 1967, Ayn was engaged in writing the last major assignment of her career, a monograph titled *Introduction to Objectivist Epistemology*, published in monthly installments in *The Objectivist* (later published in book form by The Objectivist Press and subsequently by New American Library). In this monograph, she brilliantly addressed one of the great issues in philosophy—the nature of concept formation. This work is one of her most original and important achievements. I was grateful for the opportunity to discuss its ideas with her, not only because of my enthusiasm for what she had done but also because it was a way to be close to her in safe territory. During one of our "honeymoon periods," as Ayn called them, she laughed and said, "I don't know whether it's good or bad, but for you my brain really is an aphrodisiac!"

When I told Ayn that Patrecia was to appear in *The Sign in Sidney Brustein's Window,* in Philadelphia, she immediately responded, as I had known she would, "We must go to see her."

Ayn was fond of Patrecia, and it was a fondness I hoped to cultivate in her. I was convinced that if Ayn grew to know Patrecia before discovering that my feelings were romantic, she would see in Patrecia what I saw. My goal was to be with Patrecia openly and to integrate our relationship into my Objectivist life. I was convinced that my desire was a rational one, and I hoped that in the end Ayn's own rationality would assert itself. But it was imperative that Ayn come to this conclusion on her own. I wanted her to accept that our time as lovers had come and gone. I wanted her old benevolence and basic sanity to come back to her. I wanted her to grasp that I had to have a private life apart from her and that this life included a woman who was my contemporary. And I wanted her to be the one to tell me these things.

I hated the calculations and manipulations that this strategy entailed, but I felt that my back was to the wall and that my survival was at stake. Another, previously unrecognized self had emerged within me. It was not the younger self that Patrecia had reawakened, or the adult, masculine self that had fallen in love with her, but someone ageless, androgynous, and utterly ruthless who had no purpose other than to assist me in realizing my aims and who was willing to blast through any obstacle or impediment.

This self smiled pleasantly at Ayn and said, "Yes, of course we must go to see Patrecia's play. It might be fun."

On the stage, Patrecia was, as Ralph Roseman would say, "electrifying," a being of energy, light, and devastatingly innocent sexuality who projected a stylization that clashed with the naturalism of the other performers and made it impossible to look away from her.

I sat between Ayn and Barbara with a number of our friends around us, plus a number of NBI students who had driven down for the event. "She's wonderful!" Ayn whispered in my ear with great excitement. "Oh, this girl is an actress!"

Later, backstage, Ayn threw her arms around Patrecia and proceeded to praise her in terms that even I found extravagant. But this was like Ayn—nothing in moderation. Everyone crowded around, congratulating Patrecia, whose face was flushed with somewhat dazed happiness. Then Ayn said something astonishing and preposterous: "Patrecia, what is magnificent is that you have taken the philosophy of Objectivism and applied it to the art of acting!" I saw the blank expression on Patrecia's face. Her glance said to me silently, "What has Objectivism got to do with this?" But then the moment was swept away as more people forced their way into the room to extend praise and good wishes.

"Now I see more clearly why you say she is someone very unusual," Ayn announced to me as we drove back to Manhattan. Frank, who had aged enormously in this past decade and whose faculties were already beginning to slip—a result both of his drinking and of early senility, neither of which anyone grasped—muttered, "Marvelous. Marvelous."

A few weeks later, Patrecia and I stopped by Ayn's apartment, declaring that Patrecia had sought my guidance in a scene she was preparing. Ayn and Frank accepted this as normal and unalarming, as I had calculated they would. That evening, Patrecia and I had in fact been working on scenes from Ibsen's *Master Builder*—simply for our own pleasure— and, at their prompting, we read one of those scenes now. We were all in relaxed high spirits. Then Ayn hurried into her office and came back with the script of *Ideal*. She asked us to do a dramatic reading of the climactic scene between Kay Gonda and Johnny Dawes. After two or three faltering attempts, Patrecia succeeded in locking onto Gonda's psyche and persona, and the result was mesmerizing.

"How did you do that?" Ayn demanded afterward. "What did you do to capture her?" There was something almost intimidating in Ayn's intensity, and I saw Patrecia freeze. I knew that she could not explain her own internal processes in doing Gonda, not now, neither to Ayn nor to herself. I also knew that because the person asking her for an explanation was Ayn, she would blame herself for her inability.

As she stammered and groped for words, unable to say much more than "I just *felt* her," I saw some of the eagerness and warmth disappearing from Ayn's eyes. I saw Patrecia noticing it too, but there was nothing I could say and no way I could help.

"You must do better than just talk about feelings," Ayn said to her, and Patrecia replied with awkward conscientiousness that she was trying to learn.

"I think you were magnificent," Frank said abruptly, loudly, and defiantly. The evening ended on a note of emotional flatness.

Meanwhile, the work on behalf of Objectivism went on.

Early in 1967, I received a phone call from psychologist Albert Ellis, founder of Rational-Emotive Therapy, who explained that many of his followers were pushing for a rapprochement with Objectivism because, they believed, there were so many points of agreement between us. "You and I know, of course," he said, "that our differences are much more meaningful than our apparent similarities. When we talk about the importance of reason, for instance, we do not really mean the same thing. I propose that we stage a public debate—Rational Psychotherapy [this is what he called his system at that time] versus Objectivist Psychology. This should make the facts of life clear to everyone." After some hesitation, I agreed. I was not a debate enthusiast, but I felt this would be an interesting experience.

Ellis proposed that each of our institutes sell tickets to our respective followings and that we each keep our own proceeds. On Friday evening, May 26, approximately eleven hundred people crowded into the New Yorker Hotel. Ellis had sold about two hundred tickets, NBI had sold about nine hundred. Our mutual friend, psychologist Lee Shulman, was the moderator.

Although I was pleased with our large ticket sales, I did not like that the room was weighted so heavily in my favor. This made Ellis the underdog, a role I much preferred for myself when intellectual combat was involved. Several times, I had to join Lee in requesting that the audience show more courtesy to Ellis, who I thought generated antagonism almost instantly with a kind of provocative abusiveness and haranguing that seemed to be the trademark of his lecture style.

At one point, when he attacked the "unrealism" of Ayn's heroes and heroines—in a radical departure from the subject of the debate—Ayn leaped up from her seat and shouted, "Am I unreal? Am I a character who can't possibly exist?" It took Lee some time to restore order.

For Ellis, it was not a good evening. He became angrier and angrier as the event progressed, inspiring the audience to laugh. After this debate, Ellis began attacking Objectivism and my psychological ideas with unfailing regularity.

Although I hardly appreciated this at the time, I came to see that some of his concerns about the attitudes and behavior evident in the Objectivist subculture—fanaticism, dogmatism, oppressive moralism—were justified, his misrepresentations of Objectivist theory notwithstanding.

Even though the Scotts had not yet publicly announced their separation, Patrecia moved out of the penthouse and into a studio apartment a block away at 165 East Thirty-Fifth Street, where Barbara and I had once lived.

One evening, at a party at Wilfred's, Patrecia sat quietly beside me in a corner of the living room while Allan Blumenthal, who had joined us, unexpectedly began to talk about how much I had contributed to his and Joan's lives and how much everyone in the Collective had been helped by me. I struggled between wanting to appreciate his words and finding his manner subtly self-abnegating and sycophantic, as well as feeling cruel for having my perspective. "You gave me my career," he was saying. "You taught me to believe in myself. You made my marriage to Joan possible. You contributed so much to our happiness. I hope you know how appreciative I feel." I thanked him and squeezed his shoulder, and he moved away. When I glanced at Patrecia, I was astonished by her look of protectiveness. Later she said, "You looked so young and lonely."

I felt more loved by Patrecia than I had ever felt loved before, in the terms that mattered most to me. I also felt better understood, in just those respects I most badly needed now.

I did not feel blindly worshiped; she was completely unsentimental and straightforward in calling me on my faults any time she believed I was thoughtless, unfair, unkind, or self-indulgent. I felt absolutely supported by her. But when she looked at me, I saw a consciousness that was not afraid to look at what she saw.

Perhaps because of her youth, perhaps because that was what she was most sensitive to in people, Patrecia seemed especially keyed in to the younger part of me, the part untouched by my experiences with Barbara or Ayn, the part most open, receptive, and unarmored. In all our interactions, it was as if she were constantly calling me back to that younger self, as if to remind me of an identity that I had allowed to become submerged. "At times," I said, "I feel almost as if you have been sent to me— don't ask me by whom—to help me remember who I truly am."

"Isn't it funny?" she remarked. "You draw out the most adult side of me—and I draw out the youth in you."

"We give each other what each of us most needs right now," I answered.

I paid for the joy I experienced with Patrecia in guilt, anxiety, and depression. My worst crime was that I obliged Patrecia to pay, too.

"Run for your life," I once burst out to her. "Run away from me and from this world. Your kind of spirit can't survive intact here. I'm sinking into horror, and I'm afraid for you." She shook her head calmly and said, "I love you." "What am I doing to you?" I cried to her. And she stroked my face and said simply, "I do not admire what you are doing. I hate what I am doing. But I admire everything about you, and I will stand by you, I will stand by us, as long as I can."

"It keeps getting harder," she said to me in the summer of 1966. "I never really believed that the secrecy would go on this long. It bothers me that I still have not told Larry the truth, even though our marriage is finished. It bothers me, every time I see Barbara or Ayn, to smile and be friendly and know that everything I say and do is a lie. I feel awkward whenever I'm around anyone in the Collective or at NBI. I act strange. I exaggerate being young and confused to cover up what I'm really feeling, and then I see Joan or Barbara looking at me oddly, and I know they're thinking how immature I am, and it's so humiliating, but I don't know what else to do. I'm no good at lying. I don't feel like myself anymore. Sometimes I'm so angry with you, I want to run away. Or else I want to give you an ultimatum—either you announce the truth publicly or I will leave you. Only, I'm afraid to give you an ultimatum, because I don't think you're ready, and I'm afraid of losing you. I can't leave you. I don't want to. I ask myself which is the real courage: to leave you, taking a chance that one day we might be together again, or to hang on, to absorb everything and give up parts of who I am, as the price I have to pay for having you."

When I finally told Barbara of my relationship with Patrecia, there was no drama or shock on Barbara's part. I told her, because it had become intolerable not to. "It was obvious and inevitable," she said, her voice subdued and noncommittal. "Do you expect it to last?" she asked, and I said that I did not know. "It won't," she declared flatly, perhaps because she could not grasp what the relationship was about, or perhaps because it did not fit our official theories of sex and love. She agreed that Ayn must never know about Patrecia, "because you're right, that would be the end of everything."

She felt strongly, some of the time, that Ayn should be told once and for all that a resumption of our affair was impossible. The rest of the time, Barbara fell into uncertainty, shuddering and saying things like, "God knows how she'll handle the rejection. God knows what you should do. What a mess."

Barbara continued to bewilder me. When we met, she would often turn the subject to our future and to her conviction that it would be a tragic mistake if we did not reconcile. "We had everything," she said to me. "We mustn't lose it all." My sister Elayne told me that, a few years earlier, on a day when Barbara had been out walking with Joan and her, Barbara had declared, "I have everything I ever wanted. A beautiful apartment in New York. Exciting and important work. Wonderful friends. And marriage to a great man." In spite of everything that had happened, in spite of Ayn, Wilfred, and Patrecia, some part of Barbara still seemed to be clinging to that vision. I had moments when that vision still had power over me, but not often.

She continually reminded me of the life we had shared at its best, as if our staggering incompatibilities required only goodwill to be resolved. Gently, almost compassionately, she continued to insist that, whatever the short-term rewards of my relationship with Patrecia, I was inviting long-term calamity, even without Ayn in the picture. I let her plead her case, out of some last, lingering notion of fairness and objectivity.

After much indecision and turmoil, I agreed to go away with Barbara for a weekend in the Poconos, a resort area in Pennsylvania. "Let's give ourselves this last chance," Barbara had implored. Just as I had hung on to a vision of what our relationship might be, long past the time when it made any sense to do so, I knew that now it was Barbara who could not let go, in spite of her love for Wilfred. Perhaps in some respects she was as bonded to me as I was bonded to Ayn and for similar reasons. And perhaps because Wilfred was still married and because his relationship with Barbara was not without conflict, at some deep level she felt alone in the world and fearful of an unknown future.

"Go," Patrecia had ordered. "You haven't said good-bye to each other yet, anyway. So I hope you give each other your best. Then maybe you'll know more clearly where you are."

At the resort, holding Barbara in my arms, I had little enthusiasm for what we were doing, and I feared that it showed. Barbara seemed almost frenzied, as if she were determined to bring everything to this one sexual encounter that she had withheld through the length of our marriage. Then, suddenly and violently, she began to cry, in great moans of pain beyond anything I had ever heard from her.

"I can't stand it!" she sobbed. "I can't stand it! I'm going to die! This is too much!" Utterly bewildered, I begged her to tell me what was the matter. She then cried, "I can't stand the idea of your sleeping with Patrecia! It's killing me!"

The suffering she conveyed was devastating. I felt almost as if my own sanity were slipping away. Where had this explosion come from? I implored her, "What are you talking about? Please calm down and help me understand what you're saying."

She kept repeating hysterically that she was tormented by mental pictures of Patrecia and me making love. "The pictures are unbearable!" She was weeping and holding herself.

Finally, I said the only thing that seemed relevant: "Barbara, why do you care? I was never what you wanted sexually. Why do you begrudge my being happy?"

She said that she loved me and that she would never resent my happiness, but that she could not bear the idea of my sleeping with another woman. She was oblivious to the contradiction in this statement.

"What about my sleeping with Ayn?"

Barbara answered, her voice rising, "That was different! Ayn was different! Ayn was another world—much older and a great genius. I couldn't think of rivalry with Ayn. And besides, Ayn never meant to you sexually what Patrecia means to you! Don't you suppose I know that?"

Again I asked helplessly, "But why do you *care?*"

And then, at last, after eighteen years of a tortured relationship, she finally told me, in a voice broken by sobs, "Because I know what sex means to you! I know your kind of intensity; it's more than just sexual. *I know you!* I know the look on your face, and I can't stand your giving that to anyone else!"

I thought of all the nights during all the years of lying in bed, my fists clenched in an agony of frustration and loneliness, while Barbara lay beside me reading a book.

I thought of one night in particular, long ago in Los Angeles, when we were still at UCLA. It was the night she confessed that when I showed any suffering, she felt uncomfortable and disappointed. It was a statement she would repudiate as the opposite of her convictions several decades later, but by then I had lived with the memory of it for a long time.

I told myself that I deserved all the pain I had endured in our marriage because I had not left it long ago.

Were there times when we had been happy together? Yes, there were. Even times when we were sexually happy. But that was not enough to justify what each of us had endured in the course of our relationship. It was time to wake up.

Looking at her tear-streaked face, I thought that probably I would never understand her and that I did not need to. This was a thought that was immensely liberating.

I proceeded to comfort her as I would comfort a child, feeling nothing except leaden tiredness.

Later, I asked Patrecia if in any sense she had known what would happen.

"No," she said. "I thought you might discover you were still in love with her."

"Patrecia, you are a brave person."

In September 1967, less than a year before our world was to shatter irredeemably, NBI leased eight thousand square feet of office space on the lower level of the Empire State Building. We were now offering lecture courses in eighty cities, and people all over the world were asking us to bring our courses to them. Wilfred negotiated a fifteen-year lease. It was the biggest financial commitment I had ever made—almost half a million dollars. *The Objectivist* moved in as our subtenant. It was here that we began to hold our Saturday night dances.

"Are we *crazy?*" Barbara said to me apprehensively. "Everything can explode at any minute! It's only a matter of time until you have to tell Ayn the truth; we both know that. Wouldn't it be better to tell her *before* signing the lease?" Eight thousand square feet in the Empire State Building to house all of our projects—I wanted that. "I am going to find a solution," I said. I did not grasp that by now I was almost totally out of control.

The realization of how many of my own principles and convictions I was violating filled me with anxiety. I sensed in me the rage of an animal pacing a cage and roaring impotently.

I had not felt effective with Barbara since the first months of our relationship, I no longer felt effective with Ayn, and I was failing the one person with whom I did feel effective.

But when I looked at the doors of our new offices and saw the gleaming letters, NATHANIEL BRANDEN INSTITUTE, I felt I was still the man and the mind who had launched a philosophical movement. I looked at the stage, the auditorium, the conference room, the glass partitions, the desks, the filing cabinets. I thought of my first letter to Ayn and of everything it had taken to come from that day to this sight. And I thought, I can't walk away from this. I can't give this up. Why should I have to? There is so much I want to accomplish. I love this battle. It's the crusade I always wanted. Am I damned because I want Patrecia as my reward?

Sometimes Patrecia and I came to NBI late at night when the staff had gone, and we would walk through the rooms together. One time, I stopped in the middle of the auditorium where I lectured on philosophy and psychology, and I cried to her, "Patrecia, what I want is right! I want you, and I want all of this! And I have a right to want it!"

I was shocked by the expression on Patrecia's face; it revealed a depth of anger I had never seen in her before. It was a look of the most profound moral indignation. "Nathan," she said, her voice shaking, "I have always loved and admired Ayn, and I have always felt compassion for her. But what I saw that first night at your lecture was real—the twisted side of her. When it comes to this issue, the issue of you, Ayn is totally out of her mind. She's as irrational as any of those mystical loonies who scared me in childhood. She is insane."

I did not cut her off, did not forbid her to speak as I once had. I did not answer. But this time, she knew I had heard her.

Still, was it not I who was helping to *make* Ayn "insane"?

Barbara and Wilfred's breakup had been coming for a long time, as the frictions that had plagued their relationship since they were teenagers surfaced in new forms with increasing frequency and heat. They were incompatible in some basic way, it seemed to me.

As it turned out, Barbara developed a friendship some months later, early in 1968, with a new man. That friendship would eventually become a romance lasting several years, and Barbara would describe it as the happiest relationship of her life up to that time. His name was Robert Berole, and he was a thoroughly likable and kind human being with a very positive outlook on life. For Barbara, he seemed just what the doctor ordered. His effect on her was wonderful. In his presence, her spirits soared.

I was glad to see Barbara in a happier state. She became more serene, more whole. And she no longer talked about the redemption of our marriage.

Since her marriage to Larry, Patrecia had worked professionally as Patrecia Scott. Now, she discovered that there were at least six Patricia Scotts in New York in the worlds of modeling and acting, and she decided to change her last name. One evening, discussing the question of names with Ayn and a few other of our friends, she asked for an opinion of several alternatives she had been considering.

"If I can make a suggestion," Ayn said, "how about Patrecia Wynand? I think it has a good sound, don't you?"

"After Wynand in *The Fountainhead*?" Patrecia said thoughtfully. Then she nodded. Professionally, she became Patrecia Wynand.

I never explicitly discussed with Patrecia the strategy I was pursuing with Ayn. Patrecia and I had a silent understanding about it. But I knew that to put the issue fully into words would only make her more self-conscious in Ayn's presence. "It will take a long time," Patrecia informed me solemnly, "to recover from all the consequences of what we are doing now. Even if we end up together, we won't come out of this undamaged. I hope you think about that."

I knew there were times when she resented me for the position in which I placed her. I did not blame her. My guilt for doing what I was doing to her dwarfed the guilt I felt concerning the pain I was causing Ayn.

As the end of 1967 approached, Ayn asked me what we might do on New Year's Eve. No one was in the mood for a large party. "I don't feel like spending New Year's with Barbara and her boyfriend at a Collective event," I told her, knowing that was a feeling she would have to respect. "And I don't want an evening alone with you and Frank; it'll be hard on me, and I'll drag you both down." I was determined to spend New Year's Eve with Patrecia.

I said that I was feeling rather depressed and not really in the mood for festivities. I had been complaining of depression a good deal; it was obvious to Ayn that I was often unhappy. I was attributing this to the breakup of my marriage; to the exhaustion of overwork; to an odd sense of deadness that made it exceedingly difficult to think of resuming a romance with her; to the lingering trauma of her past devastating reproaches; and to the lack of any kind of personal pleasure in my life apart from work. I mentioned all of these reasons to account for my moodiness, withdrawal, and the real despair moving through my body like a sickness.

"I have an idea," Ayn said brightly. "Why not ask Patrecia to be your date? Perhaps Alan Greenspan could ask Leisha, and the six of us could have an evening together." After considering her proposal carefully for a few minutes, searching Ayn's face for any sign of a trap, I said that it might be a good idea. "There's only one thing you must be careful about," Ayn said. "I suspect that Patrecia already has a little crush on you. You must watch yourself not to encourage her. You don't want to hurt her."

We celebrated New Year's Eve at the Plaza Hotel. As if in rebellion against the insanity of the occasion, Patrecia decided to enjoy herself, to be simply and openly who she was, without weighing her every statement. She did not retreat behind her usual protective facade of semi-inarticulate teenager; she allowed herself to be a confident twenty-seven-year-old woman and to treat me in every sense as her date of the evening. If I sat too long at the table in deep conversation with Ayn, she would grab my arm possessively and cheerfully and say, "Let's dance!"

Ayn and Frank seemed truly to enjoy themselves, as if they, too, were glad to be away from the somberness of what our Collective parties had deteriorated into.

Dancing with Ayn, I told her, "This was really a good idea."

"Yes," she replied, "both girls are pleasant to be with, don't you think?" Frank was dancing with Leisha, and Alan was dancing with Patrecia. "I think Alan likes Patrecia more than Leisha," Ayn said. "Do you suppose it could develop into something?"

I shrugged. "Who knows?"

A week or two later, in an irritable mood—perhaps because her subconscious mind had registered a signal that her conscious mind had missed—Ayn stated angrily, "There's not a single person in the Collective who would dare to interrupt, if you and I were talking, and ask you to dance. I'm afraid Patrecia is pushy. That's not the way an idealist behaves." I knew that what I was hearing in that moment was not self-esteem but egomania.

My conversations with Ayn focused increasingly on what was wrong with me, why I was so emotionally repressed, and into what dimension I had disappeared.

I knew that I was putting her through hell. I had given her no way to understand me. At times, when I was not immersed in my own pain, I was tormented by the suffering I was causing. Yet I took no action to change anything. I delayed facing the fact that nothing in our situation would change until and unless I made it change. And because I delayed, I caused needless suffering and humiliation to us both. I avoided a responsibility that was mine to take. It was as if I were waiting for a miracle to deliver me.

She could not doubt the enormous esteem in which I held her mind and her achievements or my dedication to fighting for Objectivism. Nor could she doubt that in some sense I loved her, even though the erotic component could hardly have been more absent. "You're here but you're not here," she would say. "You're elusive. You act like a man in love one day, and on the next you're withdrawn and you have no explanation of why. Do you know what kind of torture this is for me?"

We'd had nearly eighteen years filled with wonderful memories. I had built my life around this relationship. Had I been merely indifferent toward her, or had my emotions been principally negative, I would not have been able to keep us both in a state of suspension for as long as I did. It was not romantic love, but it was love. I did not doubt that then, and I do not doubt it now. I still worshiped her as a goddess of reason. And yet the thought clearly present in my mind, but not yet manifest in words, was, If Ayn's philosophy holds that I am morally wrong to be in love with Patrecia and that I am a traitor to my values for not romantically desiring Ayn, then at least in these respects her philosophy is wrong. This was not a position I knew how to defend yet.

What I told myself consciously was that there had to be a way to fulfill Ayn's emotional needs without romance or sex and that when she and I discovered it—when Ayn accepted that our relationship was one of minds, not bodies, as it had started out to be—the road would be cleared for an emotional renaissance.

"Do you realize," I said to her, "that I've known you half my life?"

She looked at me silently and suspiciously.

I went on, "A year after I left home, I acquired a new one—in a manner of speaking. You might say I've never been really on my own. Sometimes I wonder if that's healthy."

"Getting tired of a serious, philosophical life?" she asked sharply. "You're on your own now, in every way that counts. Unless you mean you want to be free of me."

"Free of you? I want us to be friends forever."

"*Friends* is not what I'm talking about! What new irrationality is this? Do you think I would have dedicated *Atlas Shrugged* to a *friend?* I've told the whole world that you are Objectivism. Do you think I would say that about a *friend?* What's the matter with you? Don't you attach meaning to the words you speak? Where has your mind gone?"

The message was clear—if I were not in love with her, that meant my mind had gone and I was a traitor to our philosophy. This was Ayn's notion of giving me every chance to withdraw from our "romance."

We had "psychological" conversations in which she struggled to "help" me with my seeming depression and confusion, and I looked for opportunities to drop the hints that might grow in her mind toward the conclusions I desired.

"I can't see myself spending my future as the third person in your marriage to Frank," I would say, and she would answer, alarmed, "Are you asking me to leave Frank and live with you openly?" "No," I would say, "but I want you to understand how difficult our situation has become." She would respond indignantly, "You want a life with a lesser woman just because it's *easier?*"

We had adopted the term *psychoepistemology,* proposed by Barbara, to designate the study of cognition from the aspect of the relationship between the conscious and the subconscious, the volitional and the automatic, as well as individual differences in methods of cognitive functioning. We spoke of a person's psychoepistemology as rational or irrational, as reality oriented, emotion oriented, or people oriented. "Something has happened to your psychoepistemology," she would say. "Clarity was always your strongest trait. What's happened to it? Do you realize how much chaos you permit yourself?"

When we were not discussing our personal relationship, my mind functioned as it had always functioned, or so it seemed to me. There were many occasions when we were as exquisitely attuned as we had been at our best. At such times, Ayn would become optimistic about the future and announce that no problem could possibly resist our combined brains. "Haven't we been soul mates since you were fourteen years old? Think of what we have already been through together!" It was still possible for us to be happy together, to hug and laugh and say that we lived in a benevolent universe.

"Remember," she would say, sometimes cheerfully, sometimes threateningly, but always as a warning, "without you the Collective loses its meaning for me. They're the tail, but you're the comet. If anything goes permanently wrong between us, I'm finished. *Everything* is finished. You're my lifeline to the world and to any chance at happiness I'm ever going to have." What she projected—and this was the judgment I dreaded—was that if I failed her, it would be tantamount to a sin against the Holy Ghost, deserving of total damnation. A part of me shared her view, and it was a view that paralyzed me.

My attachment to NBI and to the world I was building was another trap in my dealings with Ayn. Yet another was the comparison I made between my devastating experiences with Barbara, when I was barely twenty and had my whole life ahead of me, and what I suspected I was now doing to Ayn when she was in her sixties, after a lifetime of her feeling battered by an uncomprehending world.

I felt as if my brain were imprisoned in the vice of conflicting values, all of them absolutes and all of them at war with one another.

Of our various projects at NBI, none gave me as much pleasure as a new venture I had initiated, NBI Theater. Patrecia's involvement in acting had reawakened my early love of the theater, and I wanted to produce a series of plays and to write for the theater myself. Ralph Roseman was guiding and coaching me in the various business aspects of production. Barbara had written an excellent stage adaptation of *The Fountainhead*. (Ayn told me she liked it more than her own movie adaptation.) Phillip Smith was to direct, we were talking to agents and actors, and we aimed for a fall 1968 opening.

By that time, I projected, *The Psychology of Self-Esteem* would be finished. I had a contract for the book with World Publishing, a house owned by Times-Mirror, which also owned New American Library, or NAL. Ayn had promised my editor that the book would be good and, given Ayn's importance at NAL, that had been enough, so he did not request to see any part of the book as it was being written. It was promised for delivery this year.

I was behind schedule. I was also late with many of my articles for *The Objectivist*. I found it difficult to concentrate on my writing. Today, it is difficult for me to believe that it was during the agonizing chaos of this period that I was writing my central chapters on self-esteem.

Ayn was often late with articles herself, yet she reproached me constantly for not delivering mine on time, blaming my preoccupation with the stage production of *The Fountainhead*. "I would never have given my consent to that project," she spat at me, "if I thought it would get in the way of your writing for *The Objectivist*. Nothing should come ahead of your articles. Nothing matters more."

Ayn did not want to pursue me; her self-concept demanded that I pursue her. "Tell me what's wrong. If I ask, you say you love me, and sometimes you act like a man in love, but there's no consistency to anything you do. If our romance is over, say so." When I made the most tentative move in that direction, she would immediately respond with an explosion of wrath that would last for hours.

During calmer times she would say, "Is it my age? I could accept that."

No, she couldn't. I tried to tell her more than once, and even the hint sent her through the roof.

What I actually told her was, "It's more exact to say that I would like the chance to build a life with someone who is a contemporary and with whom I could have a complete relationship."

"Where will you find a contemporary who is my equal?"

I said, "You have no equals at any age," and I wondered, Is love only a contest of philosophical grandeur?

"Well, then, what are you suggesting? Do you want to be like Goethe or any of those so-called geniuses who marry a nothing hausfrau? You know the type I mean; I despise them. Do you wish to be a hero in public life but not in your private life?" Each word was a thunderbolt of moral condemnation.

"Ayn, the world consists of more than you and hausfraus."

Her voice rose. "The man to whom I dedicated *Atlas Shrugged* would never want anything less than me! I don't care if I'm ninety years old and in a wheelchair! This will always be my view! If you are a complete and utter fraud, at least have the decency to say so, and we'll go our separate ways and you'll be out of my life for good and I'll be out of my misery! I won't have to see or speak to you again—ever!"

In her despair, Ayn had begun turning more and more to Barbara, whom she sought as an ally to her cause. This had been happening for a year. Barbara said to me, "Ayn insists that it's you who keeps pressing for a continuation of the romance. She says she knows perfectly well that she may be too old. If she's offering you a chance to withdraw, why aren't you taking it?"

I told her that I did not think she understood what Ayn meant by offering me a chance. When Barbara declared that I could not let Ayn suffer this way and that I should tell her the truth, I asked if she meant that I should tell Ayn about Patrecia. "No. Not about Patrecia. The idea that she was being rejected for Patrecia would kill her." When I pointed out that Ayn was not being rejected for anyone, that my feelings for her changed years ago, long before I ever met Patrecia, Barbara observed correctly, "That's not how Ayn will see it."

If Ayn is becoming more and more agitated and irrational, I told myself, I have contributed to it. By giving her contradictory signals. By not letting her know the limits of my feelings for her at the start of our affair. By not holding her to the original agreement of 'one or two years at the most.' By feeding her grandiosity from the day we met.

Sometimes, when I saw the enormity of Ayn's pain, my anguish and self-reproach were overwhelming. Other times, I confronted another truth within myself, one that was no less real—an attitude of cold indifference toward a suffering I was less and less able to respect.

At NBI on Saturday nights, I danced with Ayn, with Patrecia, and with a few of our friends. I struggled to maintain the appearance of normalcy while wondering why the actual facts were not obvious to everyone. I would later learn that parts of the truth were obvious, at least to some students, who suspected a relationship between Patrecia and me.

Years later, reflecting on "the old days at NBI," screenwriter Richard Danus remarked, "Seeing you and Patrecia together, it seemed natural, logical, that you two would be in love. You fit, somehow. It was Barbara and you that never fit; at least, I never thought so—no criticism of Barbara intended—and I know I was not the only person who had that viewpoint. Patrecia and you were not the puzzle. Barbara and you were the puzzle."

Ayn's conflicts with Frank were worsening. Frank's mind was continuing to deteriorate, although no one yet perceived the onset of arteriosclerosis. He would erupt against Ayn in violent rages, often in my presence, and I would see a look of helpless bewilderment on Ayn's face. "Frank, darling, are you angry with me about something you haven't told me?" They would have interminable talks about his psychoepistemology. Ayn did the talking, and Frank listened silently, except for an occasional muted response. "Do you have any suggestions," Ayn asked me, "on how I can encourage Frank to speak to me more?" I suggested that Frank might have a great deal of stored anger and resentment against her. Later she informed me, "I asked Frank about that, and he says 'absolutely not.' You're wrong."

Frank had his own studio apartment by that time, where he painted— and drank. Years later, after his death, when his studio was discovered to be filled with empty liquor bottles, Elayne would tell me, "Ayn refused to admit that he had become an alcoholic. She said he must have somehow used the bottles 'to mix his paints in.' She saw what she wanted to see."

In the early spring of 1968, still another aspect of Ayn's psychology came into focus—her disposition to use people in the most cold-blooded and hypocritical way. As our relationship continued to deteriorate, and she increasingly turned to Barbara for help, she often poured out her suffering in a way that Barbara found heartbreaking. At the same time, Ayn often spoke to me of Barbara with appalling lack of respect. Neither her moments of affection toward Barbara nor her contempt could be taken at face value; one had to know what purpose they served in the moment— or in what mood Ayn happened to be on a particular day. When, for example, she focused on the history of my marriage, she told me that it was clear that Barbara had not been the right woman for me—"not strong enough, not purposeful enough." But when she suspected that I might be attracted to Patrecia (which I denied, even though I could not stop praising her virtues), she declared that Barbara was the only "other woman" in my life she could accept. Then she virtually embraced Barbara as a spiritual sister. Barbara's guilt at deceiving Ayn, by protecting my secret about Patrecia, began to rise.

Barbara felt obliged to listen in increasing distress while Ayn spoke of her suffering. Ayn confided that she felt my objection to being the "other man" in her marriage was only a rationalization. She would say, "If he feels for me what he says he feels, and sees in me what he says he sees, he'd be willing to be part of a harem. Doesn't he know that the great proof of my love for him is that I chose him *despite* a happy marriage and the difference of our ages?" Ayn had made this remark about a harem to me, too.

Once, when I expressed to Ayn my desire for a personal life apart from NBI and our work, she immediately answered, "You mean, a personal life apart from me?" This was sufficient to throw her into a lengthy, impassioned, and indignant speech. "You have *no right* to other concerns. I placed my life's work in your hands. I told the world you were my intellectual heir. I have not gone through the hell of the past forty years, I have not fought and fought and fought and endured and endured, so that you can profit off my blood! I am not going to retire gracefully and let you reap the rewards of my agony! You have no right to casual friendships, no right to vacations, no right to sex with some inferior woman! Did you imagine that I would consent to be left on the scrap heap? Is that what you imagined? Is it?" Such tirades had become commonplace.

Throughout the spring of that year, Barbara had been pressing me to tell Ayn that I was not in love with her. At no point did she suggest that I tell Ayn about my relationship with Patrecia, perhaps partly because she still imagined Patrecia was one day going to vanish from my life.

Ayn was becoming increasingly suspicious and hostile toward Patrecia, as my feelings became more obvious, and she looked for every opportunity to find fault with her. Whereas she had once spoken positively of Patrecia as a possible mate for Alan Greenspan or Leonard Peikoff, she now conveyed that such an idea would be inconceivable and denied that she had ever thought differently.

"Don't ever permit yourself to think, even for a moment," she said to me once, her voice shaking with suppressed violence, "that Patrecia or some equivalent is going to cash in on my ambition, mind, and achievement. I have not lived as I have lived in order, now, to hand you over graciously and lie down and die."

Returning from a drive in the country, where Barbara and I had gone to talk, she said, "You look terrible. I've never seen you so unlike yourself. You look so haggard. God, how did we all get into this?" We pulled into the parking garage of our building, and my head fell on the steering wheel in total despair and misery. "I've got to tell Ayn the truth about *everything*," I said. "I can't stand this any longer. The whole situation makes me sick, and I make myself sick. I've got to tell the truth—and let everything collapse, as it's going to anyway." Now it was Barbara's turn to be frightened. She whispered gently, urgently, that I did not know what I was saying, that I was overreacting out of emotion, that I needed to think more clearly and move slowly. There was a subtle note of hard, practical calculation behind her words. "Give up NBI?" she said, as if we were discussing the end of the world—*her* world. "Give up everything we've created? Just walk away from Objectivism? Walk away from NBI? How can you possibly do that? You can't. You'd never respect yourself again."

When I saw that I felt like a fraud when facing my own students; when I realized that no aspect of my work gave me pleasure any longer; when my meetings with Ayn were reduced to long, drawn-out sessions made of nothing but pity, rage, guilt, and mutually inflicted pain; when I knew that there was no longer an ounce of dignity between us; when I heard Ayn scream her suspicions that I was falling for a "chorus girl"; when I heard

Patrecia tell me, after returning from the run of a play she had done outside New York, "I missed you, but I was glad to be away, away from everything, away from this madhouse," I knew that I could not remain passive any longer. I had to act, had to bring some reality back to Ayn's and my relationship, no matter what the consequences.

I had to communicate—clearly, explicitly, and unequivocally—that a continuation of the romance between us was impossible, that the love affair was over. I had been inexcusably passive much too long. I needed to begin taking responsibility. In my relationship with Ayn, I had badly defaulted in this area.

I decided to write a letter that I would give to Ayn personally so that she could read it in my presence. I knew that if I attempted to *tell* her my thoughts, I would not have a chance to finish; there would be an explosion within the first seconds. I was no longer afraid of her anger; I had faced it too many times, and in any event the letter would hardly spare me that. But I was afraid of never having the opportunity to be heard and understood.

A letter also allowed me to select my words carefully, to say exactly what I meant to say with no possibility of ambiguity or misunderstanding. I could put it tactfully, lucidly, lovingly. I was a writer; I knew how to express myself on paper. This was the most challenging writing assignment of my life. My purpose was to communicate that our time together as a romance had passed and that my most fervent wish was for us to be passionate, loving friends and intellectual comrades. I worked on the letter with more care than I had ever brought to any other project. I wanted Ayn to understand that I had to have a life of my own.

My words focused on our age difference, but of course there were many aspects of Ayn's personality—her rage, her grandiosity—that had long ago extinguished any romantic feelings I had for her. And deeper than any such considerations was the simple fact that at the age of twenty-four, I had confused passionate admiration with romantic love—and had not the wits to extricate myself. The letter did not address these matters.

When Barbara read it, her face showed fear and horror. But she told me that it was "a good letter, or as good as such a letter can be" and that she felt "petrified" at the thought of Ayn's reaction.

Then she made an unexpected statement, the full truth of which I recognized only later. "I don't for a minute think you really expect this letter to work. The idea that you and Ayn are ever going to be friends after this is a joke. Some part of you already knows there is absolutely no way for you to save the situation and have everything you want. I think your intention is to precipitate a crisis. I think you know exactly how all this is going to end, and I think that you're orchestrating it."

On an evening toward the end of June, Ayn came to my apartment for dinner. When she entered and took one look at me, she embraced me with concern and said, "Darling, what's the matter?"

I told her that I needed to speak to her. We decided to try to eat first, but it was impossible. Alarmed by my manner, Ayn became her most caring, sympathetic self. I told her that I had written a letter in which I attempted to convey my understanding of the core problem in our relationship. As soon as she heard these words, the warmth disappeared from her eyes, and I knew it would not return, not toward me, not ever again. "Have you written that you're not in love with me?" she demanded harshly. I handed her the letter.

It was several pages long. In it, I apologized for not conveying to her sooner the truth of my feelings. I acknowledged the great joy and love I had experienced with her over the years. I spoke of feeling that I was an outsider in her and Frank's marriage, as I properly had to be, and of my need for a personal life entirely my own. I said that the twenty-five-year difference in our ages now made sex with her impossible for me. And that I wanted us to be again the great friends we had once been.

Within ninety seconds, she was screaming at me with a violence that exceeded my worst projections. "You *bastard,*" she kept shrieking. "You bastard, you bastard! You nothing! You fraud! You contemptible swine!" Then she leapt up and said, "I don't want to be alone in the same room with you! I want Barbara here! I want Barbara to know about this *obscenity!*" She ran to the telephone, called Barbara's apartment, and said, in a trembling voice, "Come down at once and see what this monster has done!"

When Barbara arrived, Ayn held up my letter—her entire body now shaking—and asked, "Have you seen this *vile thing?*" Feigning bewilderment, Barbara did not reply. When she finished reading it, she nodded her head at Ayn with an expression that could have meant anything and gave a long sorrowful sigh.

"Everything you have ever professed to be," Ayn stated, her face twisted in hatred, "is a lie!" My love of *Atlas Shrugged* was a lie, she informed me. My dedication to Objectivism was a lie. My idealism was a lie. Even my work in psychology was fraudulent. "Everything was stolen from me. When did you ever have an original idea of your own?"

I realized that I was hearing nothing I should not have expected. My mind flashed to previous examples of Ayn's rewriting history regarding other people.

No matter how tactfully my letter was worded, the basic message that came through to her, and all that she would register, was that she was too old to inspire romantic feelings in me. All of her energies were now being mobilized to deny her suffering.

The intimately personal meaning of what was taking place between us, the devastation she was experiencing, was swept aside. It was easy to track her internal process: since I was a bastard and a scoundrel, clearly I could not have the power to cause her pain; therefore, what she was feeling was not pain; it was moral indignation.

I had witnessed this kind of rationalizing in Ayn before, when I had not been personally involved. I was thoroughly familiar with the way she pushed away feelings that threatened her idea of who she was.

She paced the room while Barbara and I sat silently, watching her. Her first impulse was to break with me totally and on the spot. "I will denounce you in *The Objectivist*!"

Deeper than my anguish, I felt a strange, almost light-headed calm. I had been right, I told myself; I had been right. I had understood Ayn correctly. She did not yet know about my love affair with Patrecia; all she knew was that I did not want the continuation of a romance with her— and she was prepared, on the basis of that information alone, to repudiate me publicly, to deny the value of my work, and to tell our followers, as she now announced to Barbara and me, that I was a "traitor to Objectivism" and "a complete fraud."

"What am I going to do?" she moaned, almost as if we were there to help her. "I've given him my public sanction. I've dedicated *Atlas* to him. If he can do this, he's capable of anything. How do I know what he might say or do publicly that will embarrass me?" I had the sense that her greatest fear was that I would retaliate against any attack by disclosing the secret of our affair. "If I can't have some guarantee that I am going to be protected from him, I'll disgrace him. I'll ruin his name. It doesn't matter what happens to him now—I've got to protect myself!"

I did not attach literal meaning to any of her words; even in my state, I thought them ludicrous. I also knew that sooner or later, a more practical-minded side of her would make her aware that, in order to denounce me to the world at this point, she would have to say what my letter had been about. Looking at Barbara, I imagined that she was having the same thought.

When Ayn began to speak of canceling all plans for the stage production of *The Fountainhead*, I listened almost indifferently, as if she were referring to some project that had mattered to me in some other lifetime.

She had begun to calm down, and it was obvious that she had realized the practical difficulties in denouncing me publicly at this time. She could hardly say to the world that she repudiated Nathaniel Branden as a spokesman for Objectivism because he failed her romantically, because he refused to sleep with her. If the denunciation was ever to happen, she would have to find other grounds.

Almost incoherently, she spoke to Barbara—as if I were not there—of "giving him one more chance." Our personal relationship, she announced, had ended, but perhaps "he can show me that he is still competent and trustworthy to represent Objectivism." How I was to establish this to her satisfaction, she did not say, and I did not ask.

When they had gone and I was alone in the apartment, my most urgent desire was to talk to Patrecia. But she was away from New York, working in summer theater. I clung to her image in my mind—a sole point of support in a collapsing world.

I was in agony. And yet, in the midst of remorse, anxiety, and the worst suffering I had ever known, I was glad this evening had taken place. Glad I had given Ayn the letter. And passionately sorry I had not done so years earlier.

It was the first step toward a confrontation that would be far more terrible than the one tonight. But it was also the first step toward a return to reality and the rebuilding of my self-esteem.

After that night, Ayn and I spoke infrequently and almost always about business concerning *The Objectivist*—until the day we saw each other for the last time.

During July, we had a few working sessions, which were awkward and somewhat formal. Our exchanges about my mental and emotional state were detached, strained, and impersonal. After eighteen years of intimacy, we had lost the art of talking easily and naturally together.

When we met, our eyes were dry. We did our crying alone. We acknowledged this once to each other. I was touched by Ayn's candor in admitting that she, too, wept, even though there was a total absence of emotion in her voice when she said it.

"How are you feeling?" Ayn asked once, and I answered that I was in hell. "But a better, cleaner hell than I was in a month ago." She nodded in understanding, and I said, "And you?" She answered, "Just as you see. In hell." We spoke dryly and factually, like two accountants comparing the figures in our ledgers.

I saw that there were times when, in response to her own pain and mine, Ayn wanted to reach out to me. I also saw that she needed me to make the first move, to make it easier for her to melt against the resistance of her official intellectual position against me. But I was still withholding the truth about Patrecia, and I knew that soon that truth would have to come to light. Until it did, to allow further warmth between Ayn and me was a fraud I was no longer willing to tolerate. If we were ever to be close again, I wanted that closeness to be based on honesty.

Ayn needed time, I told myself, to absorb and accept the fact that I was not in love with her. I hoped that our relationship could restabilize in this new context. Then I would tell her about the affair I had been having with Patrecia for the past several years. I hoped she could make peace with these facts.

As foolish as it seems to me today, while one part of me yearned to be out of this environment entirely, another part could not relinquish the idea that a happy conclusion might still be possible. That part felt that I was rational and right in wanting to continue my work with NBI and *The Objectivist,* to have an intimate friendship with Ayn, and to have my life with Patrecia, and I felt as if we were all trapped in some vast, tragically unnecessary mistake.

Yet a voice within me said that this embittered woman sitting opposite me on her living room sofa was not the person I had fallen in love with when I had first read *The Fountainhead*—and that Ayn Rand no longer existed.

I sensed a corresponding conflict within Ayn. There were moments when she looked at me with hatred, and moments when her dark, pain-filled eyes said, "But this is Nathan! This is the man with whom I shared everything!"

To Barbara, she said, "There is nothing for me to look forward to, nothing to hope for in reality. My life is over. He has forced me into a permanent ivory tower. He took away this earth."

Ayn said that I obviously needed to talk to someone who would be emotionally uninvolved in the problem. She suggested Allan Blumenthal. I agreed, not because I imagined that Allan could help me "clarify my thinking" but because I thought that if he knew the actual facts, he might be able to influence Ayn in a saner direction. I knew that whatever I said to Allan would go directly to Ayn. Both Allan and Ayn communicated this to me at the outset. No one suggested that I should have the right to privacy in this matter, and I did not ask for it.

Ayn gave me permission to discuss with Allan all the details of our affair. She recognized that there was no way Allan could participate effectively without this knowledge.

I recall the first moment of entering Allan's apartment. Allan and Joan looked at me with guarded and noncommittal eyes. Joan's expression conveyed a hint of satisfaction. For some months, the Collective had sensed the presence of trouble. No one could imagine what it might be, only that it involved some conflict between Ayn and me. Now, Joan's eager anticipation at learning the nature of the conflict seemed palpable. I recall thinking with indifferent astonishment, as I walked with Allan into his study, that Joan's accumulated resentment toward me had to be enormous and that all her protestations of undying gratitude were empty and meaningless. If I had been paying attention I would have known it sooner.

Whatever her grievances were, she was never to tell me. All I ever heard from her was how much I had helped her with her personal problems.

As I related the story of Ayn's and my relationship, I had to keep from laughing when I saw the involuntary, fastidious wrinkling of Allan's nose, which was so typical of him when his sensibilities were offended. It was obvious that he did not approve of the affair. When I observed his growing sympathy and concern for me, I allowed myself a flicker of hope.

"But this is monstrous!" he finally exclaimed. "What's the matter with Ayn? How can she not see how irrational and unfair she's being? Ayn should never have allowed your affair to begin in the first place! She's twenty-five years older—it was her responsibility to know better at the start! Disaster was inevitable! And never mind you, look what she's done to Frank and Barbara!"

When I protested that I was hardly an innocent victim, the impatient gesture of his hand brushed my statement aside. "Oh, Nathan, you're so naïve!" He went on to express the view that for some time, he and Joan had been troubled by Ayn's near paranoia, violent temper, and general blindness to any context but her own. He insisted that he was prepared to take my side and do whatever he possibly could to help Ayn see reason. He said that we had to "save her" for her own sake, as well as mine.

"My heaven," he said. "And to think that sometimes Joan or I faulted you for being tense or abrupt or insensitive! I think it's incredible that you've been able to function at all, to do all that you've done, carrying the weight of these ridiculous burdens all these years! I'm more in awe of you than ever now!"

It was not awe that I needed from him now but strength. Our meeting took place on a Sunday, and I knew that tomorrow, Monday evening, he had an appointment with Ayn to hear her version of our relationship. When he repeated that I could count on him absolutely, I pointed out that he had not yet spoken to Ayn. He drew himself up in his chair and said, as if he imagined I would find his words encouraging, "You can trust me, and I'll tell you why. I'm more afraid of you than I am of Ayn."

I did not hear from him on Tuesday morning, when he had promised to telephone, so I called him. His first words were, "Now, I know you're going to think I've been brainwashed," and then I knew that he had been.

I listened, with the old, familiar sense of heaviness, as he said, "Ayn gave me an entirely different picture of the situation. I had no idea that it was you who has been chasing her all these years, when she gave you plenty of opportunities to withdraw from the romance. To tell you the truth, I'm shocked at your cruelty! You obviously do have serious psychological problems!"

At our next meeting, I told him that I had not been chasing Ayn, as she had declared to him, although this was a fantasy in which she was heavily invested, and I explained the actual progression of events and the nature of my complicity. His own knowledge of Ayn's psychology inclined him to believe me, he said. He suggested that of course Ayn had her own biases and blind spots, and the truth was no doubt more complicated than either she or I appreciated.

I wanted to tell him about Patrecia—first, because she was an essential element of the full context, and second, because I thought his own regard for her would make it possible for him to understand me better. The problem was, I was not prepared to ask Allan to deceive Ayn on my behalf. Barbara agreed. "You can't put Allan in that position." I decided to communicate my love for Patrecia but not the affair.

I began by telling Allan the story of my relationship with Barbara, because that was where it all began, and I spoke of the years of loneliness and sexual frustration, both before and after the romance with Ayn. "The trouble with you, Nathan," Allan informed me, "is that you attach too much importance to sex."

Why am I telling this eunuch anything? I thought in revulsion. But then, impatient for some kind of resolution, I proceeded to acknowledge the depth of my feelings for Patrecia.

"You'll have to give her up," he announced, as if it were self-evident. If I did, I asked him, would that make her importance to me go away? He shrugged. "You'll have to solve that on your own."

When I remained silent, and Allan realized that it was not a foregone conclusion that I would be as submissive as he had expected, he said, "Otherwise, what do you imagine will happen? You're absolutely dependent on Ayn. Your whole reputation is as 'Mr. Objectivism,' and for that you need Ayn's sanction. How will you earn a living?"

I smiled inwardly and wondered, Does he really think I'm trapped? For the past several summers, I had been spending six weeks in California, lecturing in Los Angeles and San Francisco; I had developed a fondness for Los Angeles, and recently I had begun to think of moving there with Patrecia, if I could not rescue the situation in New York. At the same time, the thought of leaving this city was painful. I answered, "I will move to L.A. and open a practice in psychotherapy."

Allan looked at me as if I had abandoned all reason. "But Nathan, Ayn won't let you."

It was not Allan for whom I now felt contempt but myself: for sanctioning Allan as a psychiatrist, for imagining that he could ever be any sort of ally in a battle of this kind, for crediting him with any significant amount of independence or integrity. I felt thoroughly worn and battered, but I could not control myself. I said, "How do you think she will stop me?"

Up till this time, in an effort to protect me, Allan had given Ayn fairly sanitized reports of our conversations, not mentioning the depth of my estrangement from her or the strength of my feelings for Patrecia. I can only speculate as to what his own agitation and torment must have been during this period; at the time, I was in no position to think about it. In any event, all that now came to an end.

When Allan finally told Ayn of my love for Patrecia, she immediately announced that under no circumstances would she ever speak to me again. I was informed by both Allan and Barbara that Ayn had ascended to a higher level of rage. "You don't want to know what Ayn is now saying," Allan told me. We discontinued our meetings, as we recognized that they had no purpose. All further communications to or from Ayn, Barbara said, were to be channeled through her.

"Judgment day is coming," I told Patrecia, and when she asked what I meant, I answered, "The day when everything will be out in the open." Patrecia observed that when I said it, I looked relieved. "Judgment day is coming for us all," I added. "For everyone involved. Ayn likes to say, 'Judge, and be prepared to be judged.' Fair enough. I guess every day of our life is judgment day, and our own ego is the judge."

As a condition of continuing to support NBI—that is, give it her "sanction"—Ayn demanded a letter from me in which I admitted that I had behaved inconsistently with the principles of Objectivism. Indifferently, in a note consisting of one or two sentences, I obliged. To acknowledge that I was not a perfect Objectivist had no importance to me at that point. My letter mentioned no specific act or person. I saw myself as calming Ayn's paranoia, placating her morbid fantasies that I would do something to disgrace her and Objectivism—as if my note could protect her or mean anything to anyone but her.

I listened calmly as Barbara informed me of Ayn's newest "terms," which included that I now devote my life exclusively to Objectivism, forswearing all other interests and goals and somehow persuading her that my mind was still reliable and that I could be trusted to represent her. I gathered that neither she nor Ayn was struck by the absurd contradiction of a man's teaching Objectivism while practicing the kind of selflessness Ayn demanded. Abandon my ego and preach the morality of egoism? If my sin had been hypocrisy, was my atonement to embody a new form of it?

"You need to know," Barbara said, "that Ayn is not really enthusiastic about your continuing the work for NBI under any circumstances. She says she thinks it's imperative that she denounce you in *The Objectivist*. But on what grounds—that you're in love with Patrecia? That's the truth, but she can hardly say it. All that's protecting you is Ayn's fear for her own reputation."

I recognized finally and irrevocably that any hope of reconciling with Ayn had been foolish self-delusion, another instance of refusing to see what was staring me in the face. I knew that the next step was to announce to Ayn that Patrecia and I had been having an affair. I did not take it. I was afraid—and I could not have said precisely of what. Afraid of Ayn's wrath, to be sure, but that was not all. Afraid most of all, perhaps, of facing cleanly and inescapably that I had betrayed myself for nothing. Had I told the truth from the beginning, the outcome would have been the same—of that I had no doubt—but I would have spared everyone a great deal of suffering. It was difficult now even to recall the reasons that had once made my choices seem imperative.

I was beginning to hear the first rumors of new charges against me, originated by Ayn and now spreading among our friends. They struck me as so preposterous that I felt my whole world had become a madhouse. I was sinking deeper and deeper into a waking nightmare. Leonard Peikoff, now returned from his exile in Denver and proudly reinstated with Ayn, looked at me tensely as if I were an unpredictable disaster that could happen at any moment. Other members of our circle spoke to me carefully, tentatively. I looked like hell, I told myself, and that was responsible for at least part of their response.

I thought more and more about breaking with everything and leaving with Patrecia for a new life. However, Patrecia was not particularly eager to leave New York. She loved the stage and saw the East Coast as the center of theatrical activity. It was primarily Leisha's interest in acting that made a move to California tempting for Patrecia. "Leisha and I have talked about it," Patrecia told me. "Since we're identical twins, we both can't hope to make it here. Maybe we'll divide up the country; she'll try to succeed in New York, I'll try movies and television in California. If it comes to that."

By early August, I knew that it would come to that. I merely did not know the specific steps that would make it happen.

One day, Barbara announced, "Ayn is wondering if I could run NBI without you." She did not say this as if it were a prospect she especially relished. I suspected she was already having her own daydreams of escape. "Of course I was," she told me later. "I saw what your 'glory' cost you."

"Run for your life," I said to Patrecia, as I had said it before, and she answered, "Not now and not ever." I had not allowed anyone—not Ayn, not Barbara—to see the depth of despair I disclosed to Patrecia. I wanted her to see the worst, to see me at my lowest, with every possible illusion stripped away. She said, "We are going to survive." She did not attempt to influence me in any particular direction; it was as if she, too, were merely a spectator of a drama unfolding before her. "The only choice I have to make right now," she said, "is the one I've made—to stand by you and to wait. Do what you have to do. Your job is to get through this. When it's all over, I hope you'll condemn yourself less than you are doing now."

I spent long, tortured hours of self-examination in my study, looking out the window, leaving to Barbara and Wilfred the daily business of NBI.

On an evening in August, Barbara came to my apartment, visibly shaken. "I've reached the end," she stated. "Ayn is about to make me her heir." Up to that time, I was the beneficiary in Ayn's will, after Frank, just as I was the beneficiary in Frank's will, after Ayn. Ayn had informed Barbara that she had made an appointment with her lawyer to change her will. "Ayn intends for me to inherit everything!" Barbara said, as if it were a disaster. "I can't live with that. The guilt is too much. And it's too late for you to tell her the truth about Patrecia. She refuses to speak to you now, under any circumstances. I have to do it."

At least give me a chance to save myself, she was saying, a chance to save my integrity.

What was to happen now seemed inevitable. From the night I had heard Barbara's comment that my goal was to precipitate a crisis and had given Ayn my letter, some part of me had known precisely what I was doing and how all this was meant to end. I had engineered it.

"Tell her," I said.

Barbara telephoned Allan Blumenthal and asked him to accompany her. They went together to Ayn's apartment on the sixth floor while I waited in mine on the twentieth.

Barbara proceeded to tell Ayn that I had been lying about my relationship with Patrecia, that we had been in love and having an affair since 1964, and that for the past two years Barbara had known about it and collaborated with me in deceiving Ayn. This, Barbara explained, is why I had been in such a bad way for such a long time.

They talked for less than an hour when, leaping furiously to her feet, Ayn demanded that I be summoned at once.

It was Allan, Barbara told me later, who advised Ayn against the confrontation, declaring that my state was so terrible and my remorse so profound that no one could be as hard on me as I was already being on myself. Barbara supported Allan in this position. "Don't think Allan took pleasure in what happened," Barbara told me later. "He was concerned for you. More than once, when I was telling Ayn the story, Allan ran into the bathroom to throw up."

"Get that bastard down here!" Ayn hissed.

It was Allan who telephoned me. "Nathan, Ayn wants you to come down."

Riding down in the elevator, I felt my mind dividing, felt part of my consciousness splitting off from the exhausted and battered rest of me, to observe what was about to happen and to guide me through it.

I entered and looked at them—Ayn, Frank, Barbara, and Allan. Ayn and Barbara sat opposite each other on the sofa. Frank lay stretched out in a chair, looking a little more present than usual. Allan let me in and returned to his chair.

"I don't want you in my living room," Ayn said, standing to face me, her body trembling. She pointed to a straight-backed chair in the foyer between the living room and the dining area that was halfway to the door. "Sit there." And I did.

"What a loathsome creature you are!" she said, and I watched her carefully as the tirade began. She poured abuse on abuse, drowning her suffering in self-righteous anger. "You have rejected *me? You* have dared to reject *me?*" I watched and I listened and I thought, There is nothing I need to do now, only sit and wait and endure. Everything has been set in motion—now let it play itself out. Let her say whatever she needs to say. I owe her that.

I cannot say what I felt as I watched and listened. I was beyond feeling. In moments of great crisis, the mind and body protect themselves by moving into a state that feelings cannot reach.

"Do you *begin* to know what you've done?" Ayn was shrieking. "Do you *begin* to know what you've thrown away? May you be damned to the hell you put me through! You rotten hypocrite!"

And I thought, Patrecia, I *am* guilty. Guilty for what I put you through— for the sake of protecting my relationship with the people in this room. Ayn is right—I do warrant condemnation, only hers aren't the reasons, not the most important ones. . . . What does it matter, the pain Barbara, Ayn, and I caused one another? We're all crazed animals anyway, and none of us has clean hands. But you, Patrecia—you never brought me anything but good, and I betrayed you by not shouting out my love for you from the first day I became aware of it.

Listening to Ayn, I felt a combination of pity and contempt for her beyond anything I had imagined possible. The sounds of her denunciation went on, as if she wished that her words could turn to blows. It took all of my energy to hold my body erect in the chair.

I noticed that, even now, it was important to Ayn that I agree with her, that I share her verdict, that I see myself as the "depraved monster" that she insisted I was. "Do you realize . . . ?" her sentences began. "Do you admit . . . ?"

I thought, If I really were the rotten human being she was describing—if, as she claimed, I had no sense of moral principles—her rebukes would mean nothing to me. And if I were willing to give my sanction now to what she was doing, wouldn't my willingness be the very error she cautioned against in *Atlas Shrugged*? The "sanction of the victim," she called it—the error of granting moral validity to the premises of one's own adversaries and thus collaborating in one's own destruction.

"You are an irredeemably rotten human being," she was saying. But if I were, why was she telling it to me? Was she not still counting on a virtue she would not admit I possessed?

"Objectivism never meant anything to you! Not *The Fountainhead,* not *Atlas Shrugged,* not any value you pretended to share with me! You passed yourself off as my soul mate, God damn you, and you're less than Peter Keating or James Taggart! You've damaged me worse than any of my enemies ever could!"

I thought that in a sense that last sentence was true. Barbara had said to me, "She had weapons against her intellectual adversaries, but you hurt her as a woman, hurt her at the point of her greatest doubts and insecurities. She never liked her body or her appearance. She hates the fact that she doesn't resemble her heroines. So what do you imagine she will feel visualizing Patrecia?" Was that the image that was driving her now to wilder and wilder frenzy?

"Your whole act is finished! I created you, and I'll destroy you! You won't have your career or money or prestige! You'll have nothing! I'll stop the publication of *The Psychology of Self-Esteem*! I have the influence at New American Library to do it! I'll remove your name from the dedication page of *Atlas Shrugged*! You would have been nothing without me, and you will be nothing when I'm done with you!"

Suddenly, in the voice of a five-year-old, tears rolling down her cheeks, Barbara began to tell me, "I'm *proud* I could never really respond to you! *Proud* I never gave you what you wanted!"

Poor Barbara, I thought. Look at what you are now doing to protect your self-esteem, to rationalize this insanity, and to survive.

I told myself, Do not argue, do not fight. Study these people, and learn, once and for all. These are the people you have not wanted to let go of all these years. These are the people to whom you sacrificed Patrecia and your own integrity.

My attention shot back to Ayn when, at the edge of my vision, I saw a new thought hit her consciousness. Taking two steps closer to me, she asked ominously, "Did you tell Patrecia about our relationship?"

I answered that I had and that I'd had to, in order to help Patrecia understand my context and my requirement of secrecy.

Ayn gasped as if she had been struck, and then it was she who struck out, slashing her hand twice against my face, while screaming, "God damn you! God damn you!"

It would have been easy to avoid her blows. I chose not to. I wanted her action to stand there, naked and unobscured.

When she stopped, I felt my body straightening and my shoulders relaxing. I leaned forward almost eagerly, as if an important revelation about Ayn were in the process of disclosing itself.

"Oh, well," she said, and chuckled grimly. "What does it matter? No one is going to believe you, anyway. Not when I am through with you. It won't matter what you say or to whom. The whole world will brand you as a liar—I'll see to that."

But in this matter, I would be telling the truth if I chose to talk. Ayn knew that, and everyone in the room knew it.

Lies had been part of our life—at Ayn's insistence—since the start of our affair, when I was twenty-four years old. And Ayn was about to embark on a new campaign of lies to conceal from her friends and from the world the real cause of our break. Everyone in the room knew that. And if Leonard or the rest of the Collective were ever to learn the truth, it still would not matter to them. They would twist their brains into pretzels of rationalization to protect their vision of Ayn.

Frustrated by my long silence, Ayn demanded, "Well? Do you have anything to say?"

"I am deeply sorry," I answered truthfully, "for the pain I have caused you."

"Well, I have one more thing to say to you!" Ayn stated. And then she left me her final legacy: "If you have an ounce of morality left in you, an ounce of psychological health, you'll be impotent for the next twenty years! And if you achieve any potency sooner, you'll know it's a sign of still worse moral degradation!"

I welcomed the long moment of silence that followed. I wanted everyone in the room to hear what she had just said.

I looked deliberately at Allan. I thought, You are a psychiatrist. How do you assess the mental and moral state of a human being who would say what Ayn just said? This is the person you have now chosen to stand by.

I looked at Barbara; she was still crying.

I looked at Frank; his eyes were open, staring at me, revealing nothing. Would anyone ever know what all this meant to him? Would he permit himself to know?

"Now get out!" Ayn ordered.

I got up and walked to the door. I turned, knowing this was the last time I would see her.

I thought of the night Frank had greeted me at the door, more than eighteen years ago, when I had entered their home for the first time. I had then waited for Ayn Rand to walk toward me. "How do you do, Mr. Blumenthal."

I thought of her reminiscences of that evening, and of Ayn's saying to me, her eyes intense with happiness, "Walking into the living room, seeing you for the first time, I thought, He's got my kind of face. And then I told myself, Don't start that again, meaning, Don't start hoping. I'd met too many alleged admirers who seemed intelligent and serious in their values and who turned out to be phonies. But, you see, this time it didn't end in disappointment. This time I was right."

"Good-bye, Ayn," I said, standing at the door. I nodded to Frank. Then I left.

17

AYN FORGAVE BARBARA.

She told Barbara that although it was wrong to deceive her, it was an understandable mistake in that Barbara legitimately had conflicting loyalties. "You chose the man you had married," Ayn had told her. "I can understand that. And eventually you did come to me with the truth."

After reporting their reconciliation, Barbara presented me with Ayn's new demands. Ayn wanted me (1) to withdraw from any and all participation in NBI and its various affiliates; (2) to turn over, without compensation, full ownership to Barbara; (3) to transfer, without compensation, my 50 percent ownership of *The Objectivist* to Ayn; and (4) to inform all our friends, as well as the NBI and *Objectivist* staff, that I was doing so, and that Ayn was breaking with me, because of immoralities I had committed. Barbara was obviously unhappy about what she was reporting.

If I agreed to these demands, Barbara told me, Ayn would write only a brief statement in *The Objectivist*—"a single paragraph stating that because of moral failures on your part she has terminated your personal and professional relationship and that you no longer speak for her or for Objectivism." If I did not agree to these demands, Barbara said, Ayn would "create a public scandal."

Even in the depths of my misery, I could not help smiling at the foolishness of this threat. I had no fear of a scandal; Ayn did. Did Ayn really think the world cared if Nathaniel Branden slept with a woman who was not his wife? Did Ayn not appreciate that the next question in everyone's mind would be, Why is Ayn Rand so interested in Nathaniel Branden's sex life? If the full truth about our conflict were revealed, Ayn—by her own admission—had the most to lose, because it was she who was fanatical about protecting her reputation.

Barbara knew that the threat of scandal meant nothing to me and that the only power Ayn had over me was moral, which was made possible by my own feelings of remorse for how I had handled things. She said that she, too, thought the scandal threat was nonsense. Nonetheless, she believed that I should agree to Ayn's demands. She saw me as having no alternative in the circumstances.

In a detached, impersonal voice that revealed nothing of her own emotions, she pointed out that it was to my advantage to sign over NBI because my lease with the Empire State Building still had fourteen years to run. Without receiving rent from *The Objectivist,* even if I tried to operate a more modest NBI on my own, I would not be able to meet my monthly obligations. "You'll be stuck with an enormous debt," she observed. "This is a way out."

And you and Ayn will receive the benefits of all my work of the past ten years, I thought, without it costing either of you a nickel. I did not say it because I truly did not care. If they wanted NBI, they could have it; it meant nothing to me any longer. A fair trade, I told myself. I will have my freedom and Patrecia. And you, Barbara, God help you, will have Ayn and all the burdens of NBI. At that moment I did not know the extent to which Barbara did not want any of it, either.

On the evening of August 25, 1968, Barbara came to my apartment accompanied by Wilfred and Hank Holzer. My sister Florence, whom I had telephoned in Toronto, was with me; she had flown to New York at my request, knowing that I wanted someone outside the situation to talk to. Hank, Barbara, and Wilfred had been sent to my apartment by Ayn; they had brought the papers transferring to her my half interest in *The Objectivist.* I said to Hank, "As my lawyer, are you advising me to sign these papers?" He answered that he could not continue to act as my lawyer. He handed me a letter of resignation. I said, "Without notifying me in advance that you had resigned, and without counseling me to get a new attorney?" Only Florence looked shocked. Barbara and Wilfred gave no sign of finding the situation abnormal. In this and in everything that followed, it seemed clear that Hank was presenting Ayn's idea of the arrangement.

I felt sick with contempt. Whatever my past errors, I knew that this whole situation—Ayn's demand and their complicity—was despicable. On the other hand, what was *The Objectivist* to me now? Let Ayn have it, I thought. Let her have whatever she wants. I prepared to sign—and then I stopped.

I remembered the copyrights to my *Objectivist* articles. As a matter of convenience, Ayn's and my pieces were all copyrighted in the name of the magazine, with the understanding that each of us retained full rights to our material. So long as we were co-owners of *The Objectivist,* we had never felt the need to put that understanding on paper. But now?

I said that I would not sign the transfer papers until rights to my articles were assigned to me in writing. Hank telephoned Ayn, and she told him that she agreed that my articles would remain my property, but she wanted *The Objectivist* turned over to her that night. "You have Ayn's word," he urged. "You have my word in front of witnesses. What more can you ask for?" I looked at Barbara. "Sign, Nathan," she pleaded. "Sign. Ayn is still Ayn. She would never renege on a promise of this kind." I did not doubt that she was speaking with absolute sincerity. Barbara is right, I told myself. Such a betrayal would be too much for Ayn, even in her present state. I was thinking of her respect for property rights. "Sign," Wilfred urged. "We had to talk Ayn out of wanting to send Bob Teague up here with us to make you sign." Teague was a man who worked for us; he had a brown belt in judo. Involuntarily, I laughed and asked, "You mean the idea was that Bob would strong-arm me into signing?" Looking miserable, Barbara and Wilfred nodded.

Somehow, this idea did not lower my spirits; it raised them. In this moment, all four of them, including Ayn, struck me as absurd. Seeing my hesitation, Hank then began talking about "financial improprieties" that I could be charged with. These comments seemed to me as ludicrous as Ayn's idea that Bob Teague might use physical coercion to obtain my signature. I felt swept clean of every emotion but one, for which *contempt* is too weak a word. Its object was Hank and Ayn.

To Florence's silent horror, I took the documents over to the dinner table and signed them.

The next evening, I was visited by Florence's sons, Leonard and Jonathan Hirschfeld, twenty and eighteen respectively. I had asked them to come. Both had been brought up as Objectivists, reared to the sound of my lecture voice on tape in the basement of their home, where Florence held NBI classes in her capacity as NBI's Toronto representative.

For the past year or two, Leonard had lived in New York and attended NYU, and Jonathan, who had only recently arrived here, was to begin at NYU this fall. I was attached to them both and felt deeply concerned about the emotional impact that my break with Ayn would have on them. I felt it imperative that I discuss it with them personally.

When I interviewed Leonard for this memoir, he remembered this about the evening:

We arrived at six o'clock. No lights on in the apartment. You looked worn and altogether wrecked, as if you had been crying or in horrible pain for a long time. It was shocking to see you that way. Could this be my Uncle Nathan? But I thought it made you look more vulnerable, more human. You said that you had bad news, that you had committed immoral actions, betrayed your Objectivist principles, and that Ayn had broken with you. I was touched by the fact that you cared that much about how we would be affected; you seemed very protective of us. You didn't want us to lose our idealism or become disillusioned. I can't remember how many of the facts you told us that night and how many I learned over the next several weeks. I think you told us about Patrecia. That made me happy. I thought she was a fantastic human being, and I didn't care about anything else. I was glad she and my uncle were in love. Later, when I heard the things people were saying about you, I thought they had gone crazy. Nothing you did justified what was said. That was the hardest for me to absorb—not what you did, but how people reacted, and how hysterical they became.

After I met with him, Leonard wrote a long, detailed letter to his parents in which he dissected the irrationality of Ayn and her various spokespersons with a lucidity and insightfulness truly dazzling for a person his age. Jonathan recalled:

You told us that you had done something immoral, that you had betrayed Ayn. You seemed most concerned that the break between you and Ayn would lead us to doubt the validity of Objectivism. None of it made any sense to me—I am sure I was in shock. . . . You were the embodiment of virtue; it was impossible for me to grasp that you had been lying about your relationship with the woman you loved. Throughout my adolescence, I had eagerly awaited my departure for New York, the center of the world, the center of Objectivism. I was eighteen, I had just arrived, and this world with you at the center had crumbled. I was far less concerned with Ayn's behavior or the justice of the attacks on you than I was with my own overwhelming disappointment. In the end, I did ask the necessary questions of your enemies, and then they betrayed themselves, and my perspective changed—in your favor.

Jonathan, too, wrote a letter to his parents, profoundly moving in its depiction of his feelings of personal letdown and betrayal by the uncle he had so much admired. Rereading it decades later, I am still moved to sadness by its quiet dignity and luminous anguish.

For more than a year, my nephews would be at odds with each other over their conflicting perspectives. Because Jonathan and I cared for each other deeply, our estrangement was painful for both of us.

Leonard, Florence, and Hans rallied to my support. Leonard did so fully and immediately, which created a unique bond between us that continues to this day. Florence and Hans did so with some ambivalence at first, although I believed that their basic instincts were with me. Some of their hesitation in opposing Ayn was due to the fact that they admired her enormously and had learned a great deal from her. Also, perhaps, they were influenced by the fact that their younger son was very critical of me. As his parents, they wanted to be open to both sides. Whatever she was struggling with internally, though, Florence was very protective of me, indignant about the growing lynch mob atmosphere, and quite helpful in our discussions. Of my three sisters, she alone stood by me. She persisted in asking questions until she was satisfied she had the truth.

A crucial turning point for Florence was a meeting with Ayn. After several hours of evading questions about whether she had ever had an affair with me, Ayn finally lost her temper under the pressure of Florence's questioning and shouted, "If Nathan were the man he professed to be, he would be in love with me and not with that harlot!" At this same meeting, Ayn vigorously denied that I had ever made any contribution to her on a personal level. Yet years earlier, Florence had heard her say more than once that in the period after the publication of *Atlas Shrugged,* I had saved her life. Ayn's denial of this following our break struck Florence as particularly graceless and ugly. Thereafter more vehement in championing me, Florence, too, became a pariah in the eyes of Ayn's supporters.

Increasingly outraged by the dishonesty and malice of these supporters in their campaign against me, she said to Jonathan, "No sense in our arguing about this. Go talk to Allan and Joan, Leonard Peikoff, and Ayn's lawyer. Listen to what they've got to say, and decide for yourself if they're people you want to stand with."

I did not expect Jonathan's sympathies for Ayn and his antagonism toward me to last, and they didn't. He was repelled by the way Ayn's supporters demanded the blind acceptance of her pronouncements and their resentment at almost any questions, which they took as evidence of "irrational hostility." Also, he had a number of talks with Barbara, who spoke on my behalf, arguing that I had been caught in "an impossible trap."

On August 28, five days after my final meeting with Ayn and two days after my meetings with my nephews, I assembled the staffs of NBI and *The Objectivist* to announce the break formally. My chief concern was that their work on behalf of Objectivism continue. I knew that many of them would be devastated by the news of my withdrawal and my repudiation by Ayn. I did not want them to collapse into disenchantment and cynicism. Also, I wanted to take responsibility—openly and honorably—for the mistakes that I had committed. "I have taken actions I know to be wrong," I said. "I have failed to practice the principles I taught to all of you. Ayn is fully within her moral rights in severing our relationship. But I ask you to remember that a philosophy is not to be judged by the behavior—or misbehavior—of any of its exponents. Objectivism is as worthy of your support as it ever was." Barbara stood near me, weeping.

"While you were speaking to our staff," Barbara told me later, "something inside was screaming that this was a mistake. You gave Ayn and the others a terrible weapon that they all used again and again. 'Nathaniel Branden himself admits he acted improperly,' they said. 'What else do you need to know? He stands convicted out of his own mouth.'" Florence, who was also at NBI the day I made that statement, shared Barbara's apprehension. "I wanted to shout to you," she said, "'Nathan, don't do this.'"

Word of the break shot through the Objectivist subculture in New York and then across the country, virtually overnight. The problem was, no one knew what I had done wrong. Was I a secret drinker? A drug addict? A child molester? What did Nathaniel Branden do that was so terrible as to be beyond redemption? There was no way to stop—or answer—the rumors that were now spreading like wildfire.

Although I was prepared to share the full truth with members of my immediate family and a few friends, I had no intention of disclosing to the world the story of my past affair with Ayn and its relevance to our break. However, if I did not reveal that information, my affair with Patrecia would merely seem like a personal issue without any relevance to the matter. An extramarital relationship might be questionable but hardly a sin of major magnitude. If nothing more was said by Ayn or me, our break would remain essentially unfathomable to people. I do not know what was in Ayn's mind; evidently, she imagined that her admirers would require no more information than that she had repudiated me, that I had admitted to doing "something wrong," and that on the basis of no more than this, I would become persona non grata, a moral outcast.

As far as the Collective went, Ayn's assumption was correct; no one was willing to talk to me or to hear my response to any charges.

Elayne and Harry were an exception. I did discuss the situation with them briefly. They informed me that I was entirely responsible "for getting into this mess" and that their allegiance was to Ayn and Objectivism.

When I informed them of my affair with Ayn, explaining that it was the background to the entire conflict, they were clearly shocked and appalled, but it made no real difference to them. I was unable to communicate adequately the context in which I had made my choices—or they were unable to hear. "Why didn't you come to us sooner?" they demanded. "Why didn't you ask for our advice and help?" I could not make them understand that I had been sworn to lifelong secrecy by Ayn and had felt bound by that. It was obvious that they were deeply hurt that I had not confided in them years earlier. I thought it possible that, if I had, they might now be responding differently. I would never know. Having worked with Ayn at close quarters, through her involvement in *The Objectivist,* Elayne was already disenchanted with Ayn, although I was not aware of this at the time. Nonetheless, she felt that Objectivism represented the best hope for the future and that, if they were to build a better world, the work must continue. This meant that Ayn must be supported. Harry held this viewpoint even more strongly.

In Toronto, Reva and Sholey communicated that they stood with Elayne and Harry. My father had died some years before. In the last days of his life, he had been showing *Who Is Ayn Rand?* to the nurses in the hospital and boasting about his son's work. Hearing that Ayn and I had severed our relationship, my mother was bewildered by snatches of information she could not grasp and kept asking questions no one wanted to answer. Seeing the issue exclusively in terms of family solidarity, she tormented Elayne with phone calls and reproaches: "Why are you still working for that woman?" I wanted to comfort my mother and had no idea what to say to her.

When I had my first opportunity to tell my brother-in-law Hans the full story myself, he made a comment I have never forgotten—one that shocked me profoundly, because he said it about Ayn Rand and because I knew it was true. Referring to Ayn's desperate desire to hang on to me romantically and her virulent antagonism to my love for Patrecia, he exclaimed, "But it's so *antilife!*" This spoke to the core of my own deepest feelings. Nothing could have been more helpful for me to hear.

When I told Patrecia of the way Elayne, Harry, Reva, and Sholey had responded, she was incredulous. "Your own *family?*" she asked. "Two of your own sisters and brothers-in-law have repudiated you because you weren't honest and aboveboard about our relationship? Nathan, what's happening to people?" I replied that if there were other, additional reasons, they had not spelled them out.

For years, I had done every kind of violence to myself, because I could not let go of my youthful vision. I saw that they could not let go of their visions, either.

Meanwhile, Barbara and Wilfred were working long hours to prepare a plan for restructuring Nathaniel Branden Institute without Nathaniel Branden. I had not yet signed over ownership to Barbara, and she had not pressed me to do so. Her first step was to gain Ayn's approval of the plan that she and Wilfred had formulated at Ayn's request. I was not surprised when Barbara told me later, "Even while I was working on the project, I wanted to fail. I did not want to remain in that world. I wanted to be free."

Hank Holzer studied the plan and told Ayn it was reasonable. However, she barely looked at it. Evidently frightened of allowing any organization to be associated with her name again, she announced with great agitation that she wanted no part of it. Later, Barbara and Wilfred told me they were relieved.

In the days that followed, Ayn reversed her decision about writing only a single paragraph about our break. She decided to publish a long denunciation aimed at completely ruining my reputation.

To destroy me, Barbara later told me, had become Ayn's obsession. She spoke of little else. How will she do it, I kept wondering, when she's terrified of anyone's learning about our affair?

Barbara was particularly distressed to hear Ayn mention, once again, her intention to stop the publication of *The Psychology of Self-Esteem* through her influence at NAL. "He'll never be published!" Ayn raved.

Having heard Ayn praise my book as a "work of genius," Barbara was stunned by Ayn's vindictiveness. "Over that issue more than any other," Barbara later told me, "my view of Ayn crashed." I nodded, in understanding and gratitude.

Ayn's attacks against me were becoming more and more frenzied. New accusations were materializing daily. Barbara confided her growing alarm to a couple of friends, expressing concern both about the state of Ayn's mind and the risk of my "professional destruction."

Barbara's worries were instantly transmitted back to Ayn, and Barbara was summoned, via Hank Holzer, to appear before Ayn and a few members of the Collective to answer charges of having made false and immoral accusations against Ayn. Barbara telephoned Ayn and told her, "I am willing to discuss with you anything you care to discuss. I am not willing to appear before a jury of my peers to answer charges." Ayn's only response was to ask whether Barbara were coming to the meeting. When Barbara answered no, Ayn slammed down the telephone. Their friendship of eighteen-and-a-half years had ended.

When Patrecia asked me if I were surprised that Barbara and Ayn had broken their relationship, I answered, "Not for a minute. Barbara has been too close and seen too much. She would not have the stomach for what's going to be happening around here from now on."

Some weeks earlier, when I saw that my own relationship with Ayn was spinning toward final dissolution in precisely the way that I had foreseen, I telephoned Allan Blumenthal and told him, "Here is what is coming next. I want to go on record as saying this now—before it begins. Ayn will soon be saying, and then the rest of you will be saying, that I never originated anything, never contributed anything, that every idea of mine is really Ayn's."

Allan answered, "Don't be paranoiac, Nathan. That's ridiculous. No one has ever denied that you're a clever fellow."

I was not yet impervious to shock. I said, "A *what?* 'A clever fellow'? Is that what the party line—meaning Ayn—now says I am? I'm too late for a prediction, then. The process of rewriting history has already begun."

Years later, as the new "leader" of the Objectivist movement, Leonard Peikoff would do everything possible to make Ayn's admirers forget that Nathaniel Branden Institute—or Nathaniel Branden—had ever existed or had any significance in Ayn's life.

Patrecia and I were making arrangements for our move to Los Angeles. Barbara told me that she and Bob Berole, the man she was planning to live with, were also going to relocate there. Shortly after that, I learned that Wilfred and his family were intending to do the same. Patrecia liked all of them—Barbara, in particular—but she wanted a total break from the kind of life we'd had in New York and expressed the hope that a new "mini-Collective" would not form in Los Angeles. I assured her that it wouldn't, and it didn't.

NBI was now closed. The task of liquidating it entailed selling off equipment and as much of our stock of books and art prints as we could. Wilfred performed this project heroically. He handled everything with extraordinary grace and competence. He found someone who would take over our lease with the Empire State Building, and he handled all the negotiations. Because we had kept pouring almost all of our earnings back into the expansion of NBI, we did not have large cash reserves. At the end, the corporation had only about $45,000, and Wilfred, Barbara, and I divided it equally. That was what was left of ten years of work. I had no other personal savings.

Throughout September, students kept rushing into the NBI offices, desperate to learn what had happened. They arrived in anger, they arrived in tears, they arrived in agonizing bewilderment. No more NBI? It was as if their world had shattered. Ayn Rand and Nathaniel Branden no longer together? It was as if their mother and father had divorced violently. No intelligible explanation as to why? It was as if their worst fears about an irrational universe had come true.

One day, when Elayne and Holzer were in the office, supervising the removal of some files and equipment, I shouted to her, "Do you think our students are stupid? Do you think they will never figure out what this conflict really concerns? Do you think you people can go on spreading lies about Barbara and me without our fighting back? What is Ayn counting on? If I'm the monster she says I am, how come she's so certain I'll remain a gentleman, keep silent, and protect her reputation?" Several of Ayn's people heard me shout this; now, a new story circulated: "Nathaniel Branden is showing evidence of a nervous breakdown."

Ayn went to our literary agents, Curtis Brown, and demanded that I no longer be represented by that firm. Alan Collins had died, and the new head was Perry Knowlton. Gerry McCauley, who represented me at Curtis Brown, announced that he would quit if any writer were allowed to exert such pressure. As Gerry told me, there was never a question in Perry Knowlton's mind—or in anyone else's—of yielding to Ayn's demand.

With NAL, she was evidently more successful. Its sister company, World Publishing, informed me that my contract was terminated shortly after I passed the promised deadline without submitting a completed manuscript. All but three chapters of the book were finished, and no publisher would normally terminate at that point without even asking to see any of what I had written.

I watched the flow of events, sometimes feeling pained, indignant, or enraged and sometimes feeling numb and disoriented. I was able to think ahead to my life in California; I found it difficult to concentrate on the events in New York.

I had once thought that the most painful loss would be the loss of Ayn's esteem. Now I discovered that far worse was my inability to feel the esteem I had once felt for Ayn. This loss was like an unhealing wound at the center of my universe. Since childhood, I had longed to feel admiration above all other emotions.

Barbara came to me in dismay, reporting that when she passed people on the street whom she had known for a decade or more, they turned and looked away. I would tell her some new rumor I had just heard about myself. But I rarely felt horror; more often, I felt pain, lethargy, anger, sadness, or detachment.

"You've got to understand," Barbara beseeched me, "that Ayn wants you dead! The Ayn out there now is not the Ayn you were in love with. The craziest, worst side of her is now totally in control. You've got to get this through your head. You've got to fight back. You've got to defend yourself. Ayn wants you dead. That's all that's moving her now."

Long ago, on the night of March 2, 1950, when I sat facing Ayn for the first time, I had thought, I'm home, I'm home, I'm home. Now, I asked my brain to absorb the fact that the woman who had been my idol was plotting my annihilation.

A friend who was particularly helpful to me during this period was psychologist Roger Callahan. Roger had moved to New York from Detroit, because he wanted to learn what Objectivism had to offer, philosophically and psychologically, and because he wanted to deepen his association with me and with our circle.

I did not know how he would react to the news of Ayn's and my break, because about two years earlier, sometime after the dissolution of his own marriage, he came to my office one day and began to confide his feelings of love for Patrecia. I had not known that he felt this way, and I sat listening in considerable distress, wondering if he would feel betrayed by me when he found out that Patrecia and I were lovers, as he would eventually. It was an excruciatingly difficult meeting.

"What's going on, Nathan?" he asked, when the first rumblings reached him, and I told him the whole story. There was not a beat of hesitation; instantly, he was totally committed to defending me—not only against my critics but also against what he regarded as my overly severe judgment of myself.

"Your own sense of morality is being used against you," he said indignantly. "You're still not thinking clearly. It's admirable that you don't want to evade responsibility for your mistakes, but your attitude is blinding you to the seriousness of the mistakes the other side is making. Granted, you didn't handle Ayn and Patrecia as you should have. Granted, it would have been better if you had told the truth from the beginning, regardless of consequences. But there were reasons you didn't; there were mitigating circumstances. For one thing, you knew exactly what you would be up against. The mistakes you made were not evil. But trying to block the publication of your book, taking *The Objectivist* from you the way they did, lying about your achievements, literally trying to destroy you—all that is evil. They accuse you of betraying Objectivism. What is your betrayal compared to Ayn's and the others'? What is your deception compared to the multiple deceptions they're all conspiring in right now? Can't you see that? Is this some kind of perverse egoism on your part that makes you place your vices—if that's what you call them—above everyone else's? If the great Nathaniel Branden does something wrong, that makes him worse than anyone? Wake up, Nathan. For Christ's sake, wake up!"

That conversation took place thirty years ago. I am still grateful for it.

Roger's practice as a psychotherapist was fed largely by students of Objectivism. He knew that, in supporting me publicly, he would draw enormous antagonism. Nonetheless, he invited me to guest-lead several of his therapy groups and gave me a forum to answer his clients' questions about my break with Ayn. And he lost a sizable percentage of his practice. Anyone who went to him was labeled a "traitor to Ayn Rand and Objectivism." When I expressed appreciation and concern for his loss of business, Roger answered, "I've had a large practice for many years without referrals from Allan Blumenthal and the others, and I will again."

When my psychologist friends Lee and Joyce Shulman from Detroit came to New York for a visit, I filled them in. Lee telephoned Ayn to ask for a personal meeting; he felt strongly that Ayn was on the verge of making a colossal mistake that would damage both her and the Objectivist movement. He intended to urge her not to go public with our conflict but rather to settle it privately, without scandal. As soon as he told Ayn about his concerns, she told him to talk to Allan Blumenthal, who was authorized to speak for her on this matter.

When Lee and Joyce met Allan and Joan for dinner, the Shulmans were told that Ayn absolutely must repudiate me publicly. Then Allan and Joan made the same accusations against me that Ayn would subsequently publish. They urged Lee and Joyce to join them in condemning me. When the Shulmans declined to do so, Allan said, "You're trying to judge a situation about which you don't really have full knowledge." Why, Lee wanted to know, is a judgment *against* Nathan without full knowledge acceptable but a judgment *for* Nathan isn't? Allan's response was to lean on Ayn's authority: "You must choose between Nathan and the author of *Atlas Shrugged*."

Ayn refused to release the rights to my articles in *The Objectivist*. I needed those rights to publish *The Psychology of Self-Esteem*.

Ayn had not refused to release my copyrights, declared Hank Holzer, but there were "conditions." Hank sent me a memo stating her terms: (1) neither Barbara nor I could ever answer the charges in "To Whom It May Concern" (Ayn's denunciation of us in *The Objectivist*), (2) we could never discuss Ayn Rand or our relationship with her with anyone, and (3) Hank could never be charged with unprofessional behavior in his dealings with me. There were other demands, but these were the main ones.

I refused. I knew that this was plain, undiluted evil.

"What happened to property rights?" I asked. "Either the articles belong to me, or they don't." The answer was that Ayn's offer was the only deal I was going to get.

And the answer that came back to me, via the grapevine, was that "normal standards are inoperative when dealing with a moral criminal such as Nathaniel Branden."

"This," I said to Patrecia, "is what all their talk of reason, justice, and integrity comes to. This is what their ideals mean in the real world. And this is what they will have to live with and lie to themselves about from now on—all those who know about Ayn's demands and still choose to stand by her."

"Can Ayn really keep your rights to those articles and prevent the publication of your book?"

"Hell, no. The first thing I'll do when we get to California is find a lawyer who will blast through all this garbage. Then I'll find a new publisher. I promise you—nothing will stop the publication of *The Psychology of Self-Esteem.*"

One evening Barbara burst into my apartment highly agitated. "I've been on the phone with Peter Crosby," she said. Peter and his wife Jan were our Los Angeles representatives, in addition to being personal friends. "Leonard and the others are already busy on the telephones, coast to coast, spreading the word that no good Objectivist should deal with either one of us. We are officially declared 'enemies.' Since everyone is afraid of what you might choose to tell—I don't just mean Ayn, I mean other people, too—the strategy is to spread the word that Nathaniel Branden is a confessed liar and is not to be believed on any subject."

I told Barbara that except with the die-hard believers, I did not think the strategy would work. "Ayn has always had such contempt for her own followers. She thinks they'll believe anything she tells them. I think she's wrong."

Barbara expressed surprise at my seeming lack of anger. I shook my head sadly. "Barbara, I would never have done what these people are doing now—or I don't believe I would—but still, how angry can I get? I'm Dr. Frankenstein, and they're my goddamn monsters."

"But you *are* angry!" said Patrecia when we discussed it. "You're furious! And you should be!" I knew she was right, and I said so. She went on, "If there's one thing I hate in this world more than anything else, it's malice—and malice is what I see everywhere. These people worshiped you, and they never forgave you for the fact that they were not as important to you as you were to them! Now we're seeing the envy and hatred that are on the other side of adulation! I've always sensed this, and it's always made me wary of any kind of fame. It's not just Ayn who thought she owned you. It's all the people who are now going berserk."

"Patrecia, I set myself up for it."

"No, you didn't. I was at NBI, too. I saw and heard the same things everybody else did. I never thought you owed it to me not to do anything I might think was wrong. You are a human being. You are entitled to struggle and stumble and do whatever you have to do. I love you. But I never thought you were a divinity."

I knew that she was suffering her own shocks, as longtime friends withdrew from her. I did not know if she were aware of the things being said about her by the other side—by Joan Mitchell Blumenthal, for example, who had once spoken of her love for Patrecia with tears in her eyes, or by Ayn, who had told her the night of the power blackout, "You have such an air of benevolence; that's why I love you." I guessed that she wasn't aware. And yet, at another level, she would have to have known. Not the concretes, not the specifics, but the gist of their accusations.

I held her in my arms, I pressed her head against my face, I thought of what still lay ahead, and I told myself, Just hang on a little while longer.

But already, like music growing louder and louder, the feeling of liberation was surging within me. It towered above pain, rage, or any sense of loss. It towered above the whirlwind of madness, rising to greet the future.

It would be coming in the next issue of *The Objectivist*, Ayn's definitive statement to her following—and to the world—about her break with Nathaniel and Barbara Branden.

It was in the May issue, which actually appeared in October, because we had fallen so far behind in our schedule. Through an acquaintance, we obtained an advance copy, directly off the printing press, two weeks before publication.

"To Whom It May Concern" was six pages long. It began:

> This is to inform my readers and all those interested in Objectivism that Nathaniel Branden and Barbara Branden are no longer associated with this magazine, with me or with my philosophy.
>
> I have permanently broken all personal, professional and business association with them, and have withdrawn from them the permission to use my name in connection with their commercial, professional, intellectual or other activities.
>
> I hereby withdraw my endorsement of them and of their future works and activities. I repudiate both of them, totally and permanently, as spokesmen for me or for Objectivism.

Following this introduction, Ayn launched into a long list of accusations, primarily against me and secondarily against Barbara. It seemed obvious to Barbara and me that the article was libelous.

One of the charges against me was financial malfeasance—which stunned Martin Coblenz, who was the accountant for both NBI and *The*

Objectivist and who knew every detail of our financial life. "I can't believe this," he said. "I can't believe I am reading this. What has happened to Miss Rand?"

Ayn's article ended with the following statement:

FOR THE RECORD

We, the undersigned, former Associate Lecturers at Nathaniel Branden Institute, wish the following to be on record: Because Nathaniel Branden and Barbara Branden, in a series of actions, have betrayed fundamental principles of Objectivism, we condemn and repudiate these two persons irrevocably, and have terminated all association with them and with Nathaniel Branden Institute.

Allan Blumenthal
Alan Greenspan
Leonard Peikoff
Mary Ann (Rukavina) Sures

Our judgment that Ayn's article was libelous was supported by George Berger, an attorney in the Louis Nizer office, whom we consulted. Either he had never heard of Ayn Rand or he knew only the name, but halfway down the first page of her article, he turned to me and asked, "How old is Miss Rand?" At the bottom of the page, he asked, "And how old are you?" After reading a paragraph or two of the second page, he said, "A woman scorned." Barbara and I flashed astonished glances at each other. Was it that obvious to an outsider?

He encouraged us to initiate a lawsuit. "I promise you, this will be one of the easiest cases I ever had to try. I would love to have Miss Rand explain in court, to impartial listeners, how she justifies the things she says in this piece. I don't understand how her own attorneys ever allowed her to do this."

After some reflection, Barbara and I decided against the suit. The thought of spending the next two years of my life in the sewer of a libel action appalled me; I wanted to get on with my future in Los Angeles. Barbara felt the same way. We decided instead to write a detailed answer to Ayn's accusations. I would answer the charges against me, and Barbara would answer the charges against her. Because Ayn's attacks were so ill reasoned and ill founded, and because we saw them as easy to refute, this seemed the most rational course of action. We would send our answer to all the people on the *Objectivist* mailing list.

I experienced extreme distaste at the thought of writing about my affair with Ayn, although I knew that if I did not communicate the actual nature of our relationship, people would never understand the conflict. I did not realize the extent to which I had internalized Ayn's obsession with secrecy. I could not fight her at that level, I told myself, and I did not think I needed to. The thought of the shame and embarrassment I would cause her and Frank was repugnant to me, in spite of everything that had happened.

I was relieved when George Berger advised me not to disclose the affair in my published "Answer to Ayn Rand" but rather to address Ayn's charges, point by point. "But what do I do about this?" I asked him, pointing to a paragraph in Ayn's piece about an "irrational" and "offensive" written statement of mine that had compelled her to break off our association. Ayn was referring to the letter in which I explained that a resumption of our affair was impossible for me. But she gave no indication of the content of my letter. Many people would later comment on how incomprehensible they found this omission.

"My advice," said Berger, "is to follow Miss Rand's lead and to say as little as possible. Answer this point briefly, stating only the *content* of the key paragraph she found so 'offensive.'" After a long process of reflection, I decided to accept his counsel.

After answering Ayn's various accusations—which included loss of serious interest in philosophy; financial improprieties; and vague, unspecified intimations about my "sordid" personal life—I ended my answer with this statement:

> I believe it is apparent, to any thoughtful reader of Miss Rand's article, that whatever the truth or falsehood of any of her specific charges, the real and basic reasons for her condemnation are not given in that article. . . . A major part of the story is obviously missing.
>
> She does provide one indirect clue—and I must confess I am astonished that she chose to include it.
>
> She writes: "About two months ago (at the beginning of July), in an apparent attempt to terminate the discussions he himself had initiated, Mr. Branden presented me with a written statement which was so irrational and so offensive to me that I had to break my personal association with him."
>
> In writing the above, Miss Rand has given me the right to name that which I infinitely would have preferred to leave unnamed, out of respect for her privacy. I am obliged to report what was in that written paper of mine, in the name of justice and of self-defense.
>
> That written statement was an effort not to terminate my relationship with Miss Rand, but to save it in some mutually acceptable form.

It was a tortured, awkward, excruciatingly embarrassed attempt
to make clear to her why I felt that an age distance between us of
twenty-five years constituted an insuperable barrier, for me, to a
romantic relationship.

The charges against Barbara chiefly had to do with alleged financial
exploitation. Ironically, these accusations completely disregarded the fact
that it was Ayn's announcement of her intention to make Barbara her heir
that prompted Barbara to tell Ayn the truth. Barbara's written response
was devastating in its quiet dignity and in the facts she marshaled to
counter Ayn's accusations (our complete responses may be found on my
Web site at www.nathanielbranden.net).

We knew, however, that for many of Ayn's followers, this would not be
a trial of facts, evidence, or logic. Someone said to us, "Regardless of what
Ayn Rand or you say or write, roughly one-third will take Miss Rand's
side, one-third will take your side, and one-third won't take sides." We
thought that this was probably true.

If students could not accept Ayn's charges merely on the basis of her
written statement, they were told sternly by Ayn's fervent supporters,
"You are challenging the judgment of the author of *Atlas Shrugged*."
When one of Allan Blumenthal's therapy clients expressed a desire to meet
with me and hear my side, Allan informed him, "After Miss Rand's article, there are no sides." I began to hear of clients' being expelled from
therapy with Allan because they refused to agree that Ayn Rand was
entirely in the right. I heard similar stories about Hank Holzer's clients,
including draft cases he was defending. "You are asking," people told
Holzer and Allan, "that I condemn a man without any hard, objective evidence—a man who has made a gigantic contribution to my life." "You
are asked," they answered, "to demonstrate your loyalty to Ayn Rand and
to Objectivism."

Anyone who professed any reservations about Ayn Rand's being right
in the matter of her conflict with Nathaniel Branden was declared an
enemy. Decades-long friendships shattered over disagreements in this matter. Marriages and families broke up. Former lovers no longer acknowledged each other.

I heard the rumors from various sources: "Separated from Ayn Rand,
Nathaniel Branden will now disappear into oblivion." "Ayn Rand says
Nathan was a gigolo." "Branden is an embezzler." "Branden was only in
Objectivism for the money." "Branden hurt Ayn Rand; that's all anyone
needs to know to condemn him." "Branden will become a bum; he's fin-
ished." "The only moral thing Nathan can now do is commit suicide."

"No one should discuss the situation with Nathaniel Branden or Barbara Branden." This was the word sent down by Ayn, passing to Leonard Peikoff, Allan and Joan Blumenthal, and Hank Holzer, then to our students, our readers, and an ever-widening network. Some people obeyed. Others did not. Some came to me, and I answered their questions as best I could. I did not tell them about my affair with Ayn. However, when I told them what they would later read in my published "Answer to Ayn Rand," many of them guessed.

When people asked me if I minded if they talked to the other side, I urged them to do so. I especially urged them to talk to Leonard Peikoff; he was so hysterical now in his defense of Ayn and in his denunciations of me that I knew he would win converts for me. This happened again and again. People said to me, "If they had a good case, foam wouldn't be coming out of Leonard's mouth." I laughed when I heard this and said to new inquirers, "Don't just hear my side. Talk to Leonard Peikoff."

"This war," I said to Patrecia, "is going to split the Objectivist movement in two. The setback is going to last a long time. It may take two decades, and a whole new generation of readers, for the movement to recover fully—assuming there's anyone competent to focus it then."

"Why do people care so much?" she asked. "Why are they so tortured about it?"

"Because to them, Ayn and I were the proof that the Objectivist vision is possible. We were the evidence that it was not just a dream. Now, either they will have to stand by Ayn as uncritical, conformist true believers, or they will have to rethink the philosophy on their own, without mother and father figures to make it easier. They'll have to make a new judgment about its validity. For them, also, this is judgment day."

"What do you think will happen to the Objectivist movement?"

"Short-term, I think it will go into something of a decline. Long-term, I think that it will have a major impact culturally and politically and that its biggest growth will happen after Ayn's death."

" 'After Ayn's death.' . . . What do imagine you'll feel?"

"I'm already feeling it."

We talked about the Collective and my predictions for its future. I said, "For a while, everyone will be closer and nicer to each other. Ayn will be especially warm, securing everyone's loyalty. Some of them will scramble to win points with her by dredging up any bad memory about me or Barbara to prove Ayn right. There will be endless discussions of my psychology, and every kind of theory you can imagine will be put forth, principally by Ayn. Then, whatever the idea is, she will discard it a week later for some new idea. Eventually, she will drive the Collective crazy with her psychologizing. God knows what she'll write about me in her journal—she's kept one for years—but I promise you, it will not be primarily governed by considerations of truth."

Years later, I learned of the accuracy of my predictions. She spent many hours speculating about my psychology with the Collective. I heard that she wrote many papers to herself on my "psychology" and "psychoepistemology." She was obsessed with questions such as the following: Was Nathan always evil, or did some strange transmutation occur during the course of our relationship? If Nathan had always been corrupt, how had he been able to fool everyone? How could he master Objectivism so well if he did not really care about ideas? Yet at no time did she tell the Collective the truth about our relationship. Knowing Ayn as well as I did, I was sure that in her private notes, not meant for the Collective's eyes, she would be rewriting the history of our relationship in order to explain and justify her own "errors of judgment" and to account for my "collapse into evil."

I said to Patrecia, "I don't know how long anyone will last, but the Collective will not stay together. One by one, for one reason or another, they will leave or be thrown out. Holzer won't last; he's too abrasive. The Blumenthals won't last; they never belonged in that environment in the first place, even at its best. Elayne and Harry won't last; sooner or later, their basic sanity will rebel. Maybe one day we'll be friends again. I don't know whether Mary Ann Rukavina will remain with Ayn or not. I can't see Alan Greenspan breaking with Ayn, or Ayn with him. My guess is that after a while, he'll simply fade away without ever severing the connection officially. But Leonard Peikoff will last, because he truly has no identity apart from his relationship to Ayn."

I made this forecast in public lectures on more than one occasion because I wanted to be on the record. It all came true.

In later years, Leonard would be anointed Ayn's "intellectual heir," as well as financial heir, and would surround himself with a group of true believers. They would rise to new heights of ruthlessness and hysteria in excommunicating deviationists and people who asked threatening questions. In converting the Rand legacy into personal cash, Leonard would also display an imaginativeness that few people would have anticipated. For example, he published highly personal notes of Ayn's, taken from her journals, that were never meant to be shared with the world. The impression conveyed was that, after years of obsequious self-abnegation in Ayn's service, it was payback time for Leonard. He felt entitled.

One afternoon toward the end of October, shortly before Patrecia and I were to leave for California, I received a phone call from a man I did not know in Dallas. I gathered that he was a fairly wealthy businessman with intense convictions about the importance of the Objectivist message for civilization. "You can't retire and withdraw from all this, Mr. Branden. My friends and I are prepared to put up any amount of money you think you need to start up a new organization, anywhere in the country, to teach the Objectivist philosophy."

I was stunned and touched. "Haven't you heard," I asked, "that Miss Rand has repudiated me as a spokesman for Objectivism."

"The reason I started admiring you wasn't because Miss Rand told me to, and I don't plan to stop admiring you now because Miss Rand tells me to. I won't presume to speculate about what's gone haywire with that woman, although I do have my own, private opinions, but you were the greatest teacher I ever heard, and the job you started out to do is still waiting to be done."

I thanked him and said, "I've got a life of my own to pursue now that goes beyond Ayn Rand and Objectivism. I agree about the job that needs to be done, but it's not my problem any longer."

"What do you want for yourself now?"

"A private life."

I was not concerned about reestablishing myself professionally or financially. I would contact the people on the NBI/*Objectivist* mailing list (which Barbara had had the foresight to copy) who lived within commuting distance of Los Angeles and inform them that I was opening a psychotherapy practice; I knew that my appointment book would be filled very quickly. Nothing Ayn or her supporters might attempt would really matter. John Hospers, now head of the philosophy department at the University of Southern California, had already arranged a job for me there; I would lecture on the philosophical foundations of the biological and psychological sciences. My mind was filled with plans for future books.

The primary challenge awaiting me in California was not economic but intellectual and spiritual. I faced the task of rethinking my philosophical convictions down to their base and of redefining myself and my goals outside the context of my relationship to Objectivism and Ayn Rand. I knew I would need time. At the age of thirty-eight, I had to create a new foundation for my existence and a new direction. I felt excited and inspired at the prospect.

On the morning of October 31, 1968, I rode with Patrecia down the elevator at 120 East Thirty-Fourth Street for the last time. A car was waiting to take us to the airport.

I stood on the street looking up. Six floors above was Ayn's apartment, and fifteen floors above that was Barbara's. I thought about everything I was leaving behind, and I felt immensely solemn. I sensed a vast, ecstatic emptiness within me, an emptiness of unlimited possibilities.

I got into the car and took Patrecia's hand. She was smiling. There was earnestness in the total stillness of her body and in a serenity and strength that seemed to flow from her spirit. I thought of what she had given me and felt gratitude and love. I knew that she read in my face the same thought I read in hers: We're free.

I paused to reflect: What were the appropriate words for this occasion? Signaling the driver to go, I said, "Thank you for waiting, Patrecia."

EPILOGUE

DURING OUR FIRST YEAR in Los Angeles, free from outside conflicts or pressures, Patrecia and I had the opportunity to explore and deepen our relationship, confirming and strengthening our earlier assessments and intuitions about each other. My feelings of being connected to her more deeply than I had ever felt connected to anyone grew even more powerful.

On November 7, 1969, a year after leaving New York, Patrecia and I were married. We decided not to invite anyone to the wedding. The ceremony was a height we wanted to experience alone. I remember the breathless solemnity of our mood, the touch of Patrecia's hand in mine as we rode back to our hotel suite. I remember thinking that my strength had come back to me in full and that I needed nothing more to guarantee our future.

"I want us to grow old together," I said to Patrecia. I felt sure that the worst was behind us. Our life was exquisitely simple, organized around our two cardinal values: work and love. "No more obstructions," I declared. "Now we're free to concern ourselves only with what matters."

"To grow old together," Patrecia repeated. "Could anything be more wonderful?"

I was instantly busy with my new office practice, and my economic recovery was as rapid and relatively effortless as I had predicted. Nine months after arriving in California, we moved into the house where I still live. For me, the house was the symbol of our freedom and of my victory over the past. Standing in our glass-enclosed living room, we looked at the city and the sky stretched out before us.

"What a fool I was," I said, holding Patrecia in my arms, "to hang on to the past so long. Now, everything is ahead of us."

I would awaken in the morning eager to begin the day and conscious of feeling none of the weight of duty and obligation to which I had become accustomed in New York. I did not have to wonder how Ayn was feeling or if she needed me for anything. I had no organization for which I was responsible, no staff or large overhead. I did not have to spend time with people I did not like. I felt the tension that had accumulated over years draining from my mind and body.

The simplest outings—a drive down to the ocean for lunch, a walk through Beverly Hills, a day's visit to Santa Barbara—were occasions of great exuberance. To sit at my desk and think of nothing but my own work felt like a magnificent luxury. To anticipate an evening with Patrecia and to know that our time was ours to spend in any way we wished felt intoxicating.

When working as a model in New York, Patrecia had lightened her hair to blond; now, she allowed it to return to its natural brown, which I preferred. As she stood in the swimming pool in our backyard, it glistened in the sunlight, showing faint traces of auburn. I flung my arms around her and lifted her body out of the water and into the air, shouting "Patrecia Branden!" And she shouted back, "Nathaniel Branden! My husband, Nathaniel Branden!"

I addressed a number of Objectivist audiences and almost always received a warm and benevolent welcome. On some occasions, Barbara accompanied me, stood by me, defended me against false accusations, and was altogether a good friend to me. This was our most comfortable role—not lovers but partners in battle.

Notwithstanding Patrecia's and my happiness, there were times when we were hit by pain, anger, or depression about the past. Some mornings, I would wake up with my jaw tightly clenched and the heavy awareness that my dreams had taken me back to Ayn and my life in New York, and I felt consumed by rage. When these attacks came, I did not fight them. I accepted them, knowing that they were inevitable and that Patrecia and I both needed time to heal.

The Psychology of Self-Esteem was published by Nash Publishing Company in the fall of 1969. It was subsequently contracted to Bantam Books and went on to sell about a million copies worldwide. The central importance of self-esteem to human well-being, so ignored and neglected when the book was first published, is widely accepted today as incontrovertible.

In 1970, I published *Breaking Free,* which explores the childhood origins of negative self-concepts, illustrated by brief case vignettes. It reflects the beginning of my interest in the developmental aspect of psychology, which I had largely neglected. With this book, I began thinking, more deeply than I had before, about the role of parents in nurturing or subverting the growth of healthy self-esteem.

During this period, people asked me, "Do you still consider yourself an Objectivist?" I answered, "If, by an 'Objectivist' you mean someone who agrees with every idea or position Ayn Rand takes, then I am emphatically not an Objectivist. If, however, you mean someone who agrees with the *essentials* of her philosophy—the supremacy of reason; opposition to any form of irrationalism; an ethics of rational or enlightened self-interest, in contrast to the advocacy of self-sacrifice; individualism as opposed to collectivism; inalienable rights, political and economic freedom, and laissez-faire capitalism as opposed to any version of statism—then I am an Objectivist." Sometimes I laughed and said, "You must understand that Ayn Rand would say that I am definitely *not* an Objectivist. Perhaps I am a neo-Objectivist."

Over the years, I encountered many men and women who, in the name of idealism (Objectivist or otherwise), crucified their emotional life to conform to their professed values. Inevitably, this entailed massive self-repudiation, which students of Objectivism are appallingly expert at, notwithstanding their talk of "selfishness." (This seems to be much less true today.) Hearing their stories, I thought of my own history and of what I had learned from it. In my therapy and lectures, I said, "No one has ever evolved to a higher level of development by repudiating and damning what he or she is." I had come to see how supremely important self-acceptance was to healthy self-esteem.

The Disowned Self, published in 1972, is an examination of the widespread problem of self-alienation, in which an individual cuts himself off from his deepest emotions and highest possibilities. This book, which stands as a kind of sequel to *The Psychology of Self-Esteem,* represents a shift in emphasis from the purely cognitive aspects of self-esteem development toward a wider focus that embraces feelings, emotions, and the problem of self-disowning via denial and repression. It was intended not to replace but to supplement my early book. *The Disowned Self* illustrates, far more than the previous two books, the kind of therapy I was practicing during the 1970s.

Writing it, I was acutely aware of my former students at NBI; it was almost as if I were writing them a letter. In offering them a better understanding of emotion than I had provided in the past, and in emphasizing the supreme importance of self-acceptance, I hoped to undo some of the harm I might have caused them.

During this same period, I went back to school and, in 1973, I received my doctorate from the California Graduate Institute.

When I reflect on the early years in Los Angeles, the memory that remains most powerful with regard to my own development is that of awakening to an internal sense of efficacy far greater than I had ever experienced in New York. In addition to the joy and satisfaction I found in writing, I loved the practice of psychotherapy, loved experimenting with new and different procedures, and was excited about the results I was achieving. Nothing seemed more interesting to me than the process by which human beings *change*.

After publishing *The Disowned Self*, although I continued to write for myself, I did not publish again for seven years. "I am learning so much so rapidly," I told Patrecia, "that I don't want to publish for a while. I feel that by the time I finish a project, I will have already moved too far beyond it."

Apart from my theoretical work in self-esteem and of course in Objectivism, I was identified for a while with a technique I developed for self-understanding, self-exploration, self-acceptance, and self-healing. It was a sentence-completion procedure I first wrote about in *The Disowned Self*, which I then brought to a higher level of sophistication and taught in my seminars. I did not originate the technique per se but greatly expanded its power by identifying new ways of using and applying it. Many years later, I elaborated on the technique in *If You Could Hear What I Cannot Say* (1983) and *To See What I See and Know What I Know* (1986). The basic idea is to give a client an incomplete sentence, a sentence stem, and ask that it be repeated aloud again and again, each time with a different ending. The art consists of knowing which stems to select and how to build a structure from one stem to another, often in a long chain. It involves pursuing a course that may be subtle, complex, and indirect and using subconscious associations along the way, in the attempt to access knowledge and resources of which the client may be quite unaware. I received many invitations to demonstrate and teach the particular ways in which I worked with this method. Almost every week, in one or another of my therapy groups, I would have visiting psychologists or psychiatrists who had asked to sit in and observe. It delighted me to see their amazement at what the sentence-completion technique could accomplish. It remains the simplest and fastest instrument I know for rapid access to blocked or disowned aspects of the self. The procedure can be integrated into virtually any therapeutic approach. Almost all of my later books in psychology contain illustrations of its power.

I did not miss the world I had left in New York, but sometimes I missed the intellectual intensity of that world. I did not miss Ayn as a person (or not often), but I missed the stimulation of our philosophical conversations at their best. I did not miss the Collective, but sometimes I missed the sense of community we had shared.

In reflecting on my relationship with Ayn, I came to see that I had wanted an older person who would teach me things, help make life and the world understandable, and be a point of security and stability while I was forming my own identity. I had wanted a hero to admire. I had not known I'd wanted that. Growing up, I had told myself I didn't need anyone. Because I disowned the need, its power over me became all the greater, blinding me to dangers in my relationship with Ayn that I might otherwise have seen.

In the early years in California, Barbara reproached me for not condemning Ayn harshly. Although Barbara's attitude toward Ayn later softened enormously, in the period after the break she took the position that Ayn was a monster who was utterly destructive in her dealings with people. "You don't realize what a victim you were," she told me repeatedly. I said that I did not think that I or she or anyone else in the Collective was Ayn's "victim," and, in any event, that I was far more interested in understanding the roots of my own behavior than in focusing on how terrible Ayn was. There were occasions when we briefly reversed roles; she would become more sympathetic to Ayn, and I would become more condemning. But predominantly, it was she who urged me to take a more severe perspective.

I said that as far as Ayn's philosophy was concerned, the challenge was not to throw out the baby with the bath water, not simply to rebel against everything we had learned but to take the time to rethink our ideas so as not to lose what was valuable. Barbara did not disagree with this. I was concerned because I saw students of Objectivism, hurt and disillusioned by the divorce of their philosophical parents, rebelling against philosophy as a whole, discarding any serious interest in ideas, and collapsing into bitter cynicism.

In retrospect, I would say that where Barbara and I differed, we each had a valid point. I was slow to appreciate fully the destructive side of Ayn's character and to see that, according to her own code of morality, she merited the sternest condemnation for her hypocrisy, dishonesty, and megalomania. But I was also right in insisting that self-examination be our number-one priority—and in warning of the danger of backing off from philosophy.

In *The Passion of Ayn Rand,* Barbara suggests that not long after the break, her anger at Ayn faded and her love reasserted itself. Actually, she and I remained at loggerheads for eleven years over the issue of how one should feel about Ayn. On an evening in 1979, in the living room of my home and in the presence of about fifteen people, Barbara began to speak with great pain and anger—once again—about how Ayn had almost ruined her life.

I had long ago confronted what my own rewards were for remaining with Ayn (I have discussed them throughout this memoir) and had hoped Barbara would at last examine her own motivations. We had an intense discussion in which, to her credit, she finally did acknowledge the payoffs: the position she (and I) occupied as a leader and teacher; the adulation she received; the ego-intoxicating conviction that she was participating in history; the sense that her existence had unique moral meaning in the Objectivist cause; and the fact that, quite simply, she enjoyed the personal friendship and confidence of a woman she regarded as one of the greatest thinkers in the world. Thereafter, she spoke of Ayn more sympathetically and much less angrily. She still lapsed into her old perspective, but less often.

In later years, she would come to see herself as the champion of Ayn Rand and me as the enemy—a complete reversal of our previous discussions. However, she specifically asked me to state in this book that she no longer regards me as Ayn's enemy.

Sometimes, when I talked with Patrecia about the future, I saw the faintest suggestion of a shadow flicker across her face. When I asked her about it, she said, "I don't know. All my life I've fought against that feeling of doom my mother raised us with. The sense of some terrible catastrophe— an earthquake or a war or some other cataclysm—that will devastate everything. God, how I hated hearing about that! Sometimes, when I'm very happy, as I am now with you, that old message comes back just for a moment, like something cold and evil chasing after me. Then it's gone, and I'm all right again." This was an aspect of Patrecia I had not seen before, and I did not know what to think of it. I held her in my arms to create an island of safety.

But those brief moments seemed to vanish almost immediately, and she was her fast-moving, high-energy, laughing self again. She said often, "I love you so much, it's frightening."

I knew what she meant; the intensity of what I felt sometimes frightened me, too. I had never been this happy. But I would laugh and say, "What is there to be frightened of?"

Patrecia, 33, in Beverly Hills, California, home, 1973

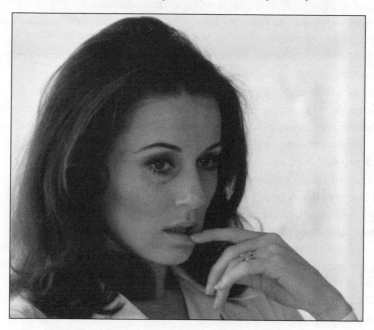

I never ceased to reflect on Ayn's philosophy and the aspects I was convinced needed rethinking. I found myself dwelling on the inadequate attention she paid to benevolence, mutual aid, generosity, and simple kindness as ethical desirables. If life were the standard of the good, these issues were not marginal but important. These issues deserved a more prominent place in Objectivist doctrine. I knew many Objectivists who understood this, practiced it in their personal lives, and took it as self-evidently implied by their philosophy, even if Ayn had remained too silent on the subject. Had she developed this theme fully and explicitly, I think it would have made it easier for people to understand what she meant by "rational selfishness."

I thought about Ayn's concept of justice. One of the most significant things she had to say on this subject was that we should not think of justice only in terms of dealing with the guilty but also in terms of appreciating the good, of acknowledging and rewarding the virtuous and admirable. In *Atlas,* this theme is central. However, Ayn also urged her followers not "to withhold contempt from men's vices." Hence the violently abusive language with which she and her followers characterized actions of which they did not approve. After our break, I came to understand, more deeply than I had before, that even if what people are doing is wrong, even if they are being irrational and committing errors of morality, we do not lead them to virtue and rationality by projecting contempt. We do not make people better by telling them they are despicable. If the goal is to inspire positive change, a better strategy than scorn and abusive condemnation is required.

Asked constantly by people to discuss my current perspective on Ayn's philosophical system, I began to realize that Ayn had not formulated a philosophical system in the full sense; she had sketched the outlines of one. Some of the elements were filled in rather specifically, whereas others remained vague or entirely missing. What she provided was an overarching vision of man's place in the universe, man's relationship to existence, and some brilliantly argued support for certain key ideas (such as her views concerning concept formation, her metaethics, the morality of self-interest, and her justification of natural rights), and some dazzling insights on a wide variety of philosophical issues (such as the nature of sensory perception, the irrationality of conventional ethics, the value and meaning of art, and the virtues of freedom and the evils of statism).

Viewing her writing as a whole, I thought she was right far more often than she was wrong. I thought her work abounded with philosophical wisdom, even if I was now sometimes antagonized by her form of expression. I thought her writing contained the ingredients and clues out of which a true philosophical system could be developed—if her followers had the mind to do it. These are still my convictions today.

My greatest area of disagreement is in the field of psychology, where I see her as being wrong far more often than she was right, especially when she was "psychologizing" about her opponents. Although I share her opposition to mysticism, I think that her analysis of "the psychology of mysticism" is ill informed and essentially absurd. I later presented my own critique of mysticism in The Art of Living Consciously (1997).

On a Sunday afternoon in 1975, in the living room of our home, I was sharing some of my ideas about Objectivism with a group of students who were interested in Ayn's work. I said, "Ayn Rand knew far more than she wrote. Having participated in hundreds of philosophical discussions with her and having been present at her discussions with gifted professional philosophers, I know she could have argued far more cogently for her ideas and answered many more objections than she ever did in print. I think she was a far better philosopher than almost anyone fully knows. She believed that all she had to do was fling her inspired thunderbolts into the world and that any decent mind could do the rest. Her achievements are enormous. But in the sphere of technical philosophy, she needed to give more than she gave if her purpose was to leave behind a comprehensive system. However, I do not believe that was her purpose; her purpose was to formulate only what she needed for *Atlas Shrugged*."

Someone asked how I felt about the fact that Ayn had instructed her publishers to remove all references to me in *Atlas Shrugged*—the dedication in the front and the statements in the back about Nathaniel Branden's being "as rational and independent a mind as I could conceive of" and "my intellectual heir." I answered that I would always remember my joy and excitement when Miss Rand first told me of her intention to dedicate *Atlas* to me—and that her subsequent repudiation felt less important to me. "Just the same, it's difficult to think of Miss Rand without sadness."

When they had gone, I stood with my arm around Patrecia on our garden terrace and overlooked the city. "I'm happy," I told her simply. "I'm really happy. When I was a teenager, I had two ambitions: to be able to earn my living doing work I cared about and to have the woman I loved. Ever since *The Disowned Self* was published, I've felt that life doesn't owe me anything. I mean, I hope there will be many more books and more great years together, but if I had to die now, I don't feel I've missed anything."

"I wish I could feel that." She sighed. "I do feel that about you, but not about work. I still feel unsettled about what I'm going to do with my life. The most important thing I've learned since coming to California is something I knew before, but I know it better now. It's that love is not enough. Living through you is not enough. Nothing will ever be enough until I know what to do with my energy, until I have an outlet, a way to use what I am. Will I achieve that in acting? I don't know. . . . What's the most important thing you've learned since moving here?"

I answered, "How disastrous it was to allow my self-esteem to become involved with my relationship with Ayn. Whatever it was that made me write to Ayn and whatever it was that knew how to talk to her when I was not yet twenty years old; whatever launched me into the affair with her, with all of its madness, and gave me a particular kind of certainty; whatever made it possible for me to create NBI and to accomplish the things I've accomplished in psychology—I had all that long before I met Ayn. Her great gift was that she helped me see it. Back in New York, she tried to take it back—to make me forget it. In the end, she couldn't do it. There are gifts that, once given, cannot be taken back."

"You are today," Patrecia answered, "as I saw you in that first moment at NBI—only much more relaxed and cheerful."

One day that fall, as I walked from my office to the elevator, a voice inside my head told me, It's time to telephone Ayn.

"Tell me what you hope to accomplish by calling her," Patrecia said when I told her at dinner.

"In one sense," I answered, "I don't hope to accomplish anything. I don't think Ayn will be willing to talk with me. In all likelihood, she'll hang up on me. I am thinking of all the years in New York when I could have been fully truthful with her and wasn't. I was afraid then, but I am not afraid now. I don't know whether calling is the right and rational thing to do or whether it would be wiser not to call, to let the past remain the past. But if I have to choose without full certainty, then at least I'll know it's not fear that's motivating me this time. It feels important to do it—important for my self-respect, important for my self of those years. The way Ayn reacts is really not the point. This is between me and me."

"What would you like from the conversation, ideally?"

"Not a resumption of our friendship but a better ending—one with more honesty and dignity between us."

I telephoned Ayn on a morning in January 1976, during a week when I was in New York to conduct a psychotherapy workshop. Here is the conversation verbatim.

"Hello?"

"Hello, Ayn. This is Nathaniel." To my ears, my voice sounded relaxed, almost gentle, as if to soften any shock.

"Who?"

I smiled at the sharp intake of her breath.

"This is Nathaniel."

Now in the tone of a prosecutor, a tone I remembered too well: "To whom am I speaking, please?"

"Nathaniel Branden."

"Well, you didn't really think I would speak to you, did you?" That old familiar contempt, the contempt reserved for enemies.

"I didn't know. But I think it would be a loss for both of us if you refused to. I feel there are things we need to say to each other. So I hoped we could talk."

An ugly chuckle. "Well, no. Good-bye." She hung up.

I began to laugh. I got up and began to dance around the hotel suite, feeling released from an enormous weight. Pulling out some hotel stationery, I wrote down what Ayn and I said to each other. Then I called home and told Patrecia what had happened. "How do you feel?" she asked.

"Just as I sound—wonderful! It was odd—even as I was dia
number, I was feeling absolutely serene, almost light-headed, as
going through the motions because I needed to, just to finish something
once and for all. But it was already finished. I had felt that, but I wanted
to be certain, and this was the final confirmation."

That was not the end of my reflections about Ayn or my efforts to understand my behavior in our relationship. Increasingly, I saw to what extent
my personality had become distorted through our association. It was
sometimes a difficult struggle to sort out my own thoughts, feelings, and
responses and to differentiate between those that were authentically mine
and those that were, in effect, Ayn's voice speaking through me and influencing me in old ways. I came to appreciate the importance of separation
and individuation, not only in infancy and childhood but also at every
stage of development. I did not rebel against that which seemed valid and
important in Objectivism, but I learned to ask, "And what else is true?"

As my reflections and meditations continued, I felt a spirituality emerging within me, one that had nothing to do with religion and everything to
do with love. A love of life and of the life force that I saw manifested
wherever I looked. A love of the world as a place of wonder, enchantment,
and unlimited possibilities. A love of Patrecia's face in the first light of
morning when I thought how lucky, how incredibly lucky, I was. A love
of all the simple daily activities that supported our existence.

One evening in 1975, Patrecia and I were having dinner with Dale Wasser-
man and his wife, Ramsey. I was talking to her, and Dale and Patrecia
were discussing theater. My attention was divided between having my
own conversation and eavesdropping on the one I was missing, since both
interested me. Whenever Dale reflected on stage plays he had written, such
as *Man of La Mancha* or *One Flew over the Cuckoo's Nest,* or difficulties on the way to production, I was always intrigued. Dale sometimes
conveyed that he was not overly enthusiastic about actors and actresses
as a group; he was, however, always warmly supportive of Patrecia. She
had been talking very earnestly for a long time when he said to her, "Are
you sure you want to be an actress? For an actress, you think too much.
The way your mind works is more that of a writer or a director."

A month or so later, Dale telephoned to say that the Los Angeles Free
Shakespeare Company was staging a production of *Macbeth.* He suggested that Patrecia audition for the role of Lady Macbeth. As she had no
background or training in Shakespeare, she was both flattered and taken

Nathaniel, 45, and Patrecia, 35, with Takara, in Aspen, Colorado, 1975

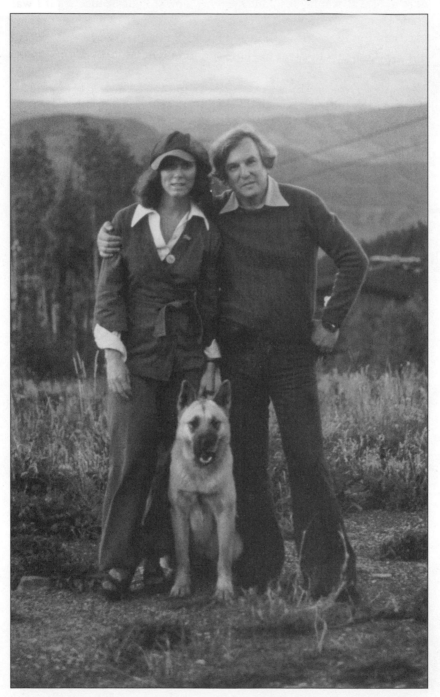

aback. When she protested that she did not think she was qualified, Dale said with great authority, "Patrecia—just do it." He gave her the name of the director, David Alexander, whom he knew, and said he would make a call on her behalf, simply to introduce her. Then she would be on her own.

Patrecia was called back to audition for the part three times. David Alexander and his associates were impressed by her work but wondered if they would not be wiser to go with a "name." After the third audition, they told her the part was hers.

The production was well received, and Patrecia was praised for her performance. Seeing her on stage, I knew that with Shakespeare, Patrecia had found herself as an actress. I recall an English literature professor's raving to me about the depth and originality Patrecia brought to her interpretation and wanting to know where she had received her Shakespearean training.

Later that same year, we read that a major production of *Macbeth* was being staged at the Los Angeles Music Center, with Charlton Heston and Vanessa Redgrave in the leads. It was scheduled to open early in 1976. Before Patrecia could check out the possibility of auditioning for a smaller role, her agent at William Morris called to say that he had already been contacted by the producer's office about Patrecia's auditioning for Lady Macduff, as well as the part of Redgrave's understudy.

She was quickly hired. John Ireland played Macduff. The director was Peter Wood. We later heard that Redgrave was known to get sick during performances and that Patrecia had been hired specifically to take over the role of Lady Macbeth if necessary.

Several weeks into the production, it happened. On a Wednesday morning in February, Patrecia received a call instructing her to come to the theater immediately to prepare for the Wednesday matinee; Redgrave was ill, and Patrecia would be going on as Lady Macbeth. I wanted to cancel my therapy appointments so I could go that afternoon, but Patrecia asked me to wait for the evening performance, saying she would be more in control by then. Not wanting to add to her tension, I agreed. Immediately after the performance on Wednesday afternoon, she telephoned in a state of unreserved rapture and told me that the show had gone beautifully without a single problem. Everyone was excited, Heston and the rest of the cast were enthusiastic and complimentary, and Peter Wood seemed pleased.

Sitting in the theater that evening, watching the authority and passion of Patrecia's performance, remains to this day one of my most thrilling memories. All my life, the longing to admire had been powerful in me, nowhere more so than in the context of romantic love, and that longing now felt supremely fulfilled. I love you, I said to her silently, feeling the emotional sum of all the steps from our first meeting at NBI in New York to the performance in this theater tonight.

When we were alone after the performance, I told her what I was feeling while she was on stage: "I am so proud of you. I felt awe at what you were doing. Your certainty was magnificent. You brought a quality of ecstatic consciousness to everything you were doing, down to the smallest gesture. It was there underneath your scenes of worst suffering, just as you bring it to your life. I love you so much."

Redgrave did not return for the rest of the week, and Patrecia played Lady Macbeth through Saturday night. She then resumed the role of Lady Macduff. The critics had been invited back to see her, and although Charles Champlin of the *Los Angeles Times* had reservations about the production as a whole, he compared Patrecia's performance favorably to Redgrave's.

I wondered, sadly, if she would ever have an opportunity to play so satisfying a role again—and what she would be feeling when she next auditioned for the movie or television female role that was then typically being offered.

She, too, had been thinking about her future. She was keenly aware of the emotional cost, to her personally and to our relationship, of pursuing an acting career. She did not feel optimistic about finding satisfying work in Los Angeles, and she did not want to seek work elsewhere in the country, because she did not want us to be separated for any length of time. "I feel totally boxed in," she said. Prior to the recent production of *Macbeth,* she had decided to enroll in Antioch College, first to complete a bachelor's degree, then to obtain a master's in psychology. Ever since New York, she had dreamed of one day completing her education. *Macbeth* had not changed her mind.

Once, I asked her, "What does acting mean to you?" She thought for a moment, then said, "Ordinary reality is too slow. In art, everything is condensed, stylized, and reduced to essentials. So when I'm acting, I'm in a world where nothing is accidental, everything has a purpose, every gesture and word has to count, life is speeded up, everything is much more intense. And that intensity feels like my natural state."

On November 7, 1976, we celebrated our seventh wedding anniversary. It was almost sixteen years since we had seen each other for the first time. "I looked at you," she said, smiling, "and I thought, I will never have him. He will have to remain an abstraction."

"I looked at you," I answered, "and I felt I had stepped out of ordinary reality into a dream."

In February 1977, Patrecia was contacted by the Old Globe Theatre in San Diego, notified of the Shakespeare festival being planned, and invited to audition. She had been waiting for this event for a year. The central conflict of Patrecia's life came into focus most sharply at this point—the conflict between love and career. If she were accepted, she would have the opportunity to play Kate in *Taming of the Shrew* and Gertrude in *Hamlet,* plus a smaller role in a third play. This prospect filled her with rapture. However, the commitment meant being away from Los Angeles for six months—five months in San Diego and one month in Scottsdale, Arizona.

We both felt it imperative that she audition. "If you get the job," I said, "I'll drive to San Diego on weekends. We'll manage. This is important to you." She spoke to Antioch and was assured that, if necessary, she could take a leave of absence without academic penalty.

Meanwhile, I was on fire with a project of my own.

Since the beginning of my career, the central focus of my interest had been self-esteem. Since coming to California, I had been researching what might be accomplished when working with groups. In the spring of 1976, I began to consider conducting a therapeutic-educational program that could accommodate as many as one to two hundred participants at a time. Its purpose would be to generate psychological growth, particularly in the area of self-esteem. The workshop, to be called an "Intensive," would be spread over three-and-a-half days.

I saw this as an opportunity to create an event that would combine didactic elements—straight teaching—with participatory, experiential learning; psychological exercises; and processes aimed at raising consciousness, stimulating self-awareness and self-acceptance, and leading to increased self-expression, assertiveness, and personal integrity. I wanted to take the participants on a journey that would reflect some of the key elements of my own evolution.

At first, I both resisted the project and felt drawn to it. I knew that if the Intensives succeeded, I might again be obliged to create an organization, and I liked the current simplicity of my life with an office and one secretary. I was afraid that, through their own momentum, the Intensives could become the center of my professional life, demanding more of my time than I wished to give. But they represented a challenge that was difficult to say no to. Could the kind of psychological truths that interested me be effectively transmitted in an Intensive in such a way as truly to change lives? Could I create the kind of experience I imagined, that would draw on everything I had learned?

When I thought of the Intensive, called "Self-Esteem and the Art of Being," and what I wanted the program to contain, I thought of my own struggles since leaving New York to free myself of old perspectives that no longer served me, to free myself of pain and anger, to be more sensitive to my own needs, to be more empathic in dealing with others, to be more balanced as a total human being. Never for a moment did I imagine that the process was finished. I still carried too much tension, was still too impatient and too remote when I didn't intend to be, and was still not in a harmonious relationship with my body. I thought that in giving this Intensive, I would advance my own development as well as that of my students.

On the evening of March 17, 1977, I conducted "Self-Esteem and the Art of Being" for the first time in Los Angeles. The class consisted of about one hundred seventy-five students. The assistants scattered around the room were all psychotherapy students of mine. Patrecia and her father were sitting among the other students. The Intensive was emotionally powerful for everyone, including me. I felt that I had attained a new height of effectiveness in working with people and in generating change, and I was thrilled by the many demonstrations of honesty, self-confrontation, and personal growth I was witnessing. It works! I thought triumphantly.

"What an incredible breakthrough this is!" Patrecia said happily at the end of the weekend. "I feel as if I've taken the most fantastic leap in my own development—as if I've risen to a higher level of autonomy."

Two students who had known me at NBI came over to tell me how much they thought I had changed. "You have all your old power," one of them said, "but now you're *human*."

The next morning, while Patrecia was still in bed, I sat down beside her and said, with unexpected tears, "Whatever I became that allowed me to do what you saw at the Intensive, I saw that Nathaniel Branden reflected in your eyes when you were twenty-one years old at NBI. You gave me that vision and helped me to achieve it all these years. You said once that I've been your protector. Do you understand that you have also been mine?" She listened with an expression of quiet gratitude and pride that matched my own feeling.

A week later, some friends of ours invited us to join them for a few days of skiing at Aspen. At first, I was going to go alone, because Patrecia was running late on some school assignments. At the last moment, she decided to come with me; if she got the Old Globe job, it would be a long time before we would have another vacation. Between her studies at school and her preparation for the audition, she was exhausted; her eyes had a bright intensity that showed she had pushed herself past her limits. She was now anxiously awaiting final word from the theater, which would not come for another week.

Flying to Aspen, I smiled when I saw her writing in her diary. She kept diaries all her adult life, and she kept one throughout our relationship. To my surprise, in our lodge that night, she volunteered to show me a few pages, which she had never done before. "Nathaniel, stretched out, peaceful and serene, soon to fall asleep into his own private bliss. The touch of his hand holding firm on my leg will soon be slipping off. . . . I have work to do, and it *will* get done, but I didn't want to sit alone in my big empty house, longing to be with Nathaniel. . . . 'The hand' has slipped off. I miss its warmth. I shall pick it back up and do with it what I will." I pulled her into my arms and told her how happy I was that she had decided to come with me.

For some years, we had known that she had a mild epileptic condition, possibly a consequence of slight oxygen deprivation during her eleven days in an incubator. On three occasions in the past decade, she had had seizures and lost consciousness for a minute or two; that was the only symptom. We had been told that the condition was easily controllable with medication. On the second day of our trip, I saw her looking at a medicine bottle with some concern; she had taken her last pill. In her unexpected rush to leave Los Angeles with me, she had not noticed that the bottle was almost empty. Neither of us was aware that if one has been taking that medication regularly, it is dangerous to stop abruptly, because this can lower one's seizure threshold. Incredibly, we had not been told this, and I learned it only much later.

In the day we skied. Patrecia was a faster skier than I was, and on difficult slopes she would go down first, then wait below, waving her pole and smiling, as if to say encouragingly, "Nothing to it!" In the evening, we talked about Intensives, the Old Globe, and Patrecia's studies at Antioch. The strain that vanished from her eyes on the ski slopes reappeared when we focused on the future.

We arrived home on Wednesday, March 30, and went out for dinner. We were both exhausted from skiing all day and talking late into the night. I recall that we could hardly hold our heads up in the restaurant. Patrecia remarked that first thing in the morning, she would refill her prescription. She looked tense—tomorrow was the day she expected to hear from the Old Globe.

I encouraged her to talk about her feelings, but she was uncharacteristically reticent. "What can I say that you don't know?" she asked.

The next morning, she seemed in better spirits. We lay in bed for a long time, holding each other. "How is it possible," Patrecia said, "that after so many years I still love you so much?" I shook my head in wonder. "I don't know," I answered. "I look at you now, and I feel as I felt when I saw you fifteen years ago, as if you were a miracle that had been sent to me. For fifteen years, whenever I have seen you, the lights in the universe have grown brighter."

At 2:30 that afternoon, she telephoned me at the office. I remember the hushed, solemn quality of her first words: "Well, Nathaniel, I got it." She had just heard from the Old Globe. She reported to me the compliments she had been paid on the quality of her work. The quiet happiness in her voice had a quality of muted intensity; I thought how much I loved the sound of her voice.

"Oh, Patrecia," I said, "I am so glad that you are getting the appreciation you deserve. I am so happy for you."

She answered, "I wish you were home right now. I've got classes at Antioch. I don't know how I'll concentrate, but I've got to go. See you around seven-thirty or eight." We said we loved each other and hung up.

Later, someone who saw her at school at 4:30 that day would report, "She looked so happy, she looked like she was going to blow a fuse."

Driving up the winding road to our house at 7:15, having just had an early dinner with friends, I wondered whether, in her excitement, Patrecia had remembered to feed our dog, Takara. We usually fed her each day around 5:30. When I pulled into our driveway and saw Patrecia's car, I smiled and thought, She couldn't stand to be in classes today; she's come home early.

Inside the house I shouted, "Patrecia!" When she did not answer, I called her name again. I moved through the house, looking for her. When I stepped into her study and saw her bag lying on the floor, I felt sudden alarm; she never went anywhere without her handbag.

Then I became aware that Takara was in the room, jumping up on me, but how was that possible? If Patrecia were not home, Takara would be locked outside. Then I saw that the door to the yard was open, and I ran out, my eyes rapidly sweeping the area.

When confronted with unbearable reality, the brain sometimes tries to protect itself. As I looked into the swimming pool, for some small fraction of a second I wondered how a tree branch could have fallen to the bottom of the pool. Then, in a moment of unspeakable horror that has never left me, I grasped that it was not a tree. Through the dark water, I discerned the shape of Patrecia.

I shouted, flung myself in, dived beneath the surface, and grasped her body in my arms. I pulled her to the side of the pool and struggled to resuscitate her, searching my mind desperately for everything I knew about

Patrecia, just turned 37, six weeks before her death, 1977

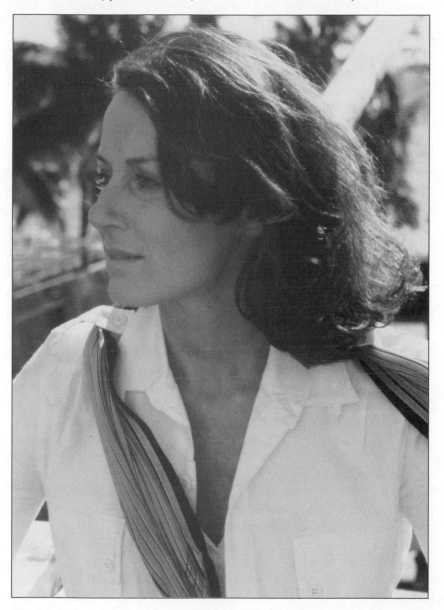

treating drowning victims. She did not respond. I went on trying, pleading with Patrecia to come back to me. No response. Her eyes were open. Her face had the peacefulness of absolute emptiness. Patrecia was not there.

I do not recall the details of the next sequence of events. I know I shouted for help and tripped the house alarm to summon the police. I know I kept returning to the body, fighting to give it breath and life, weeping like a child and begging Patrecia to wake up. At some point, I felt a neighbor's hand on my shoulder and heard his voice saying, "It's no use. She's dead."

I prowled through the house like a wounded animal, moving from room to room, shouting, "Patrecia!" Then I collapsed on the living room sofa, whispering her name again and again, like a prayer never to be answered.

What could have happened? Why and how did she die? For a brief moment, the thought flashed through my mind that Patrecia had somehow had a seizure and lost consciousness while standing too close to the pool. What other explanation could there be? My next thought was that if she had *not* had a seizure, she had been murdered—by someone from "the old days" who imagined he would be avenging Ayn Rand.

Later, there was an autopsy, and the coroner's verdict was death by accidental drowning. Patrecia had evidently left school early and come home. Following normal routine, she would have been feeding Takara by the swimming pool around 5:30 in the afternoon. At that time, the bright sun would have been pouring down into our yard through leaves and branches, reflecting off the glass windows of our home, as well as off the water in the pool, toward which Patrecia would have been facing. As a physician explained, the result presumably was a "flicker phenomenon," a pattern of change in the frequency of light, hitting her eyes, triggering electrically unstable brain cells, and precipitating a seizure. Had she been feeding Takara a foot or two back from the pool, she would merely have lost consciousness. All this was conjecture. It was the most logical explanation anyone could produce and the one most in accord with the evidence.

Later, I learned that a "psychological autopsy" was also performed. They checked into details of Patrecia's life to discover if her death could have been a suicide, difficult as suicide would have been in a swimming pool. This possibility was ruled out entirely. Murder also had to be considered, but there was absolutely no evidence of foul play—although my nephews Leonard and Jonathan, on hearing of the death, found themselves wondering, as I had, about some lunatic from our past. The only rational interpretation of events was that Patrecia had died in a freak accident, caused by the interaction of several factors, including her lack of medication, photic stimulation from sunlight, physical exhaustion and emotional stress, and proximity to the swimming pool.

The night of her death, Thursday, March 31, 1977, I lay in my bed-room, dreading falling asleep because I dreaded waking up, dreaded the first moments of consciousness in a world in which Patrecia no longer existed. Trying to make my brain absorb what it could not absorb, I said aloud to the empty room, "I found my wife's body in the swimming pool. I found Patrecia's body in the swimming pool."

I kept repeating these sentences, in a voice I had never heard before, pleading with an indifferent universe for some response. Everything inside me seemed to be disintegrating, as if the entire structure of my mind and body were crumbling and as if I were falling endlessly through space. I had no center; I was only endlessly falling.

That was twenty-one years ago.

I shall not attempt to describe the agony of the long mourning process. Nor shall I attempt to describe the terror—and the miracle—of falling in love again. I briefly address both these issues in *The Psychology of Romantic Love*, published in 1980, three years after Patrecia's death, and then again in a book that I wrote with my wife, Devers, *What Love Asks of Us* (originally titled *The Romantic Love Question-and-Answer Book*), published in 1982.

A few weeks before her death, Patrecia and I visited with Barbara one evening, and the two women spoke of their affection for each other with a warmth that touched me deeply. At the time of the death, Barbara performed extraordinarily. She took care of all the funeral arrangements. She was there for me in the most magnificently caring way. On that score alone, I will be grateful to her for the rest of my life, even though our closeness during that period was not something we were able to sustain in later years.

The struggle to rebuild my life, the development of my love for Devers, and her heroic support of me through the long grieving process are not part of this memoir. But I will not end this book here, because I do not want to leave my memoir a tragedy—and because there was one last incredible development in my relationship with Ayn Rand.

In the fall of 1980, Devers and I were flying to New York to give a new Intensive, "Self-Esteem and Transformation." An hour into the flight, I was reading, and she was sitting silently, thinking. Occasionally, I glanced up to look at her profile outlined against the window. I thought that I was blessed beyond what a man has a right to expect of life.

I have been given another chance, I thought. Against all probability. It is three-and-a-half years, and there are still times that are very difficult, but I am learning to be happy. The strength of my love for Devers helps break through the barriers.

Watching her now, I thought of how we met. She came to my office for a job interview shortly before the accident. I had been looking for a person who could take responsibility for promoting and marketing the Intensives, as well as the day-to-day administrative work, and an acquaintance called to say that he wanted me to meet a woman who might be right for the job. Her background was in business, sales, and management. She had an unusual work pattern; she typically moved into a new field for two or three years, worked as an efficiency expert or ran an office or got an ailing business on its feet, trained her own replacement, and then took a sabbatical for several months. Then she would move on to another field entirely.

She was tall, with long brown hair that fell straight back, and she possessed the quiet unstressed authority of a business executive. It was difficult to assess her age. Physically, she could have been in her early thirties; only her quality of mature assurance suggested someone older. She was slender and strikingly good-looking with a somewhat angular face and a bearing that reflected natural, unboastful pride. She held herself like a woman who knew her own value and who had no need to flaunt it.

I was astonished when she said that she was forty-three. I was then forty-six. I was still more astonished when she mentioned that she had two grown daughters whom she had raised alone; she had been widowed at the age of twenty-four. "That's when I went into the business world. I had to find a way to survive."

In the late spring of 1977, Devers began sitting in on all my therapy groups and attending all my Intensives. She then launched into a comprehensive reading program in psychology, aiming to master every aspect of my work with people, which she did with a speed and proficiency that far excelled those of any student I'd ever had. She took many programs and workshops offered by psychotherapists of other schools and displayed the same skill at rapidly assimilating their work. She brought to the world of psychology and psychotherapy the same luminous intelligence and self-assurance that she had previously brought to the world of business. I learned that, for two years in her thirties, she had taken troubled teenagers into her home and worked with juvenile authorities. Now, in 1980, she was beginning to colead Intensives with me and teach my approach to mental health professionals. She was already innovating and introducing new therapeutic procedures of her own, involving work with subpersonalities, which I would write about briefly in *The Six Pillars of Self-Esteem* (1994). (This book would be the culmination of my lifetime's work on self-esteem.)

When I looked at Devers, I saw energy, self-confidence, an absolute commitment to the vision of life as joy, and a balance and internal harmony that I had never seen in a woman before. I admired these qualities enormously. What I found extraordinary about her from the beginning was the degree to which the various aspects of her were integrated—the career woman, the lover, the inner child, and the mother, as well as the healthily selfish, generously compassionate, feminine, and masculine parts of her personality. Balance, she said often, was her cardinal value. I was drawn to the serenity and excitement that united at the center of her being. What remained unspoken between us in our early encounters was "You're my idea of a woman" and "You're my idea of a man."

I recall my incredulity when she informed me that she was a grandmother. Shortly before Devers and I met, her daughter Vicki had a son—whom she named Brandon! How could Devers, this beautiful woman who moved through the world like a slightly impatient dancer, be a grandmother? "Very easily," she had explained. "By having Vicki when I was not yet eighteen." I learned that Devers's maiden name was Israel and that her ancestors had emigrated to Greece from Spain.

Leaning back in my seat in the plane, I allowed my mind to drift. I recalled the day of our wedding, December 10, 1978. I felt absolutely sure of myself and of what I was doing. I knew I was not free of pain, but I loved Devers totally and unreservedly, and I wanted the commitment to her, through marriage, to establish a new beginning for me. I would need time, because I was still grieving for Patrecia, the spiritual companion of my youth. With Devers, I felt I was embarking on the great love affair of my full adulthood.

But the transition had not been easy. There was no way I could hide my suffering from Devers, and she had to witness it for a long while. Devers made me look at pictures of Patrecia and talk about her for hours—not once but many times. Devers did nothing to hasten the mourning process but encouraged me to go through it completely, holding back nothing, including, on some days, my desire not to awaken to a world in which Patrecia did not exist. From the depths of my private hell, some part of me would marvel at Devers's courage and tenacity. My admiration and love for her went on growing, and the life force within me slowly began reasserting itself.

Now on the airplane, I became aware of Devers's looking at me. "What are you thinking about?" she asked.

"I'm thinking that I have been graced by a miracle."

"We both have," she answered.

"There is such joy in you, and such joy for me in looking at you. You're like a walking affirmation of life."

I thought of the many nights Devers had watched me while I slept, my body shaking with nightmares about the accident. I remembered the long tortured process by which I had come back to life. And I said, "We've been through some tough times together."

She reached over and hugged me. "It was worth it. I love you very much."

"I love you—and I don't think I would have survived without you."

"You would have made it with me or without me. But I'm glad we went through it together."

When she picked up a book and began to read, I sat thinking for a long time, my mind going back to the years in New York. An hour or so later, I noticed her putting her book down, and I turned and said, a little meditatively, "So much of my life has been focused on work and long-range goals. There's been so little time for play."

She laughed. "Look at what you've had in your life. You're a man in love with drama, and look at the last thirty years. What do you think you've missed?"

It was then—for the first time—that I saw the plot structure implicit in all that had happened since the day I first picked up *The Fountainhead*. When I told Devers what I was thinking, she said instantly, "You must write it."

A day or two after our arrival in New York, as we were out for a walk, we stood in front of 120 East Thirty-Fourth Street, the building that I had made a prison for so many years. "Here it is," I said to Devers. "Here is where so much of it happened. Six floors up—6G—is Ayn's apartment, where she still lives. And look down there—that white brick apartment building on Thirty-fourth and Third. On top is the penthouse where Patrecia and Larry lived."

"Ayn is alone now?"

"Yes. Frank died last year."

"What do you feel, standing here?"

"I wonder . . . where is he, the Nathaniel of then? The man who didn't want to let go of Ayn or Barbara. I don't pretend he's not part of me, but I feel as if I'm in a different incarnation."

"You are."

"After everything that has happened—after so much pain and struggle—I'm an incredibly happily married man. It's still frightening at times how much you mean to me. I'm so aware of our mortality."

"And when you were younger?"

"When I was younger, I thought we were all indestructible."

I glanced at my watch. Time to move on. We had a dinner date with Elayne and Harry. The reconciliation had happened at the time of Patrecia's death. A day and a half after the accident, all three of my sisters had appeared at my home, and our old conflicts suddenly seemed unimportant. Not long after that, Elayne and Harry terminated their relationship with Ayn. Devers asked me how I felt about seeing them tonight. "I wish our reunion had happened in different circumstances," I answered, "but I'm glad we're friends again."

Later in 1980, Devers and I were in New York again. On this particular day, I was scheduled to tape a television interview at 6:00 P.M. We separated at noon; I had a meeting with my publisher. Devers said she wanted to do some shopping and have her hair cut. We agreed to meet back in our hotel room at 4:00. When she did not appear by 5:20, I became agitated. She knew I had to be at the television studio. What could have delayed her? It was unlike her to be late and not to call. She finally telephoned at 5:28, and I could hear the exaggerated calm in her voice as she said, "I know, I know, but don't wait for me. I'll meet you at the station." "But where are you?" I asked, and she answered, "With Ayn. I've been here all afternoon." There was a long moment of silence. Then I said, "See you soon."

I hung up the phone and began to laugh.

At the television station, everything seemed to be happening in slow motion. I was impatient to be alone with Devers and to hear what had happened. When the interview was finally over, we rushed off to a restaurant for a dinner we barely touched.

Devers said, "I was at Ayn's for more than five hours! Toward the end, she was reluctant for me to go. That's why I was so late."

"Take your time," I urged. "Try to tell me everything."

"I arrived in Ayn's apartment building around 12:30. I lied; I told the doorman I was a journalist and had an appointment with Miss Rand and had arrived early. He said Miss Rand had gone out, and I asked if I could wait for her inside. Reluctantly, the doorman agreed. Taking the elevator to the sixth floor, I waited down the hall from 6G for an hour and a half—until the elevator door opened, and I saw an elderly lady with a scarf around her head walk to the door of 6G. I recognized that it was Ayn. Nathaniel, I didn't want to tell you about this in advance. I didn't want you to try to talk me out of it. I just wanted to do it."

"But why?"

"Because you two never had the kind of ending you deserved."

"I know. I wanted a different ending, too, once. That's why I telephoned her a few years ago. But it's hopeless. Well, anyway, tell me what happened."

Devers continued, "At the sight of her small figure and somewhat disheveled appearance, I was surprised. Could this be the giant about whom I had heard so much? Stepping forward, I said, 'Miss Rand?'

"Ayn's key was in the lock. She looked up abruptly. 'Yes?'

"'May I speak to you? My name is Devers Branden.'

"'What do you want?' Ayn asked, instantly suspicious. 'What did you say your name was?'

"'I'm Nathaniel Branden's wife—Devers Branden. I would very much like to speak to you.'

"I knew that my only chance of success was to be completely natural and straightforward—and that my only hope would be Ayn's curiosity."

Fascinated, I hung on every word.

"Ayn looked shocked, but her eyes were studying me even as she growled, 'What do you want? Did he send you here?' She did not say your name.

"The door of the apartment was now half-open, and I moved in slightly, blocking her from entering. I leaned against the entrance with an air of authority, and I said that I had come here on my own and that you knew nothing about it. I could see that in spite of being disoriented and taken aback, Ayn was a little intrigued.

"Right away, she began denouncing the doorman and threatened to have him fired. I told her it was not the doorman's fault, I lied to him, and when I explained what I had done, she smiled, almost in spite of herself, and said, 'Ingenious.'

"We talked about this for a few more minutes, and I could see her softening. Then I opened the door slightly and said, 'Do we have to remain talking in the hall? It's a little chilly. Won't you invite me in?'

"She said, 'What's your purpose in being here?' I didn't answer immediately but asked again if we could go in.

"Looking disoriented, she led me into the apartment. Like Ayn herself, the living room seemed faded and in disrepair; perhaps it had once been beautiful, but now it appeared dingy. To establish my presence more firmly, I immediately took off my coat.

"I sat on the sofa, and Ayn again demanded to know what I wanted. I got up, walked around the room, and studied Frank's paintings on the walls, conscious that Ayn was watching me. I was not going to let her set the rhythm or pace. She asked if you still had that painting of Frank's—you know, the large nude—and whether you wanted to sell it. I answered that it was special to you, and that you would not part with it. She asked that I tell you that if you ever wanted to sell it, she wanted to buy it. Then I sat down again and told her that you had not sent me and that my purpose here was my own.

"I began to talk about my understanding of what Ayn and you had once meant to each other and how sad it was that your relationship had ended as it did, with so much pain and anger. Ayn began to protest, denying that she'd ever felt any pain—which I ignored. I said to her, 'The ending deserved more honesty and dignity than either of you brought to it. I would like to see, not a new friendship between you two—I understand that's impossible—but a different ending. That's really all I'm here for.'

"She said angrily that you and she could never be friends, and I told her again that that was not what I was proposing. 'I'm proposing that you meet in person or talk on the telephone—just once. No one else need ever know. This is not for the public. It's for the two of you—just to acknowledge what those eighteen years you were together meant and to say goodbye properly.'

"'Did he tell you that he meant something to me?' Ayn demanded harshly, and I answered, 'Yes, but your behavior at the time of the break and afterward told me much more eloquently.'

"Ayn looked at me as if I were a strange creature from another planet and demanded, 'What did he tell you about me?' I looked directly into her eyes, and said, 'Everything.'

"She was sitting across from me in a chair. She got up and stood over me, almost threateningly, and asked again, 'What did he tell you?' I answered, 'I'm only here because Nathaniel told me so much about those eighteen years and how much they meant to him. How much he learned. How you were his mentor, his friend, his partner.' I deliberately did not say 'lover'—not that early in our meeting. I wanted to leave it abstract.

"'You see, Ayn,' I said to her, 'if Nathaniel had spoken of those years primarily as painful, or if he had spoken of you primarily in the negative, there would be no reason for me to be here. But he conveyed so many happy and positive memories. You two loved each other and . . .' She interrupted and demanded, 'Did he tell you that?' I replied that you had, and she said, 'I never loved him—never!' Then she demanded, 'Why would I wish to communicate with him now?' I answered that at the time of the break, there were a lot of false accusations, a lot of things said that weren't true, and a lot of anger that wiped away everything wonderful from the earlier years. I said that in the world as I understood it, this was wrong, and that a better ending to the story deserved to be written for both of you.

"She asked—her voice shaking—if I knew what you had done. She would not say your name. I said, yes, I did. She said, 'And you still expect me to communicate with him?' I answered, yes, that was what I wanted.

"Then she became angry and said that she would not discuss you, that there was nothing to discuss, and that if I wanted to remain, I must not mention your name again." Recounting this, Devers smiled. "When she said, if I wanted to remain, I knew we had made a connection. Even when she shouted, she kept studying me; her eyes never left me. She was curious about you—and about me.

"I got up again and went back to Frank's paintings. She was impressed by the things I said about them. She told me that Frank had died the year before. I said I knew that, and she began speaking of him with great sadness. Pointing to stacks of papers and letters scattered throughout the apartment, she said, 'I'm not able to do anything. I don't write, I don't answer letters, I don't look at contracts. There are important matters here, and I do nothing.' Then, as if realizing how intimately she was speaking, she became angry again and demanded to know why you had sent me here. Again I assured her that you knew nothing of this meeting. She was skeptical. At the same time, I could see she was becoming increasingly intrigued.

"I think she liked my straightforwardness; she could see that I was not afraid of her.

"Then she asked if I had read your interview in *Reason* magazine and began to speak of it with great indignation—almost as if that were the worst offense you had ever committed. This completely bewildered me. I told her that I didn't recall the piece too clearly. I also said I could think of nothing in it to distress her that much.

"I wanted to cut that off, so I stood up and said I was thirsty and did she mind if I helped myself to a drink of water or juice. Then I walked into the kitchen. 'What are you doing?' she cried, following me. I located a glass, opened the refrigerator, and was pouring myself fruit juice. She protested that I was a guest in her house and that if I wanted juice, she would serve it to me. I told her I didn't want to bother her. She could see that all her shouting meant nothing to me.

"She reminded me of my mother—difficult and irascible and always trying to intimidate—and I had years of experience in coping with this behavior.

"She asked me what I knew about Objectivism, and I said, 'I've read your novels, naturally, but I'm no expert on philosophy.'

"'How could you be,' she asked scornfully, 'if he was your teacher? He certainly is not qualified to instruct anyone in Objectivism!'

"I just looked at her, raised an eyebrow, and said, 'Miss Rand, that really is a foolish remark to make about a man to whom you dedicated *Atlas Shrugged* and whom you described as your intellectual heir. A man who was your spokesman to the world for Objectivism.'

"She stared back almost menacingly. She began to question me about myself and was fascinated by my background in the business world. We talked for a long time about that, and she became much warmer and friendlier. 'That's why I like you!' she exclaimed. 'That's why I can talk to you! You're a businessman!' It was the strangest thing—she kept calling me a 'businessman.' But now and again, she would remember whose wife I was, and then she would become suspicious all over again. Several times, when she became impatient because I didn't see things her way, she called me 'young woman,' until I finally objected, informing her that I was a grandmother, which she couldn't seem to absorb at all. I also told her that I did not appreciate the tone of voice in which she spoke to me, and, interestingly enough, she quieted down.

"At one point, she began to speak abusively of you, and I stopped her. I said, 'You're talking about my husband. I will not allow it—not in my presence.' She stopped immediately. 'I appreciate your position,' she said. And I felt she was looking at me with respect.

"She wanted to know in detail what you had told me about the past, and I could see her registering the fact that you had not spared yourself. That you had acknowledged what you had done without defensiveness or alibis or evasion. And in the course of telling her, I was also able to communicate what she had meant to you, how important she was in your life."

Feeling grateful for what Devers wanted to accomplish, I interrupted, "She won't retain it. Not Ayn. She would have to reexamine too much."

"It was funny—she would tell me not to mention your name, but it was always she who brought the conversation back to you. She wanted to know what you were doing professionally, how we lived, and whether you were still interested in ideas. She said, 'You're not the kind of woman I expected him to marry.' When I asked what she expected, she answered, 'A nonintellectual hausfrau. But you, you're intelligent, you have self-confidence, you're a businessman. It took courage for you to come here, even if I do not approve of your manner of doing so.'"

Knowing Ayn as well as I did, it was easy to imagine the scene and to understand Ayn's response to Devers.

Devers went on, "Ayn continued probing and asking questions. I told her about the home we had bought in the mountains, in Lake Arrowhead, and mentioned that that's where you do most of your writing. I told her that I wanted you to have an atmosphere where you could think and create away from the world and where we would have a lot of time alone together. She remarked that I was a wife as well as a 'businessman,' and she was impressed by that. The details of our life clearly fascinated her; she kept pressing for more information.

"She asked about your dog, Pussy Cat, and when I told her she had died, Ayn said, 'Now, that I feel sorry about. I know how much he loved Pussy Cat.' I was stunned. I said, 'You express sympathy about Pussy Cat and say nothing about the death of his wife Patrecia?' She glowered at me and did not answer. I didn't care what kind of genius she might have been or how much she might have been hurt by you. To me, this lack of simple humanity was sickening. I wondered, What am I doing here? Everything Nathaniel and other people have told me about her dark side is true. I must remember this about her, because I feel a liking for her. I was caught up in the drama of our encounter, just as I think she was.

"In the midst of everything that was happening, several times she asked if I were hungry and whether she could get me something.

"Throughout the afternoon, there was a lot of sparring between us, almost as if she were testing me. She said, 'I like the fact that you are not afraid of me.' I answered that I was not afraid because I had nothing to lose. Then I spoke of what you had told me about the anxiety she had created in the Collective years earlier, and she protested, 'I never knew anyone was afraid to speak to me plainly and openly! I would have welcomed honest confrontation!' I answered that she and her work had become their whole world and that they did not want to be 'excommunicated.' Again, she protested that she knew nothing of their fears, and I answered that she was a supremely intelligent woman and that it was not possible for her not to have known. She dropped the subject and looked unhappy.

"At some point in the conversation she said, 'I'm not sure yet how rational you are, but you appear to be a realist. You have a good sense of reality.' Later, she stunned me by saying, 'You can come back and talk to me again if you like, providing you don't mention his name.'

"She spoke about her philosophy and her writing, which I enjoyed, and when I asked questions, she answered in great, very precise detail.

"Whenever I tried to convey sympathy for how hard the break must have been for her, she became rebellious and chastising. How dare I think that you had the power to cause her suffering? That's how she would talk: 'How dare you this? How dare you that?' Then she would turn mellow and friendly again. I said several times that I should go, and she encouraged me to stay. She struck me as desperately lonely.

"I mentioned how sad it was that most of the Collective had disappeared from her life, that most of her old friends had gone, and she said, almost pathetically, 'Leonard Peikoff is my friend.' There was such suffering in the way she spoke, but I knew I should not mention this or she would explode again. I thought, This is the woman who taught all of you respect for the facts of reality?

"When I thanked her for her time and said I had to meet you back at the hotel, she suggested that I stay a while longer and meet you at the television station. Then she said, 'If only you weren't Nathan's wife!' This was the first time she pronounced your name. 'If you weren't married to him, we could be friends!'

"Finally, I knew I had to go, and I stood up and put on my coat. At the door, I didn't think. I just reached out and put my arms around her, and for a moment she rested her head against my chest. She seemed so tired. I leaned down and kissed her. Then she realized her position and pulled away. She looked shy, young, and embarrassed.

"She said she enjoyed me and that if I wanted to call her from California, I could telephone her collect. I told her, gently, that calling collect was not necessary, that you had done quite well for yourself, and that if she didn't mind, of course I would call her. And then we said good-bye."

I felt assailed by a mixture of emotions: admiration for Devers, appreciation for the love that had motivated her, sympathy for Ayn, fascination with the sheer drama of the encounter, nostalgia for the world of my youth, amusement at the two women's interactions, happiness in contemplating the contrast between my life today and the life I'd had with Ayn.

Devers said, "I don't think she'll ever believe you didn't send me. And yet, she had a good time. I kept saying, over and over again, that no one need ever know if you two were to communicate. And that I was not out to exploit her and that I had no secret agenda."

"Will you call her again?"

"I don't know. There is so much pain and denial in her about the breakup. Maybe she needs that to survive, and I shouldn't try to tamper with it."

"If she is now maintaining that she never loved me, never suffered over our break, that means that in all these years, she has only grown worse. Still, you decide what you want to do."

"It's funny, there was only one thing I felt guilty about—as if I were betraying her. And that was that I didn't tell her that Barbara was writing a biography of her. I know it's not really my business, and I owe her nothing. And yet I felt badly about not telling her, because she spoke so much about people's betraying her and because, to a degree, she trusted me enough to become a little vulnerable." (I later learned that Barbara herself eventually told Ayn about the biography.)

We were silent for a long time. Then I noticed a faint smile on Devers's face, and I asked her about it.

"I'm thinking about how pleased she looked—in spite of herself. She was pleased at the simple level of feminine self-esteem when I told her how warmly you spoke of your love affair with her. She looked softer, even prettier. She never admitted that there was a love affair. If only for a few moments, I know I made her a little bit happy. Naturally, she can't admit this to anyone else, but maybe, when she's alone, her memories can be a little less tragic."

Devers telephoned Ayn again a month or two later from our home in Lake Arrowhead.

"Please don't push for a meeting between us," I told her. "Just talk with her, and let whatever happens happen. But be prepared for the possibility that when you call, she may well have disowned and erased everything positive that happened between you, including her invitation that you call. She may treat you like a presumptuous intruder. That would be like her."

Ayn was surprisingly friendly and receptive. They talked about her desire to resume writing and her difficulty in doing so. They talked about Devers's growing involvement in the world of psychotherapy. Ayn once again expressed astonishment that I had married a woman of such evident character.

When Devers asked Ayn if she had seen me on a New York television show, Ayn said she had not. But two hours later, in the same conversation, when Devers made some reference to the interview, Ayn said sharply, "When that young man asked him a question, Nathan should not have smiled so much. When one discusses ideas, one must be serious." Devers did not comment.

Afterward, Devers reported with astonishment, "Out of the blue, Ayn began telling me what an excellent spokesman for Objectivism I could be, 'if you were trained properly and if you weren't his wife.' I told Ayn I had no interest in being a spokesman for Objectivism, and she demanded once more, 'Then what do you want?' And again I told her I wanted some communication between you two. Then, for the first time, I referred to your affair explicitly. 'Ayn, you two were once lovers.'

"'We were never lovers!' Ayn shrieked. 'We were never really friends! He was a student of mine! Did he tell you we were lovers?'

"'Of course,' I answered gently.

"'Why would he do that? Why?'

"I was incredulous and said, 'Ayn, I'm his wife.'

"Almost incoherently, Ayn began to rant that you and she had barely been friends and that you had meant nothing to her.

"This was too much. I said, 'Ayn, all your life you've preached the virtue of honesty. And integrity. Are you now saying that you dedicated *Atlas Shrugged* to a man who was not even important to you?'

"There was a long moment of silence. Then Ayn answered, her voice low and muffled, 'A gentleman would have carried it to his grave.'

"I answered, 'All the years when you and your supporters were attacking him, he never said a word about it. He could have caused you great pain and embarrassment and, if he had chosen to talk, it certainly would have clarified what your conflict was really about. Do you realize that?'

"'Yes,' Ayn answered grudgingly.

"Then, in one of those switches that I had grown accustomed to by now, Ayn launched into a speech to the effect that she had 'made' your reputation and that since coming to California, you had done nothing. I then informed her of the details of your career, and Ayn's efforts to conceal her surprise were obvious.

"Then, abruptly, she announced that you only stayed with Objectivism as long as you did because of the income it had brought you. I felt angry, but I answered quietly that there had never been a great deal of money for you at NBI and that you never cared that much about money. You knew you could earn more on your own. The proof was that in California, when you started over again essentially broke, only nine months after opening your office practice, your earnings were already twice what they were during your best year in New York.

"Then she said, no, you only stayed with her because it was good for your career. I reminded her of all the heat and hostility you drew on yourself from the psychology profession because of your championing of Ayn Rand and the way your career had really taken off only after you went out on your own.

"'Then why didn't he leave sooner?' she demanded irritably.

"I was stunned. 'Don't you know?' I asked her. 'Do you really not know what you meant to him? What Objectivism meant to him? What the cause he was fighting for meant to him? After all these years, you still don't understand what his conflict was?'

"'If he's so successful now,' she stormed, 'why does he keep chasing me?'

"'He's not chasing you. He shares my conviction that you two should have had a better ending, and he is open to that, but in the sense you seem to mean, he wants nothing.'

"Ayn said that she was unable to believe that you weren't after something else, and she insisted that you had sent me to her. I assured her that she was wrong, but I said that I would not raise the subject of contact between you again.

"When this issue was set aside, Ayn became friendly again and asked me when I would next be in New York. I answered, 'In a few months.'

" 'You can come and visit,' Ayn said, 'if you call first—and if you don't mention his name.' "

Although they talked again on the phone, Devers did not call her when we were next in New York.

Several months later, in New York—on June 17, 1981—Devers did call again. Ayn said to her, almost reproachfully, "You had told me you were going to see me, and you never appeared, and I never heard from you."

When Devers invited her to lunch, Ayn said, "Oh, I'm sorry, I can't. I have one appointment after another. I can't do it right now."

She went on to say that she was busy, that she had begun working again but could not discuss it because it was confidential. "But I'm writing again!" Ayn said brightly, and Devers answered, "Congratulations!"

She did not inform Ayn that she knew the "confidential" project was a television adaptation of *Atlas Shrugged*.

Ayn reported happily that her energy was coming back. Then, for the first time, she asked how I was, and Devers answered that I was in excellent health and was spending more and more time in Lake Arrowhead writing. Devers mentioned that she and I were now writing a book together—*The Romantic Love Question-and-Answer Book*. Ayn wanted to know the details of the project, and Devers told her.

Ayn expressed pleasure that Devers had called and invited her to call again.

The next day, walking up Lexington Avenue, Devers said to me, "I feel like sending Ayn flowers—to celebrate that she's writing again!" She sent an expensive and elaborate arrangement.

Knowing Ayn as I did, I should have foreseen that this was a mistake, but my critical antenna was off. It was this gesture on Devers's part that flung Ayn back into her paranoia.

Ayn knew the hotel at which we were staying, and Devers expected a phone call, if only to say thank you. When it did not come, she telephoned Ayn, who immediately said, her voice cold and brusque, "I'm very busy, Devers. You will have to excuse me."

When Devers asked if she had received the flowers, Ayn said that she had and that she had given them to a friend. "It was very improper for you to do such a thing. If you want to bribe me—for what I don't know— it's not enough."

Devers assured her that her motive was only affection, and Ayn answered that such an ostentatious display made her feel totally misunderstood. She kept talking about Devers's evident wish to "bribe" her. Utterly bewildered, Devers could not break through Ayn's wall of hostile suspiciousness.

Trying to introduce a lighter note, Devers said that she wanted to express her delight that Ayn was writing again and that sending flowers "was the American way of celebrating." Ayn answered sternly, "Do not be presumptuous. I am not accepting lectures on Americanism."

When they had hung up the phone, Devers said to me, "I should have respected my earlier impulse, which was not to pursue this beyond the first two conversations." I agreed.

Devers decided to make one more phone call, some months later, on September 25. Through our sources, we had begun to hear that Ayn was now telling her friends of Devers's contacting her, only now she was speaking of "this terrible woman who is bothering me and making a pest of herself."

"Typical Ayn Rand," I said. "OK, call her one more time. Only this time, as repellent as I find the idea, I want to tape-record the conversation. I want you to ask her point-blank about what she's saying to her friends about you." I knew even then that the gesture was futile and that, regardless of what happened, we would never be able to bring ourselves to play the tape for anyone; we never have. We destroyed it.

We knew that when Ayn first heard Devers's voice, she would be cold and possibly angry and that Devers would have to keep her on the phone long enough to activate some small part of the old warmth between them. It took her almost twenty minutes to accomplish this. Finally, Ayn said, "Look, I can only think of you as Nathan's wife. We can only make trouble for each other."

Devers then said that she could accept that but that there was one last question she wanted Ayn to answer.

She then repeated the things Ayn was reported to have said about her, and Ayn interrupted, "I never said any of that! I never said anything but good about you! I told you I thought you were intelligent and seemed honest! Who's been spreading these lies?"

Then Ayn said that although she had not made the allegations Devers had heard, she had "told everybody" that Devers's purpose was to achieve a reconciliation between Ayn and me, which I wanted. When Devers protested once again that I wanted no such thing and asked why Ayn imagined that I wanted it, Ayn answered that I had realized that I needed her and that I could amount to nothing without her.

They talked a few minutes longer, during which time Ayn denied that she had ever invited Devers to call her. Ayn then said good-bye.

Recounting the conversation, Devers shook her head a little sadly. "Well," she asked, "what do you think about all this?"

"I'm glad you had some experience of Ayn Rand. What is there to say? The story is finished."

Here is what I believe: Ayn was a great thinker and a great woman. She was also a struggling human being, as we all are. If one cannot understand her in her humanity, shortcomings included, one cannot fully appreciate her greatness; one cannot know Ayn Rand.

Some months later, in December 1981, Elayne telephoned me to say that Ayn was very ill and that her death was imminent.

For some weeks, I had been expecting this phone call. Despite Ayn's efforts to keep the information secret, I had heard a few years earlier of her lung cancer and of the surgery that followed. A subsequent operation for gallstones worsened her condition. I knew that her health had been deteriorating recently.

"Ayn never fully recovered from the conference in New Orleans at which she spoke last month," Elayne said. The event to which she referred was the annual conference of the National Committee for Monetary Reform, an organization whose aim was to reestablish the gold standard and to enlighten the public about the benefits of a free market. Ayn had been the star speaker. The world understood her political ideas better in 1981 than when *Atlas Shrugged* was originally published. In the years ahead, her profound, if largely subterranean, impact on the culture would be still more evident. Her influence would be acknowledged, for instance, in the explosive renewed appreciation of capitalism in the late 1980s. And beyond the arena of politics and economics, the lengthened shadow of *The Fountainhead* and *Atlas Shrugged* appeared socially in a growing respect for self-fulfillment as a proper life goal. The vision in her books seems less controversial today.

"She was ill coming home," Elayne continued. "I think she caught a cold. Anyway, she developed cardiopulmonary problems. When she checked into New York Hospital last month, it was obvious that she didn't have long to live. There was nothing more the doctors could do. So, at her own request, she was allowed to go home a few days ago with round-the-clock nurses. The most she's got is a few months. I thought you'd want to know."

I sat in my office for a long time, talking about my feelings with Devers. "I'm seeing the two of us as we were in January 1955 when the affair began. Why couldn't we have had the courage to be kinder to each other? And why are questions like these never usually asked except at a time of death? Why did we both behave so goddamn stupidly?"

On the afternoon of March 6, 1982, Elayne telephoned agai
time to tell me that Ayn had died a few hours earlier.

Now they were both gone: Patrecia and Ayn. That night I felt that finally
and irrevocably my youth had died.

Later that night, sitting in my study with Devers, I said, "I'm thinking
of what Ayn's and my world was really about. There's a profound need
that psychology has never adequately studied—the need to experience an
ecstatic state of consciousness. An experience that shatters the ordinary
walls of reality and lifts a person to another plane and entirely another
level of feeling. Some people seek that experience in religion and in the
promise of union with God. Others seek it in sex or in passionate love
affairs. Some seek it in drugs or in military battle or in music or in creative work or in an athletic performance that seems to break the bounds
of the possible. Ayn heard the most ecstatic music inside her own head.
And she never fully learned what to do with it here on earth, except
through her writing."

Devers nodded in silent understanding. I saw in her expression a reflection of my own, a solemnity beyond sorrow, beyond tears.

"Nietzsche said somewhere, 'I love those who know not how to live
today.' That was Ayn. And that's why I made too many allowances for
her—because some part of me struggled with the same problem. Not just
Ayn and me, but all of us—we were ecstasy addicts. No one ever named it
that way, but that was the key. People can't understand Ayn, or her appeal
to people, or the force that held all of us together back in New York if they
don't understand that human beings have that need for an ecstatic state of
consciousness. That's what Ayn transmitted through her novels, and that's
what we fell in love with and fought against leaving. It was through her
that we first entered that other plane. It was a spiritual hunger. A hunger
that inspired the best in us, and sometimes the worst. After breaking with
Ayn, I knew that the task was to find other forms of fulfillment for that
spiritual longing—not to disown and renounce it. I have found it—in my
work and with you. In the intensity of what we have together. And in the
simple fact of feeling the preciousness of life each day."

In February 1986, Devers and I flew to Scotland. Her daughter Vicki had
moved there with her son, Brandon, and had remarried. He was now nine
years old, and I wanted to introduce him to skiing. He was not ready for
the lift, so I pulled him up the hill by his poles while he yelled, "Faster,
Grandpa!" He evoked feelings in me I had never experienced before.
"How much does Grandpa love you?" I would ask him. Spreading his
arms wide, he would shout, "A whole skyful!" I watched him shooting

Nathaniel, 52, and Devers, 49, married since 1978, authors of the then newly published *The Romantic Love Question-and-Answer Book*, 1982 down the slopes like a runaway train, aimed straight at Devers, who was waiting for him at the bottom, and I laughed a good deal.

"You have given me so much," I said to Devers, "and one of the wonderful things you've given me is today. The paradox is, being Brandon's grandfather doesn't make me feel old—it makes me feel young."

Later, back at the house, Brandon looked at me a little wonderingly, almost wistfully, and said, "You laugh so much, Grandpa. I love the way you laugh."

Devers was standing beside me when he said it. When I looked at her, I had tears in my eyes—and a sense of overwhelming gratitude to Brandon.

Devers and I often talked about the greatest challenge of life—the challenge to remain vulnerable. To remain open, receptive, and feeling. Not to retreat with our bruises into a shell. To remain responsive to life and to the possibilities of joy. Brandon's statement meant to me that this was a battle I was winning.

But unfortunately, it is a battle that must be fought many times. There is no final victory. Nine years from now, at the age of eighteen, Brandon would be killed in an automobile accident. A new, terrible challenge awaited us—against which in the end we would prevail. However, that is not part of this story.

To return to 1986 and the flight home from Scotland: Devers turned to me and said, "Well, Grandpa, how are you enjoying life on earth?"

I would soon be celebrating my fifty-sixth birthday. Devers's daughter Lorin was pregnant and in a few months would give birth to a girl she named Ashley. Devers and I looked forward to being present at the hospital for the birth.

I answered, "How am I enjoying life on earth? I feel that everything is just beginning."

"Do you realize," Devers said, with love and a hint of humor in her eyes, "that right now everything is absolutely right? No major conflicts for us, no drama, no 'theater' anywhere in your life. Can you stand that? Have you had enough of the other? Can you just relax and surrender to being happy?"

I looked at the face that was the center of my universe. I marveled at the capacity of joy to regenerate itself.

"Yes," I answered.

THE AUTHOR

WITH A PH.D. IN PSYCHOLOGY and a background in philosophy, Nathaniel Branden is a practicing psychotherapist in Los Angeles. He also does corporate consulting, conducting seminars, workshops, and conferences on the application of self-esteem principles and technology to the challenges of modern business.

He is the author of many books, including *The Six Pillars of Self-Esteem, The Art of Living Consciously*, and, most recently, *Self-Esteem at Work* and *A Woman's Self-Esteem*. His books have been translated into fourteen languages, and there are more than 3.5 million copies in print.

In addition to his in-person practice, he consults worldwide over the telephone. He can be reached at his Los Angeles office in the following ways:

P.O. Box 2609
Beverly Hills, CA 90213
Telephone: (310) 274-6361
Fax: (310) 271-6808
E-mail: NathanielBranden@compuserve.com
Web site: http://www.nathanielbranden.net

INDEX